THE POLITICS OF PARENTAL LEAVE POLICIES

Children, parenting, gender and the labour market

Edited by Sheila B. Kamerman and Peter Moss

This edition published in Great Britain in 2009 by

The Policy Press
University of Bristol
Fourth Floor
Beacon House
Queen's Road
Bristol BS8 1QU
UK

Tel +44 (0)117 331 4054
Fax +44 (0)117 331 4093
e-mail tpp-info@bristol.ac.uk
www.policypress.org.uk

North American office:
The Policy Press
c/o International Specialized Books Services (ISBS)
920 NE 58th Avenue, Suite 300
Portland, OR 97213-3786, USA
Tel +1 503 287 3093
Fax +1 503 280 8832
e-mail info@isbs.com

© The Policy Press

British Library Cataloguing in Publication Data
A catalogue record for this book is available from the British Library.

Library of Congress Cataloging-in-Publication Data
A catalog record for this book has been requested.

ISBN 978 1 84742 067 1 hardcover

Cover design by The Policy Press
Front cover: image kindly supplied by Sheila Campbell
Printed and bound in Great Britain by MPG Book Group

Contents

List of tables and figures

Tables

Figures

Acknowledgements

This book is a collective effort from a group of authors drawn together by a common interest in leave policy and by membership of an international network on leave policies and research. We would like to thank all of the contributors to the book for freely contributing their expertise and knowledge to the common cause. We would also like to recognise the collegiality and commitment of all members of the leave network, which has created a climate conducive to collaborative working, cutting across national and disciplinary borders. Finally, and very sadly, one of the authors in this volume, Pentti Takala from Finland, died just before the completion of the book, in July 2008; he will be much missed.

Sheila B. Kamerman and Peter Moss

Notes on contributors

Berit Brandth (Norway) is Professor of Sociology in the Department of Sociology and Political Science at the Norwegian University of Science and Technology in Trondheim.

Deborah Brennan (Australia) is Professor of Social Policy and Deputy Director of the Social Policy Research Centre, University of New South Wales.

Anders Chronholm (Sweden) is Senior Lecturer in the Department of Technology and Society at Skövde University.

Andrea Doucet (Canada) is Professor of Sociology at Carleton University in Ottawa.

Thorgerdur Einarsdóttir (Iceland) is Associate Professor of Gender Studies at the University of Iceland.

Daniel Erler (Germany) is a research consultant for *pme Familienservice GmbH*, a large German employee assistance provider.

Anna Escobedo (Spain) is Associate Lecturer on Family, Work and Comparative Social Policy at the Department of Sociology of the Universitat Autònoma de Barcelona.

Jeanne Fagnani (France) is Research Director at the National Centre for Scientific Research and is a member of le Centre d'Economie de la Sorbonne, University of Paris 1.

Bernard Fusulier (Belgium) is Senior Research Fellow at the Belgian National Fund of Scientific Research and Professor of Sociology at l'Université catholique de Louvain, Interdisciplinary Research Group in Socialisation, Education and Training.

Sheila B. Kamerman (United States) is Compton Foundation Centennial Professor for the Prevention of Children's and Youth Problems at Columbia University School of Social Work, Director of the University's Institute for Child and Family Policy, and co-director of the website-based Clearinghouse on International Developments in Child, Youth and Family Policies.

Marre Karu (Estonia) is an analyst in the Labour and Social Policy Programme of PRAXIS Centre for Policy Studies and a PhD student in the Department of Sociology and Social Policy in the University of Tartu.

Jiřina Kocourková (Czech Republic) is Assistant Professor at the Department of Demography and Geodemography, Faculty of Science, Charles University of Prague.

Marta Korintus (Hungary) is Head of International Relations at the Institute for Social Policy and Labour in Budapest, and is involved in research concerning children and families.

Elin Kvande (Norway) is Professor of Work and Organisation int the Department of Sociology and Political Science at the Norwegian University of Science and Technology in Trondheim.

Johanna Lammi-Taskula (Finland) is Senior Researcher at the National Institute for Health and Welfare, Finland (formerly STAKES, National Research and Development Centre for Welfare and Health, Helsinki).

Lindsey McKay (Canada) is a PhD student in the Department of Sociology and Anthropology at Carleton University in Ottawa.

Antoine Math (France) is a researcher at the Institut de Recherches Economiques et Sociales (IRES) in Paris.

Peter Moss (United Kingdom) is Professor of Early Childhood Provision at the Thomas Coram Research Unit, Institute of Education, University of London and co-coordinator of the International Network on Leave Policy and Research.

Katre Pall (Estonia) is Head of Benefits Policy in the Social Security Department in the Ministry of Social Affairs.

Gyda Margrét Pétursdóttir (Iceland) is a PhD student in Gender Studies at the University of Iceland.

Janneke Plantenga (the Netherlands) is Professor of Welfare State Economics at the Utrecht University School of Economics, and co-coordinator of the EU Network of Experts in the fields of employment and gender equality (EGGE).

Chantal Remery (the Netherlands) is Assistant Professor at the Utrecht University School of Economics, and co-coordinator of the EU Network of Experts in the fields of employment and gender equality (EGGE).

Nada Stropnik (Slovenia) is Senior Researcher at the Institute for Economic Research, Ljubljana.

Pentti Takala (Finland) was Senior Researcher at Kela, the Social Insurance Institution of Finland, until his death in July 2008.

Diane-Gabrielle Tremblay (Canada) is Canada Research Chair on the Socio-Organizational Challenges of the Knowledge Economy and Professor in Labour, Economics and Management at the Télé-université of the Université du Québec à Montréal.

Karin Wall (Portugal) is a Senior Research Fellow at the Institute of Social Sciences (ICS) of the University of Lisbon.

ONE

Introduction

Peter Moss and Sheila B. Kamerman

Entitlements to job-protected leave for parents are an important part of social policy in most developed countries, a necessary part of the tool-kit for running a modern state. With very few exceptions, today's parent in these countries can expect the right to take leave at and around the time of childbirth (or, in most countries, adoption), then for a period of the child's early years, and often to be paid by the state while taking that leave. In some cases, the parent can also expect to have the option to work reduced hours or to take time off work, often with pay, if a child is ill. This strand of social policy, which recognises the care responsibilities of members of the labour force, began in the late 19th century as a health issue for employed women, maternity leave being introduced for women workers to protect their health and that of their newborn infants; indeed, when the European Union (EU) introduced minimum standards for maternity leave across all member states in 1992, it did so on health and safety grounds (see Chapter Fifteen). But as leave policies have developed and broadened, so too have their rationale and goals become more diverse.

Maternity leave rights were first introduced, in Germany, in 1883, alongside health insurance and paid sick leave, part of a new social insurance system intended to bind workers to the state. By the outbreak of the First World War, 21 countries had established maternity leave policies, covering 4 to 12 weeks, and 13 of these were paid. In 1919, the International Labour Office adopted the first Maternity Protection Convention, subsequently ratified by 33 countries. This specified that a woman working in the public or private sector:

   (a) shall not be permitted to work during the six weeks following her confinement;
   (b) shall have the right to leave her work if she produces a medical certificate stating that her confinement will probably take place within six weeks;
   (c) shall, while she is absent from her work in pursuance of paragraphs (a) and (b), be paid benefits sufficient for the full and healthy maintenance of herself and her child, provided either out of public funds or by means of a system of insurance ...;
   (d) shall in any case, if she is nursing her child, be allowed half an hour twice a day during her working hours for this purpose. (ILO, 1919, Article 3)

Gradually, this right to paid maternity leave was implemented across most industrialised countries, though in some cases not for many years (the UK, for example, did not introduce statutory maternity leave until 1976). In a couple of cases (Australia and the United States), implementation is yet to take place, although, as Chapter Two makes clear, the situation in Australia may change soon.

Since the 1970s, another form of leave entitlement – parental leave – has emerged, preceded by the development of childcare leave in Hungary in 1967, a post-maternity leave intended for women. Parental leave, however, is for both parents; usually following on from maternity leave, it is available equally to mothers and fathers and is intended to enable working parents, men as well as women, to give time to the care of their young children. It can be defined therefore as a social care, rather than a health and welfare, measure.

Sweden was the first country to introduce parental leave, in 1974 (discussed in more detail in Chapter Fourteen), followed soon after by Slovenia, then part of Yugoslavia (see Chapter Nine). By 1983, the European Commission was proposing minimum standards on parental leave across member states and although this proposal was blocked for some years, mainly by the veto of the UK government, by the time it was eventually agreed, in 1996, most member states had introduced their own entitlements (see Chapter Fifteen for the history of the EU directive on parental leave). Alongside parental leave, other forms of leave have been introduced in some countries, including paternity leave, entitling fathers to take time off work at and around the time of childbirth and reflecting a growing attention to fathers' inclusion in, and use of, leave policies; leave to care for sick children; and, increasingly, leave covering parents of adoptive children as well.

These developments, with parental leave at the centre, can be seen as part of the redesign of the welfare state that has emphasised its role in encouraging and supporting employment of both men and women, although, as we shall see, there remains considerable ambivalence about the employment of women with very young children, especially infants less than one year of age. The relationship between employment, care and gender is still contentious, going to the heart of beliefs about childhood and parenthood, men's and women's roles. In an age when employment is seen, at least by governments, as an unqualified good – economically, morally and socially – leave policies are part of the battery of policy measures needed to assure continuity of employment, or, to use the European Union's term, to 'reconcile employment and family responsibilities'.

Overview of leave policies today

Table 1.1 shows statutory entitlements to various forms of leave across the member states of the EU and the Organisation for Economic Co-operation and Development (OECD) included in this book, as well as some details of the policies. The table, like this book, is focused on legal entitlement, so gives only a partial picture of access to leave, omitting any reference to leave benefits arising from collective bargaining or benefit packages offered by individual employers to members of their workforce. These supplements to statutory rights are more significant in some countries than others (for example, where there remains a strong tradition of collective bargaining), but they are not legal rights, nor universally available. Neither are legal entitlements necessarily universally available; eligibility criteria usually apply, excluding some working parents, often those in more marginal and precarious forms of employment (see, for example, Chapter Three on Canada).

As the table shows, coverage of maternity and parental leave is nearly universal across the countries included in this volume, Australia (for maternity leave) and the United States (for maternity and parental leave) being the exceptions. The table also indicates that Iceland, Norway and Sweden have no distinct maternity leave, but this needs some qualification. There is leave available to mothers before and after the time of birth, but it is part of a generic leave (included in the table under parental leave), some of which is earmarked for women, some for men, with the remainder to be used by the family as the parents choose. In these countries, the distinctions between maternity, paternity and parental leaves are increasingly dissolving, at least in law (see Chapters Ten, Twelve and Fourteen).

But if most countries now offer maternity and parental leaves, there is far more diversity in the details, especially for parental leave; major dimensions of diversity include length of leave, payment (whether unpaid or paid and, if paid, at what level), flexibility in use (especially whether leave can be taken on a part-time basis and in several blocks of time), and whether leave is a family or an individual entitlement (that is, whether leave is an entitlement for the family, to be divided between parents as they choose; an individual and non-transferable entitlement for each parent; or a mixture of the two approaches). In practice, therefore, countries with an entitlement to parental leave can differ enormously in the details, and therefore effects, of that leave policy. For example, compare the situation in 2008 in three countries: Iceland, with a 9-month 'birth leave' entitlement, paid at 80% of earnings, divided equally (in 3-month sections) between mother, father and family; the Netherlands, with 16 weeks' maternity leave followed by 13 weeks of parental leave per parent, the former paid at 100% of earnings from public funds, the latter unpaid, although parents can save for their leave period through a 'life course savings scheme' that attracts some tax relief (see Chapter Eleven; the length of parental leave was doubled from January 2009 and payment, at 50% of minimum wage, extended to all parents taking leave); and France, which offers leave until a child's third birthday, 10–12 weeks being maternity leave paid at full earnings, the rest being parental leave as a family entitlement, parents taking leave being eligible for a low, flat-rate benefit payment – though only for 6 months if there is only one child (see Chapter Seven).

Table 1.1: Provision of statutory leave entitlements (2008) and childcare services for children aged under 3 years (2005)

	Maternity leave	Paternity leave	Parental leave	F	Postnatal leave (months) Total	Postnatal leave (months) Paid**	Leave for sick children	% of children under 3 years in formal childcare***
Australia	✗	✗	✓	F	12	0	✓✓✓	No information
Canada[1]	✓✓✓	✓	✓✓✓	F	12	11.5 [0]	✓ [+]	No information
Québec	✓✓✓	✓✓✓	✓✓✓	F	12	11.5 [6-10]	✓ [+]	
Czech Rep[2]	✓✓✓	✗	✓✓*	I	36	36 [6.5]	✓✓✓	2 [2]
Estonia	✓✓✓	✓✓✓	✓✓✓	F	36	36 [19]	✓✓✓	12 [3]
Finland	✓✓✓	✓✓✓	✓✓✓	F	36	36 [11.5]	✓	27 [8]
France[3]	✓✓✓	✓✓✓	✓✓*	F&I	36	36 [4]	✓ [+]	32 [16]
Germany[4]	✓✓✓	✗	✓✓✓*	F	36	14 [14]	✓✓✓	16 [8]
Hungary[5]	✓✓✓	✓✓✓	✓✓✓	F	36	36 [24]	✓✓✓	7 [2]
Iceland	✗	✗	✓✓✓	F&I	9	9 [9]	✗	No information
Netherlands[6]	✓✓✓	✓✓✓	✓	I	8.5	2.5 [2.5]	✓✓✓ [+]	40 [36]
Norway	✗	✓	✓✓✓	F&I	36	12 [12]	✓✓✓ [+]	No information
Portugal[7]	✓✓✓	✓✓✓	✓✓	I	35	5 [5]	✓✓✓ [+]	29 [3]
Slovenia	✓✓✓	✓✓	✓✓✓	F	14	14 [12]	✓✓✓ [+]	24 [2]
Spain	✓✓✓	✓✓✓	✓	I	36	3.5 [3.5]	✓✓✓ [+]	39 [25]
Sweden[8]	✗	✓✓✓	✓✓✓	F&I	36	16 [13]	✓✓✓	53 [22]

Source: Moss and Korintus, 2008; Social Protection Committee, 2008, Table 10

Notes

[1] Canada – There are differences in length of leave between provinces and territories; three provinces allow 3 to 5 days of unpaid leave to care for members of the immediate family.

[2] Czech Republic – Parental leave may be taken until child is 3 years, but benefit is paid until child is 4.

[3] France – Parental leave payment to parents with one child until 6 months after the end of maternity leave. Leave is an individual entitlement, the benefit payment a family entitlement.

[4] Germany – Parental leave payment after maternity leave until child is 2 years and means tested.

[5] Hungary – For insured parents, leave is paid at 70% of earnings until a child's second birthday, then at a flat rate; only the mother is entitled to use in a child's first year. For non-insured parents, leave is paid at a flat rate for the whole period. Either of the parents in a family with three or more children may take leave during the period between the third and the eighth birthday of the youngest child leave for non-insured parents.

[6] Netherlands – Doubling in length of parental leave and wider coverage of payment introduced in January 2009.

[7] Portugal – Extension of paternity and of maternity leave, linked to fathers taking more of this leave (renamed 'initial parental leave'), and enhanced payment for parental leave introduced in January 2009.

[8] Sweden – 480 days of paid leave per family (divided between individual entitlements and family entitlement), 390 days at 80% of earnings and 90 days at a low flat rate; each parent also entitled to 18 months' unpaid leave.

Key

X = no statutory entitlement; ✓ = statutory entitlement, but unpaid; ✓✓ = statutory entitlement, paid but either at low flat rate, or earnings-related at less than 50% of earnings, or not universal, or for less than 6 months; ✓✓✓ = statutory entitlement, paid to all parents at more than 50% of earnings (in most cases up to a maximum ceiling) for at least 6 months; F = family entitlement; I = individual entitlement; F&I = some period of family entitlement and some period of individual entitlement.

* Payment is made to all parents with a young child whether or not they are taking leave.

† Total postnatal leave includes maternity, paternity and parental leave.

** Unbracketed figures indicate total length of leave in months to nearest month during which some payment is made; bracketed figures indicate length of leave paid at two thirds of earnings or above.

[+] Additional leave entitlements covering a wider range of family members than young children and/or situations of serious illness.

*** Bracketed figures indicate the percentage of children aged 0–2 in services for less than 30 hours a week; where this figure is a high proportion of the total, for example, in the Netherlands, it may indicate extensive part-time services.

In an attempt to bring some system to the great individual differences between national parental leave policies, Wall (2007) has suggested six main 'leave policy models' in Europe, defined in terms of length of leave and, equally important, their rationale – what values and goals they assume and support:

- the one-year-leave gender equality-orientated model (for example, Iceland, Slovenia, Sweden);
- the parental choice-orientated model (for example, Finland, France);
- the long leave mother home-centred model (for example, Hungary, Czech Republic);
- the short leave part-time employed mother model (for example, the Netherlands)
- the short leave male breadwinner model (for example, Spain);
- the early return to full-time work model (for example, Portugal).

Table 1.1 also shows the availability of paternity leave and leave for sick children, the latter more common than the former, and both less widespread than parental leave. Once again, there are considerable differences in leave schemes, in these cases mainly concerning length (for example, how many days of leave can be taken for a sick child) and payment.

The diversity revealed by this table, elaborated in much greater depth for many of the countries in the chapters that follow, makes an important point. International organisations today have an increasing influence on the formation of social policy. The EU, as we see in Chapter Fifteen, has actually set minimum standards for maternity and parental leaves through legislation (directives) that apply to its member states – and all other countries subsequently wishing to join. This legislative involvement by the EU is continuing. In October 2008, the European Commission announced a proposal to improve maternity leave standards, while in July 2008, the social partners (European organisations representing trades unions and employers) agreed to launch formal negotiations to update EU standards on parental leave as part of a recognised EU procedure for policy making in this area.

Other international organisations exert 'soft' power. They proffer recommendations or guidelines for policy; the International Labour Office, for example, updated its original 1919 Maternity Protection Convention in 1952 and 2000, enhancing standards that apply to countries ratifying the Convention. Others create expectations through conducting international comparative studies, such as the recent *Babies and bosses* and *Starting strong* reviews conducted by the OECD (OECD, 2001, 2006, 2007). All of these organisations provide international meeting places, where governments and others with an interest in social policy meet to discuss issues, exchange experience and contemplate policy developments.

Yet despite these increasingly potent international influences, social policy, including leave entitlements, remains largely the remit of nation states. While most accept the principle of regulating the labour market in the interests of children, parents and families, the practice of that principle is subject to national differences. In short, practice remains the product of the nation state, and its particular circumstances and politics; globalisation, including the growing presence of international bodies, is just one influence on national policy.

Bringing politics into the social policy arena

This book will enable the reader to make many comparisons between national social policies in a particular field – that of leave entitlements for parents. But this is not its main purpose. Its main purpose is explanatory, in particular to better understand *how* and *why* leave policies are shaped by political processes, ending so differently. The book does this through a series of national case studies, most focused on individual countries, but with two chapters that each compare two countries (Chapter Nine on Hungary and Slovenia, and Chapter Thirteen on Portugal and Spain). These cases, we hope, will cast some light on the politics of leave policy and, in that way, enable a better understanding of how and why countries create the distinctive national profiles for leave policy that Table 1.1 hints at and that the subsequent chapters will reveal in more detail. We can readily note the large differences between, for example, Iceland and France. But how and why did these differences come about? Which interests and which purposes influence policy formation, which processes and institutions are involved? What is the relationship between welfare state developments generally and the development of parental leave policies? And why have some countries, for instance Iceland and Germany, strayed away from the path they were originally following to make major changes in policy direction?

Consideration of national social policy differences has often focused on structural and institutional explanations arrived at through the application of typologies or statistical analyses seeking relationships between variables. One example of the former is relating national policies to Esping-Andersen's well-known typology of welfare regimes (Esping-Andersen, 1990): social democratic, conservative and liberal. In this case, leave policies appear to be most developed in countries defined as having social democratic regimes (for example, the Nordic states) and least developed in liberal regimes (for example, English-speaking countries), while conservative regimes (such as France and Germany) occupy the middle ground. Another example is gender welfare regimes, where analyses attach central importance to the association of policies with legitimated and supported gender relationships, for example dual earner, one-and-a-half earner and male breadwinner households.

Another approach is to relate policies to political and economic institutions, using quantitative methods. For example, a recent analysis develops an index of 'maternal employment policy', incorporating leave and childcare provision, and then looks statistically at the relationship of this index to various indicators of economic and political institutions across 20 countries. The conclusion is that:

> ... political and economic institutions that fragment and decentralise interest representation are significant impediments to the expansion of maternal employment policy. Specifically, a higher number of veto points and decentralised employer organisations greatly increase the chances that those opposed will be able to veto the introduction and expansion of these policies. I also find that having women in power is consistently associated with more generous child care and parental leave policies. (Lambert, 2008, p 317)

Our focus in this book is different. We attempt more detailed consideration of political process, working at the level of the individual country. This case study approach is not offered as an alternative to the other approaches outlined above, but as a complement. Case studies focused on the process of policy formation enable a more nuanced exploration of national and historical variability, to qualify the generalisations that flow from studies of welfare regimes or statistical analyses of the relationship between policies and institutions.

For instance, there are a number of broad commonalities between leave policies in Nordic states, including relatively generous payments to parents taking leave. These states are the main proponents of social democratic welfare regimes; they also have high levels of women in power as measured by female representation in parliament. So it is tempting to generalise, associating generous leave policies with a particular welfare regime and certain institutional features. Yet more careful excavation of leave policies reveals major differences between these countries. Some (Iceland, Norway and Sweden) have policies that actively promote take-up by fathers, for example, a 'father's quota' in parental leave; others (Denmark and Finland) do not (for a more detailed examination of the differences between Scandinavian countries on this issue, see Rostgaard, 2002). Iceland, at one extreme, has now introduced a '3 + 3 + 3' policy, dividing a total of 9 months' leave equally between women, men and family use and covering all periods by a benefit pitched at 80% of earnings. At the other extreme, Finland has a 3-year leave period, divided between maternity leave, parental leave and childcare leave, much covered only by a flat-rate benefit. To make sense of these differences, we need to go beyond the structural and the institutional to the processual and the political (see the Chapters Six, Ten, Twelve and Fourteen for a more detailed comparison of policies in Finland, Iceland, Norway and Sweden respectively).

Another example, this time of historical variability, is Germany, a country usually identified as having a conservative welfare regime, and until recently having a leave policy characterised by a long period of low-paid or unpaid leave, seemingly intended to support the maternal care of young children. Yet recently there has been a major shift of policy (see the Chapter Eight for a more detailed account). The leave period remains 3 years, but now benefit is paid at a far higher level – but only for a maximum of 14 months and with a strong incentive for fathers to use at least part; this is associated with a new priority to create more childcare places for children under 3 years. There has been a clear change of thinking about the purposes of leave, which has produced this reorientation of policy. To understand this, it is necessary to follow the political process that led to this change.

In Chapter Eight, Daniel Erler suggests that Germany has taken a 'Nordic turn'. But these recent changes may also be seen as the former West Germany, confronted by demographic and labour market problems, belatedly moving to adopt many of the policies and goals of the former East Germany (it has also initiated a large increase in childcare provision). In this area, therefore, the conservative welfare regime has conceded much ground to social democratic and perhaps, too, socialist welfare regimes.

Conflicting goals and interests

Adopting a political perspective for the study of leave policy formation recognises the many competing goals and interests involved. The relative strength of these interests and goals and how they interact will be specific to each country – hence the value of case studies. Leave policy, more than many other social policies, is at the intersection of the economic (since it bears on labour force participation and labour market regulation), the social (since it bears on children, families and gender equality) and the demographic (since it bears on fertility). This generates a complex situation of different potential objectives and potential conflicts between objectives, even within the same broad field; for example, an opposition can be set up between objectives for child well-being and objectives for gender equality in those cases where it is presumed that the former require a prolonged period of maternal care, which parental leave may be designed to promote. But as this example illustrates, conflicts or synergies are to some extent constructed; whether or not a long leave targeted at mothers is proposed will depend in part on predominant understandings of a good childhood and what it means to be a good mother or father, understandings that may change over time (Cameron and Moss, 2007).

Different objectives can in turn be represented by different interest groups, whether formally constituted (for example, employer organisations, family associations, trades unions) or informally represented (for example, through women in parliament). An important question here is which interested parties have a voice in policy making, and how loud that voice is – in other words, who is included and who excluded. One group noticeably absent in our case studies are children themselves, who are represented in policy making neither directly nor indirectly through adult advocates; the language of children's rights is yet to make its presence felt.

Nor can we assume uniformity of view and position among similar interest groups across different countries. Esping-Andersen's work on welfare regimes encourages us to think in terms of differing political and cultural values in different countries, producing different normative views and expectations about welfare. Thus, for example, employers in social democratic Sweden may adopt somewhat different views about the role of the state in relation to the labour force and labour market, and therefore about leave policy, than their counterparts in the liberal United Kingdom.

Different political and economic institutions may also play their part here, creating different ways for conflicting goals and interests to be negotiated, each with distinctive patterns of inclusion and exclusion. In Finland, for example, recent leave policy has developed through very particular institutions linking social partners with government; these groups have played a leading role in creating policy, though perhaps to the exclusion of some others (Chapter Six on Finland). Similarly, the EU parental leave directive was first negotiated and agreed under the Social Agreement procedure of the Maastricht Treaty – 'social dialogue' in Euro-speak – between European social partners, representatives of employer and trade union interests, before being adopted by the EU itself.

What we are sketching here are political processes of policy formation constituted by the interplay and friction of different goals and interests, and mediated by the values embodied by particular welfare regimes and by the form and composition of economic and political institutions. But there is one other element to be taken into account. This particular equation of actors and forces is not immutable; it is prone to occasional reconfiguration. An obvious example is the recent history of much of Central and Eastern Europe, where countries have experienced a rapid and often traumatic transition from authoritarian socialist to democratic capitalist regimes, removing certain constraints on policy making, but replacing them with others (see Chapters Four, Five and Nine on the Czech Republic, Estonia, and Hungary and Slovenia). Another example, provided by Portugal and Spain, involves transition from fascist dictatorships, and all countries covered in this book have been subjected to the rapid economic changes resulting from a potent mix of new technologies, consumerism, globalisation and market capitalism.

The role of complementary policies

This book goes deeply into one area of policy. But no policy exists in isolation; it is always influenced by and influencing other policies. In the case of leave policy, this is particularly the case with early childhood education and care (ECEC) services, which provide for children up to compulsory school age and come in many forms and with many names (for example, nursery, *crèche*, *kindergarten*, nursery school, *école maternelle*, childminder). An important question to be asked of any country is how policies on leave and ECEC services articulate; for example, does the end of one lead seamlessly into the start of the other or are parents left with a gap in provision when leave finishes?

The relationship is often at the heart of political debate. For those who believe young children should be cared for at home by a parent (almost invariably the mother), leave should be longer and ECEC services should not be developed for the youngest children. For those who believe that gender equality is compromised by this solution and also believe young children can benefit from services, leave should be shorter (as well as well paid and encouraging use by fathers), followed by an entitlement to an ECEC service from the end of leave (contrasting arguments and policies are vividly illustrated in Chapter Nine on Hungary and Slovenia).

So although this book is not focused on early childhood services, many of the chapters tell stories that give this policy field a supporting role and tell of debates about the relative merits and preferred relationship between these two areas of policy. The politics of leave is intimately connected with the politics of ECEC services. (See Table 1.1 for levels of these services for children under 3 years.)

Outlining the book

This book has been born of international collaboration, namely a network of scholars interested in leave policy and research. With members from more than 20 countries – mostly in Europe, but also in Australia, Canada and the United States – the network has provided a forum for exchange, dialogue and reflection about leave, with an annual seminar providing a regular meeting point, as well as the opportunity to develop projects like this book (for more information, visit the network's website at www.sfi.dk/sw46603.asp). It was at one of these seminars that one of the co-editors of this book expressed an interest in the topic of the politics of leave, and soon a group had come forward sharing that interest and willing to contribute to the book.

We recount this background in part to show how such networks of interested individuals can play an important role in fostering knowledge and cooperation at an international level. But it also explains to some extent the inclusions and exclusions of the subsequent chapters; most are chapters offered by network members, though in a couple of cases the editors actively sought authors to fill particularly glaring gaps in coverage. Most of these chapters offer case studies of individual countries, and the politics of leave in those countries, although, as already noted, two chapters each compare two neighbouring countries: Chapter Nine on Hungary and Slovenia and Chapter Thirteen on Portugal and Spain.

The final selection of countries gives, we believe, a good spread, whether judged in terms of welfare regime, type of leave policy, recent history or geographical coverage. It is not, however, perfect. The United Kingdom is an obvious omission, a particularly interesting case as a liberal welfare state that has come consistently late to the introduction of leave policies, after sustained political resistance, and that has ended up with a distinctly unusual leave profile, including the longest maternity leave in the developed world and the most limited parental leave. The United States is another glaring omission, although this has come about largely because of the paucity of its policy developments, in particular the absence of any national policy regarding paid leave, and the short duration of the unpaid, albeit job-protected leave. Other notable omissions are countries from within the former Soviet Union (with the exception of Chapter Five on Estonia) and from East Asia, such as Japan, Korea or China. Our focus, too, is on relatively rich countries, leaving out the situation in the many relatively poor countries, where leave policies, if in place at all, are at a much earlier stage of evolution.

What we do include, however, is a chapter about the European Union's role in developing standards for parental leave, an important study of the role of this unique international body.

After some discussion, we decided to organise the chapters by alphabetical order of country (using the English name for each country), ending with the EU chapter. To order them according to some external criterion – for example, welfare regime – is to beg the question of whether or not this criterion is relevant to understanding the politics of leave – or whether it presupposes some explanatory relationship that does not in practice exist. Readers may, of course, choose to read the chapters in whichever order they choose, and decide whether pre-existing categories prove helpful to understanding the politics of leave.

Each national case study chapter begins with a box summarising key features of leave policy in 2008, followed by a short text covering take-up of leave. Readers interested in more detail on policies and take-up are referred to the annual review of the network, which includes detailed notes on 25 countries (Moss and Korintus, 2008). The performance of each country on a range of demographic, employment and gender equality indicators is shown in the Appendix at the end of the book, giving the reader a rapid reference point for making contextual comparisons. Before that Appendix, however, we provide a concluding chapter where we review the main themes that have emerged from the preceding chapters, as well as offering some tentative comments and conclusions on the politics of leave.

References

Cameron, C. and Moss, P. (2007) *Care work in Europe: Current understandings and future directions*, London: Routledge.

Esping-Andersen, G. (1990) *The three worlds of welfare capitalism*, Cambridge: Polity Press.

ILO (International Labour Organisation) (1919) *Maternity Protection Convention, Number 3, 1919*, Geneva: ILO.

Lambert, P. (2008) 'Comparative political economy of parental leave and child care: evidence from 20 OECD countries', *Social Politics*, vol 15, no 4, pp 315-44.

Moss, P. and Korintus, M. (eds) (2008) *International review of leave policies and related research 2008 (Employment Relations Research Series No 100)*, London: Department for Business Enterprise and Regulatory Reform, available at www.berr.gov.uk/files/file47247.pdf (accessed 20 October 2008).

OECD (Organisation for Economic Co-operation and Development) (2001) *Starting strong: Early childhood education and care*, Paris: OECD.

OECD (2006) *Starting strong II: Early childhood education and care*, Paris: OECD.

OECD (2007) *Babies and bosses: Reconciling work and family life. A synthesis of findings for OECD countries*, Paris: OECD.

Rostgaard, T. (2002) 'Setting time aside for the father: father's leave in Scandinavia', *Community, Work and Family*, vol 5, no 3, pp 344-64.

Social Protection Committee (2008) *Child poverty and well-being in the EU: Current status and way forward*, Luxembourg: Office for Official Publications of the European Communities.

Wall, K. (2007) 'Leave policy models and the articulation of work and family in Europe: a comparative perspective', in P. Moss and K. Wall (eds) *International review of leave policies and related research 2007 (Employment Relations Research Series No 80)*, London: Department for Business Enterprise and Regulatory Reform, pp 25–43, available at www.berr.gov.uk/files/file40677.pdf (accessed 20 October 2008).

TWO

Australia: the difficult birth of paid maternity leave

Deborah Brennan

Maternity leave[1]: none.

Paternity leave: none.

Parental leave: 52 weeks per family with no payment; the mother may start to use this leave up to 6 weeks before the birth and 6 weeks can only be taken by mothers.

Leave to care for sick children: 10 days per person per year at 100% of earnings + 2 days with no payment for each 'permissible occasion'.

Other: none.

Australia is a federal state. It has a high level of part-time employment among women. Just over a third of mothers who worked in the 12 months prior to birth used some paid maternity leave and a quarter of fathers used some paid paternity leave; mothers are more likely than fathers to use unpaid leave. Overall, two thirds (68%) of mothers used some maternity or parental leave, but only 30% of fathers used any paternity or parental leave. These figures include non-statutory leave benefits.

Introduction

The absence of a national system of paid maternity or parental leave in Australia presents a puzzle: how is it that a country once regarded as a 'social laboratory' and renowned for its progressive social and industrial legislation (Roe, 1976; Castles, 1998) does not provide this basic entitlement for working parents? Even if a minimalist scheme of paid leave is introduced in the next year or two, as seems likely following the election of a Labor government,[2] the lack of such leave to date requires explanation, especially since 'work–life balance' and 'family policy' have been prominent political issues for at least two decades (Pocock, 2003; Brennan, 2007). In seeking to explain this puzzle, one may locate Australian approaches to paid family leave (including maternity, paternity and parental leave) within the historical traditions of the welfare state in this country and the distinctive industrial relations regime that prevailed for much of the 20th century. These historical and institutional characteristics help to explain the absence of paid leave in this country, but they do not fully account for it. Both cultural values and party politics also matter a great deal.

The normative strength of the male breadwinner family has been critical in shaping Australian debates and policies on family support. Despite comparatively low levels of female labour force participation, Australian policy makers have eschewed 'in-work' benefits such as earned income tax credits. Instead, Australia's main family allowance programme, Family Tax Benefit A, provides means-tested support to households with dependent children regardless of parental labour force status. A smaller programme, Family Tax Benefit B, provides additional support to families reliant on a single earner, effectively imposing a penalty on workforce participation by second earners, almost always mothers.

A focus on women as mothers, rather than workers, is deeply (though not unambiguously) embedded in Australian institutions and values and has been reflected in the debates about paid family leave, especially maternity leave. Prominent individuals – ranging from female trade union leaders to conservative male politicians – have resisted the International Labour Organization (ILO) definition of maternity leave as leave from paid work, insisting that motherhood itself, rather than absence from employment, should be the basis of entitlement to support. The argument that paid maternity leave is discriminatory because it provides no support to mothers outside the workforce is an example of this attitude.

The politics of paid statutory leave in Australia have played out in many arenas: political parties, trades unions, women's organisations, workplaces and, indeed, the national parliament. Supporters disagree about whether an effective scheme requires income replacement or whether a flat-rate social security payment – similar to the payments that apply to other contingencies such as unemployment – is adequate. Opinions vary (even among trade unionists) about whether employers should contribute to the cost of paid family leave and, if so, what the appropriate mechanism for this might be. There are divergences about whether eligibility should be limited to those who can demonstrate strong attachment to a single employer or whether less restrictive criteria would be more appropriate given the changing labour market. And there are strongly held views about whether Australia should aim, first, to meet the ILO standard of 14 weeks' paid maternity leave.

The success of the Australian Labor Party (ALP) at the federal election in late 2007 ended more than 11 years of government by the socially conservative Liberal and National Parties. The ALP election platform centred on the needs of 'working families' and placed considerable emphasis on expanding early childhood education and care services. The platform also committed a future Labor government to introducing "a paid maternity leave scheme for all mothers with no cost burden to small business". The ALP thus had a broad commitment to maternity leave but no clear policy about how it would be funded, who would be eligible or what level of support would be provided. Not long after its election, the government asked the Productivity Commission (a research and advisory body on economic, social and environmental matters) to identify the costs and benefits of providing paid maternity, paternity and parental leave. In September 2008, the Commission issued a draft report recommending the introduction of 18 weeks' parental leave paid at the minimum wage and funded by government (Productivity Commission, 2008). Responding to the draft report, the Prime Minister said it was time to "bite the bullet" and introduce paid leave. However, the characteristics of the scheme – including the basis of entitlement, level of financial support and mechanisms for funding – remain subject to lively contention (Maiden, 2008).

This chapter begins by outlining the distinctive features of the Australian approach to social protection and industrial relations. The second section considers Australia's support for families with children and indicates some of the mechanisms Australia has adopted to meet its international obligations under the United Nations Convention on Elimination of all Forms of Discrimination against Women (CEDAW) and the ILO Convention on Workers with Family Responsibilities. This section also describes current patterns of access to maternity and parental leave and other forms of family income support. The chapter then turns to the politics of paid maternity leave, examining the ways in which political parties, women's groups, trades unions and employer groups have framed the issue of financial support for new mothers (and, more recently, fathers). The chapter concludes with an assessment of the prospects for paid parental leave in Australia.

The breadwinner/homemaker household in law and social policy

In the late 19th and early 20th centuries, Australia was regarded as one of the most socially progressive countries in the world. Women gained the franchise in 1902 (compared with 1920 in the US and 1928 in the UK), the first Labour (left) government in the world was elected in 1904, and Australian working men were among the first in the world to win an 8-hour working day (Castles, 1998; Castles and Uhr, 2005).

The establishment of quasi-judicial systems of arbitration to resolve disputes between employees and employers and to determine wages was central to Australia's approach to labour relations. Arbitration institutionalised the role of trades unions, giving them power to bring their employers before an industrial tribunal. Together with tariffs on imported goods and restrictions on non–white immigration, arbitration ensured relatively high wages for male employees. In the *Harvester* judgment of 1907, the Commonwealth Conciliation and Arbitration Court (later to become the Australian Industrial Relations Commission (AIRC)) determined that an unskilled labourer should receive a 'fair and reasonable' wage sufficient to enable him to support himself, his wife and two or three children 'in frugal comfort' (Macintyre, 1985). Similar rulings were made in state jurisdictions (the Commonwealth of Australia includes six states and two territories). Thus, gendered assumptions about workers and their needs were built into the system from its earliest days.

The 'family wage' brought substantial benefits to working-class households, although it was never adequate to meet the needs of a family comprising two adults and several children (Cass, 1983; Nolan, 2003). Further, adoption of the family wage principle relegated women to the status of secondary earners. For several decades, the basic wage for women was set, by the Arbitration Court, at 54% of the male rate. It rose to 75% in 1950 but not until 1969 was the notion of 'equal pay for equal work' accepted. In 1974, the 'family' component of the male minimum wage was finally discarded and equal minimum wages for men and women were introduced.

Historically, most disputes heard before the AIRC related solely to the parties involved. Some, however, were identified as particularly significant and given the status of 'test cases'. Interested groups could apply to participate in these proceedings, and unions not party to the initial action could seek to have their awards varied in line with the Commission's rulings. Through this mechanism, therefore, the Commission was able to set standards for the whole country. From the late 1970s, test cases became an important means for extending different types of family leave to workers throughout Australia. Indeed, since the Constitution did not give the national parliament direct power over the terms and conditions of employees in private employment, the AIRC was more important than the parliament in extending workers' entitlements (Baird, 2005).

In contrast to the insurance-based systems of social protection established in many European countries, Australia (and New Zealand) focused far more on wage protection. Castles coined the term 'wage earners' welfare state' to encapsulate this approach, arguing that the essential difference between Australia and most other nations was that, throughout much of the 20th century, "wages policy ... substituted for social policy" (Castles, 1994, p 124). However, as indicated above, this 'wage-earners' welfare state' focused primarily on the needs of working men. Women, regardless of their actual circumstances and responsibilities, were assumed to be dependent on men.

Despite emphasis on wages rather than social insurance, Australian governments did not neglect other forms of social protection. The Commonwealth (or federal) government introduced taxpayer-funded age and disability pensions in 1908 and, at least in some states, 'boarding-out' allowances helped unmarried and deserted mothers to support their children. In 1912, following sustained advocacy by Labor Party women, a non-means-tested Maternity Allowance was introduced, equivalent to several weeks' wages for a woman factory worker and seen by women as partial recognition of their 'maternal rights' (Lake, 1993). The allowance was also an expression of Australia's preoccupation with increasing its white population or, in the words of the *Australian Medical Gazette*, "breeding ... a stronger and sturdier race". Aboriginal and Asian mothers were not eligible to receive the benefit (Lake, 1993).

In the 1940s, in the aftermath of the Depression and the Second World War, the Commonwealth introduced widows' pensions and unemployment benefits. Like age and disability pensions, these were means-tested, taxpayer-funded benefits, paid at a low, flat rate. In the 1920s and 1930s, the possibility of moving towards European-style social insurance requiring contributions from employers and employees was raised. Such schemes were promoted by the conservative side of politics, but resisted by a coalition of the ALP, the labour movement, the self-employed and various welfare organisations (Butlin et al, 1982; Watts, 1987). Australian social security arrangements have undergone many changes, especially in the past decade, but all the major income support payments, including unemployment and disability benefits, pensions and payments to low–income sole and partnered parents, are similar: flat-rate benefits, with eligibility determined on the basis of family (rather than individual) income and assets, and funded from general taxation rather than earmarked taxes or individual contributions. The absence of a tradition of social insurance makes it extremely difficult to argue for income replacement for maternity or parental leave and the fact that family income tests are applied to almost all Commonwealth payments further complicates the situation.

The election of the Whitlam Labor government in 1972, following 23 years of conservative rule and coinciding with the efflorescence of second-wave feminism, led to a surge of interest and activity in policy areas relating to women's domestic and employment circumstances. Childcare, equal pay, access to education and employment, and protection from domestic violence were central issues for the new government. Maternity leave was less central, but it was the subject of quiet, sustained attention from the Women's Bureau, a small section within the federal Department of Labor. Maternity leave also featured increasingly in debates within the trade union movement. In 1973, the Whitlam government introduced 12 weeks' paid leave and 40 weeks' unpaid leave for female Commonwealth (federal government) employees, and 2 weeks' paid paternity leave for men. Most state governments had already introduced maternity leave for their public servants and teachers and Whitlam's initiative brought the Commonwealth into line. The Women's Bureau noted that maternity provisions around Australia "clearly [fell] short of those described under international standards" and pointed out that "employee associations are taking an increasingly active interest in the subject" (DLNS Women's Bureau, 1973, p 11).

From the mid-1970s onwards, the assumption of women's economic dependence was increasingly contested and women entered the labour force in ever greater numbers, especially married women whose participation rate rose from 13% in 1954 to 33% in 1971 (Whitehouse, 2004).

Meanwhile, an emerging group of women activists and officials was beginning to make an impact on trades unions, building on the historical traditions of feminist advocacy for equal pay. Many of these young women were employed in the growing public service and professional unions, while others held positions in more traditional, blue-collar unions (Booth and Rubenstein, 1990). In 1975,

International Women's Year, women unionists adopted a Charter for Working Women calling for equal employment and education, childcare, flexible work hours and maternity and paternity leave. The Charter became a touchstone of feminist activism within the union movement and put the spotlight on contentious issues such as the family wage.

Many male unionists did not welcome the activities of this new breed of young, tertiary-educated women. They resented campaigns for equal pay, seeing them as undermining the family wage and pushing women into paid work. But the leadership of the union movement as a whole was increasingly aware that unions faced new challenges, including a dwindling base of male industrial workers, and that women represented an important source of recruits.

In the wake of a conference called by the Australian Council of Trade Unions (ACTU) to discuss the Working Women's Charter in 1978, Jan Marsh, a young research officer who would later become Deputy President of the AIRC, was charged with advancing the Charter's aims. Marsh took a 'test case' on maternity leave to the Arbitration Commission on behalf of the Electrical Trades Union. The Maternity Leave Test Case (1979) established 12 months' unpaid leave as the standard for eligible women in the private sector, bringing them into line with the 52 weeks' unpaid leave available to Commonwealth public servants. Adoptive mothers gained access to similar leave in the Adoption Leave Test Case in 1985.

Over the ensuing two decades, further cases considerably extended family leave entitlements. The Parental Leave Test Case in 1990 transformed 'maternity leave' into 'parental leave', making it a shared entitlement between the parents. This case also resulted in new fathers gaining a week's unpaid paternity leave at the time of birth (or 3 weeks at the time of adoption). Eligible parents could thus take a total of 51 weeks' unpaid leave (Baird et al, 2002; Owens, 2005). In two subsequent cases (the Family Leave Test Case and the Personal/Carer's Leave Test Case), the Commission extended to employees the right to use their own entitlement to sick leave and bereavement leave to care for members of their immediate family who were ill. For most workers, this resulted in 11 days' paid personal leave, up to 8 of which could be used to care for others. This leave is not restricted to those with responsibilities for young children; it can be used to care for ageing relatives, same-sex partners, siblings and grandchildren, but these individuals must be seen as part of the 'immediate family' and be a member of the worker's household.

As part of its drive to make the Australian economy more competitive, the Liberal Party, in power from 1996, introduced radical changes to the legislative framework governing labour relations. These reduced the power of trades unions by moving away from the centralised wage determination and dispute resolution that had prevailed since early in the 20th century and placing the emphasis on enterprise bargaining and individual contracts (Campbell and Brosnan, 1999). Liberal leaders argued that an enterprise focus in industrial relations would allow work–family balance matters to be negotiated at the workplace.

In 2005, the Family Provisions Test Case (also known as the Parental Leave Test Case) awarded employees a number of new rights: a 'right to request' an extension of unpaid parental leave from 52 weeks to 2 years; a right to 8 weeks of parental leave that parents could take simultaneously; and a right to request part-time employment, following parental leave, until a child reaches school age. Employers could refuse these requests 'on reasonable grounds' relating to their effect on the workplace or the employer's business. About 20% of industrial awards were varied to incorporate these provisions before the Howard government introduced legislation (WorkChoices) that prevented the extension of test case determinations in this way. WorkChoices also removed parental leave from the list of matters that could, in future, be included in industrial awards, although it did not remove existing entitlement to such leave. Opposition to WorkChoices was the single biggest issue behind the defeat of the Howard government in November 2007.

Employment, family payments and parental leave

Given Australia's history as a 'male breadwinner' society, it is not surprising that the employment patterns of men and women are very different, especially for those with young children. Motherhood, especially the presence of very young children, has a significant impact on the employment of women, especially when children are young. Mothers are far less likely to be employed than fathers, much less likely to work full time and more likely to be engaged in casual work. By contrast, Australian men work among the longest hours in Organisation for Economic Co-operation and Development (OECD) countries with over one third working 45 or more hours per week (Lee, 2004; ABS, 2005). Fathers of young children are especially likely to work overtime and/or 'unsocial' hours.

There are contradictory assessments of the Australian government's support for families. An analysis of support for working mothers in 20 OECD countries (based on data collected in 1999) placed Australia near the bottom, with only New Zealand, Mexico and Turkey ranked lower. This assessment was based on a set of measures including paid parental leave, flexible working-time arrangements, childcare subsidies and the taxation of second earners (Jaumotte, 2004). Yet only a few years later, Australia's performance on key work and family indicators – including the proportion of children under 3 years in publicly funded childcare, female employment, the gender pay gap, child poverty and total fertility – was assessed as at or above the average of the 13 countries included in OECD's *Babies and bosses* review (Adema, 2008).

A social policy analyst, Peter Whiteford, has shown that the Australian system "privileges part-time work and ... penalises second income earners in couples" (Whiteford, 2008). He emphasises, however, that these negative aspects of Australian performance are not the whole story. Australian expenditure on families as a percentage of gross domestic product is among the highest in the OECD; the system is generous to lone parents and jobless families; and Australia is relatively successful in reducing child poverty (Whiteford, 2008).

But there is no doubt that Australian men and women are poorly served when it comes to the provision of paid family leave. Depending as it does on industrial awards and employer policies, and there being no statutory entitlement to paid leave, access to such leave is "patchy and unfair", with the most vulnerable workers missing out almost entirely (Work + Family Policy Roundtable, 2008, p 6). In 2008, 53% of female employees and 50% of male employees were eligible for some paid maternity or paternity leave. But only 34% of female part-time employees had access to such leave, compared with 69% of full-time workers; and only 17% of male part-time employees compared with 56% of full-time workers (ABS, 2008). Paid leave is also far more likely to be available to those on high incomes. Up to 65% of female managers and 54% of professional women have access to paid maternity leave, compared with only 18% of clerical, sales and service workers and less than 1% of casual workers (Baird and Todd, 2005). Access to paid leave is heavily skewed towards public sector employees: 74% of women in public sector employment have access to paid maternity leave compared with only 32% of those in private sector employment (Baird and Todd, 2005). A survey of parents in 2005 revealed that at least 27% of mothers and 35% of fathers of newborn babies were not eligible for parental leave, paid or unpaid, either because they were self-employed or because they had not worked for the same employer for 12 months (Whitehouse et al, 2006).

Even for the minority who do have paid leave, the duration is often short. Very few women in Australia have access to the 18 weeks' paid leave recommended by the ILO as a minimum (Work + Family Policy Roundtable, 2007). Perhaps for this reason, 14 weeks' paid leave has become the benchmark for many of those lobbying for paid leave.

A survey conducted as part of the Australian government's Longitudinal Study of Australian Children (Whitehouse et al, 2006) enables us to look not just at overall patterns of entitlement for men and women, but at the actual leave entitlements and take-up of paid leave by men and women who became parents in 2005. In this study, just over a third (37%) of mothers who were employed in the 12 months prior to the birth of their child made use of some paid maternity leave. Around 60% used some unpaid leave (with approximately a quarter of this group taking *only* unpaid leave). On average, women took 40 weeks' leave and, of all the maternity leave taken, around 27% was paid. Confirming the international evidence on the importance of leave being paid (especially if men are to be encouraged to use it), the survey showed that over 80% of fathers who took some leave, took only paid leave. In stark contrast, less than 15% of mothers took *only* paid leave (Whitehouse et al, 2006).

The survey also probed parental preferences. Nearly half (46%) of Australian mothers who took leave and returned to work within 15 months would have taken a longer period if they had had access to *paid* leave. Only 6% said that access to more unpaid maternity leave would have led them to take a longer period off work (Whitehouse et al, 2006).

The politics of paid maternity and parental leave

Political interest in financial support and industrial protection for mothers has a long history in Australia, predating the ILO Maternity Protection Convention of 1919 (Huntley and Ramsay, 2006). However, activism around *paid* maternity and parental leave did not get under way until the early 1990s. In the period 1983–96, ACTU entered into a series of agreements (or Accords) with Labor governments, in which unions agreed to moderate their wage demands in return for increases in the 'social wage' – that is, through extending healthcare, superannuation, social security and community services. It was in this context, and "in the spirit of ILO Convention 103 (Maternity Protection)", that Labor made a commitment to provide 12 weeks' paid maternity leave to all Commonwealth government employees (Cass, 1994). Part of the political context for this was that Australia had ratified CEDAW in 1983 but had entered a reservation to the provision concerning maternity leave, stating it was "not at present in a position to take the measures required … to introduce maternity leave with pay or with comparable social benefits throughout Australia" (cited in HREOC, 2002, p 29). Australia had also ratified ILO Convention 156, Convention Concerning Equal Opportunities and Equal Treatment for Men and Women Workers: Workers with Family Responsibilities, in 1990.

Women's organisations and trades unions were keen for the government to withdraw Australia's reservation to CEDAW and give full effect to ILO Convention 156. Family policy debates also took place during 1994 under the auspices of the National Council of International Year of the Family, which had propelled all forms of family support into the centre of national political debate. Against this background, in 1995 the government introduced the Maternity Allowance, a means-tested, lump-sum payment, equivalent to about 6 weeks of social security benefits, and payable to mothers regardless of their labour force status (Cass, 1994). Although ACTU accepted this as a step towards paid maternity leave, key women's organisations condemned it (Brennan, 1995). The Women's Electoral Lobby was particularly affronted by the means testing of the benefit. It argued that this was "not a principle the ACTU should embrace lightly" for a payment that should have been available to all women workers (MacDermott, 1996).

The politics surrounding paid maternity leave took a new turn with the election of the conservative government in 1996. John Howard, the Prime Minister, was known for his support of the 'traditional' family. Among the first acts of his government were cuts to childcare funding and the reshaping of family payments to benefit households with a stay-at-home parent while penalising those in which paid work and care were shared. This was achieved primarily through the design of Family Tax Benefits A and B, described in more detail above.

The renewed campaign for paid maternity leave thus took place against the backdrop of a conservative government determined not to 'advantage' women in paid employment in comparison with women in the home. Prime Minister Howard drew on the argument of the UK sociologist Catherine Hakim, that women fall into one of three groups: home-based, work-centred or adaptive (Hakim, 2000). Hakim was invited to Australia to meet with policy makers and to address a major conference. The message taken from Hakim's work was that the government should eschew measures such as paid maternity leave that were said to benefit only 'work-centred' women (Hakim, 2003).

The Human Rights and Equal Opportunity Commission (HREOC) has been a major source of institutional support for paid maternity leave. Established in 1986, this independent statutory authority has the job of fostering and protecting human rights and overseeing the implementation of various laws. These include the Sex Discrimination Act, which gives effect to Australia's international obligations including CEDAW and ILO Conventions. Given this remit, HREOC has taken a strong interest in women's employment, especially ways of combating discrimination in employment. A HREOC report on pregnancy and work noted that the limited availability of paid maternity leave was a major problem for women in paid employment and urged the government to look further into this issue and to consider removing the reservation that Australia had entered to CEDAW (HREOC, 1999).

Three years later, under a new Sex Discrimination Commissioner, HREOC again entered the maternity leave debate, publishing a carefully researched discussion paper exploring the issue of paid maternity leave (HREOC, 2002) and following this with consultations around the country. At the end of this process, HREOC put forward a proposal for a government-funded maternity leave scheme that would meet the minimum ILO standard without putting pressure on business. Under the proposal, employed mothers who were not eligible for employer-funded paid maternity leave, including self-employed, casual and contract workers, would receive 14 weeks' pay at the minimum wage rate, funded by the Commonwealth government. The proposal was deliberately minimalist because, in the words of the Sex Discrimination Commissioner, "the debate had made it clear that Australia was still struggling with the concept of mothers working as a moral issue; there was no point in muddying the waters further by devising a scheme that could be dismissed because it was 'unaffordable'" (Goward, 2005, p 179).

The government made no formal response to the proposal, but individual ministers were outspoken in their condemnation. Workplace Relations Minister Tony Abbott announced that paid maternity leave would only be introduced "over this government's dead body" (ABC Radio, 2002a). Finance Minister Nick Minchin attacked the proposal as "middle-class welfare", saying he had received many calls from people asking "why should I have to pay for somebody else to go on leave to have a baby?" (ABC Radio, 2002b). In fact, the HREOC proposal was clearly structured to provide a safety net for vulnerable, low-income women.

The sticking point for the government seemed to be that women not in the paid workforce would miss out, an outcome it perceived as 'discriminatory'.

Many of the arguments, indeed the phrases, used by government ministers who opposed the principle of paid maternity leave appeared to draw on a paper published by the Centre for Independent Studies, a libertarian think tank founded in 1976. Its main argument was that "working mothers and at-home mothers should be treated equally in public support for their dependent children" and that "a special benefit restricted to employed women would be discriminatory against mothers engaged in home production" (Maley, 2002, p 7). Rejecting the claim that women had "'no choice' but to give up work", Maley insisted that "[w]orking mothers … always have the option of not working. The decision to work is a free one, as is the decision to have a baby, and both have foreseeable consequences" (Maley, 2002, p 5). He also implied that only women working full time would benefit from paid maternity leave; since most mothers of pre-school children either work part time or do not have paid work, they would miss out. This misrepresented the HREOC proposal for maternity leave, which was explicitly designed to cover both part-time and full-time workers. Maley's comments echoed Catherine Hakim's contention that "it is mainly work-centred women …who benefit from maternity leave and related job rights – that is, women who have the lowest fertility and are least likely to need it" (Maley, 2002, p 12).

Within the parliament, the Australian Democrats, a small political party with representation in the Senate (or upper house) but not the House of Representatives, were the champions of paid maternity leave. The Democrats' leader Natasha Stott-Despoja, the youngest woman elected to the parliament, introduced two private members' Bills supporting 14 weeks' leave at minimum wage for all eligible working women.

In lieu of paid maternity leave, the government introduced a maternity payment – the 'Baby Bonus' – currently set at AU$5,000 (€2,615)[3] and payable to all women in fortnightly instalments on the birth or adoption of a child. This payment, an echo of Labor's 1912 Maternity Allowance, provided assistance with the costs of a new baby, especially for household reliant on low incomes. It was, however, worth much less than 14 weeks' pay at the minimum wage and fell far short of the proposal put forward by HREOC. The maternity payment appeared to be an example of the kind of policy advocated by Hakim; that is, "designed to be neutral" as between work-centred, home-centred and adaptive women.

In fact, the maternity payment was not neutral. While the payment was of clear benefit to women outside the labour force, it could have been developed alongside, rather than as an alternative to, a genuine maternity leave scheme. It seems, however, that concerns about declining fertility trumped the rights of employed women. During a post-budget press conference, the Treasurer linked the maternity payment to the economic implications of population ageing, urging Australians to have three children, "one for your husband and one for your wife and one for your country".

To the dismay of many trades unions and women's groups, the Labor Party's initial response to the Baby Bonus appeared to end the campaign for a wage-related payment for working women at the time of childbirth. In the 2004 election campaign, Labor advocated a Baby Care Payment, similar in structure to the government's measure but subject to a family income test. Such a scheme, it proclaimed, would "deliver on Labor's commitment to introduce 14 weeks paid maternity leave" (ALP, 2004, p 2). Yet the structure of the proposal, the level of payment and the fact that it would be means tested on family income, all undermined this claim. The contrast with other work-related leave entitlements was stark. The leadership of the ALP appeared to have accepted the argument for 'equal treatment' of women in the labour force and those outside it – a principle that undercuts the notion of leave as a workforce entitlement and that would never be tolerated in respect of the forms of leave from which men benefit the most (for example, annual leave).

Meanwhile, the Howard government advocated workplace bargaining, rather than national legislation, as the key to extending paid maternity leave. But, unsurprisingly, the individual agreements that the government promoted in place of collective bargaining, were an ineffective vehicle for achieving paid maternity leave. In 2004, only 11% of Australian workplace agreements contained any reference to maternity leave, and only 7% referred to *paid* maternity leave (Baird and Todd, 2005).

A late delivery?

The Productivity Commission inquiry into paid parental leave, initiated by the Rudd government in early 2008, was the catalyst for a new round of ideas about paid parental leave to be expressed. Business and government representatives made clear that they would not countenance a scheme involving major costs for employers and this position, combined with the lack of a social insurance tradition in Australia, seemed to rule out a scheme based on income replacement. Other issues – including the primary objectives of a statutory, paid parental leave scheme – remain unresolved. Participants in the inquiry put forward many possible objectives for paid parental leave including the health of mothers and babies, gender equity at work and in the home, the promotion of work–family balance and enhanced fertility (Productivity Commission, 2008, para 1.5). The proposals embodied different ideas about the objectives of paid parental leave and different understandings of what is possible in the current political and economic environment.

The Commission itself adopted an unequivocal stance, stating that paid parental leave should be a workforce entitlement, not a generalised form of support for parents with newborn, or newly adopted, children. It proposed 18 weeks' leave, paid by the Commonwealth government at the minimum adult wage to 'primary carers' who had worked for an average of 10 hours per week in the preceding 12 months. Eligible parents could share the leave between them, with an additional

2 weeks' paid leave available if fathers or other partners shared the leave. Those who shared care would have a total of 20 weeks' paid leave. Since many parents already have access to some paid leave, the Commission estimated that 'the vast majority of children' could be cared for exclusively by their parents for at least the first 6 months after birth. Employers would be required to pay superannuation (that is, private pension) contributions on behalf of employees on paid parental leave. Those outside the labour force and employees not eligible for paid parental leave would receive a maternity allowance equal in value to the current Baby Bonus.

The recommendations of the Productivity Commission had a mixed reception. Unions and women's organisations welcomed the proposals, on the whole, but those who advocated a longer period of paid leave and/or a higher level of remuneration saw them as too cautious. Conservative politicians attacked the recommendations for distinguishing between mothers in the home and mothers in the paid workforce. The opposition spokesman on families, for example, claimed that paid parental leave would create "first and second class mothers" (Lunn, 2008a). This claim was echoed in *The Australian* by a critic who argued that paid parental leave would create "two classes of families and two classes of mothers" (Shanahan, 2008). Government ministers responded cautiously. Senior women, such as Deputy Prime Minister, Julia Gillard, and Minister for Families, Jenny Macklin, expressed support for paid maternity leave in principle, but joined conservative commentators in expressing concern about measures that differentiate between women in paid work and those caring for children at home. Not a single Labor parliamentarian offered unequivocal support for paid maternity or parental leave as a workforce entitlement.

Conclusion

Late in 2008, the Treasurer indicated that the impact of the global financial crisis on revenue would almost certainly cause a delay in the introduction of paid maternity and parental leave until at least 2010 (Lunn, 2008b). In an earlier era, an announcement of this type might have provoked a storm of protest from women Labor MPs, but, disappointingly, there was not even a gentle rebuke (at least in public). Describing paid maternity leave as 'something we believe is important', the Deputy Prime Minister, Julia Gillard, has said it would have to be "weigh[ed] in the budget process" (Maguire, 2008). The Minister for the Status of Women, Tanya Plibersek, added, "when we were elected we didn't predict the global financial crisis and everything we do … has to be in the best interests of the whole community" (Dunlevy, 2008). Even when a $42 billion 'stimulus package' passed through the parliament in February 2009, not one member of parliament suggested that a paid maternity leave scheme should be included. The Sex Discrimination Commissioner, along with advocacy groups such as the National Foundation for Australian Women, worked hard to promote the benefits of paid leave as part of the stimulus package, describing it as "social infrastructure which will improve national productivity and increase women's attachment to the workforce" (Dunlevy, 2008), but to no avail.

Aspects of the male breadwinner tradition continue to be embedded in Australian culture and institutions. If the Rudd government announces the introduction of a statutory scheme of paid leave during its first term of office, it will be a scheme of relatively short duration with a low level of remuneration (closer to minimum wage rather than income replacement). Australia is a long way from achieving a system of paid parental leave that recognises men and women as equal (or potentially equal) partners in the workplace and in the home. Nevertheless, even a modest scheme of paid parental leave will be a considerable advance on current arrangements, especially for low-paid women.

Postscript

On Mothers' Day 2009, the Australian government announced that a government-funded Paid Parental Leave (PPL) scheme would come into effect on 1 January 2011. Under the scheme, eligible primary carers will receive the minimum wage (currently $544 per week) for 18 weeks. The scheme will apply to wage and salary earners, including casuals, contractors and the self-employed, who have been in paid work for at least 10 of the past 13 months and who have worked at least one day per week. Primary carers who are not eligible for PPL because of the work test may receive the Baby Bonus of $5,000. Both payments will be subject to an income test excluding primary carers who earned above $150,000 in the previous financial year (fewer than 1 per cent of mothers earn this amount). Critics have argued that the income test makes this a welfare payment rather than a maternity or parental leave scheme. However, since eligibility for PPL is tied to workforce participation and payments will be made through employers, the scheme has been widely welcomed by women's groups and trades unions as representing the arrival, at long last, of paid maternity and parental leave in Australia.

Notes
[1] Leave provision described here refers to statutory entitlements.

[2] See postscript at end of chapter.

[3] Converted into euros at exchange rate on 21 October 2008, rounded up to the nearest 5 euros.

References
ABC Radio (2002a) 'Abbott embroiled in baby brawl', Transcript of PM (evening current affairs programme), 22 July, www.abc.net.au/pm/stories/s613611.htm (accessed 8 November 8).

ABC Radio (2002b) 'Howard rejects claim paid maternity leave too costly', ABC News Online, 15 September, www.abc.net.au/news/politics/2002/09/item20020914000556_1.htm (accessed 21 November 2006).

ABS (Australian Bureau of Statistics) (2005) *Australian labour market statistics (Cat. No. 6105.0)*, Canberra: ABS.

ABS (2008) *Employee entitlements and trade union membership*, Australia *(Cat. No. 6310)*, Canberra: ABS.

Adema, W. (2008) 'Work and family reconciliation in OECD countries: an overview', Keynote address to 10th Australian Institute of Family Studies Conference, 9-11 July, Melbourne.

ALP (Australian Labor Party) (2004) 'Balancing work and care: Labor's Baby Care Payment', Election Statement.

Baird, M. (2005) 'Parental leave and the industrial relations system', *Work, Family and the Law. Special Edition of Law in Context*, vol 23, no 1, pp 45-64.

Baird, M. and Todd, P. (2005) 'Government policy, women and the new workplace regime: a contradiction in terms and policies', in E. Davies and V. Pratt (eds) *Making the link 17: Affirmative action and employment relations*, Sydney: CCH Australia Limited, pp 61-4.

Baird, M., Brennan, D. and Cutcher, L. (2002) 'A pregnant pause: paid maternity leave in Australia', *Labour and Industry*, vol 13, no 1, pp 1-19.

Booth, A. and Rubenstein, L. (1990) 'Women in trade unions in Australia', in S. Watson (ed) *Playing the state*, Sydney: Allen & Unwin, pp 121-35.

Brennan, D. (1995) 'Current directions and future prospects', in R. Batten, W. Weeks and J. Wilson (eds) *Social change in the Australian family* (2nd edn), Melbourne: Longman, pp 303-15.

Brennan, D. (2007) 'Babies, budgets and birth rates: work and family policy in Australia, 1996-2006', *Social Politics: International Studies in Gender, State and Society*, vol 14, no 1, pp 31-57.

Butlin, N.G., Barnard, A. and Pincus, J.J. (1982) *Government and capitalism: Public and private choice in twentieth century Australia*, Sydney: Allen & Unwin.

Campbell, I. and Brosnan, P. (1999) 'Labour market deregulation in Australia: the slow combustion approach to workplace change', *International Review of Applied Economics*, vol 13, no 3, pp 353-94.

Cass, B. (1983) 'Redistribution to children and mothers: a history of child endowment and family allowances', in B. Cass and C. Baldock (eds) *Women, social welfare and the state*, Sydney: Allen & Unwin, pp 54-88.

Cass, B. (1994). 'Expanding paid maternity/parental leave through family income support: supporting early infant care as a social responsibility', *Social Security Journal*, no 3, pp 3-18.

Castles, F. (1994) 'The wage earners' welfare state revisited: refurbishing the established model of Australian social protection, 1983-1993', *Australian Journal of Social Issues*, vol 29, no 2, pp 120-45.

Castles, F. (1998) 'Social laboratory', in G. Davison, J. Hirst and S. Macintyre (eds) *The Oxford companion to Australian history*, Oxford: Oxford University Press, pp 592-3.

Castles, F. and Uhr, J. (2005) 'Australia: federal constraints and institutional innovations', in H. Obinger, S. Leibfried and F. G. Castles (eds) *Federalism and the welfare state: New world and European experiences*, Cambridge: Cambridge University Press.

DLNS (Department of Labour and National Service) Women's Bureau (1973) *Children of working mothers*, Women in the work force series, Booklet no. 7, Melbourne: DLNS.

Dunlevy, S. (2008). 'No leave for mums', *Daily Telegraph*, 25 November.

Goward, P. (2005) 'Reforming the policy framework', in P. Grimshaw, J. Murphy and B. Probert (eds) *Double shift: Working mothers and social change in Australia*, Melbourne: Melbourne Publishing Group.

Hakim, C. (2000) *Work–lifestyle choices in the 21st century: Preference theory*, Oxford: Oxford University Press.

Hakim, C. (2003) 'Competing family models, competing social policies', Paper presented to the annual conference of the Australian Institute for Family Studies, 12 March, Melbourne.

HREOC (Human Rights and Equal Opportunity Commission) (1999) *Pregnant and productive: Report of the national pregnancy and work inquiry*, Sydney: HREOC.

HREOC (2002) *Valuing parenthood: Options for paid maternity leave. Interim paper*, Sydney: HREOC.

Huntley, R. and Ramsay, J. (2006) 'Never made to follow, never born to lead: women in the NSW ALP', in D. Brennan and L. Chappell (eds) *'No fit place for women'? Women in New South Wales Politics, 1856–2006*, Sydney: University of New South Wales Press.

Jaumotte, F. (2004) *Female labour force participation: Past trends and main determinants in OECD countries (Economics Department Working Paper)*, Paris: Organisation for Economic Co-operation and Development.

Lake, M. (1993) 'A revolution in the family: the challenge and contradictions of maternal citizenship in Australia', in S. Koven and S. Michel (eds) *Mothers of a new world: Maternalist politics and the origins of welfare states*, New York, NY: Routledge.

Lee, S. (2004). 'Working hour gaps: trends and issues', in J. Messenger (ed) *Working time and workers' preferences in industrialized countries*, London: Routledge, pp 29-60.

Lunn, S. (2008a) 'Maternity leave "income substitute, not welfare"', *The Australian*, 4-5 October.

Lunn, S. (2008b). 'Economic crisis may delay baby leave', *The Australian*, 6 October.

MacDermott, T. (1996) 'Who's rocking the cradle?', *Alternative Law Journal*, vol 21, no 5, pp 207-12.

Macintyre, S. (1985) *Winners and losers: The pursuit of social justice in Australian history*, Sydney: Allen & Unwin.

Maguire, T. (2008). 'Pregnant pause in maternity promise delivery', *Daily Telegraph*, 24 November.

Maiden, S. (2008) 'Rudd backs paid maternity leave but won't commit to 18 weeks', The Australian Online, 29 September, www.theaustralian.news.com.au/story/0,25197,24418877-601,00.html (accessed 21 October 2008).

Maley, B. (2002) *Families, fertility and maternity leave*, St Leonards, NSW: Centre for Independent Studies.

Nolan, M. (2003) 'The high tide of a labour market system: the Australasian male breadwinner model', *Labour and Industry*, vol 13, no 3, pp 73–92.

Owens, R. (2005). 'Taking leave: work and family in Australian law and policy', in J. Conaghan and K. Rittich (eds) *Labour law, work, and family*, Oxford: Oxford University Press.

Pocock, B. (2003) *The work/life collision*, Annandale, NSW: The Federation Press.

Productivity Commission (2008) *Paid parental leave: Support for parents with newborn children*, Draft Inquiry Report, Canberra.

Roe, J. (ed) (1976) *Social policy in Australia*, Sydney: Cassell.

Shanahan, A. (2008) 'Maternity leave is ok for some', *The Australian*, 4–5 October.

Watts, R. (1987) *The foundations of the national welfare state*, Sydney: Allen & Unwin.

Whiteford, P. (2008) 'Assistance for families: an assessment of Australian family policies from an international perspective', Keynote address to 10th Australian Institute of Family Studies Conference, 9–11 July, Melbourne.

Whitehouse, G. (2004) 'From family wage to parental leave: The changing relationship between arbitration and the family', *Journal of Industrial Relations*, vol 64, no 4, pp 400–412.

Whitehouse, G., Baird, M. and Diamond, D. (2006) *Highlights from the Parental Leave in Australia Survey, December 2006*, Brisbane: University of Queensland, available at www.polsis.uq.edu.au/index.html?page=55767 (accessed 21 October 2008).

Work + Family Policy Roundtable (2007) 'Benchmarks: work and family policies in Election 2007 Work + Family Policy Roundtable', available at www.familypolicyroundtable.com.au/pdf/benchmarksFINAL.pdf (accessed 21 October 2008).

Work + Family Policy Roundtable (2008) 'Submission to the Productivity Commission Inquiry into paid maternity, paternity and parental leave on behalf of the Work + Family Policy Roundtable', available at www.unisa.edu.au/hawkeinstitute/cwl/documents/WFPRoundtableSubmission.pdf (accessed 16 April 2009).

THREE

Canada and Québec: two policies, one country

Andrea Doucet, Lindsey McKay and Diane-Gabrielle Tremblay

Maternity leave[1]: Québec – 18 weeks at 70% of earnings or 15 weeks at 75% of earnings, both with an earnings ceiling of CAN$60,500[2] (€37,665) per year. Rest of Canada – 15 weeks at 55% of earnings, with an earnings ceiling of CAN$41,100 (€25,585), but no payment for the first 2 weeks of leave.

Paternity leave: Québec – 5 weeks at 70% of earnings or 3 weeks at 75% of earnings, both with an earnings ceiling of CAN$60,500 (€37,665). Rest of Canada – none.

Parental leave: Québec – 32 weeks, 7 weeks at 70% of average earnings and 25 weeks at 55%, or 25 weeks at 75% of earnings, both with an earnings ceiling of CAN$60,500 (€37,665). Rest of Canada – 35 weeks at 55% of earnings with an earnings ceiling of CAN$41,100 (€25,585).

A 'Family Supplement', increasing wage replacement to 80% for all types of leave, is available throughout Canada for low-income families with a net annual income of less than CAN$25,921 (€16,135).

Leave to care for sick children: Québec – 10 days per year unpaid for the health or education of one's child or partner's child. Rest of Canada – provinces of British Columbia and New Brunswick allow 3 to 5 days of unpaid leave a year to care for immediate family members.

Other: none.

Canada is a federal state, with marked differences in leave policy between one province, Québec, and the rest of Canada. These include flexibility and level of payment, but also eligibility (see below). Nationwide, a quarter of mothers are not eligible for leave. In 2006, 56% of fathers in Québec took a period of leave. This mainly accounted for an increase across Canada in fathers taking leave, rising to 20% in 2006. Just over half of all mothers (51%) take 12 months or more of leave, compared with only 4% of fathers.

Introduction

Within 3 miles of each other, two distinct policy regimes influence the first year of parenting in 2 Canadian families. On one side of the Ottawa River, in the city of Ottawa in the province of Ontario, Bill and Sarah Rogers welcomed their baby daughter Naomi 14 months ago. Sarah took 15 weeks' maternity leave and most of the 33 weeks of parental leave (both at 55% of earnings); this is partly because she is breastfeeding and partly because Bill is the higher income earner and they need his full earnings. Like the majority of Canadian fathers, Bill did take some time off work when Naomi was born – 2 weeks of vacation time – and he also took 2 weeks of parental leave at the end of the year, as Sarah was returning to work and they were trying to find childcare for Naomi. They finally settled Naomi into a nursery, where they pay over CAN$10,320 a year (€6,425) in fees.

Across the river, in the city of Gatineau in the province of Québec, Marie and Serge are also new parents to a 14-month-old baby, Luc. Serge took 5 'daddy weeks', non-transferable paternity leave at 70% of his earnings, to spend the first weeks of parenthood with Marie and Luc. Like Sarah, Marie had access to maternity leave and she also took most of the parental leave; yet, compared with Sarah, Marie received both of these entitlements for 25 weeks at a higher rate of 70% of her earnings and the remainder at 55%. Marie and Serge were able to receive $18,000 more in benefits because of a higher earnings ceiling. Just after his birth, Luc was put on a list for a childcare place, which came through when he was one year old; Serge and Marie pay CAN$1,680 a year (€1,045), about 15% of what Bill and Sarah pay in Ontario.

These two families live in neighbouring provinces in Canada, a country with two distinctly different approaches to parental leave and childcare: one in Québec, one in the rest of Canada. This chapter offers two case studies, a national one of Canada, and a provincial one of Québec. In the case of Canada, statutory leave entitlements are split between federal and provincial jurisdiction. Québec is the only province that has made a significant investment in funding childcare and parental leave. This chapter highlights the distinct historical and political development of the two leave regimes, while also pointing to some of the effects of these different approaches to parental leave in Canada.

Jurisdictional divisions

This vast country is a federation with an increasingly decentralised division of power between federal and provincial levels of government. There are 14 jurisdictions in total: ten provinces, 3 territories and the federal government, although territorial authority is largely subsumed under federal jurisdiction. Many dimensions of social policy fall under provincial jurisdiction, such as education, social assistance and childcare, while social security is a matter of federal jurisdiction. Healthcare is constitutionally federal but delivered by the provinces. The federal government nonetheless funds and delivers specific programmes in areas of provincial jurisdiction as it sees fit (for example, post–secondary student loans).

When it comes to leave policies, all 14 jurisdictions have separate employment standards legislation, with different periods of job protection for unpaid caregiving leaves, and human rights statutes, containing anti–discrimination clauses. Canada's maternity and parental leave *benefit* programme (that is, payments to leave takers) is federal because it is part of the federal Employment Insurance (EI) programme. Québec is the only province with its own leave benefit programme, established in 2006 following a legal battle over jurisdiction. Québec also has its own pension programme and immigration policy, unlike any other province, presenting an instance of what has been termed 'asymmetrical federalism', where one province has greater jurisdictional scope than others (Evans, 2007).

Canadian and Québec contexts

As in many Western countries, the social terrain in Canada and Québec is characterised by rising labour force participation of mothers of young children. Unemployment – for men as much as women – can contribute to stay-at-home parenting. But most children live in dual-earner families (Marshall, 2006; Statistics Canada, 2007) and the majority of women with children under 3 years (64%) are employed. Today, women are the main breadwinners in nearly a third of Canadian two-earner families (Sussman and Bonnell, 2006) and the proportion of single-earner families where the father is the stay-at-home parent has increased from 2% (in 1976) to 13% (Statistics Canada, 2008).

Except for Québec, and unique programmes for Aboriginal peoples, Canada does not have a universal childcare programme. It is widely acknowledged that across most of the country childcare demand exceeds supply, quality is uneven and the cost is expensive. Investment in early childhood education and care is low and there are regulated childcare spaces for less than 20% of children under 6 years with working parents. This helps to account for the relatively high numbers of stay-at-home parents in Canada; the decision on the part of Canadian parents to have one parent stay at home with pre-school children is part of a strategy to balance work and home for both parents in a country where, outside Québec, childcare has never been a viable option for many parents.

The history and politics of two parental leave benefit plans

Canada: federal government leave benefits within Employment Insurance

A defining feature of maternity/parental leave benefits in Canada, outside Québec, is the location of this earned financial entitlement as a 'special benefit' within the EI programme, managed by the Canadian Department of Human Resources and Social Development. Unemployment Insurance (as the programme was called prior to 1994) was established in 1940 as a labour market-based income security measure. It was founded on a policy of full employment and "designed to fit the industrial post-war 'male breadwinner' model in order to replace earned wages temporarily" (Bernstein et al, 2001, p 155). Payment for maternity, parental and other leaves are add-ons. As a result of its location, changing ideas about how to address regular unemployment have, by default, affected important features of special (maternity and parental) leave benefits.

In Canada, there are three significant dates in the development of leave policy: 1971, 1990 and 2001. In 1971, maternity leave (along with sickness leave) was implemented as an individual entitlement, which provided mothers who had 20 or more insurable weeks of employment with 15 weeks of benefits at 67% of wage replacement to a maximum of CAN$100 per week (Warskett, 2007). According to Pulkingham and van der Gaag (2004, p 116), this change "represented a signal victory for Canadian women's labour rights". In the 1980s, adoptive parents also gained rights to benefits, and a successful court case at the end of the decade gave birth fathers entitlement to leave benefits (see Porter, 2003). Some argue that this legal requirement was the impetus behind the introduction of 10 weeks of parental leave benefits in 1990 (Porter, 2003; Calder, 2006; Campbell, 2006). The official rationale, however, was the need to care for newborn children. A family entitlement period added to maternity leave enabled mothers to extend time off, and for the first time allowed fathers to take time off work to care for an infant.

Finally, in 2001, new legislation significantly modified Canada's parental leave scheme by adding 25 weeks of paid parental leave to make a total of 35 weeks. When mothers take maternity leave plus all of the parental leave, this change doubles their total compensated care time from 25 weeks to 50 weeks. At the same time, there was a lowering of eligibility conditions, cutting the required number of annual employment hours from 700 to 600, and a reduction in the 14-day unpaid waiting period before payment commences (from applying to each parent when leave is shared to one waiting period per couple).

Overall, the trend in leave entitlements is positive, with significant gains in 1990 and 2001. Less visible is the erosion in overall level of EI benefit payments and coverage. Since hitting a peak at 67% in the 1970s, the wage replacement rate has slowly declined to 55% (McKeen and Porter, 2003). In the mid-1990s, a set of "fundamental changes to Canada's unemployment insurance system" (Kerr, 2005) was made as part of a neoliberal restructuring of the welfare state (McKeen and Porter, 2003; Porter, 2003). First, the 1996 Employment Insurance Act sharply reduced eligibility: the hours required to qualify for benefits more than doubled from 300 to 700. This resulted in eligibility for regular and special EI "plummeting" from 83% in 1990 to 44% in 1997 (Battle et al, 2005). Since 'special benefits' statistics were not separated out until 2000, the number of parents disqualified is unknown.

Lodging a criticism that continues today, a coalition of trades unions and women's organisations protested that the jump in hours of work required to be eligible for EI benefits disproportionately disqualified women, given their higher rates of part-time and short-term employment (Townson and Hayes, 2007). In response, the federal government in 2001 reduced the hours for 'special benefits' from 700 to 600. There followed a small rise in mothers qualifying for these benefits, from 54% in 2000 to 61% in 2001 (Marshall, 2003a), but this proportion has subsequently shown little change, increasing to only 62% by 2006 (Perusse, 2003).

Pulkingham and van der Gaag (2004) have posed an important question: why did leave benefits improve in 2001 during a period in which social security generally declined? The official rationale for increasing the period of paid leave was the promotion of child development, followed by helping parents balance work and care, long-term economic gain, gender equality, and supporting businesses to retain employees (Human Resources and Skills Development Canada, 2005). However, as Patricia Evans (2007) points out, this investment was not necessarily a forward-looking strategy, but rather use of a window of opportunity.

As a result of cuts to EI expenditures, with little reduction in employee-employer premiums, an unprecedented surplus accrued in the Employment Insurance Account from 1994 onwards (House of Commons Canada, 2000). Rather than improve eligibility or restore benefit levels for all unemployed persons and parents, the governing Liberal Party reallocated funds to "those who are perceived to have legitimate reasons to be away from their jobs" (Evans, 2007, p 121). Creation of 'compassionate care benefits', allowing time off work to care for a dying family member, similarly served to reduce the "embarrassing" size of the surplus and "insert a presence in expanding, rather than retrenching social programmes" at no cost to general revenues (Evans, 2007, p 121). According to Evans, "the decision by the federal government to extend parental benefits in 2001 was made, quite simply, because it was compellingly easy to do so" (Evans, 2007, p 121). Following Evans, it is important to note that there was no specific call for the extension of parental leave. This action could, therefore, be interpreted as an offering made in place of the provision of childcare, which remains a long-standing demand by social actors and an unfulfilled promise at the federal level.

The Canadian women's movement and its allies have continually pressed over the past few decades for a national childcare plan, but this goal remains elusive. The federal Liberal Party, which formed a majority government in 1993, made a commitment to a national childcare programme in its 'Red Book' party platform. No action was taken during four consecutive majority governments, from 1993 to 2004. One explanation for the expansion of parental leave benefits in 2001, in fact, is to compensate for the lack of investment in childcare. However, by 2005, the Liberal government had negotiated bilateral cost-sharing arrangements with the provinces to significantly expand childcare spaces in a plan modelled after Québec's CAN$7-a-day system (Barton, 2007). But the agreements stood unsigned at the time of the federal election of 2006, only to be cancelled by the incoming minority government, led by the right-of-centre Conservative Party.

Between 2006 and 2008, the current federal government took two key actions in relation to childcare policy. First, an annual cash benefit of CAN$1,200 (€745) per child under 6 years of age (paid in monthly instalments) was introduced, called the 'Universal Childcare Benefit'. The policy emphasises 'choice' without acknowledging that the amount of money falls far short of the cost of childcare and does nothing to resolve a chronic shortage of spaces. 'Choice' is, therefore, structured to support one parent at home caring for children.

Second, while still avoiding the creation of a new national programme, the CAN\$5 billion (€3.1 billion) amount allocated by the previous government for childcare agreements was replaced with a transfer of CAN\$250 million per year to provinces and territories "to support their priorities for childcare spaces" (Government of Canada, 2008). This reflects the Conservative Party position of greater provincial autonomy.

As a result of changes in parental leave policy, most Canadian children born in the 2000s are now receiving a longer period of full-time care, overwhelmingly from their mothers. Moreover, many more are experiencing a father at home for some of the time, since more fathers are taking leave; the 25-week extension of parental leave has led to use by eligible Canadian fathers increasing from 3% in 2000 to 18% in 2005 (Marshall, 2008). An increase to 23% in 2006 is explained by the dramatic increase in Québecois fathers taking leave under the new regime in that province, up from 32% of eligible fathers in 2005 (under EI) to 56% in 2006 (under the Québec Parental Insurance Plan) (Marshall, 2008). As explained below, this jump in participation is best explained by the implementation of a non-transferable paternity leave for fathers in 2006.

Québec: historical context of family policy

Family policy in Québec is largely the result of strong mobilisation and capacity building by social actors such as trades unions (especially the women's committees within the four largest unions), women's groups such as Fédération des femmes du Québec, and some progressive family groups (for example, the Fédération des associations de familles monoparentales et recomposées du Québec). The current complement of family policies were implemented after many years of social debate and, more specifically, lobbying by two large coalitions that are still active today; a coalition for the development and support for childcare with some 50 participating groups, and a coalition on the development of parental leave, which included many of the same groups (compare Giroux, 2008). In addition to these two groups, two consultative governmental bodies, the Conseil du statut de la femme (Status of Women Council) and the Conseil de la famille et de l'enfance (Council of the Family and Children), played an important role in stimulating the debate on family policy and work–life integration.

The history of family and work–family policies in Québec is generally divided into four periods: the period prior and leading up to 1987, 1987–96, 1997–2002 and 2003 to the present (Tremblay, 2008a; Conseil de la famille et de l'enfance, 2007, revised 2008). The first period began in the early 1980s when, in the midst of a difficult economic climate, social actors exerted pressure for the development of an explicit family policy. In 1981, the government mandated a minister to identify the problems of Québec families and elaborate a general policy (Conseil de la famille et de l'enfance, 2007, revised 2008). An interdepartmental committee was created and, following extensive data collection, produced a 'Green Book' for public consultations, which ran from October 1984 to May 1985. During that period, 13 forums were held in different regions of Québec, guided by the Québec government's objective of taking "the pulse of the population in all its diversity and its plurality, on family issues and the choices that the Québec society must make, the measures and priorities to be adopted in order to implement the family policy" (Comité de la consultation sur la politique familiale, 1986, p 11, authors' translation). The report, produced in April 1986, concluded that it was not only the government that had to adapt to the new context: "other actors are responsible for collective support to families, amongst which are economic agents, workplaces, educational establishments, professional corporations, unions, employer associations, as well as those responsible for housing, environment, leisure activities, public services and others" (Lepage et al, 1989, p 11, authors' translation).

The second period (1987–96) follows the adoption, in December 1987, of a coherent 'family policy'. To this end, a Family Secretariat was established, to coordinate family policy with all government departments, as well as a Family Council. This period was centred on social debate about families as well as creating financial support for families. Consultations were held with public, private and community sector bodies.

A distinct transformation in family policy occurred during the third period (1997–2002), which was during the time that the Parti Québecois led a majority government in the province. Beginning in 1997, Québec took steps to adopt a parental leave plan that was distinct from that of the federal government; this was fuelled by demands from the community, unions and women's groups during the 1990s. The government produced a 'White Book' for family policy, which integrated the various elements put forward in the new regime.

Accelerating the development of childcare and the desire to create a parental insurance plan for Québec were central features of this period. This was the result of an important social mobilisation for public support of childcare (Cleveland, 2008). Many services had been set up by families and communities, but public support was requested from the government with the objective to create 200,000 childcare spaces for children aged 5 years and under. Part of the rationale for these demands was the view that childcare would support women's participation in the labour market, reduce child poverty, and improve equality of opportunity for all children, regardless of social class (Marois, 2008). As noted by Marois (2008), political support from the Québecois government, including its head, the Premier, was essential to the implementation of public childcare. The results stood in stark contrast to elsewhere in the country: from 1992 to 2004, Québec increased childcare spaces by 310% compared with 33% in nine other provinces, including a 7% drop in Alberta (Human Resources and Skills Development Canada, 2007,

Appendix VII). Finally, the fourth period (2003 to the present) is characterised primarily by the adoption of the new Québec Parental Insurance Plan (QPIP) in 2006. From 2003, there was a strong mobilisation of social actors to support the childcare system, especially when the Conservative Party took power in Ottawa and the Liberals in Québec, with party policies that potentially threatened the orientation of family policy in Québec. At the same time, to establish a better parental leave benefit plan, the Québec government requested that the funds needed for this purpose be transferred to it from the federal scheme. Following a court case, in March 2005, the federal and provincial governments arrived at a financial agreement that allowed Québec to withdraw from the federal EI Maternity and Parental Benefit Plan. Ten months later, in January 2006, the province of Québec initiated a separate parental leave programme. For social actors, the discussion during this period centred on the importance of supporting families with childcare services, rather than lump-sum payments such as the federal Conservative government introduced, and that a new party, the Action démocratique du Québec, proposed for Québec.

The main objectives of the Québec Parental Insurance Plan are to ensure equity of access for the majority of women and men, whatever their employment status, and to offer more flexibility and better income. The point of reference in Québec for family policy as well as work–life balance issues, and even for fertility issues, is not Canada or the United States but Europe – Scandinavia for work–life balance and France for family policy and fertility issues, since France has had a consistently higher fertility rate than Québec in recent years as well as a high rate of women in the workforce (Barrère-Maurisson and Tremblay, 2009a, 2009b). However, fertility was never the only objective of Québec family policy, and the large social mobilisation around the issue mainly arises from concerns about equity, such as equity of women in employment and equity of rights of children, as well as fathers' participation in family responsibilities.

Employers' organisations have remained opposed, the most vocal being the Fédération canadienne de l'enterprise indépendante, representing some 20,000 small businesses in Québec. Other employer organisations such as the Conseil du patronat du Québec (mainly large businesses) and the Association of Manufacturers and Exporters of Québec, agreed in principle with the idea of a Québec Parental Insurance Plan, but differed over some details, particularly related to the supplementary costs to be assumed by employers (and employees) in order to have a more generous regime.

Québec: the new Québec Parental Insurance Plan

This new plan has a number of advantages in terms of the population covered, flexibility in taking the leave and the income replacement rate, all elements requested by the various social actors active in the debate over the past 15 years or so. Funding is based on contributions paid into the plan by employers, employees and self-employed workers (at the same time they continue to contribute at a lower rate to the federal EI programme for 'regular' unemployment insurance coverage). The new regime has been so successful in terms of parent participation, especially that of fathers and newly eligible groups such as self-employed workers, that discussions are now under way about increased contributions. Compared with other provinces and territories in Canada, more Québecois parents are eligible, leave is more generous and flexible (either a shorter leave with a higher income replacement rate or a longer leave with a lower income replacement rate); moreover, 3–5 weeks of the entire leave period (of almost one year) are reserved for fathers.

Québec's 2006 Parental Insurance Plan contains four major changes from EI. The first change, paternity leave, has been implemented in the form of non-transferable rights for fathers. Similar to policy measures in Scandinavia, this provides for 3–5 weeks of non-transferable leave for fathers ('daddy weeks'), with higher benefits than was the case under the federal plan, since the income replacement rate and earnings ceiling have also been increased. As noted above, the implementation of these 'daddy weeks' has led to a dramatic increase in fathers taking leave, with over

Table 3.1: Comparison of Canada (EI) and Quebec (QPIP) Parental Leave Benefit Plans, 2008

	Canada Employment Insurance	Québec *basic plan*	Québec *special plan*
Eligibility	600 hours	$2,000 earnings	
Self-employed workers	Not covered	Covered	
Basic replacement rate	55% for 50 weeks	70% for 25 weeks 55% for 25 weeks	75% for 40 weeks
Low income replacement rate[1]	Up to 80 %	Up to 80%	
Maximum insurable earnings	CAN$41,100 (€25,575)	CAN$60,500 (€37,540)	
Waiting period	2 weeks (per couple)	None	
Duration[2]	15 weeks maternity 35 weeks parental No paternity leave	18 weeks maternity 32 weeks parental 5 weeks paternity	15 weeks maternity 25 weeks parental 3 weeks paternity

Adapted from 'Child Care Spaces Recommendations', Report from the Ministerial Advisory Committee on the Government of Canada's Child Care Spaces Initiative, Government of Canada, January 2007.

Notes:

[1] Under both plans, a net family annual income of less than CAN$25,291(€15,755) is required in order to be eligible.

[2] Maternity and paternity leave are non-transferable individual entitlements. Parental leave is a shared entitlement.

half of Québécois fathers taking some or all of this leave; however, the average duration of leave has reduced for Québecois fathers taking leave, from 13 weeks in 2005 to 7 weeks in 2006 (Marshall, 2008). One interpretation is that since more fathers are taking the 3 to 5 weeks of leave reserved for them, this brings down the average length of leave. Meanwhile, in the rest of Canada, the average length of leave taken by fathers increased from 11 to 17 weeks (Marshall, 2008). Here, the duration of fathers' leave time could be partly related to mothers' lower eligibility.

The second change is more flexibility. Québec parents now have two options: a basic plan (longer leave with lower benefits) or a special plan (shorter leave with higher benefits). The basic plan includes benefits of 70% of average weekly earnings for 18 weeks of maternity leave, 5 weeks of paternity leave and 7 weeks of parental leave, then 55% of earnings for the remaining 25 weeks. The special plan provides benefits equivalent to 75% of earnings for 15 weeks of maternity leave, 3 weeks of paternity leave and 25 weeks of parental leave. Under the special plan, biological mothers can receive benefits for a maximum of 40 weeks (versus 50 in the basic plan) and biological fathers can receive benefits for a maximum of 27 weeks (versus 37 weeks). Adoptive parents are ineligible for maternity or paternity benefits. Under EI, adoptive parents are eligible for the same period of parental leave as biological parents. Under QPIP, adoptive parents can choose a version of the basic plan (37 weeks, with 12 weeks at 70% and 25 weeks at 55% of shared leave) or the special plan (28 weeks at 75% of shared leave).

The third change is the increased income offered by the plan. In addition to the abolition of the EI's 14-day waiting period without benefits, the Québec plan increases the replacement rate to periods of 70% and 75% of wages and the maximum insurable income to CAN$60,500 instead of CAN$41,000. In both plans, families earning less than a net family income of CAN$25,921 qualify for a 'family supplement' increasing the wage replacement rate to 80%. Higher replacement rates and ceilings are considered favourable to men's participation. Fourth, and finally, it is important to note that there is greater accessibility to parental leave for both women and men in Québec. The criteria for eligibility in Québec are broader than in the rest of Canada. This important change is addressed below.

Discussion and analysis

Accessibility

Both the Québec and the Canadian programmes are contributory wage replacement insurance schemes funded not through the tax system but through a separate pool of funds raised through payments by employers and employees in formal employment relations. Although the two plans have radically different eligibility criteria, both are premised on attachment to the paid labour force and are only available to parents with insurable employment. However, the eligibility requirements beyond this minimum are radically different: in the federal scheme, parents must have worked a minimum number of hours (600) over the past year, compared with a minimum level of earnings (CAN$2,000 or €1,245) in QPIP. Also, under EI, unlike QPIP, self-employed workers are excluded.

In 2001, the extension of parental leave by the Canadian government to 25 weeks overlooked calls by Québec groups to extend coverage rather than the length of leave. Many groups were asking that students and the self-employed be covered, something which is now possible with QPIP's low earnings qualification. Data show that the Québec system gives greater accessibility. As mentioned above, more Québécois mothers were eligible for parental leave in 2006 than other Canadian mothers; put differently, under EI, 38-40% of Canadian women have been consistently ineligible for parental leave in the past few years (Canada Employment Insurance Commission, 2005). Reasons for ineligibility include not being in the paid workforce (often due to full-time care work for older children), self-employment or not working the requisite number of hours (common for part-time and contract workers) (Marshall, 2003a). The percentage and reasons for fathers' ineligibility is unreported. (The Statistics Canada survey used to generate this data interviews mothers only.)

As mentioned earlier, a growing body of literature criticises EI for its weak coverage of that part of the population – predominantly women, immigrants, people of colour and young workers – with non-standard employment relationships: several employers instead of just one, limited-term employment contracts, and often part-time or casual employment (see Vosko, 2000, 2006; Clement et al, forthcoming). Studies of both 'regular' and parental leave EI applicants report insufficient working hours as a major cause of ineligibility (Bertrand and Bédard, 2002; Marshall, 2003a).

Although nationally nearly 80% of full-time students in 2005 were in the labour force (Canadian Association of University Teachers, 2007), students are highly unlikely to work sufficient hours to qualify for EI leave benefits. By comparison, under QPIP, earning CAN$2,000 over the previous year is a far easier threshold to pass and will enable more students to access parental leave benefits. National scholarship-granting agencies now provide parental leave, extending the funding period by one term, but this covers only a small percentage of graduate students (www.sshrc.ca). Taking a range of differences among women into account, Calder (2006, p 116) argues that a gendered script written into EI "has led to the benefit being delivered in a manner that does not enhance the equality of women in Canada". Data flowing from the implementation of QPIP over the next few years will enable researchers to study the extent to which QPIP reduces inequality of access.

Gender and class equity

According to Plantenga and Remery (2005), one of the key determinants in the take-up of parental leave by fathers in 30 European counties is a high level of payment while on leave. This is especially important for families where fathers are the primary breadwinners and for low-income families. Wage replacement rates closer to normal earnings improve the ability of lower earners to afford to take a longer period of leave. In spite of the 'family supplement' raising wage replacement rates to 80%, a study by Marshall (2003a) found that short leave-takers (returning 5 months after childbirth) had an annual income below CAN$16,000 (€9,960) and lived in a household with a total income under CAN$40,000 (€24,900). Mothers' earnings were found to be "clearly the overriding factor" in determining the length of leave mothers take from employment (Marshall, 2003a, p 9). Employer top-ups available often but not always in unionised workplaces similarly influence which parent's income the family can afford to sacrifice. While earnings-related benefits will always retain the stratification of the labour market, low wage replacement levels reinforce class inequality into the next generation.

International research studies have further confirmed the link between wage replacement and gender equity while also highlighting the class differences between families who take leave and those who do not. As described recently by Margaret O'Brien (in press, 2009): "Countries with high statutory income replacement father-care policies may promote gender equality but reinforce income inequalities, as cash transfers are being made to families which are already well-paid". She argues that this increases the risk of greater economic polarisation between "parental leave rich and parental leave poor households" (in press, 2009). Canadian research confirms this point; Evans argues that the current system of parental leave in Canada "implicates class/gender in ways that exacerbate inequalities between men and women, and among women differently situated" (Evans, 2007, p 127).

Data on parental leave show that the majority of users are still women, despite increasing participation on the part of fathers in childcare, infant play, children's sports and educational activities (Doucet, 2006). Although the extension of parental leave to one year in 2001 was viewed by some in Canada as constituting considerable progress in terms of employment equality, this policy could very well further reinforce traditional mothering roles without having a strong influence on the participation of fathers in parenting, and thus rather negatively affect the goal of labour force equality. This was indeed one of the reasons why the Québec coalition on parental leave called for a more inclusive and flexible programme, rather than just longer leave. In contrast, in Québec, low-cost childcare is a progressive measure that seems to have raised female employment rates and childcare enrolment.

Why do two regimes continue to exist within the same national context?

The jurisdictional divide in policy making between federal and provincial levels of government could be argued to be a structural weakness that undermines the efforts of social actors at the federal level. It is at the local level that parents seek solutions to work–life balance challenges and there is evidence of limited success in improving the quality and, to a lesser extent, availability of childcare in Vancouver, Calgary and Toronto independent of the provincial or federal government (see Mahon, 2009). Overall, however, the federal government holds the purse strings while the provinces deliver most social policy. Due to this divide, social actors are separated by province. Another contributing factor is the weakening of social actors since at least the 1990s through cuts to previously state-funded advocacy and women's groups as well as advisory bodies (McKeen and Porter, 2003).

One feature of Québec politics that sets it apart from other provinces is that it has continually sought to exercise greater autonomy. In family policy, greater provincial control can be attributed in large part to the very active role that unions and women's groups have played. The history of family policy in Québec is dominated by the active role of such social actors and, as we have shown, it is evident that the mobilisation of social actors and the building up of various coalitions and consultative bodies on family policy have been critical. They asked the Québec government to support childcare systems developed by community and women's groups, and then to offer a better parental leave plan than was offered at the federal level (Tremblay, 2008a, 2008b).

This active role of social actors is particularly characteristic of Québec, especially in the North American context (Tremblay, 2008a, 2008b, forthcoming) but also in comparison with many European countries. Barrère-Maurisson and Tremblay (2009a, 2009b), comparing Québec with France, conclude that in Québec organisations of social actors – 'intermediate organisations' – have been very vocal and active in parental leave, childcare and family policy debate; while in France, as in many other European countries, it is more traditionally the state that has developed family policy, with less civil society involvement.

Conclusion

It is clear that Québec parents receive more public support for balancing employment and the care of children than parents in the rest of Canada, and that QPIP enhances accessibility and equality more than EI. For these reasons, our view is that some version of the Québec plan would be welcomed by families elsewhere in the country. However, while incremental change may occur, there are a number of indicators that significant change is unlikely to occur at the national level or in any other province any time soon.

First, it could be argued that family policy is not high on the national political agenda, while it is on the provincial agenda in Québec. During the October 2008 federal election, party platforms included childcare and parental leave reforms, but overall these issues were considered minor, receiving a low media profile and surpassed by other topics in leadership debates. By contrast, the three Québec parties propose different options, but at least two of them (Parti Québécois and Parti libéral) both agree on the importance of maintaining the childcare and leave policies. The third party, Action démocratique du Québec, proposes a scheme similar to that of the Conservative Party at the national level, the direct cash transfer of CAN$100 (€60) a month per child. This scheme has the support of some parents, generally those who have one caregiver parent at home, but it has been strongly criticised by family and women's groups in Quebec (Marois, 2008; Tremblay, 2008b).

One reason for the low profile of family policy at the national level may be the fact that Canada does not have as many women parliamentarians (22% as of 14 October 2008) as some other countries, especially in Scandinavia (see Newman and White, 2006). Québec, on the other hand, has a history of more women legislators than the federal parliament, most other provinces and many industrialised nations (France, for example), peaking in 2003 at 30.9% compared with a provincial average of 21.3% (www.cbc.ca). Moreover, many of these women have exercised important responsibilities and convinced their male counterparts to support progressive family policies. At present, half of Quebec Cabinet ministers are women. In the Parti Québécois government, in power from 1996 to 2003, Pauline Marois, a former Finance Minister and now the party leader, proposed and championed the new parental leave system (introduced formally by a Parti libéral government in 2003) and implemented the childcare system (Marois, 2008).

Second, addressing the demographic challenge of an ageing population does not point only towards policies that encourage a higher fertility rate. Historically, labour shortages have been addressed in Canada through immigration policy and increasingly by recruiting temporary foreign workers. A good example is the federal 'Live-In Caregiver Program'. It allows parents – many of whom cannot find or afford childcare – to employ a foreign nanny to care for their children with the requirement that the nanny must live in the home of her employer (www.cic.gc.ca). Québec has a lower immigration rate than in the rest of Canada and immigration has never been a main policy objective; this may contribute to greater interest in the impact of family policies on fertility rates.

Third, several critical factors that contributed to QPIP do not exist in other provinces. As we have argued, family policy in Québec is largely the result of strong mobilisation and capacity building by social actors such as trades unions (especially the women's committees within the four largest unions), women's groups and some progressive family groups, as well as an important public debate on the issue. Social actors are not mobilised to the same degree for parental leave or childcare in the rest of Canada. Newman and White (2006) argue that the women's movement in Québec has focused on provincial politics far more than elsewhere in the country. Also, if English-speaking provinces have a comparator it is not Europe but the United States, against which Canadian leave policy is generous; and, no other province shows any interest in assuming responsibility for additional policy areas from the federal government, including parental leave. For these reasons, among others, there are no signs of significant improvement to EI leave policy in Canada anytime soon.

Having said this, if there is a glimmer of hope for parents in the rest of Canada, it comes from two sources. First is an election promise made by the winning Conservative Party to allow self-employed workers to opt in to EI maternity and parental benefits. Second is a court case currently under way, launched by a coalition of unions that have asked for a legal ruling on the constitutionality of federal government use of EI surplus funds to reduce general revenue debt. The unions argue that the surplus should be channelled to improving access and benefit rates for 'regular' and 'special' benefit recipients. If the new minority Conservative government follows through, a larger proportion of parents currently ineligible for benefits will qualify. If the court case succeeds, all parents, like Bill and Sarah, may attain more generous benefits, closer to those available to Marie and Serge, their Québecois neighbours.

In conclusion, this chapter has shown that it is mainly because of the more inclusive characteristics of the parental leave plan in Québec that QPIP should be envisaged for implementation elsewhere in Canada. QPIP provides more parents with coverage (such as the self-employed, students and part-time workers) and a greater probability that fathers will participate. Parental leave benefit policy is not the only condition needed to facilitate work–family articulation; others include childcare, flexible working time and tele-work (Tremblay et al, 2007; Tremblay, 2008a, forthcoming). As these policies and programmes vary both between and within provinces, it is clear that the Canadian approach to gender, work and family remains complex and diverse. Nevertheless, to date, only one Canadian province, that of Québec, has developed a comprehensive family policy that focuses on issues of infant and child well-being, gender equality, women's employment and the promotion of fathers' involvement.

Notes

[1] Leave provision described here refers to statutory entitlements.

[2] Converted into euros at exchange rate on 23 February 2009, rounded up to the nearest 5 euros.

References

Barrère-Maurisson, M-A. and Tremblay, D-G. (2009a) 'La gouvernance de la conciliation travail-famille: comparaison France-Québec', in *Santé, société et solidarité*, No 1-2008, pp 85-95.

Barrère-Maurisson, M-A. and Tremblay, D-G. (2009b) *Concilier travail et famille: Le rôle des acteurs*, Québec-France. Québec: Presses de l'université du Québec.

Barton, N. (2007) 'Conservatives give child care report a time out', Capital News Online, vol 20, no 5, 30 March.

Battle, K., Mendelson, M. and Torjman, S. (2005) 'The modernization mantra: toward a new architecture for Canada's adult benefits', *Canadian Public Policy/Analyse de Politiques*, vol 31, no 4, pp 431-7.

Bernstein, S., Lippel, K. and Lamarche, L. (2001) *Women and homework: The Canadian legislative framework*, Status of Women Canada's Policy Research Fund, Ottawa, ON: Status of Women Canada.

Bertrand, J.-F. and Bédard, M. (2002) *EI benefit coverage of the unemployed according to work pattern prior to unemployment*, Ottawa: Applied Research Branch, Strategic Policy, Human Resources Development Canada.

Calder, G. (2006) 'A pregnant pause: federalism, equality and the maternity and parental leave debate in Canada', *Feminist Legal Studies*, vol 14, pp 99-118.

Campbell, A. (2006) 'Proceeding with «care»: lessons to be learned from the Canadian parental leave and Quebec daycare initiatives in developing a national childcare policy', *Canadian Journal of Family Law*, vol 22, no 2, pp 171-222.

Canadian Association of University Teachers (2007) *Almanac of Post-Secondary Education 2007*, Ottawa: Canadian Association of University Teachers.

Canada Employment Insurance Commission (2005) *Employment Insurance 2004 monitoring and assessment report*, Ottawa: Canada Employment Insurance Commission.

Clement, W., Mathieu, S., Prus, S. and Uckardesler, E. (forthcoming, 2009) 'Restructuring work and labour markets in the new economy: four processes', in N. Pupo and M. Thomas (eds) *Interrogating the 'new economy': Restructuring work in the 21st century*, Toronto: Broadview Press.

Cleveland, G. (2008) 'Bénéfices et coûts des centres de la petite enfance du Québec', in N. Bigras and G. Cantin (eds) *Les services de garde éducatifs à la petite enfance du Québec. Recherches, réflexions et pratiques*, Québec: Presses de l'université du Québec.

Comité de la consultation sur la politique familiale (1986) *Rapport du Comité de la consultation sur la politique familiale: le soutien collectif réclamé pour les familles québécoises, première partie*, Québec: Gouvernement du Québec, Comité de la consultation sur la politique familiale.

Conseil de la famille et de l'enfance. (2007, revised 2008) *La politique familiale au Québec: Visée, portée, durée et rayonnement*, Québec: Conseil de la famille et de l'enfance.

Doucet, A. (2006) *Do men mother? Fathering, care, and domestic responsibility*, Toronto: University of Toronto Press.

Evans, P.M. (2007) 'Comparative perspectives on changes to Canada's paid parental leave: implications for class and gender', *International Journal of Social Welfare*, vol 16, pp 119-28.

Giroux, M.-È. (2008) *La lutte pour un régime québécois d'assurance parentale*, Cahiers du Crises No MS0803, Montréal, Crises UQAM.

Government of Canada (2008) 'The Universal Child Care Plan provides spaces: new child care spaces', available at www.universalchildcare.ca/eng/spaces/index.shtml (accessed 17 April 2009).

House of Commons Canada (2000) *Public accounts of Canada 1999–2000*, Ottawa: House of Commons Canada.

Human Resources and Skills Development Canada (2005) *Summative evaluation of EI parental benefits*, Ottawa: Human Resources and Skills Development Canada.

Human Resources and Skills Development Canada (2007) *Supporting Canadian children and families: Addressing the gap between the supply and demand for high quality child care*, Report from the Ministerial Advisory Committee on the Government of Canada's Child Care Spaces Initiative, Ottawa: Human Resources and Skills Development.

Kerr, K.B. (2005) *Employment Insurance premiums: In search of a genuine rate-setting process*, Ottawa: Library of Parliament.

Lepage, F., Bérubé, G. and Mailloux, T. (1989) *Les congés parentaux au Québec: Analyse de la situation actuelle*, Québec: Conseil du statut de la femme, Direction de la recherche et de l'analyse, Service juridique.

McKeen, W. and Porter, A. (2003) 'Politics and transformation: Welfare state restructuring in Canada', in W. Clement and L.F. Vosko (eds) *Changing Canada: Political economy as transformation*, Montréal: McGill-Queen's University Press.

Mahon, R. (2009) 'Of scalar hierarchies and welfare redesign: child care in four Canadian cities', in R. Keil. and R. Mahon (eds) *Leviathan undone? Towards a political economy of scale*, Vancouver: University of British Columbia.

Marois, P. (2008) 'L'adoption d'une politique familiale au Québec; priorité aux centres de la petite enfance', in N. Bigras and G. Cantin (eds) *Les services de garde éducatifs à la petite enfance du Québec. Recherches, réflexions et pratiques*, Québec: Presses de l'université du Québec.

Marshall, K. (2003a) 'Benefiting from extended parental leave', *Perspectives on Labour and Income* (Statistics Canada Catalogue no. 75–001–XIE) vol 4, no 3 (March) pp 5–11 (NB No volume number).

Marshall, K. (2003b) 'Parental leave: more time off for baby', *Canadian Social Trends*, (Statistics Canada Catalogue no. 11–008–XPE) No 71 (Winter), pp 13–18 (NB No volume number).

Marshall, K. (2006) 'Converging gender roles', *Perspectives on Labour and Income* (Statistics Canada Catalogue no. 75–001–XIE) vol 7, no 7 (July), pp 5–17 (NB No volume number).

Marshall (2008): Marshall, K. (2008) 'Fathers' use of paid parental leave', *Perspectives on Labour and Income* (Statistics Canada Catalogue no. 75–001–XIE) vol 9, no 6 (June), pp 5–14 (NB. No volume number).

Newman, J. and White, L.A. (2006) *Women, politics, and public policy: The political struggles of Canadian women*, Don Mills, Ontario: Oxford University Press.

O'Brien, M. (in press, 2009) 'Fathers, parental leave policies and infant quality of life: international perspectives and policy impact', *The Annals of the American Academy of Political and Social Science*.

Perusse, D. (2003) 'New maternity and parental benefits', *Perspectives on Labour and Income* (Statistics Canada Catalogue no. 75–001–XIE) vol 4, no 3 (March), pp 1–4 (NB No volume number).

Plantenga, J. and Remery, C. (2005) *Reconciliation of work and private life: A comparative review of thirty European countries*, Luxembourg: Luxembourg, Office for Official Publications.

Porter, A. (2003) *Gendered states: Women, unemployment insurance, and the political economy of the welfare state in Canada, 1945–1997*, Toronto: University of Toronto Press.

Pulkingham, J. and van der Gaag, T. (2004) 'Maternity/parental leave provision in Canada: we've come a long way, but there's further to go', *Canadian Woman Studies/Les Cahiers de la Femme*, vol 23, nos 3,4, pp 116–25.

Statistics Canada (2007) *Women in Canada: Work chapter updates 2006*, (Statistics Canada Catalogue No. 89F0133XIE), Ottawa: Statistics Canada.

Statistics Canada (2008) *Labour Force Survey*, Unpublished Data. Ottawa: Statistics Canada.

Sussman, D. and Bonnell, S. (2006) 'Women as Primary Breadwinners', *Perspectives on Labour and Income*, vol 7, no 8, pp 10-17.

Townson, M. and Hayes, K. (2007) *Women and the Employment Insurance Program. Growing gap*, Ottawa: Canadian Centre for Policy Alternatives.

Tremblay, D.-G. (2008a) *Conciliation emploi–famille et temps sociaux*, Québec/Toulouse: Presses de l'université du Québec et Octares.

Tremblay, D.-G. (2008b) 'Les politiques familiales et l'articulation emploi-famille au Québec et au Canada', in N. Bigras and N. Cantin (eds) *Les services de garde éducatifs à la petite enfance du Québec: Recherches, réflexions et pratiques*, Québec: Presses de l'université du Québec.

Tremblay, D.-G. (forthcoming) 'Quebec's policies for work–family balance: a model for Canada?', in M. Cohen (ed) *Women and public policy in Canada*, Toronto: University of Toronto Press.

Tremblay, D.-G., Paquet, R. and Najem, E. (2007) 'Work–family balancing and working time: is gender determinant?', *Global Journal of Business Research*, vol 1, no 1, pp 97-113.

Vosko, L.F. (2000) *Temporary work: The gendered rise of a precarious employment relationship*, Toronto: University of Toronto.

Vosko, L.F. (ed) (2006) *Precarious employment: Understanding labour market insecurity in Canada*, Montréal: McGill-Queen's University Press.

Warskett, R. (2007) 'The legal regulation of maternal and parental leave benefits in the context of Canadian labour market polarization', Paper presented at Workshop on Gender and Social Politics in an Era of Globalisation, 27-28 April, Carleton University, Ottawa.

FOUR

Czech Republic: normative or choice-oriented system?

Jiřina Kocourková[1]

Maternity leave[2]: 28 weeks at 69% of daily earnings up to a ceiling of CZK479 per day.

Paternity leave: none.

Parental leave: until child is 3 years; leave is an individual entitlement but only one parent can receive parental benefit. There are 3 options for benefit payment: CZK11,400 (€400)[3] per month until the child is 24 months; or CZK7,600 (€265) until the child is 36 months; or CZK7,600 until the child is 21 months, then CZK3,800 (€135) until the child is 48 months.

Leave to care for sick children: 9 days per parent per illness of a child under 10 years at 69% of earnings up to a ceiling of CZK441 (€15) per day; there is no limit on the frequency of taking leave.

Other: none.

The **Czech Republic** is a member state of the European Union (EU). It became an independent state in 1993 after Czechoslovakia separated into two states. It has a low level of employment among women with children under 3 years and a low level of part-time employment among women workers. There is no information on how much time women or men take for parental leave, but the number of men taking leave is very low; in 2006, men accounted for 1.4% of recipients of parental benefit. There is a very low level of formal childcare provision for children under 3 years.

Introduction

Until 1992, the Czech Republic was a part of Czechoslovakia. Czechs and Slovaks shared the whole communist period as one country, as well as the onset of the fundamental economic and social changes that followed the collapse of this regime. The period of common history is taken only as the starting point for the main focus of the chapter: an analysis of policies in the Czech Republic since 1993. The pronatalist population policy practised before 1990 in Czechoslovakia is contrasted with the development of family policy after 1990.

The chapter is divided into two sections. The first is historically organised and consists of several parts reflecting the changes on the Czech political scene up to 2008. Developments in maternal and paternal leave policies are systematically presented; paternity leave has not so far been established in the Czech Republic. The second section is devoted to discussion of cross-cutting issues related to leave policy: work, fertility and gender. Finally, current policy development in the Czech Republic is considered as searching for a balance between normative and choice-oriented approaches.

The short history of leave policies in the Czech Republic has undoubtedly been influenced by overall European trends in family policy, particularly increasing support for women's employment and for the involvement of men in childcare. Nevertheless, during this period some elements specific to the Czech Republic can be distinguished in both politics and practice. Development of leave policies cannot be properly understood without taking into account the whole political context as well as changes in family policy objectives made by successive Czech governments.

Although the political resurgence of Catholicism has not been so apparent in the Czech Republic as in some other countries, like Slovakia or Poland, a 'traditional' approach to family policy has become dominant since 1990. It has been apparent in the character of all leave policies adopted in the Czech Republic and could be understood as the main reason why, until now, there has been a lack of political interest in the important contribution that leave policies could make to gender equity.

Changes in leave policy since 1945

Maternity leave policy before 1990

After the Second World War, maternity leave was considered to be an important part of pronatalist population policy in Czechoslovakia. During the period from 1945 to 1990, maternity leave was extended three times: in 1964 from 18 to 22 weeks, in 1968 to 26 weeks and in 1987 to 28 weeks. Women were given the possibility of taking unpaid additional leave, initially until the child's first birthday in 1964, then up to the second birthday in 1969. In addition, in the late 1960s, a new form of leave was prepared as a part of a 'pronatalist package' of measures. In 1970, Czechoslovakia became one of the pioneers of paid extended maternity leave or what might be termed 'childcare leave'; when first introduced it lasted until the child's second birthday and was available to women with at least two children. Until 1984, a woman having one child was entitled only to an unpaid 2-year additional leave. From 1985, however, such women became entitled to paid additional maternity leave until their child was one year old, while from 1987, a woman with at least two children could take extended leave until her youngest child was 3 years old.

So, before 1990 two types of paid maternity leave were widely used by women in the former Czechoslovakia. The first was an insurance-based maternity leave that was reserved for the first months after birth, the final extension taking place in 1987. Maternity benefit was income-related and paid at 90% of a woman's net average earnings before starting maternity leave. The second was a form of childcare leave called 'additional maternity leave', during which time all women had job security and retained full pension entitlement. Payment was not insurance-based and took the form of a flat-rate benefit. Length of leave and benefit was related to numbers of children, providing a strong pronatalist incentive (Kocourková, 2002). The policy encouraged women to have a second child as soon as possible after the first one.

This additional maternity leave became the basis for the parental leave system developed in Czechoslovakia after the change in political regime in 1989.

Discontinuity in family policy after 1989

In the late 1980s, Czechoslovakia was singled out as a country with an explicit and comprehensive family policy (Gordon, 1988): 'explicit' in terms of interventionist policies aimed directly or indirectly at encouraging fertility and 'comprehensive' in terms of the range and generosity of the benefits provided to families. However, this pronatalist orientation was not in tune with the goals of the new liberal-conservative government in Czechoslovakia in the early 1990s or the liberal-conservative government that took over in the Czech Republic in 1993. Moreover, the social security system of the former communist regime was criticised by the new political elite for being excessively redistributive (Cornia, 1991).

As a result, during the first half of the 1990s the former extensive state support to all families was both substantially reduced and no longer explicitly pronatalist; for example, the amount of family benefit paid no longer increased with the number of children in the family. Initially, there was a strong tendency to limit state support only to families considered most in need. Later, the political effort of the liberal Civic Democratic Party (ODS) to make all family benefits means-tested was somewhat diluted and only child allowances have been means-tested since 1995. After the adoption of a new social security law in 1995, no improvements occurred in the family policy system until the end of century. Family policy issues were of no further interest to the liberal governments of that period.

But at the end of the 1990s, a change of government raised expectations that family policy would gain more political attention. The Social Democratic Party (ČSSD) replaced the liberal government in 1998 and expressed concern about the extremely low fertility level in the Czech Republic. The political scene was opened up to public debates and initiatives of non-governmental organisations. It was a Christian interest group called the National Centre for Families that took the first initiative, by making proposals about how to improve the situation of families with children. Starting in 1999, this group organised a yearly conference on family policy topics; at these events, representatives from political institutions in

Germany and Austria presented their views on how the Czech Republic should develop family policy. Through this influence, a tendency to apply the German traditional model of family policy was strengthened.

Although the Social Democrats led only a minority government, with the help of representatives from the Christian and Democratic Party (KDU-ČSL) they were able to introduce new measures to support families in 2001. During the subsequent government, from 2002 to 2006, the Social Democrats together with the Christian Democrats introduced further improvements to family benefits, particularly related to parental benefit, child allowances and birth grant. In addition to these initiatives, the National Family Policy Concept was accepted in 2005. Although the need for a greater variety of tools for family support was stressed in this document, this has not been realised up to the time of writing. Since 2006 the main Czech liberal party, ODS, has led the government and has not accepted this document as binding on it.

Leave policies in the 1990s

The history of a parental leave system in which the father is also taken into account as a potential carer started in 1990 in Czechoslovakia when the previous 'additional maternity benefit' was renamed 'parental benefit'. At the same time the pronatalist element of parental benefit was scrapped as all parents became entitled to this benefit for a period of 3 years irrespective of the number of children they had (see Table 4.1 for details of changes in parental benefit since 1990). In 1993, the Czech Republic took over the legislation of Czechoslovakia, with no fundamental changes until the new law on the social and family system was approved by the Czech Parliament in 1995. Before this law came to a parliamentary vote, there was a strong discussion in the media about the range of proposed cutbacks. Due to strong public protest only child allowances became means-tested; the parental benefit remained universal since it was acknowledged as a priority.

To ensure regular increases in parental benefit, the new law indexed the benefit to the cost of living. However, the main change introduced by this law was an extension of the period of entitlement to parental benefit by one year. Parents now had the possibility of receiving parental benefit until their child's fourth birthday. This was a concession by the liberal ODS party to the Christian Democrat KDU, both members of the government coalition. In exchange, the KDU approved the introduction of means-tested child allowances into the same law, even though this was not in its election manifesto.

Extension of the period of payment of parental benefit was fully in line with the aim of supporting women to stay at home with very young children for as long as possible. Nevertheless, it has caused an anomaly in the system that continues up to the present day: according to the Employment Code, parental leave can only be taken until a child's third birthday (it was called 'additional maternal leave' until 2001); but according to the Social Security Code, the parental benefit is granted until the child's fourth birthday. As job security is ensured only for 3 years, women

Table 4.1: Development of parental benefit since 1990

Valid from	Period of entitlement (years)	Benefit level in CZK (per month)	Benefit level in euros (per month)	Benefit level as % of average wage	Maximum income for entitlement to parental benefit (CZK per month)
1 Oct 1990	3	900	36	27.4	800
1991	3	900	36	23.7	800
1 Apr 1992	3	1200	48	25.8	1000
1 May 1993	3	1360	54	23.0	1000
1 Feb 1994	3	1500	60	21.4	1800
1 Oct 1994	3	1740	70	24.8	1800
1 Oct 1995	4	1848	74	22.2	1680
1 Jan 1996	4	1980	80	20.2	1800
1 Oct 1996	4	2112	85	21.5	1920
1 July 1997	4	2222	89	20.6	2020
1 Apr 1998	4	2343	94	19.9	2130
1999	4	2343	94	18.3	2130
1 Apr 2000	4	2409	96	17.7	2190
1 Oct 2001	4	2552	102	17.3	3480
2002	4	2552	102	16.1	3480
2003	4	2552	102	15.1	3480
1 May 2004	4	3573	143	19.8	*
1 Jan 2005	4	3635	145	19.1	
1 Jan 2006	4	3693	148	18.5	
1 Jan 2007	4	7600	304	37.2	

Notes: 1 EUR = 25 CZK. * Since 1 January 2004 the income limit for a parent on parental leave has been abolished.

taking leave who do not want to lose their jobs can effectively use only 3 out of the 4 years of parental benefit payment.

In the late 1990s, some interest was expressed in simplifying the parental leave system. A right–wing party, the Freedom Union (US–DEU), proposed shortening the payment of parental benefit to 3 years while, at the same time, increasing the flat rate to make parental benefit a better substitute for earnings (Kocourková, 2001). But as the Christian Democrats (KDU-ČSL) have been in government for most of the time, in coalition either with liberals or with Social Democrats, all efforts to shorten the period of entitlement to parental benefit proved unsuccessful. Hence the persistent influence of catholic conservative policy has contributed to sustaining traditional gender roles in society.

While the additional maternity leave scheme, subsequently the parental leave scheme, has changed a lot since 1990, basic maternity leave recorded fewer changes. There was no public call to extend its length as, at 28 weeks, it already exceeded the minimum standard laid down in the EU directive. Maternity leave benefit was generous in Czechoslovakia, at 90% of net average earnings. However, in the Czech Republic this rate was lowered to 69% in 1993 when reform of the sickness insurance system took place. Moreover, the ceiling placed on maternity benefit was very low for quite a long time in the 1990s, while it was not indexed until 1998, which caused a considerable drop in benefit levels particularly for women with higher incomes. By 1998, the highest possible benefit payment had fallen to less than 50% of average earnings.

One explanation for this decline in maternity benefit could be found in the economic difficulties that the Czech Republic was facing in the second half of the 1990s. In 1997, the then liberal-conservative government adopted cuts in public spending known as the 'Klaus package' after Prime Minister Vaclav Klaus, which also had an unfavourable effect on state support to families. For this reason, it was unrealistic to expect improvement in maternity benefit. Only since 1999 have several adjustments occurred to the maternity benefit ceiling, and currently the highest benefit payment is equivalent to about 60% of average earnings.

The new political context since 2001

Although the Christian Democratic Party has always been relatively weak in the Czech Republic, it has managed to keep its influence on political decision making by its participation in coalition governments for most of the period since 1990. It was expected that, after the division of Czechoslovakia in 1993, the influence of Catholicism would be weakened in the Czech Republic. During the common history of both nations in one state, Catholicism was always a stronger influence among Slovaks than Czechs. However, the political reality has developed differently. When Social Democrats came to power at the end of the 1990s, the position of Christian Democrats was even strengthened as the Social Democrats looked to them for support when introducing family policy measures.

Historically, both parties have had different aims for family policy measures. Christian Democrats advocate a traditional family, as they see the mother's role as essential for the socialisation and well-being of children. Social Democrats, on the other hand, tend to support families by promoting the individualisation of family members and making work and family responsibilities more compatible. Despite these different orientations, these two parties have not been much opposed, as there has been no great pressure to facilitate female employment through public childcare. The Czech Social Democrats, therefore, have focused their efforts on improving financial support to families, as this proved highly relevant.

With the accession of the Czech Republic to the European Union and the accompanying process of harmonising Czech legislation with EU regulations, family policy issues topical elsewhere in Europe have featured more on to the political agenda in the Czech Republic since the turn of the century. Accordingly, greater emphasis has been put on policies that could contribute to better balance between work and family. While public childcare facilities for children less than 3 years of age continue to receive little attention, an already well-developed network of childcare facilities for children between 3 and 6 years of age has been further improved and adapted to meet a greater variety of family needs. As a result of meeting EU requirements, in 2001 Czech men formally gained equal rights to use the extended maternity leave that was then renamed parental leave. Moreover, a new tendency to support family-friendly forms of employment, such as part-time work and flexible working hours, became visible, with the new employment law facilitating such possibilities.

A more favourable political climate for the adoption of family- and work-friendly policies was created when Vladimir Spidla became the Czech Minister of Work and Social Affairs, from 1998 to 2002, then the Czech Prime Minister between 2002 and 2004. His influence was particularly felt in the preparation of Social Democratic Party's election programme. He argued for following the Swedish path towards the achievement of a more egalitarian model of family life. In his view, government should take full responsibility for the support of families, and particularly of working parents, by creating better conditions to allow women to combine paid employment and family responsibilities more easily and to allow fathers to take a larger role in childrearing. However, any aspirations for a Swedish type of family policy were put aside in the declaration by the new government in 2002 because of the need for coalition with the Christian Democrats. Since 2004, Spidla has been the EC Commissioner responsible for Employment, Social Affairs and Equal Opportunities, following his replacement as the Czech Prime Minister. His work in Brussels suggests that he continues to promote gender equality at the supra-national level.

Parental leave policies in 2002–06

Parental leave arrangements were significantly developed during the period 2002–06, since they were a key interest of both Social and Christian Democrats as coalition partners. Most of the changes concerned the amount of parental benefit and flexibility in use. The first significant increase in parental benefit, by 40%, occurred in 2004. However, the largest increase in parental benefit was approved by the Czech Parliament at the end of 2005, during the election campaign. Although it was the Social Democratic Party that had such measures in its programme, it was the liberal ODS party that took the initiative and unexpectedly proposed the measure in parliament. Not wishing to lose face, the Social Democrats voted for it, so doubling the amount of parental benefit from 1 January 2007. As a result, during 2007 all parents with children under 4 years of age were entitled to receive a flat-rate payment of CZ7,582 (€305), equivalent to 40% of average gross earnings in 2005.

However, this level of benefit turned out to be unsustainable in the long term for the state budget. The new liberal government, voted into office in 2006, immediately approved a reform in order to reduce the costs of parental benefit, although it was the same party that had proposed the original measure before the election. This shows both the importance of family policy issues during the election campaign as well as their misuse by populists in the Czech Republic.

Nevertheless, the financial situation of parents on parental leave significantly improved in comparison with their situation before 2006.

Since it has become more and more important for women not to lose contacts with employment when they are on parental leave, flexibility in the use of parental benefit has also increased. First, in 2004, the limit on possible earnings while receiving parental benefit was abolished, so that recipients of benefit can now work. Second, the measure adopted in 2001 allowed parents to place their child in a public childcare service for a maximum of 5 days a month without any loss of parental benefit. But since February 2006, this provision has been improved for parents with children over 3 years of age, who can now have their child in a public kindergarten for up to 4 hours each day. Accordingly, parents with a child between the age of 3 and 4 years can work part time while taking advantage of both public childcare services and parental benefit.

Parental leave reform in 2008

Taking account of the growing budget constraints, further substantial across-the-board increases in parental benefit were hardly likely. Although the National Family Concept was adopted in 2005, most of the improvements made to parental leave were not directly proposed in a measured way by the government, but unsystematically by parliamentarians. Parental benefit arrangements were not adopted so as to follow any well-designed plan, this haphazard approach leading for example to the continuing discrepancy between the length of parental leave and parental benefit. Parents can receive parental benefit even if they work full time; however, if they work, they have to make private arrangements for the care of their child, being allowed only limited access to public services. Parental benefit can, therefore, be considered a kind of childcare benefit or child allowance for young children, rather than a payment linked to leave taking.

The latest reform of parental leave policy in the Czech Republic came into effect in 2008. The aim was to enable parents to choose how long they want to care for their children. Parents may select one of three possible periods for receiving parental benefit: until their child reaches 2, 3 or 4 years of age. The length of leave selected determines the level of parental benefit – the shorter the period, the higher the amount paid. If benefit is taken until a child is 24 months, it is paid at CZK11,400 (€460) per month; only parents who are entitled to maternity benefit of at least CZK380 per calendar day may request this form of arrangement. The intermediate rate, opting to take benefit for 3 years, is CZK7,600 (€310); only parents who are entitled to maternity benefit may request this form of arrangement. The longest option is CZK7,600 until the child is 21 months of age and then CZK3,800 (€155) until the child is 48 months of age.

Cross-cutting themes

Work disincentives

The aim of extending parental leave in 1990 was to release women from the labour market. At the same time, children's well-being became an argument in debates that arose about state support for childcare. Childcare in the family was presented as the best alternative for children. Parental leave changes were among the first steps outlined in Social Reform in Czechoslovakia, the programme of the first democratic government after the collapse of the communist regime, where the high employment rate of women was viewed critically and support was given to valuing the care of children. This could be seen as a form of rejection of the previous communist 'duty to be employed'.

The first post-communist government took steps towards implementing more conservative, refamilialisation policies, which supported women in their roles as mothers and made it more difficult for them to remain in the labour market. As a result, an outdated pattern of gendered and implicit familialism has been established, which places work and family in opposition (Sirovátka, 2004). Parental leaves were designed to strengthen the mother's role as the sole carer.

Public opposition was not strong when this approach was implemented at the beginning of the 1990s. Most women welcomed the opportunity to provide better care to their children. Before 1990, they were used to being employed while having access to public childcare services. When they wanted to care for their own child they had to have as least two children to be entitled to leave for a longer period. Many women felt labour market participation was something they were forced into, rather than a right they had fought for, and were consequently perhaps less likely than women in Western Europe to perceive employment as part of a liberation process. An anti-feminist atmosphere arose when the communist regime collapsed, which can explain the relative weakness of the women's movement during the 1990s in the Czech Republic. Thus the negative experience of being 'forced' to balance work and care before 1990 contributed to the acceptance of the new policy design after 1990.

The possibility of taking care of children for 4 years, even without job security, is the most evident aspect of refamilialisation policy in the 1990s. The demand for childcare services for children under 3 years of age also fell as a result of fewer children being born during the 1990s. It subsequently became unprofitable for the state to run these services and it transferred the responsibility to the local municipalities. Since (as in Hungary too) the national government did not give the local municipalities funds to continue subsidising nurseries, there followed a sharp drop in provision; most public childcare facilities for children under 3 years of age were closed down by the late 1990s, and the proportion of the age group attending them declined from 14% in 1990 to below 1% by the late 1990s.

Low fertility

When the communist regime collapsed in 1989, Czechoslovakia had one of the highest employment rates among women in the developed world and a relatively high fertility level, at approximately the replacement rate. The former comprehensive and generous family policy strongly supported both childbearing and the full employment of women through a well-developed system of institutional childcare and leave policies. From a comparative perspective, these policies to ease the tension between employment and childcare were fairly progressive, despite no measures being undertaken to encourage fathers to share in childcare and household responsibilities. According to Saxonberg and Sirovátka (2006a), a distinctive model of gender relations emerged, which combined aspects of both 'defamilialist' policies, promoting gender equality in work, and 'familialist' policies, supporting traditional gender roles in childcare.

Since the beginning of the 1990s, the impact of societal changes on family life in Czechoslovakia has been both intense and deep. People started to enjoy more options in their lives. However, economic reforms aimed at transition to the market economy exposed families to new uncertainties and risks, such as unemployment and income inequality. The risks to household welfare increased due to changes in the labour market and reforms of the social security system including family policies. Most of the childcare costs were shifted to families after 1990, most obviously following the radical reduction of state support to childcare services for children under 3 years of age. A previously well-developed childcare system was broken, which significantly affected women and their choices for combining work and family, while parental leave arrangements (still, significantly, termed maternity leave) were given more attention by government.

With all these changes, reinforcement of traditional gender roles has become apparent. There has been a clear shift from institutional care outside the family to family-based (that is, maternal) childcare. Families, and especially mothers, have confronted renewed conflicts between work and family aspirations, with rather passive state support.

During the 1990s, major changes in reproductive behaviour occurred in the Czech Republic. Young people started to postpone childbearing and fertility dropped steeply to well below replacement level. As well as the possibility of new lifestyles, typical of democratic societies, people were facing the negative consequences of socioeconomic transformation. Family policies in the Czech Republic did not appear to be sensitive enough to the new obstacles that families started to face. The weakening of policies that shared the costs of parenting and eased the tensions between paid work and motherhood seems to have had a negative effect on fertility development during the 1990s (Rychtaříková, 2000).

While the parental leave system underwent fundamental changes from 1990, these had little impact on childbearing. Czech women had the opportunity to stay at home with children, but at the same time they started to face a considerable decline in living standards because of the absence of a second income. The relative value of parental benefit was steadily diminishing and at the end of the 1990s it was equivalent to less than 20% of average gross earnings (see Table 4.1). Although social researchers as well as the media pointed out the lack of supportive family policies, no special policy attention was paid to the deteriorating situation of families until the change of government in the late 1990s.

Fathers' involvement

The renaming, in 1990, of 'additional maternity benefit' as 'parental benefit' can be seen as the first formal step to involve fathers in childcare (although already, since 1985, fathers could take 'additional maternity leave' if the mother were unable to take care of the child). From 1990, a father could receive the same flat-rate payment as the mother if he were unemployed and could stay at home with a child. Employed men, however, had only limited opportunities to use it, for example, if the mother was not able to take care of the child. Formally equal conditions for men and women were only established a decade later.

Moreover, there was inconsistent terminology between employment and social security codes: the Social Security Code used the term 'parental benefits', while the Employment Code referred to 'additional maternity leave'. Although this was often criticised, particularly by feminist interest groups, no government showed any concern until the late 1990s. Only then was the Employment Code amended, 'additional maternity leave' being renamed 'parental leave', while at the same time men were put on an equal footing with women as regards taking the renamed parental leave. Since then, both parents have been able to take parental leave at the same time; otherwise they can alternate with each other as often as they like, but with only one of them being entitled to parental benefit.

Although maternity leave is still primarily considered to be a right of women, recently there has been a tendency in the Czech Republic to distinguish between the physiological demands of pregnancy and childbirth on women and the care of children. Accordingly, it has been suggested that the first part of maternity leave should be reserved only for women, while the second part could be shared by both men and women. As a result of an effort to implement equal opportunities for men and women within family policy provisions, in 2006 the Social Democratic government proposed a redesign of maternity leave. The father of the child or husband of the woman who has delivered the child should, it was proposed, be able to take maternity leave instead of the mother from the seventh week after the child's birth. An amendment to the Sickness Insurance Act was approved, but its implementation has been twice postponed, first to 2008, then to 2009. With a change of government in 2006, wider political support needs to be gained, since the new law is much broader and part of it is not in line with the thinking of the newly elected politicians.

Gender: the gap between rights and practices

Feminist welfare state researchers have shown how a family policy package has an impact on gender relationships (Lewis, 1992; Orloff, 1993). The potential impact of policies for structuring private relationships is not immediately noticeable if we look only at the main parameters of policies (Neyer and Anderson, 2007). But gender neutrality of leave policies does not mean gender equality in practice. It is necessary to take into account the wider political background and look at the societal context in more detail.

During the 1990s, no policy makers in the Czech Republic considered any defamilialisation policies. There appeared to be little support among the population for gender equality and women's organisations did not pressure governments into introducing measures promoting gender equality (Saxonberg and Sirovátka, 2006b). The main argument was that under communism many women had been forced to work when they really would have preferred to stay at home. That is why in the 1990s women's organisations openly argued for the need for women to be able to become housewives if they so desired. No one group argued for the need to encourage men to share childrearing responsibilities. It was only in the context of harmonising the Czech Republic's regulations with EU rules that governments started to pay attention to policies on equal opportunities for men and women.

During the period of Social Democratic government, the family policy unit was established within the Ministry of Work and Social Affairs in 2003. Later on, this unit also got the remit for equal opportunities policies. Social Democrats wanted to stimulate women to be employed as a way for low-income families to improve their economic situations and to reduce economic differences between families. However, since 2008 due to new government policy, the issue of equal opportunities is no longer directly involved in family policy development. This agenda has been transferred out of the family policy unit at the Ministry of Work and Social Affairs. The current Czech government considers policies of gender equality to be connected more to women's employment rather than to their family membership.

Besides leave arrangements, women-friendly policies should include affordable childcare services and policies that stimulate fathers to make use of parental leave entitlements. Only the interaction of these measures can facilitate reconciliation of work and family. In the Czech Republic, scarcity of public childcare for children below the age of 3 years has contributed to limited family life choices. As mentioned above, although parental benefit was legislated for in 1990, truly equal conditions for both parents to make use of parental leave were established only in 2001. Until now, the right to take parental leave has not translated into a great deal of take-up by men. The number of men receiving parental benefit in comparison with women has remained negligible; currently only 1–2% of recipients of parental benefit are men. So although the potential exists for greater participation of men in childcare, realising that potential is unlikely while the gender gap in earnings continues.

The current government has signalled the need for a fundamental reform of the parental leave system. The last big increase in parental benefit caused not only some problems for the state budget but also a fear that the parental leave system would be exploited by unemployed women and would inhibit them from returning to paid work, since parental benefit outstripped both unemployment benefit and the minimum wage. The new reform, introduced in 2008, offering different options for taking parental benefit, was intended to make parental leave more connected with women's employment.

Although discussion about possible changes in the parental leave system was high on the political agenda until 2007, no political parties have initiated debates on gender equality, particularly the adoption of a father's quota in parental leave. It was left to academics engaged in gender studies to open discussion about this possibility. Vladimir Spidla, in his role as EU Commissioner, took part in a national conference about parental leave in October 2007. He presented his opinion that the Czech Republic should take Iceland as an example to follow: one third of parental leave should be kept for the mother, one third for the father and one third should be used as both parents choose. Following this, Czech feminists prepared a proposal to shorten parental leave to 18 months, of which 6 months would be reserved only for fathers. The proposal was rejected by most of the public, since it was perceived as too radical. This experience confirms that introducing a father's quota is more difficult in the case of an existing long parental leave than in the case of a short leave period where a quota can be part of both parents getting more leave.

Normative policy versus parental choice

Since the 1990s, the Czech Republic could be characterised as a representative of the 'long leave mother home-centred' policy model (Wall, 2007), based on the idea that mothers should stay at home as long as possible. The 2008 reforms suggest, however, that policy makers in the Czech Republic want to transform the 'long parental leave' model by adopting policies that make choice more available. Accordingly, parents have been allowed to choose how long they want to care for their children. At the time the reforms were proposed, there was discussion about whether the parental benefit should be related to previous earnings and which alternative non-parental forms of childcare should be developed. Nevertheless, after one or 2 years of paid parental leave based on previous earnings, a low flat-rate payment for the rest of the benefit period was strongly advocated by representatives of the Ministry of Work and Social Affairs. To shorten the length of parental leave would have gone against public opinion, as a large number of women prefer to stay at home with their children.

The newly introduced parental leave system in the Czech Republic, with its options on length and payment, comes closer to the 'parental choice-orientated' model, to be found in France, Norway or Finland (Wall, 2007). Shortening parental leave and providing childcare services after leave finishes – as can be found in Sweden, Iceland, Denmark or Slovenia – seems to be less acceptable for the Czech population. This model is strongly based on the promotion of gender equality both in work and family, which is not much in evidence yet in the Czech Republic.

To sum up, the aim of the new parental leave system in the Czech Republic is to keep women more attached to paid work, as this has proved to be a significant determinant of the living standard of families (Esping-Andersen, 2002). However, the state is rather vague about the next steps to be taken, for example, the promotion of greater participation of men in childcare or the development of various forms of childcare. The only acceptable way of supporting fathers' involvement in childcare seems to be paternity leave, whose adoption is currently discussed in the government; one week of paternity leave with wage compensation similar to maternity leave has been proposed by the Minister of Work and Social Affairs. If approved, this may be implemented during 2009.

As mentioned above, a father's quota is not considered due to its normative character. Similarly, development of childcare facilities for children below 3 years of age, required by the EU Employment Strategy (which sets a target of childcare places for at least 33% of children below 3 years of age by 2010) is perceived negatively in the Czech Republic.

Bourdieu points out that since family policies are directed towards the family, they also construct the family. In his view, family policies are those state activities that aim "to favour a certain kind of family organization and to strengthen those who are in a position to conform to this form of organization" (Bourdieu, 1996, p 24). Accordingly, parental leave policies may aim at both supporting a particular family organisation and institutionalising this family form as the norm. In the Czech Republic, the parental leave system has systematically led to the reinforcement of an outdated model of family. Most people in the country have conformed to the behaviour supported by such policies.

The EU work-friendly policies are based on promoting gender equality, which is not in line with family policy objectives of the current Czech government. Ministers do not support the earlier return of mothers to employment, which they believe will harm the well-being of children, or incentives to increase the involvement of fathers in childcare. In its current form, EU policies are not acceptable in the Czech Republic, either among policy makers or the wider public. They are perceived as pushing families in a direction opposite to that supported by recent family policies in the Czech Republic. Providing individual (maternal) home care to children is still considered to be a preferable strategy among most Czech families. However, it is perceived as a choice rather than a norm.

Conclusion

The short recent history of the Czech Republic has been in a very different political context to that of pre-1990 Czechoslovakia. Almost all women worked during the communist period. Since leave policy arrangements and a well-developed system of childcare already existed, adoption of measures to encourage men to share childcare would have brought the Czech family policy system closer to a Swedish model based on promotion of gender quality both in work and at home. Instead, reintroduction of a traditional family regime occurred through both explicitly and implicitly supported refamilialisation. Surprisingly, since the separation of Slovakia in 1993 the influence of Catholicism has not decreased; rather, it has become a stable latent political dimension.

Improvement of leave policy arrangements was preferred to the development of a mixed package of support for families. In the absence of comprehensive childcare facilities, parental leave entitlements helped to reinforce a traditional gender role model as women were encouraged to leave the labour market to raise children. The opportunity for men to take parental leave has remained rather hypothetical, mainly due to financial circumstances (in particular, the fact that men earn more than women). At the end of the 1990s, the apparent similarity with the (then) German policy and its traditional male-breadwinner model could be seen.

Most women welcomed the possibility to be full-time mothers in the 1990s. However, nowadays the post-communist refamilialisation policies seem increasingly at odds with the needs and aspirations of the younger population (Sirovátka and Bartáková, 2008). They are becoming more positive towards gender equality. Nevertheless, the current government is rather reluctant to introduce effective measures to involve fathers more in childcare. While the introduction of one week of paternity leave is being currently discussed at a government level, a father's quota is well off the agenda. A conservative approach still dominates policy making, although it is hidden behind talk of enabling parents to have choices in how to manage employment and family responsibilities.

The recent reform of the long parental leave model has, interestingly, been initiated by a conservative government and not by Social Democrats. Since 2008, it has been possible to take a shorter leave with a higher payment. However, the 4-year parental benefit has been retained among the options, as greater emphasis is still put on the supposed well-being of children rather than on the employment careers of mothers. In spite of its rather unique policy developments, different from most other European countries, the current parental leave system in the Czech Republic exceeds by far the standards set by the EU in its directives. So far, no paternity leave has been established, although its adoption has recently been several times discussed on the political level.

In contrast to recent EU trends, family-friendly policies in the Czech Republic are perceived as separate from working-friendly policies. As a result, since 2008, gender equality policies have been separated from the development of family policies. The EU requirements for childcare are viewed as renewing the 'forced' pattern of combining female employment with childcare outside the family; as such, they are widely unacceptable in the Czech Republic, given negative experiences with childcare services before 1990. That is why the possibility of taking long parental leave has been retained. Parental choice about the period of childcare at home is preferred to support for an integrated family strategy that could lead, it is feared, to the enforcement of a norm.

Notes

[1] The financial support provided by the research project MSM 0021620831 and contract no. 2D06004 is gratefully acknowledged.

[2] Leave provision described here refers to statutory entitlements.

[3] Converted into euros at exchange rate on 23 February 2009, rounded up to the nearest 5 euros.

References

Bourdieu, P. (1996) 'On the family as a realized category', *Theory, Culture & Society*, vol 13, no 3, pp 19-26.

Cornia, G.A. (1991) 'Economic reforms and child welfare: in pursuit of adequate safety nets for children', in G.A. Cornia and S. Sipos (eds) *Children and the transition to the market economy: Safety nets and social policies in Central and Eastern Europe*, Avebury: UNICEF.

Esping-Andersen, G. (2002) *Why we need a new welfare state*, Oxford University Press: Oxford.

Gordon, M.S. (1988) *Social security policies in industrialized countries*, Cambridge: Cambridge University Press.

Kocourková, J. (2001) 'The potential impact of fertility-related policies on future fertility developments in the Czech Republic: analysis based on surveys conducted in the 1990s', *AUC-Geographica*, vol 36, no 1, pp 19-48.

Kocourková, J. (2002) 'Leave arrangements and childcare services in Central Europe: policies and practice before and after the transition', *Community, Work & Family*, vol 5, no 3, pp 301-18.

Lewis, J. (1992) 'Gender and the development of welfare regimes', *Journal of European Social Policy*, vol 2, no 3, pp 159-73.

Neyer, G. and Anderson, G. (2007) *Consequences of family policies on childbearing behavior: Effects or artifacts?*, MPIDR Working Paper WP 2007-021, Rostock: Max Planck Institute for Demographic Research, available at www.demogr.mpg.de/papers/working/wp-2007-021.pdf (accessed 21 October 2008).

Orloff, A.S. (1993) 'Gender and the social rights of citizenship: the comparative analysis of gender relations and welfare states', *American Sociological Review*, vol 58, no 3, pp 303-28.

Rychtaříková, J. (2000) 'Demographic transition or demographic shock in recent population development in the Czech Republic?', *AUC-Geographica*, vol 25, no 1, pp 89-102.

Saxonberg, S. and Sirovátka, T. (2006a) 'Seeking the balance between work and family after communism', *Marriage & Family Review*, vol 39, no 3/4, pp 287-313.

Saxonberg, S. and Sirovátka, T. (2006b) 'Failing family policy in post-communist Central Europe', *Journal of Comparative Policy Analysis*, vol 8, no 2, pp 185-202.

Sirovátka, T. (2004) 'Family policy in the Czech Republic after 1989: from gendered and enforced de-familialism to gendered and implicit familialism', in P. Mareš et al (eds) *Society, reproduction and contemporary challenges*, Brno: School of Social Studies, Masaryk University.

Sirovátka, T. and Bartáková, H. (2008) 'Harmonizace rodiny a zaměstnání v České republice a role sociální politiky', in T. Sirovátka and O. Hora (eds) *Rodina, děti a zaměstnání v české společnosti*, Brno: School of Social Studies, Masaryk University.

Wall, K. (2007) 'Leave policy models and the articulation of work and family in Europe: a comparative perspective', in P. Moss and K. Wall (eds) *International review of leave policies and related research 2007*, Employment Relations Research Series No 80, London: Department for Business Enterprise and Regulatory Reform, pp 25-43, available at www.berr.gov.uk/files/file40677.pdf (accessed 21 October 2008).

FIVE

Estonia: halfway from the Soviet Union to the Nordic countries

Marre Karu and Katre Pall

Maternity leave: 20 weeks at 100% of earnings with no ceiling. If less than 30 days' leave is taken before the expected birth, leave is shortened accordingly. Taking leave is obligatory.

Paternity leave: 10 working days of unpaid leave.

Parental leave: until 3 years after childbirth, paid at 100% of earnings for 62 weeks – 'parental benefit'. There is a ceiling on payment of 3 times average earnings (€1,965 per month in 2009). A low flat-rate payment (€38.50 per month) – 'childcare benefit' – is paid from the end of parental benefit until the child reaches 3 years of age to all parents, whether employed, on leave or neither.

Leave to care for sick children: 14 days of leave can be taken by either parent for each episode of sickness of a child under 12 years at 100% of pay.

Other: mothers with a child under 18 months can take feeding breaks every 3 hours at 100% of pay, but this is not paid to mothers who receive parental benefit.

Estonia is a member state of the European Union (EU). It regained independence in 1991 after decades as part of the Soviet Union. There are no statistics on the take-up of parental leave; 10% of fathers took paternity leave in 2007, 80% of mothers take some parental leave and men account for just 3.7% of receipts of parental benefit.

Introduction

Social policies, including the leave policy of a particular country, do not develop in a vacuum. They are part of a political context and normally follow a rather consistent pathway. But in some societies, that gradual development can be sharply interrupted, sometimes when the political context undergoes a major rupture. This has happened twice in Estonia in living memory, bringing radical new directions, principles and ideals. However, despite the very different political regimes that have shaped Estonian social policies for 50 years, these policies, including leave policy, are now, at the beginning of 21st century, similar to the ones in Western Europe, particularly the Nordic countries.

The aim of this chapter is to shed light on the processes behind the development of leave policy in Estonia, to understand how the generous parental leave scheme that we have today came into being and how policy formation is influenced by the past. The analysis of leave policy in this chapter follows the major historical developments in the country. The second half of the 20th century in the history of Estonia is characterised by two major shifts in political order that brought all-encompassing changes in every aspect of the society, including social policy. First, there was a shift from democracy to a totalitarian socialist order in 1940 when the Republic of Estonia was occupied by the Soviet Union. The whole society was reorganised by rapid nationalisation, collectivisation and other restructuring of the economy; totalitarian rule regulated nearly every aspect of life; and an ideology of full employment and full support for working parents prevailed.

The second shift started when the independence of Estonia was restored in 1991. The collapse of the Soviet Union was followed by a period of rapid transition back to a free market economy and democracy. But in the process of building a new economy and society, social policy was left in the background.

Now a further shift in leave policy can be discerned, starting from the beginning of the 21st century and the establishment of a fully functioning market economy. Transition has ended, and the search for a social model and the attempt to save the nation from extinction have made leave policy the centre of attention. We concentrate particularly on the development of a new parental benefit scheme implemented in 2004.

The data sources used in the chapter include legislation dating back to 1944, media reports from 2003 and records of parliamentary proceedings. To understand the developments since the end of Soviet rule, interviews were carried out with policy makers and other experts in the Ministry of Social Affairs.

The Soviet Republic of Estonia: full support to working parents

The ideology of socialist society

The Republic of Estonia was founded in 1918 and it was occupied by the Soviet Union in 1940. The whole society was reorganised into a centrally planned economy. The USSR had centralised legislation and its policies were shaped by socialist ideology and principles. Political power was concentrated in the Communist Party and government; the policy-making process included few actors, there were no negotiations or public debates, and criticism of the state and its policies was punishable. Thus there was no civil society or active interest groups and the church had no influence. Although membership of trades unions was high, such organisations were not part of civil society, but merely tools of the government.

Thus, policies and decisions were made centrally and imposed on all member states and their citizens. Propaganda was an important tool with which to influence citizens and to spread ideological values. The aim was to build and live in a socialist state that would bring prosperity and equality to the society. According to the Constitution of the USSR, working was an obligation of every citizen and women were declared to have equal rights with men in all areas of life: economic, social, cultural and political. Working was a precondition of being a member of society, social security was only available to those who were working and a state pension depended on a record of continuous employment. Income inequality was relatively small and officially no poverty existed.

Estonia and Latvia (Zvidrins, 1979) were exceptional in terms of fertility, with no baby boom after the Second World War. The birth rate of Estonians during the second half of the 20th century stayed between 1.9 and 2.1 until the 1990s (Katus et al, 2002). Policies were aimed at raising fertility to guarantee reproduction of the military and labour force (Coser, 1951; Kutsar, 1991) and maternity was treated as a social obligation of women (Kennedy and Einasto, 2006). Childlessness was taxed and childbearing was a precondition for receiving social benefits. Having many children was supported by state policies. Large families had access to free services and access to housing was, among other conditions, determined by the number of children in a family (Nirk, 1989). In the Soviet system, human beings were regarded as 'human resources', and social functioning served production and the planned economy.

The totalitarian society was sustained by power, punishment and fear, generating a situation where the state-imposed values did not always match the population's values or practices (Lauristin, 1997; Gal and Kligman, 2000). As freedom of speech was limited, people did not express their real views about the society and the regime (Lagerspetz, 1996). The family was a public unit, with all family issues turned into state issues and regulated by the state.

In some ways, the Soviet Union had social aims similar on paper to contemporary Western societies. It advocated gender equality and full employment for both men and women. However, the meaning of these concepts, the reasoning behind them and the means of achieving them differed dramatically from democratic societies. Employment, for example, was compulsory; not working was condemned, even punished (Tiit, 1990).

But the best example is the ideology of gender equality, which was supported at the political level as an inseparable part of communist ideology – the equality of all people was one of the basic tenets of the system. In the labour market, gender equality was announced, enforced and also achieved to a certain extent. The employment rate of women was high, women were encouraged to take up physical and traditionally masculine jobs (such as driving tractors) and they were also given leading positions. There had to be no differences in the labour market behaviour of men and women.

However, equality and participation of women in the labour market were not to be achieved by greater involvement of men in housework and childcare or any other changes in men's behaviour. Traditional gender roles were encouraged and supported by the state, which produced media debates about the ideal and proper roles of women and the fundamental importance of 'natural' differences between men and women (Gal and Kligman, 2000). All in all, women were expected to participate in the labour market equally with men and at the same time assume the burden of raising children. Soviet times saw women simultaneously as wives, mothers and workers (Cerami, 2005). Men were hardly mentioned in the context of children or housework. Fathers had no rights to leave or access to family benefits, which were paid only to mothers of large families or lone mothers (Nirk, 1989).

What the state did provide was public services for families, although these were insufficient. Policies in this area did support reconciliation of family and work, but people were not free to choose between the two life areas. For instance, lone mothers were allowed to place their children temporarily in state-supported children's homes (Kutsar and Tiit, 2003) so they could participate in the labour market.

In sum, the regime's ideology of equality of rights did not lead to equality in reality. The general rhetoric was that all people are equal, but specific policies contradicted gender equality principles. Before the fall of the Soviet Union, the Estonian labour market was as gender segregated, both vertically and horizontally, as in Western capitalist countries, and a gender pay gap remained (Narusk, 2000).

Leave policies in the Soviet period

Some maternity leave existed in Estonia before Soviet rule. Women working in industry gained a right to maternity leave in 1913 and in 1920 a fully paid leave of 10 weeks (4 before and 6 after the birth) was extended to civil servants. In 1944, leave was extended to 11 weeks, but the agricultural sector was still excluded (Evart and Põllupüü, 1926; Kennedy and Einasto, 2006).

According to the Work Code of the USSR, introduced into Estonia in 1946, pregnant women could take 35 days' leave before the expected date of birth and 42 days after giving birth, prolonged if there were complications. The compensation level depended on the length of previous employment, varying from two thirds to full earnings. However, actual benefit payments in the 1940s and 1950s are hard to assess, as work in collective farms might be paid in kind as well as cash. Work conditions of pregnant women were highly regulated and employers were obliged to provide suitable and non-hazardous jobs without any loss of earnings and with no night or overtime work (Kovrigina, 1947).

Although maternity leave was short, women could add on annual holidays to stay home for a few months after giving birth. After women returned to work they were expected to use public childcare services provided either by the workplace or by the state – though, in reality these were insufficient (Tiit, 1990). Breastfeeding mothers were given facilities for feeding children at their workplace and breastfeeding breaks every 3 hours without loss of earnings (Nirk, 1989).

These leave arrangements developed significantly over time. Leave became longer and compensation more generous. By the end of the Soviet era, mothers had a right to leave of up to 3 years. The first changes were made in the 1950s when maternity leave was prolonged by 35 days and payment increased; all working mothers were granted a fully paid maternity leave of 56 days before and 56 days after the birth, with extra leave of 14 days for births with complications or for multiple births.

Further leave was added in 1959, giving mothers a right to 6 months of unpaid 'childcare leave' after maternity leave. Trades unions could give permission for the unpaid leave to be extended up to a year. The Work Code of the Estonian SSR (published in 1972) provided an additional unpaid one year's leave to all working women with at least one year of prior employment.

In 1978, there was recognition that the family ideal was in crisis. The Soviet state was concerned about the extent of divorces, births out of wedlock, disability and alcoholism (Tiit, 1990). There were concerns, too, over low fertility. The developments in leave that followed in the 1980s were part of the social policy that aimed to 'save' the family. First, in 1982, the existing one-year childcare leave was compensated by a flat-rate benefit equal to the minimum wage. Second, the unpaid leave was extended and could be used until a child reached 18 months of age. Then in 1989, paid leave – with the flat-rate benefit – was extended to 18 months and the unpaid leave to 3 years. By the end of the 1980s, just before regaining independence, the Soviet Republic of Estonia, as elsewhere in the USSR, had a long maternity and childcare leave with relatively generous benefits, although the leave was available only to mothers.

Improving leave policies and benefits was the state's way of expressing care for children, mothers and families and represented an overall increase in welfare (Nirk, 1989). It was also financially possible for the state to pay higher benefits. Nevertheless, providing such long leaves for women could be seen to contradict the Soviet ideology of full employment and gender equality. Little is known about the reasons behind policy making, for instance why a regime committed to full employment suddenly provided a long childcare leave, allowing mothers to stay away from the labour market for several years. One assumption is that reducing the number of women in the labour market was an attempt to deal with an emerging scarcity of jobs.

The transition period: construction of social policy

The transition period

The restoration of democracy began after Estonia regained its independence in 1991, and developments followed extremely quickly. But during the transition period, social policy ranked behind defence, monetary and economic policies. Many changes were reactions to the former Soviet regime; one of the main aims of building a new society and state was to turn away from Soviet ideology.

Extreme regulation was followed by extreme deregulation and a liberal approach was implemented in economy. An ideological shift from state responsibility to personal responsibility occurred and family matters became a private area, not to be too extensively regulated from outside. In addition, the employers' role was redefined – no social responsibilities were expected of them.

Families were, in many ways, left on their own. The safe, predictable and regulated life of the communist society was replaced with the uncertainties, social risks and problems of capitalist society. These fast changes were referred to as 'shock therapy' (Lauristin, 1997). Unemployment emerged as a new social risk, and the employment rates of both men and women fell by 20 percentage points (see Figure 5.1). By 1998, 40% of children lived below the absolute poverty line (Social Sector in Figures, 2005).

Figure 5.1: Employment and labour market participation rates by gender, 1989–2007

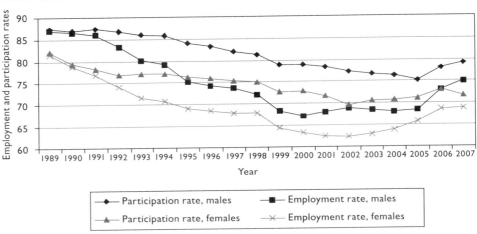

Source: Statistics Estonia (2008)

One reaction to these drastic changes in society and personal lives was a sharp fall in the birth rate (Figure 5.2). The prospect of independence and actually regaining it sparked a short-term baby boom between 1987 and 1990. Then, sudden economic changes, increased uncertainty about the future, changes in the role of the family and women and new opportunities caused the postponement of births and a declining birth rate (Ainsaar, 2000; Ainsaar and Oras, 2000; Eamets and Philips, 2000; Hansson, 2001; Kasearu and Kutsar, 2003), which dropped as low as 1.3 births per woman in the second half of the 1990s.

Figure 5.2: Total fertility rate, 1970–2007

Source: Statistics Estonia (2008)

The reaction to an era of Soviet-imposed labour market equality and compulsory female employment was the return to the traditional family model and gender roles; women were tired of forced emancipation (Kutsar, 1991). Already by the end of the 1980s, there was a campaign advocating family values that placed women at home with their children (Hansson, 2003). There were discussions about whether it would be possible to increase the wages of men to a level sufficient to support the whole family, envisaging the reappearance of single-earner households (Ainsaar, 2002). A similar trend of refamilialisation could be seen in other post-communist countries (Saxonberg and Szelewa, 2007). However, these traditional family values did not last for long.

The number of kindergartens also diminished quickly, as Soviet-type institutions, massive and impersonal, were seen as bad for children and unnecessary. At the beginning of 1990s, a maintenance allowance for parents whose children were not in kindergartens was provided to encourage mothers to stay home with children, which resulted in decreasing use of these services. Although individual rights in social security remained, changes in the tax policy in 1995 favoured single-earner households with wives staying home. Discrimination against women with children in the labour market was silently accepted.

The concept of gender equality had a negative image, tarnished by its Soviet associations. Women were tired of their burden – full-time work, home and children – as well as the social-ideological responsibilities. Family held the highest value for people and became even more important during the societal crisis of the transition (Narusk, 1996; Hansson, 2001). The ideal family was the male breadwinner model; women were to stay home with children, making full use of the 3-year childcare leave inherited from the Soviet system.

Developing a new social policy started by defining basic concepts like the 'poverty line'. According to official Soviet ideology, poverty and unemployment did not exist in the Soviet Union. So there was much preparatory work to be done to acknowledge, define and tackle these social problems.

Although conservative values dominated in the search for a social policy model, some elements were taken over from the Nordic model of social policy. Policy making was influenced by the personalities and backgrounds of particular ministers and their personal contacts with foreign experts and institutions, especially from Sweden, Finland and the World Bank (Söderling, 2001). At the beginning of 1990s, the Social Democratic Minister of Social Affairs consulted with Finnish experts with a similar political background. This may have influenced the implementation of a universal family benefit scheme in preference to a means-tested system, which was also considered. Childcare benefit was developed and the childcare leave extended to fathers. The level of family benefits, however, remained low.

Much needed to be done to restore civil society and the active involvement of citizens. After years of restricted freedom of speech and the suppression of civil society, social dialogue was largely absent. Trades unions, formerly means of exercising state power, lost influence and membership fast. Interest groups were not strong, although the first women's organisations and other new interest groups did begin to emerge during the transition period.

Leave policy in the transition period

Although new policies aimed to differ from those of the Soviet Union as much as possible, in reality the changes made to leave policy were more incremental. The principles of the system remained largely intact, the existing scheme being adjusted to correspond to the new aims and situation. Leave became longer and more generous, continuing the trend that had started already in 1980s. The main changes made in 1991 were as follows:

- Fully paid maternity leave before birth was extended from 56 days to 70; the 56 days after the birth remained unchanged.
- The 3-year 'childcare leave', partly paid and partly unpaid, became paid throughout, but at a low flat rate.
- Childcare leave was extended to fathers, first as secondary carers, then equal to mothers.
- Unpaid leave of 14 days per year was provided to parents until the child reached 14 years.

The fact that there were no dramatic changes could be seen as a result of a quite developed and modern leave policy that Estonia inherited from the Soviet Union. According to this view, there was no need for radical changes, especially as there were more urgent issues to be addressed. The existing scheme provided the opportunity to stay at home for a long time, and so met the needs and wishes of women at that time.

There was, however, a significant development in fathers' rights, as childcare leave was extended to fathers and other 'actual carers'. It is paradoxical that in the context of a return to traditional gender roles and single-earner households, for the first time in history fathers were given a right to parental leave. Yet, the Soviet society that officially advocated gender equality had given no such right to fathers. This, again, highlights the different meaning given to gender equality under the communist regime, as well as pointing to some controversies in policy making during the transition period. In practice, however, the take-up of leave by fathers remained marginal, below 1%.

In 1993, more changes were made. If the previous system divided maternity leave into two periods before and after the birth, the new leave of 126 days did not specify how many days had to be taken before or after birth. Also, parents of children under 14 years of age were provided with an extra 3 to 6 days off work per year, fully paid. The leave policies that were developed by 1993 remained intact for almost the next decade.

The capitalist society: saving the nation through policy transformation

By the end of the 20th century, a new stage in family policy was emerging. Definitions and legislation were in place and a more holistic approach was starting to develop. By 2001, the first family policy strategy was developed. Since 2002, social policy formation has been influenced by European Union goals, most notably the Lisbon Strategy; issues like women's labour market participation and gender equality reappeared on the policy agenda.

The economy recovered and the country faced rapid economic growth along with diminishing unemployment and increasing rates of women's employment. At the same time, low birth rates had become a national concern needing political involvement and action. The number of births dropped from 25,000 in 1987 to 15,000 by 1993, and showed no improvement for years. The situation was considered so critical that measures to reverse the unfavourable trend became one of the key issues during the 2003 parliamentary election campaign. All the major political parties had proposals to promote birth rate, mainly changes to parental leave and benefit. Services to families, especially early childhood education and care (ECEC), did not figure, surfacing only years later when the lack of these services was seen as a serious obstacle to women's return to the labour market. At the same time, economic growth increased labour demand and companies were struggling with a shortage of workers.

Making of a new parental benefit

The next period in the development of leave policies started with the emergence of significantly more generous leave policies. In 2002, the fully compensated maternity leave was extended by 14 days to 140 days. At the same time, 14 days of paternity leave, an individual right for fathers at childbirth, was implemented to meet the requirements of the EU directive on parental leave; this attracted a flat-rate payment equal to the level of minimum wage in 2002, approximately €4.20 per day. But the benefit was not tied to the minimum wage and was not increased until 2008, so it lost value, being worth less than 40% of the minimum wage by 2007.

More radical changes to leave policy were introduced after the parliamentary elections of 2003. In 2004, a parental benefit set at 100% of earnings, up to a ceiling, was introduced for 225 days of parental leave. Maternity and parental benefits together now guaranteed 365 days of income compensation. With this, the liberal society had made a new ideological turn towards the Nordic welfare state. We look now in more detail at this policy turn, including the process, the actors and the alternatives.

Two competing models

Two main ideas competed in the 2003 election campaign, one proposed by the right-wing liberal Estonian Reform Party, the other by the Moderates (renamed the Social Democrat Party in 2004); other parties proposed modifications of these two main models. The Reform Party proposed implementing a 'mother's wage'. The name of the scheme was confusing, since the idea was not to pay a wage but to compensate employed mothers for loss of income while they were on parental leave. As women's employment was growing, the main obstacle to having children was assumed to be a loss of income at the time of childbirth and soon after. Politicians' contact with right-wing politicians in the Nordic countries resulted in the idea of extending maternity benefit from 140 days to a full year.

The 'mother's wage' had characteristics of an insurance scheme where being on leave was treated as a risk that should be compensated at 100%. The scheme was intended to be exclusively for mothers and was seen as a part of existing maternity leave aimed at protecting the health of mothers and children. Taking care of newborn children was strongly tied to maternity, so fathers were excluded in the proposal.

The Social Democrats agreed that reconciliation of work and family should be supported by providing higher leave benefits. Their idea was to pay *parents* a wage for taking care of their children. They proposed paying a flat-rate benefit of €268 per month for a year (approximately twice the minimum wage) or €179 per month for a year and a half.

The competition between distinct positions was very visible. In addition to the Moderates, the Centre Party opposed the liberal scheme. However, the final decision was taken by the new coalition government, which was led by the Reform Party.

Debates

The creation of a new parental benefit stirred one of the most active public discussions in Estonian policy making. Paediatricians and non-governmental organisations advocating the rights of children and families joined the political debate with their own proposals, some of which were taken into account. Although there was widespread public discussion, however, the focus of discussion was quite narrow. The question was not what kinds of policies were needed to increase fertility but what should be the details of the parental benefit; eligibility criteria, duration of payment and the amount of benefit were debated. The need for parental benefit or 'mother's wage' was hardly questioned and other principles, different ideological standpoints and possible effects were not discussed.

Coalition agreements include detailed policy measures that form the benchmark for judging a government's success. The basic idea and design of the Reform Party were retained, with some detailed changes to make a more flexible scheme, including an option to work while on parental leave. But instead of being a 'mother's wage', the new measure was renamed 'parental benefit'. Parental benefit was defined as a family benefit – its purpose work and family reconciliation, very different from maternity benefit – and fathers were included as potential beneficiaries. In practice, however, the benefit is often called 'mother's wage' and is used mainly by mothers.

The initial concept had been turned, more or less, into a Nordic type of scheme, with leave and an income-related benefit available to either parent. It included another element from the Swedish model: a speed premium. In the case of another birth within 30 months of the preceding one, the new benefit payment is at the same level as the previous one. This feature, justified purely on labour market grounds, provoked no major discussion.

Some elements of solidarity were included. Non-working parents were guaranteed a flat-rate benefit set slightly lower than the minimum wage. This raised concerns about possible misuse of the system. Would it motivate women in poorer families to give birth for the sake of a short-term income? Still, paying the benefit to working parents only was felt to be discriminatory.

Wages versus benefits

The main disagreement between different parties was whether to pay a flat-rate benefit for childrearing or an income-related benefit to compensate for earnings loss while away from work. Questions about the value of children, equality and fairness were debated. Although the idea and generosity of the scheme proposed by the Reform Party could be seen as social democratic, the ideology and details of the scheme were argued to be liberal. What made the final scheme unacceptable to the opposition was its income-relatedness, with a ceiling set at three times the average wage, eight times higher than the minimum wage. This favoured higher income families, who, it was argued, could manage without such state support; the consequent large differentials in benefit payment were unethical, unfair and bound to increase inequality.

The opposition argued for a flat-rate benefit, to give equal value to all children and because bringing up a child is equally costly and difficult for every family. The advocates of income-related benefits replied that the costs of bringing up a child depend on the living standard of a family. Higher-income families cannot afford a significant drop in income, as they have higher costs, for example mortgages. Without full compensation, they may not be able to afford to have children.

The right-wing coalition government saw the parental benefit as a compensation for loss of previous earnings, while the opposition interpreted the initial proposal of a mother's wage literally and thought it unfair to pay some mothers a much higher wage than others for a similar job of childrearing. The rhetoric used when introducing the new benefit was that old policies had not worked to increase fertility, so something totally new was needed. To ease the inequality issue, the universal child allowance was also increased in 2004, although this was not part of the election promises.

Fathers' entitlements

Fathers' right to benefit was also extensively discussed, and views on this, as covered by the media, evolved over time. The initial proposals excluded fathers entirely, talking about a 'mother's wage'. After a while, it was realised that there should be a right for fathers in case something happens to the mother. Also, the media pointed out, the EU directive on parental leave stipulates giving rights to fathers. A public letter presented to the Minister of Social Affairs and the Prime Minister signed by 200 people including several social scientists and feminists suggested using a new term, 'parental benefit' instead of 'mother's wage'. The letter referred to the EU directive and pointed to the adverse consequences for gender equality of excluding fathers from childrearing. The Ministry of Social Affairs presented a draft of the Parental Benefit Act that gave equal rights to both parents. A non-transferable month of leave for fathers was discussed briefly in the ministry, although this idea found no support.

Giving equal rights for both parents was heavily criticised by doctors, especially paediatricians, who saw fathers' involvement as a neglect of children's interest. The paediatricians suggested limiting fathers' rights, reserving the new benefit to mothers until the child reaches 6 months of age. This was accepted in the parliament and was included in the final Act. The main reasoning behind this decision was to promote breastfeeding and the mother–child bond. Meeting the conditions set by the EU directive was not an issue during the parliamentary debates.

This amendment created a paradoxical situation. For the first 6 months, fathers had the right to take up parental leave but no right to claim parental benefit; they would get no payment if they took leave. As the EU directive specifies a right to leave but not to payment, no contradiction was seen to arise. But by limiting access to the benefit, fathers were deterred from taking leave and a message was sent that fathers are not equally valuable carers (Karu et al, 2007). Between 2004 and 2007, when this limitation on fathers' access to parental benefit was changed, only 1%–3% of benefit recipients were fathers.

The never-ending amendments

As hoped and expected, the number of births started increasing from 2002. Eager to measure results, the Ministry of Social Affairs and Office of the Minister for Population and Ethnic Affairs financed a study to analyse the effects of parental leave. The study suggested that there have been some changes in the characteristics of women giving birth, but it did not confirm the effect of parental benefit on the number of births (Võrk and Karu, 2006). Despite lacking evidence, politicians gave the impression that the measure had been successful, bringing fast results.

With politicians believing in its effectiveness, the length of parental benefit has been extended twice: in 2006, for another 3 months (90 days) and in 2008, for another 4 months (120 days). As of 2008, maternity and parental benefits together provide full income replacement for 575 days. With parental benefit popular among young parents, no party opposed these extensions even though the scheme has become extremely costly for the state budget and may be unsustainable in the long run.

Ways of improving the leave scheme are constantly discussed, and it is noticeable that these discussions revolve around elements of Nordic leave policies. Now that the restriction to fathers' access to benefit has been abandoned, a father's quota has been suggested, although so far politicians have seen no need for this. But the issue of fathers' involvement is not restricted to parental leave; in 2008, the Reform Party government increased payment to fathers taking paternity leave from a low flat-rate benefit to full earnings replacement. Although the idea was welcomed by young families and fathers' take-up of leave increased approximately fourfold, men are still seen as secondary caregivers. One of the first budgetary cuts of the government in response to the economic crisis was to scrap benefit payments for paternity leave as a 'luxury measure'; since January 2009, Estonia has had 2 weeks of *unpaid* paternity leave. The gender equality element in leave policy, omitted initially, has been introduced gradually during times of economic growth – only to be partially abandoned when times have got hard economically.

To sum up the third period, Estonia's family policy model, which already included universal family benefits and services provided and financed by local communities, made a significant turn towards Nordic policies. However, the transformation of policy included only certain Nordic elements, namely income compensation and a speed premium; and it had a different focus and different attitudes towards gender issues compared with Nordic countries. The aim of the parental benefit scheme was to preserve the mother's income so as to help reconcile work and family life and to increase fertility. Improvements in gender equality were neither expected nor sought, not being perceived as relevant to fertility. The outcomes could yet prove discriminatory and support traditional gender roles.

Conclusion

The development of parental leave and parental benefit in Estonia has been constantly moving towards longer duration and higher payment. A short maternity leave that already existed before the Second World War was complemented by 6 months of unpaid childcare leave for mothers in the 1950s, and then a one-year leave was established in the 1970s. Leave was extended to 3 years in the 1980s, but it was an exclusive right of mothers until after independence when fathers also got the right to parental leave. It took 12 more years until more radical changes in leave policy introduced income-related benefit payments.

At the same time, Estonian society has lived through a rapid and sweeping transformation, from a communist to a democratic regime. As society changed radically, one would expect to see a similar shift also in family and leave policies. There were changes at the political and economic level, but also in the attitudes, values and behaviour of people. While the Soviet system advocated full employment of women, regaining independence and restoring democracy brought with it a short-term return to the traditional male breadwinner model. Changes in attitudes towards family did not, however, bring about changes in leave policies and the Soviet-era 3-year parental leave remained unchanged under a very different political order.

Although Soviet communist rule has always been perceived as hostile and alien, 50 years of living in a socialist society had shaped people's values and expectations. Implementing a drastically different leave policy could perhaps have been possible right at the beginning of transition, when there was a wish to differ from the previous regime and many other reforms were made. Family policies, however, were not then the centre of attention in the process of building up the new society and leave remained almost unchanged.

Making drastic turns in family policies at a later stage of transition would have been more difficult. First, during the transition people had to adapt to new circumstances and new social problems such as unemployment and poverty emerged. Removing any existing social support in this situation would have been hard. Second, people with a background in communist society had high expectations of the state sharing responsibility (Karelson and Pall, 2003). The existing long childcare leave scheme was in line with these expectations.

At the beginning of the new century, the economy stabilised and poverty levels started to decrease. At the same time, too little attention paid to family policies, the declining availability of ECEC services, and most of all the social cost of the 'shock therapy' of transition had resulted in a low fertility rate that showed no signs of improvement. Fertility and declining population got the attention of policy makers. By 2003, all parties perceived the fertility issue to be so critical that all of them proposed changes in leave policy in the election campaign as a solution.

The income-related parental benefit that was implemented in 2004 may be regarded as a case of policy transformation towards the Nordic, and especially the Swedish, model. But although Nordic models were used as a role model in designing the Estonian parental leave scheme, only some elements were taken over and policy learning was not based on systematic analysis but, rather, informal contacts. For instance, gender equality was not a goal; fertility behaviour was the main concern.

Traditional family values found their way into the scheme through the intervention of interest groups, such as doctors, who argued in favour of breastfeeding and bonding. As a result, the access of fathers to the benefit was restricted until the child was 6 months old. This provides an example of how the debate around parental benefit stimulated the involvement of non-governmental organisations and increased public interest in social policy issues in Estonia, which was another step towards the Nordic model in policy creation.

Why were elements of a Nordic model introduced into family policy while a liberal approach prevailed in the economy? It can be argued that there are several similarities between Nordic and communist countries, such as the explicit emphasis on the role of the state, the redistribution of income and the promotion of equality among citizens (Kandolin, 1997). Already at the beginning of 1990s, Estonia was found to be in the same cluster as Nordic welfare states, making such similarity a logical and simple path to follow. Proximity to and contacts with Nordic countries also had their role to play.

Signs of a belief that a single policy measure could solve demographic problems can be detected in the debates. At the same time as placing such high hopes for increasing fertility on one new measure, other parts of leave policy were preserved. For instance, the 3-year parental leave with a low flat-rate benefit, inherited from 1980s, was retained, although it did not meet the logic of the new parental benefit scheme. But abolishing the old scheme was hardly ever discussed. Instead, additions were made to meet new requirements and conditions.

The Estonian history of leave policy shows clear signs of path dependency in policy creation. But it also demonstrates that political decisions depend not only on the circumstances of a particular moment but also on the ideology of political parties. The Nordic-oriented family policy in Estonia has been implemented by different political parties at different times, both social democratic and liberal.

Both the design and aims of the leave scheme differ somewhat from Nordic ones. The new policy model was implemented to improve the existing leave scheme. It resulted in Estonia having a long and well-compensated period of parental leave, supporting shared parental care of children and mothers' return to employment, and a second long but poorly compensated period, supporting mothers' absence from the labour market for some years. Moving towards a full

Nordic model is slow because the policy learning is selective and influenced by attitudes and values with deep roots in the past.

References

Ainsaar, M. (ed) (2000) *Laste ja perepoliitika Eestis ja Euroopas*, Tartu: Rahvastikuministri büroo.

Ainsaar, M. (2002) 'Eesti perepoliitika eesmärgid, tegelikkus ja tulemused 1993-2001', in R. Vetik (ed) *Inimarengu trendid ja poliitika kujundamine (54–62)*, Tallinn: Tallinna Pedagoogikaülikool, Rahvusvaheliste ja Sotsiaaluuringute Instituut.

Ainsaar, M. and Oras, K. (2000) 'Laste arvu mõjutavad tegurid Eestis', in M. Ainsaar (ed) *Laste ja perepoliitika Eestis ja Euroopas*, Tartu: Rahvastikuministri büroo, pp 112-133.

Cerami A. (2005) 'Social policy in Central and Eastern Europe: the emergence of a new European model of solidarity?', Paper presented at the Third Annual ESPAnet Conference 'Making Social Policy in the Postindustrial Age', 22-24 September 2005, University of Fribourg, Switzerland.

Coser, L.A. (1951) 'Some aspects of Soviet family policy', *American Journal of Sociology*, vol 56, no 5, pp 424-37.

Eamets, R. and Philips, K. (2000) *Eesti tööturu areng üleminekuperioodil*, Tartu: OÜ KTX.

Evart, H. and Põllupüü, J. (1926) *Tööstuslise töö seadus*, Tallinn: AS Ühiselu.

Gal, S. and Kligman, G. (eds) (2000) *Reproducing gender: Politics, publics, and everyday life after socialism*, Princeton NJ: Princeton University Press.

Hansson, L. (ed) (2001) *Naine, perekond ja töö 2000: pere-elu ja kutsetöö kokkusobitamise probleemidest väikeste lastega peredes*, Tallinn: TPÜ Rahvusvaheliste ja Sotsiaaluuringute Instituut, TPÜ Kirjastus.

Hansson, L. (2003) 'Women on the Estonian labour market: continuity and change', in M.E. Domsch, D.H. Ladwig and E. Tenten (eds) *Gender equality in Central and Eastern European countries*, Frankfurt am Main: Peter Lang Europäischer Verlag der Wissenschaften, pp 133-50.

Kandolin, I. (1997) *Gender, worklife and family responsibilities in Finland and Estonia – effects on economic and mental well-being*, People and Work Research Reports 15, Helskinki: Finnish Institute of Occupational Health.

Karelson, K. and Pall, K. (2003) 'Estonian self-reliance', in L. Appleton and L. Hantrais (eds) *Cross-National Research Papers, 6 (6)*, Loughborough: European Research Centre, Loughborough University, pp 55-65.

Karu, M., Kasearu, K. and Biin, H. (2007) *Isad ja lapsehoolduspuhkus, PRAXISe toimetised 29/2007*, PRAXIS Centre for Policy Studies, Study Report.

Kasearu, K. and Kutsar, D. (2003) 'Perekonna ideaalkujundid ja nende realiseerumise võimalikkus', in D. Kutsar (ed) *Millist perekonnapoliitikat me vajame?*, Tartu: Tartu Ülikooli Kirjastus, pp 88-103.

Katus, K., Puur, A. and Põldma, A. (2002) *Eesti põlvkondlik rahvastikuareng*, Tallinn: Eesti Kõrgkoolidevaheline Demouuringute Keskus.

Kennedy, P. and Einasto, H. (2006) 'Working mother in the whirlwind of times: women's changing labour market participation in Ireland and Estonia', Paper presented at the Interim Conference Gender (In)equality in the European Labour Market, European Sociological Association, Lisbon, 6–8 September.

Kovrigina, M. (1947) *Riigi hoolitsemine emade ja laste eest*, Tallinn, RK Poliitiline Kirjastus.

Kutsar, D. (1991) 'Family–gender–society: students' attitudes in Finland and Estonia', Paper presented at Gender Blending conference, Tampere, Finland, 11–10 June.

Kutsar, D. and Tiit, E.-M. (2003) 'Changing family structures and alternative paths to family formation in Estonia', in L. Appleton and L. Hantrais (eds) *Cross-national Research Papers, 6 (5)*, Loughborough: European Research Centre, Loughborough University, pp 52–9.

Lagerspetz, M. (1996) *Constructing post-communism: A study in the Estonian social problems discourse*, Doctoral thesis, Turun Yliopisto, Turku: Turun yliopisto.

Lauristin, M. (1997) 'Context of transition', in M. Lauristin and P. Vihalemm (eds) *Return to the Western world: Cultural and political perspectives on the Estonian post-communist transition*, Tartu: Tartu University Press, pp 25–40.

Narusk A. (1996) 'Gendered outcomes of transition in Estonia', *The Finnish Review of East European Studies*, vol 3, pp 10–48.

Narusk, A. (2000) 'Eesti naised ja ratsionaalsed valikud', *Ariadne lõng*, no 1/2, pp 50–9.

Nirk, M. (1989) *Soodustusi lastega perekondadele. Normatiivaktide kogumik*, Tallinn: Olion.

Saxonberg, S. and Szelewa, D. (2007) 'The continuing legacy of the communist legacy? The development of family policies in Poland and the Czech Republic', *Social Politics: International Studies in Gender, State and Society*, vol 14, no 3, pp 351–79.

Social Sector in Figures (2005) Tallinn: Ministry of Social Affairs.

Söderling, I. (ed) (2001) *Yearbook of population research in Finland, vol XXXVII*, Helsinki: The Population Research Institute.

Statistics Estonia (2008) available at http://pub.stat.ee

Tiit, E.-M. (1990) 'Perekonnapoliitikast tänapäeva Eestis', in A. Laas (ed) *Eesti perekond ja perekonnaideaal. Perekonnaprobleemid IX*, Tartu: Tartu Ülikool.

Võrk, A. and Karu, M. (2006) *Eesti vanemahüvitise mõju sündimus- ja tööturukäitumisele: hindamise võimalused ja esimeste kogemuste analüüs*, Tallinn: PRAXIS Centre for Policy Studies.

Zvidrins, P. (1979) 'The dynamics of fertility in Latvia', *Population Studies*, vol 33, no 2, pp 277–82.

SIX

Finland: negotiating tripartite compromises

Johanna Lammi-Taskula and Pentti Takala

Maternity leave[1]*:* 105 working days at 90% of earnings up to a ceiling of €46,207 during the first 56 days of leave, with a lower percentage for higher earnings; subsequently, payment is at 70% of earnings up to €30,033, with a lower percentage for higher earnings.

Paternity leave: 18 working days at 70% of earnings up to €30,034, with a lower percentage for higher earnings.

Parental leave: 158 working days per family at 75% of earnings up to a ceiling €46,207 during the first 30 days, with a lower percentage for higher earnings; subsequently payment is at 70% of earnings up to €30,033, with a lower percentage for higher earnings. A further 12 'bonus' days are available for fathers who take the last 2 weeks of parental leave. Leave can be taken part time, at 40-60% of full-time hours, but only if both parents take part-time leave and only with the employer's agreement. Benefit payments are reduced accordingly.

Leave to care for sick children: up to 4 days per child per illness, for parents of children under 10 years, with no limits on how often parents can take leave. Level and length of payment depend on collective agreements, but often at full earnings.

Other: childcare leave, referred to as 'home care leave', can be taken from the end of parental leave until a child's third birthday. A parent taking leave receives a home care allowance: a basic payment of €294.28 per month + €94.09 for every other child under 3 years + €60.46 for every other pre-school child over 3 years + a means-tested supplement (up to €168 per month). Some local authorities, especially in the Helsinki area, pay a municipal supplement to the home care allowance.

Parents can work reduced working hours from the end of parental leave until the end of the child's second year at school. The employee should negotiate the reduction with the employer, who may refuse only if the reduced working hours would lead to serious disadvantages for the organisation; in that case, working hours must be a maximum of 30 hours a week. Employees taking partial childcare leave before the child's third birthday or during the child's first and second year at school are entitled to €70 a month.

Finland is a Nordic country and a member state of the European Union. It has a high level of maternal employment. The proportion of fathers taking paternity leave has been increasing, from 46% in 1993 to 70% in 2006. In 2006, the average length of the leave taken was 14 working days. Parental leave is mostly taken by mothers and almost all mothers take leave. However, the new arrangement under which there are bonus days for fathers who take the last 2 weeks of parental leave has almost quadrupled the number of men taking parental leave, from 1,700 men in 2002 to 6,400 in 2006, about 9%; at the same time, the average length of leave taken by fathers has fallen; from 64 working days in 2002 to only 28 in 2006. The most common length of leave taken by fathers is 42 days, which means that men take all days set aside for fathers – but no more. Almost all families (86%) take advantage of home care leave, but this is used almost entirely by women; mothers take care of the child in 98% of families where one of the parents has taken leave.

There is an entitlement for early childhood education and care for children from birth.

Introduction

During the past four decades, the social partners – employers' and employees' organisations – have been significant negotiation partners with the state in designing social policy in Finland. These central labour market organisations have been involved in decisions about wages, taxes and social benefits as well as working times and schemes supporting work–family reconciliation. Social reforms have been promised by the state in exchange for moderate pay settlements that will promote employment and competitiveness.

In an international context, Finland has been a mixed case regarding the relationship between the social partners and the political institutions. For example, in pension policy, state corporatism has prevailed in Central Europe and the social partners have had their say. In Scandinavia, social partners have been strong and able to achieve schemes securing their interests through political negotiations (Esping-Andersen, 1985). In Finland, the design of pension policy – and social policy in general – has partly followed both Scandinavian and Central European models (Kangas, 2006b, pp 354-5). But in the area of parental leave policy, the corporatist model of tripartite negotiations has led the way.

The aim of this chapter is to examine how labour market partners have affected the development of family policy or, more specifically, leave policy, since the 1960s, attempting to answer a key question: why has the role of social partners been so strong in Finland? We will argue that institutional conditions were less favourable to labour organisations working through the political system, with the Social Democratic Party in a weaker position than in other Nordic countries and the Agrarian Union (since 1965 the Centre Party), the main political power in Finland, able to obstruct social reforms demanded by labour organisations. Given these political conditions, workers' organisations have regarded the labour market arena as offering more possibilities than the political one (Kangas, 2006b).

In preparing this chapter, we have drawn on interviews conducted with officials from two central employees' organisations (the Finnish Confederation of Salaried Employees and the Central Organisation of Finnish Trade Unions) and one central employers' organisation (the Confederation of Finnish Industries).

The role of labour market organisations

The Finnish model of tripartite negotiations was developed in the 1960s, as collective bargaining was combined with designing new social policies (Bergholm, 2007). Collective labour agreements already had a long history. The first general agreement between the central labour market organisations was reached in 1944, determining wage levels as well as forbidding the right to strike without advance warning (Pesonen and Riihinen, 2002). The threats of industrial action and the arbitration of the state were significant influences on collective agreements until 1960 (Bergholm, 2007). After the 1960 agreement, the two central labour organisations – the Central Organisation of Finnish Trade Unions (SAK) representing blue-collar workers and the Confederation of Finnish Employers (STK; since 1992 the Confederation of Finnish Industry and Employers, TT) representing private large-scale industries – realised they also had common interests in social policy questions. Through their participation in developing legislation on annual holiday (1960), unemployment security (1960) and earnings-related pensions (1961), the cooperative bond between them was strengthened. They were also involved in the National Health Insurance reform carried out in 1963, together with political parties.

The first general income policy settlement between central labour market organisations was reached in 1968; this covered both wages and social policy reforms (Väänänen-Tomppo, 1981; Pesonen and Riihinen, 2002). The settlement was originally negotiated between the two most influential central organisations (SAK and STK), but the state and 10 other central organisations were soon included in the negotiations (Nousiainen, 1998). (The other main trades unions were the Finnish Confederation of Salaried Employees (STTK) representing white-collar workers; the Central Organisation of Salaried Employees (TVK) representing mostly women in public sector; and the Confederation of Unions for Professional and Managerial Staff in Finland (AKAVA) representing academic professionals. The other employers' organisations were the central organisation primarily representing companies in commerce; the Commission for Local Authority Employers; and the State Employers' Office.) Although the initiative for the settlement was taken by the government, its role was rather marginal; the central organisations decided on the agenda, identified areas of disagreement and agreed solutions (Nousiainen, 2006).

Since this first general income policy settlement, union-based or local agreements on wages have been quite marginal for four decades, with the exception of the recession years in the early 1990s. Although some unions have on occasion not joined the general wage settlement, the social policy legislation linked to these settlements has been binding on all employers and employees. A special feature of the Finnish model has been the inclusion of the interests of farmers – represented by the Central Union of Agricultural Producers and Forest Owners – in the tripartite process of policy design.

The importance of trades unions grew as they recruited more members. Membership became more attractive because unemployment benefits were managed by the unions; joining an unemployment fund meant joining a union (Pesonen and Riihinen, 2002). Union membership was easy because employers agreed, as a part of the general settlement, to deduct membership fees directly from wages, and these union dues were also made tax deductible. Moreover, employment pension systems were designed so that their administration was controlled by the social partners, which was another incentive for union membership (Kangas, 2006a).

In this climate, union membership increased rapidly. In 1960, only 28% of all wage earners belonged to the four biggest central employee organisations; by 1970, this had risen to 57% and by 1988 to 90% (Borg, 1990). By the mid-1990s, more than three quarters of the total labour force were unionised, one of the highest levels in the world (Pesonen and Riihinen, 2002). At the same time as membership grew, trade unions became more professionalised and at the end of 1970s, the number of people employed by labour unions and central organisations was about 4 times higher than the number of employees of political parties (Borg, 1990). The number of organised employers increased as well; in 1950, employers in the two largest employer organisations accounted for 25% of wage earners and by 1975 this had increased to 47% (Väänänen–Tomppo, 1981).

During the 1970s and 1980s, the influence of the labour market organisations grew along with their regular and increasing participation in state committees. Temporary state committees were bodies commissioned by the Prime Minister's Office or by a ministry to clarify issues, to make proposals and to prepare legislation. Through these short-term committees it was possible to make good use of expert knowledge outside the administration. In addition, there were permanent committees, often called councils or commissions (Nousiainen, 1998). Due to the enlargement of the state, the number of committees increased from the 1950s, and through them the leaders of labour market organisations could keep in contact with decision makers, both officials and politicians (Nousiainen, 2006).

The increasing participation of the social partners in state committees caused some concern among politicians. In 1977, a survey showed that a majority of MPs thought that parliament had lost some measure of power to the labour market organisations. A quarter of MPs said the actions of trades unions and other economic organisations were too binding on the parliament especially in relation to economic and social policy. The labour market organisations were themselves aware of their power; in a survey in 1980, they regarded themselves as more powerful than either the parliament or political parties (Borg, 1990).

In addition to their large memberships, another reason for the authority of the social partners in policy design was their role in financing the National Health

Insurance fund. Benefits were funded by employers, employees and the state, which to safeguard the solvency of the insurance fund paid any shortfall as a 'guarantee payment' (Niemelä, 2004; Niemelä and Salminen, 2006). However, the size of the guarantee payment paid by the state increased annually from 1998 due to a shortfall in funding caused by lower employee contributions resulting from collective agreements (Niemelä and Salminen, 2006).

To resolve the crisis, major changes in financing the insurance system were introduced in 2006. The insurance scheme was split into two components: earned income insurance and medical insurance. The earned income insurance includes, *inter alia*, parental allowances and compensation to employers for the cost of holiday pay while employees on leave are receiving these allowances. The financing of these benefits is shared between employers (73%) and employees/self-employed persons (27%). With the social partners' financing role comes power to decide about the scheme.

Support to mothers: from child benefit to home care allowance

In the area of family policy, the social partners have been active since the creation of a child benefit system after the Second World War (Bergholm, 2003). Unlike many other countries, the child benefit system in Finland did not emerge as a result of social policy considerations but because of labour market policies (Hiilamo, 2002). In 1947, employers proposed a family wage system, which would provide a bonus or benefit for employees with children. The purpose was to avoid a general wage increase and to keep inflation under control and the proposal was supported by the industrial employees' union, with the first child benefits paid at the end of 1947. However, the Agrarian Union was strongly opposed to this measure, as a considerable number of rural families would have been excluded. As a result, the idea of a family wage was abandoned and a universal child benefit was introduced in 1948, financed from social security contributions paid by employers.

Since the 1960s, work–life policy has been a regular part of the tripartite negotiations; during this decade, the growing influence of the trades unions and the expansion of the welfare state were combined with a normalisation of mothers' employment (Julkunen, 1994). Policy reforms in the 1960s and 1970s mainly concerned the position of mothers in the labour market. Maternity insurance was delayed in Finland due to clashes of interest between industrial labour and the agrarian sector (Haatanen, 1992), but in 1963 maternity benefit was introduced as part of the National Health Insurance. Beforehand, legislation on work protection (decrees in 1917 and 1919) prohibited women employed in industry or commerce from working for 4 or 6 weeks after delivery; the duration of this unpaid maternity leave was specified as 6 weeks in the Contracts of Employment Act of 1934 (Waris, 1966; Hiilamo, 2002). Low-income mothers were entitled to a small flat-rate benefit based on the Maternity Benefit Act (passed in 1937), and this was extended to all mothers in 1949. However, the position of civil servants was better: from 1942, they were entitled to 2 months' maternity leave with full compensation (Waris, 1966; Haataja, 2008).

According to the 1963 reform, maternity benefit was paid for a period of 9 weeks, but until 1971, the length of maternity leave varied according to collective agreements in different branches of employment (Haataja, 2007, p 14). Following the example of Sweden, maternity benefit was earnings-related, amounting to about 40% of previous earnings (Hiilamo, 2002).

With the total fertility rate at an all-time low (1.5) in 1973, family policy became an essential issue in political discussions. With rising maternal employment in the 1960s, the lack of childcare services had already emerged as a social problem. These services had been provided mainly for children of poor families as a means of child protection, but the Child Day Care Act passed in 1973 was intended to support women's right to employment as well as ensuring children a safe care environment; childcare services were redefined as part of the general social care system rather than protection for children at risk.

The 1973 Act was a victory for the left parties, especially for the Social Democrats but also for the Finnish People's Democratic League (since 1990 the Left Alliance). The Act obliged municipalities to offer childcare services, with state financial support for building new centres (Anttonen, 2003). At the time, a quarter of a million childcare places were needed in Finland, but only 42,500 places were available, and 9 out of every 10 children were without a place (Mannerheimin Lastensuojeluliitto ja Väestöliitto, 1973). As a result of the Act, the importance of private provision started to decrease and the role of municipalities increased considerably.

But in the view of the centre-right political parties – mainly the Centre Party and the Conservative Party (officially called the National Coalition) – extensive investment in public childcare was not satisfying the needs of rural farming families where children were often taken care of at home. These parties – representing in particular upper and middle white-collar employees, and the interests of employers and farmers – demanded more possibilities for choice between home care for children and public childcare. As part of the collective income agreement in 1974–75, the home care of very young children was promoted by lengthening maternity leave substantially, from 3 to 7 months (Väänänen-Tomppo, 1981).

A political compromise was gradually established in the form of a cash-for-care provision, the 'home care allowance' introduced in 1985; the scheme became fully operational between 1985 and 1990. Parents with children under 3 years of age have since then had a right to choose between a home care allowance and a place in a public childcare service, available as of right from birth (Haataja and Nyberg, 2006). At the beginning of 1990, the childcare system catered for half of all pre-school children, with public provision accounting for 95% of all services (Muuri and Vihma, 1991). Most children under 3 years are cared for at home by their mothers; the home care allowance and the related right to home care leave after parental leave has finished are today highly regarded among parents of young children, but this leave is rarely taken by fathers (Salmi, 2006).

Father care emerges

As women's participation in the labour market was growing in the 1960s, the role of men was also discussed. A new gender ideology was shaped mainly among young academic radicals who demanded a renewal of gender roles (Jallinoja, 1983). Their society, called 'Association 9', was the first to propose paternity leave, in 1967 (Husu et al, 1995). The first proposal on fathers' leave rights was made in Parliament, and in 1970 the Committee on Women's Position suggested a lengthening of maternity leave with a period that could be shared between parents in order to support women's position in the labour market (Haataja, 2007).

Demands for gender equality resulted in the founding of the Council for Gender Equality in 1972. This is a permanent advisory body, originally located in the Prime Minister's Office and operating since 1986 under the Ministry of Social Affairs and Health. The tasks of the council are to monitor gender equality in society, to develop initiatives and proposals and to deliver statements on the development of legislation. The council's members are representatives of the political parties, and the aim is to promote equality across party lines. Although the council is formally a part of the ministry, it has a relatively independent status and has put forward innovative initiatives (Kantola and Nousiainen, 2008).

The Council for Gender Equality made several proposals on father care, arguing their relevance for supporting the situation of women in the labour market. A proposal in 1974 called for improved maternity leave benefits and the development of maternity leave towards becoming a parental leave. In the same year, a tripartite committee started work on the same development and proposed that 3 months of the then 7 months' maternity leave should become a period that could be shared between parents. The employers' union (Confederation of Finnish Employers STK) disagreed; it thought that long periods of leave for fathers would be dysfunctional and demanded that the transferable period should be no longer than 2 months (Haataja, 2007).

The committee also proposed a 'postnatal leave' for fathers, that is, paternity leave after the birth of a child. A year later a similar initiative was put forward by the Council for Gender Equality, motivated by the mother's need for rest as well as the development of a father–child relationship (Haataja, 2007). Subsequent negotiations resulted in the first version of paternity leave in 1978; maternity leave was prolonged by 2 weeks, and fathers were given a right to take these 2 weeks in order to participate in the care of a newborn baby. Fathers did not, however, have an individual right to leave but needed the mother's permission, and take-up of the new leave was low (Haataja, 2007). Later the same year maternity leave was further extended by 2 more weeks – this time only for mothers – and as a part of a general income policy settlement in 1979, yet another 2 weeks were added to the length of maternity leave (Väänänen-Tomppo, 1981).

Already in the 1970s, the Council for Gender Equality had also advocated a right for both parents to take leave in order to take care of a sick child. Proposals on this kind of short and temporary leave were directed to the social partners in 1975 and again in 1982. The right for temporary care leave for parents with children under 10 years was eventually introduced as part of the Employment Contract Act in 1988.

As child-related leave was no longer meant only for mothers, new terminology was needed. The official term for maternity leave had been 'birth leave', and since the introduction of paternity leave, the epithet 'or corresponding leave' was added (Haataja, 2007). As many mothers returned to employment before the end of their maternity leave period but the benefit was paid for the whole period, in 1980 fathers were permitted to take one month of the leave period with the mother's permission. As part of the 1981 general income agreement, maternity leave was extended to 158 days (about 6½ months) and the transferable period to 2 months.

The next year, maternity benefits became more clearly income-related, the income ceiling was dropped and benefits became taxable income. In order to reach a political compromise, fathers' right to use part of maternity leave was lengthened to 4 months (Mansner, 2005). In 1985, the transferable period was lengthened to the current 6½ months and the terms 'maternity', 'paternity' and 'parental leave' were adopted. Even after the adoption of the term 'parental leave' for the period that could be shared between parents, fathers' take-up was still conditional on the mother's consent.

Towards individual rights for fathers

During the 1980s, the focus in developing parental leave schemes started to shift towards fathers. The Council for Gender Equality continued to advocate father care and proposed in 1989 that parental leave should be lengthened by adding a father's quota. The first individual leave right for fathers was indeed introduced in 1991 but it was related to paternity leave. Paternity leave was lengthened from 2 to 3 weeks. Two years later, fathers gained 2 more weeks of leave, but at the expense of the whole parental leave period becoming 2 weeks shorter; families where the father did not take paternity leave, as well as single mothers, lost out (Haataja, 2007).

While these reforms on paternity leave rights were being made in Finland, the other Nordic countries were developing a father's quota for parental leave; Norway was the first country in the world to introduce a 4-week father's quota, in 1994, Sweden followed in 1995 and Denmark in 1999. The idea of the individual quota is that if the father does not take his entitlement, it cannot be transferred to the mother; in other words, the father uses it or the family loses it. In Finland, several attempts were made in the parliament during the 1990s to encourage fathers' take-up of parental leave and to create a 'father's month'. A Committee on Fatherhood – which had no representatives from the labour or employers' unions – included a Nordic comparison of fathers' leave rights in its report and proposed a lengthening of parental leave in the form of a father's quota, as well as the introduction of partial parental leave to be shared between parents (Komiteanmietintö, 1999).

The Committee on Fatherhood was one of the few state temporary committees used for preparing social policy reforms during the 1990s. These ad hoc committees were felt to be too cumbersome and slow for negotiating and designing new legislation. Instead, the use of working groups, rapporteurs, networks and consultancy assignments became more common. Social security was one sector where this new and more flexible way of preparing policy was adopted (Nousiainen, 1998; Temmes, 2001). Often, the social partners participated in the working groups dealing with social policy issues related to the labour market.

Father care re-emerged in the tripartite negotiations of 1997, as the general income policy settlement included the setting up of a tripartite working group. The task of the group was to find ways to promote a more equal take-up of parental leave by mothers and fathers, and to equalise the costs of parental leave between employers in female-dominated and other sectors. As the views and goals of the employers' and employees' central organisations were largely opposed, the working group mainly acted as a discussion forum. Common ground for new leave reforms was not found: while employees' organisations demanded more support for work–family reconciliation, employers opposed any suggestion of reduced working time or increased costs.

In the 2000s, the theme of work–life balance continued to be a part of the central income policy negotiations. In the general income agreement for 2001–02, the social partners again agreed to start a tripartite working group whose task was to clarify the challenges facing the current leave system, especially the possibilities of a father's month of parental leave and partial parental leave, both as means to promote father care. Disagreement was rife, not only between employers and employees, but also among the two employers' central organisations and among the three employees' central organisations. While employers representing the female-dominated service sector – since 1996 represented by the Employers' Confederation of Service Industries – wanted to promote a more equal take-up of leave as well as the balancing of costs of leave between sectors (so sectors with higher levels of women workers did not bear higher costs arising from leave policy), employers representing male-dominated industry – the Confederation of Finnish Industry and Employers – were not willing to accept any extra costs. A father's quota in parental leave was suggested by the employees' organisation representing female-dominated, white-collar workers (STTK), but the organisation representing blue-collar workers (SAK), as well as upper white-collar employees' organisations (AKAVA) and employers were opposed. Thus, negotiations again resulted in no leave reforms. An information campaign focusing on fathers was, however, jointly designed and carried out by the Ministry of Social Affairs and Health in 2001.

Another tripartite working group was included in the general income agreement for 2003–04. This time the group's task was more concretely defined than before: it should prepare changes to the Employment Contract Act regarding leave rights.

In 2003, negotiations had resulted in a new bonus leave for fathers, as well as a right to part-time parental leave. Consensus was reached through a series of compromises. As a result, a father could now get a non-transferable, 2-week leave bonus if he took 2 weeks of the transferable parental leave. Parents could also take part-time parental leave if both of them took this leave and worked part time concurrently. Inspiration for the bonus model came from Italy where fathers who took 3 months of paternity leave were entitled to an additional bonus month.

However, the new schemes proved less successful than hoped and there was only a modest increase in the take-up of parental leave by fathers; in 2007, 11.9% of fathers were on parental leave compared with 2.6% in 2002. The new users of parental leave mainly took a standard length of leave (that is, paternity leave + 2 weeks of parental leave + the 2-week bonus leave, that is, 3 + 4 weeks) instead of longer periods of parental leave (Hämäläinen and Takala, 2007). The consequence was that the average parental leave period taken by fathers ended up being shorter than before. The part-time solution of sharing parental leave was used only in a handful of families.

Encouraging fathers with flexibility and money

After almost a decade of tripartite negotiations on work–family reconciliation and parental leave, the social partners took a breather and left this subject out of the collective income agreement for 2005–07. The challenges, however, remained; there still existed a considerable gap between the aim of more equal sharing of childcare and the actual take-up of leave by fathers. The two ministries responsible for the administration of parental leave rights and benefits both took actions to clarify what possibilities existed for the further development of fathers' parental leave. The Ministry of Social Affairs and Health appointed a rapporteur to find ways to encourage fathers to take more paternity and parental leave and to achieve more equalisation of the leave costs of employers, while a tripartite working group was set up by the Ministry of Labour.

The key suggestions of the rapporteur (Metsämäki, 2005) were about raising the level of parental leave benefits. After hearing several experts, he proposed 100% income compensation during the first months of maternity leave, and an increase of parental leave allowance from 70% to 80% of annual earnings. The latter was intended to encourage more fathers to take parental leave, the low rate of compensation having been seen as a disincentive. The increase in the amount of the allowance would also equalise costs between employers, as firms that provided full pay would be entitled to a larger reimbursement from the state. In addition, the rapporteur suggested that a new parental insurance financed collectively by all employers should be established.

Issues addressed by the working group appointed by the Ministry of Labour (Työministeriö, 2005) included the need for greater flexibility in how the father's bonus leave could be taken. So far, the bonus leave had been tacked on to the end of parental leave. This was deemed problematic, as most mothers did not return to work immediately after parental leave, preferring instead to take some home care leave. Returning to work for a month was in most cases difficult or impossible to organise. The timing of the father's bonus leave, it was proposed, should be more flexible so that fathers could postpone their leave until the end of the mother's home care leave. Moreover, the group proposed that parents (mostly fathers) living apart from their child, but with joint custody, should have the right to temporary care leave to look after a sick child. So far, only parents living with the child had this right.

The implementation of these suggestions was negotiated in a tripartite working group set up by the Ministry of Social Affairs and Health in 2006. Although the employers' and employees' organisations had many disagreements about the desired course of action, they were both motivated to reach a compromise in order to secure their negotiating power in the future development of social policy. The Minister of Social Affairs and Health – who had previously been a chairperson of the Council for Gender Equality – had communicated her intention to present her proposal to the parliament should the working group not agree one. This would have meant the social partners being bypassed in the preparation of the leave reform and risking a loss of authority in the general area of social policy.

During the course of negotiations in the working group, a 2-month father's quota was once again put on the table by the white-collar employees and again opposed by blue-collar employees and by employers – now represented by a new central organisation, the Confederation of Finnish Industries that was formed by a merger of the Employers' Confederation of Service Industries and the Confederation of Finnish Industry and Employers. In particular, the representatives of employees in female-dominated service sectors considered that the father's quota would undermine mothers' leave rights, while employers emphasised that the decision on sharing parental leave should be left to the family (Silfverberg, 2006). Moreover, employers were holding firmly to a limit on any additional costs, especially when the government announced that the reform could not be financed by the state. This cost limit created the framework within which the compromise was to be found.

The working group did agree on a proposal that was passed by government to be approved by the parliament. It was suggested that the father's bonus leave could be used over a longer time period, and that the benefit level of both mothers (during maternity leave but not during parental leave) and fathers (during parental leave) would be higher during certain periods of leave.

Despite being a compromise, all partners in the negotiations were relatively satisfied with the proposal. For blue-collar employees, a higher benefit for maternity leave was especially welcome as it could strengthen the livelihood of young families and make full pay during maternity leave possible for more mothers, as the employer could get a higher replacement from the state. Indeed, the Service Union United was soon able to negotiate full pay during the first couple of months of maternity leave for its membership. White-collar employees were satisfied about the additional encouragement of father care (a higher benefit for one month of parental leave taken by fathers and more flexibility in the take-up of the father's month), and employers were relieved to have avoided some of the feared increase in social security contributions.

But the proposal was criticised in Parliament, on the one hand for not including a longer period of father's quota, and on the other hand for not concentrating on attitudes and values rather than modifications in leave rights. The position of single mothers was raised; these women would not benefit at all from the proposed reform. The different rate of compensation during parental leave for women and men also provoked critical comments. According to the Ombudsman for Equality, the proposal went against the Act on Equality between Women and Men. The principle of positive discrimination could not be used in this case, as men were not in a weaker position relative to women just because they used their right to parental leave less. As a result, Parliament did not accept the proposal prepared by the tripartite group. Even though the promotion of father care was seen as an important goal, fathers could not be paid a higher benefit than mothers during parental leave.

A reform was thus introduced from the beginning of 2007 with a somewhat higher benefit level (75%) for both mothers and fathers during the first 5 weeks of parental leave. Maternity leave benefit was raised to 90% during the first 9 weeks. Fathers got the option to take the bonus period of paternity leave (the 2 + 2 weeks was now called a 'father's month') until the child was about 14 months old, in case the child was cared for at home after parental leave by the mother taking home care leave. The increased flexibility and the economic incentive will probably have some effect on the take-up rates of parental leave by fathers.

The special characteristic of the reformed scheme is its complex structure. The benefit level changes several times during maternity and parental leave. A mother who takes the whole period of maternity and parental leave herself receives a 90% benefit during the first 9 weeks, then 70% for 8 weeks, followed by 75% for 5 weeks and 70% during the remaining period of about 5 months. If the father takes parental leave, his benefit is 75% of earnings during the first 5 weeks, and 70% thereafter. However, these increases in the rates do not apply to paternity leave. Moreover, high-income parents have different compensation rates due to a system of stepped progression of benefits. It is thus not very easy for parents to calculate the economic consequences of the various alternatives for sharing leave.

Conclusion

In Finland, the tripartite system has been an important framework for the processes of decision making. It would be an overstatement to say that this system, based on participation of social partners, is undemocratic, but it certainly has some limitations. A recent report by the Organisation for Economic Co-operation and Development (OECD) warns against too high an expectation being placed on the voluntary introduction of family-friendly policies based on bargaining between employers and unions: "it is probably unrealistic to expect such practices to become quasi-universal" (OECD, 2007, p 188). This kind of criticism can be applied to the Finnish system as well.

The main actors in the development of leave policy have been the central employers' and employees' organisations, and the two ministries responsible for work–family reconciliation, that is, the Ministry of Social Affairs and Health and the Ministry of Labour. In addition, the parliamentary Council for Gender Equality has had an active role in initiating measures to promote care by fathers and in promoting ongoing discussion of the topic. The role of governments and politicians has often been more passive, as negotiations have taken place outside the democratic process, and large social packages have been ratified in the parliament without much possibility for political modification (Väänänen-Tomppo, 1981).

As rationales for the reform of leave policy, labour market issues and the interests of certain occupational groups have often carried more weight than more general aims such as gender equality or the healthy development of children. An important consideration for employers' organisations in relation to leave policy has been to reduce costs, or to prevent their increase, and the problem of costs has particularly concerned employers in female-dominated sectors of the economy. Employers have also been interested in promoting work–life balance and in securing labour supply in the short run, whereas the reproduction of the labour force in the longer run has been far less of a concern. Trades unions have been interested in securing the economic interests of their members as well as promoting the well-being of employees by providing more time for personal and family needs. Since the early days of maternity protection, the rationale of health and safety at work has not been central in the negotiations. Gender equality has been referred to as an important aim more by white-collar employees than blue-collar ones. Father care has been more positively viewed by left-wing and liberal political parties than by the (Agrarian) Centre Party or the more conservative right-wing parties.

The Finnish model of tripartite negotiations has secured rather steady economic development with relatively small income differences, and the introduction of many comprehensive leave policies with a rather high income compensation level. The negotiating relationships have been quite explicit and stable, and the goals and demands of each partner have been predictable. On the other hand, the exercise of power has been centralised and bureaucratic (Borg, 1990).

During the past decade, tripartite negotiations about the reform of parental leave have been based on short-term working groups, in which it has proved more difficult to obtain an overall view of aims and means. Despite inspiration from the other Nordic countries, and ongoing negotiations in several tripartite working groups around the turn of the century, a father's quota for parental leave has not been established in Finland. Reforms to promote more equal sharing of parental leave have been based on compromises and gradual adjustments, and have made the leave scheme increasingly complicated and difficult to understand. The reforms have thus not been very satisfactory, either from the point of view of citizens or from the perspective of equality policy. For example, the adjustments made to parental leave aimed at encouraging father care have not yet had a radical impact on the gendered take-up of leave.

Governments may wish to intervene in policy design if they foresee unwanted results arising from the bargaining process. For example, policy makers may be concerned about the decline in birth rates and demographic trends, when these issues are not of immediate interest to employers and unions and are thus unlikely to feature prominently in the industrial bargaining process. Similarly, employer and employee organisations in male-dominated sectors are likely to lack incentives to pursue gender equity objectives. However, governments are interested in giving both fathers and mothers sufficient time to spend at work and with their children because this helps sustain birth rates, strengthens future labour supply and reduces child poverty risks (OECD, 2007).

In the future, changes in the economy, the labour market and occupational structure, stimulated by globalisation, will create challenges for the tripartite negotiation system. The corporatist model may not provide enough security in a context of growing insecurity and unemployment (Kangas, 2006b). General collective agreements on wages are less likely; the employers' central organisation (EK) has already declared that it are no longer interested in these centralised methods. Rather, it wants employers and employees to agree on wages at a local level. Labour unions on the other hand – at least some of them – would like to continue the tradition of collective agreements.

Despite the insecurity around collective agreements, tripartite negotiations on social policy reforms, including possible modifications of the parental leave scheme, are still seen as necessary by all social partners. The central labour market organisations are also still important partners for the state in policy design and the preparation of legislation. They remain, for the moment, key players in the field of leave policies.

Note

[1] Leave provision described here refers to statutory entitlements.

References

Anttonen, A. (2003) 'Lastenhoidon kaksi maailmaa' ['Two worlds of childcare'], in H. Forsberg and R. Nätkin (eds) *Perhe murroksessa. Kriittisen perhetutkimuksen jäljillä*, Helsinki: Gaudeamus, pp 159-85.

Bergholm, T. (2003) 'Työmarkkinajärjestöt ja Suomen lapsilisäjärjestelmän synty' ['Labour market organisations and the emergence of child benefit in Finland'], *Yhteiskuntapolitiikka*, vol 68, no 1, pp 63-76.

Bergholm, T. (2007) 'Suomen mallin synty' ['The emergence of the Finnish model'], *Yhteiskuntapolitiikka*, vol 72, no 5, pp 475-92.

Borg, O. (1990) 'Työmarkkinajärjestöt jälkiteollisessa yhteiskunnassa' ['Labour market organisations in a postindustrial society'], in O. Riihinen (ed) *Suomi 2017*, Jyväskylä: Gummerus, pp 311-36.

Esping-Andersen, G. (1985) *Politics against markets. The Social Democratic road to power*, Princeton, NJ: Princeton University Press.

Haataja, A. (2007) 'Suomalainen äitiys-, isyys- ja vanhempainrahajärjestelmä: ylistämisestä alistamiseen?' ['The Finnish maternity, paternity and parental leave system: from praise to subordination?'], in A.-M.Castrén (ed) *Työn ja perheen tasapaino: sääntelyä, tutkimusta ja kehittämistä*, Helsinki: Helsingin yliopisto, Palmenia, pp 14–37.

Haataja, A. (2008) 'Perhevapaiden ja -etuuksien käsitteistä, kohdentumisesta ja kustannuksista Suomessa' ['Concepts, targeting and costs of parental leave and benefits'], Unpublished manuscript.

Haataja, A. and Nyberg, A. (2006) 'Diverging paths? The dual-earner/dual-carer model in Finland and Sweden', in A.L. Ellingsæter and A. Leira (eds) *Politicising parenthood in Scandinavia. Gender relations in welfare states*, Bristol: The Policy Press, pp 217–39.

Haatanen, P. (1992) 'Suomalaisen hyvinvointivaltion kehitys' ['The development of the Finnish welfare state'], in O. Riihinen (ed) *Sosiaalipolitiikka vuonna 2017*, Helsinki: WSOY, pp 31–67.

Hämäläinen, U. and Takala, P. (2007) 'Isien perhevapaat ja tasa-arvo' ['Fathers' parental leave and gender equality'], in R. Lilja, R. Asplund and K. Kauppinen (eds) *Perhevapaavalinnat ja perhevapaiden kustannukset sukupuolten välisen tasa-arvon jarruina työelämässä?*, Helsinki: Sosiaali- ja terveysministeriön selvityksiä 69, pp 22–45.

Hiilamo, H. (2002) *The rise and fall of Nordic family policy? Historical development and changes during the 1990s in Sweden and Finland*, Research Report 125, Helsinki: Stakes.

Husu, L. et al (eds) (1995) *Lukukirja Suomen naisille* ['A reader for Finnish women'], Tampere: Gaudeamus.

Jallinoja, R. (1983) *Suomalaisen naisasialiikkeen taistelukaudet* [*The struggles of the women's movement in Finland*], Helsinki: WSOY.

Julkunen, R. (1994) 'Suomalainen sukupuolimalli – 1960-luku käänteenä' ['The Finnish gender model: 1960s as a turning point'], in A. Anttonen, L. Henriksson and R. Nätkin (eds) *Naisten hyvinvointivaltio*, Tampere: Vastapaino, pp 179–201.

Kangas, O. (2006a) 'Jos maalaisliitto ei olisi ollut niin vahva. Jossittelua suomalaisen sosiaaliturvan vaihtoehdoilla' ['If the Agrarian Union had not been so strong. Speculation of alternatives in the Finnish social security'], in M. Jokisipilä and M. Niemi (eds) *Entäs jos … Lisää vaihtoehtoista Suomen historiaa*, Helsinki: Ajatus Kirjat, pp 197–218.

Kangas, O. (2006b) 'Politiikka ja sosiaaliturva Suomessa' ['Politics and social security in Finland'], in T. Paavonen and O. Kangas (eds) *Eduskunta hyvinvointivaltion rakentajana*, Helsinki: Edita, pp 189–366.

Kantola, J. and Nousiainen, K. (2008) 'Pussauskoppiin? Tasa-arvo- ja yhdenvertaisuuslakien yhtenäistämisestä' ['Into the kissing room? About the merge of the Act on Equality between Women and Men and the Equality Act'], *Naistutkimus 2/2008*, pp 6–14.

Komiteanmietintö (1999) *Isätoimikunnan mietintö* [*Report of the Committee on Fatherhood*], Helsinki: Sosiaali- ja terveysministeriö, 1999:1.

Mannerheimin Lastensuojeluliitto ja Väestöliitto (1973) *Päivähoitotutkimus 72. Yhdeksän lasta kymmenestä vailla päivähoitoa. Lasten päivähoidon tarve ja tarjonta Suomessa* [*Daycare study 72. Nine children out of ten without daycare. The need and supply of daycare in Finland*], Helsinki: Mannerheimin Lastensuojeluliitto & Väestöliitto.

Mansner, M. (2005) *Suomalaista yhteiskuntaa rakentamassa. Suomen Työnantajain Keskusliitto 1980-1992* [*Building the Finnish society. The Confederation of Finnish Employers 1980–1992*], Helsinki: Elinkeinoelämän Keskusliitto.

Metsämäki, J. (2005) *Perhevapaista aiheutuvien kustannusten korvauksen kehittäminen. Selvityshenkilön raportti* [*Developing the compensation for parental leave costs*], Helsinki: Sosiaali- ja terveysministeriö, työryhmämuistioita 16.

Muuri, A. and Vihma, L. (1991) *Kuinka siinä kävikään? Lasten päivähoito ja lasten kotihoidon tuki vuoden 1990 alussa* [*And then what? Child daycare and home care support at the beginning of 1990*], Helsinki: Sosiaali- ja terveyshallitus.

Niemelä, H. (2004) 'Suomen sairausvakuutusjärjestelmän synty' ['The emergence of sickness insurance in Finland'], in K. Hellsten and T. Helne (eds) *Vakuuttava sosiaalivakuutus?*, Helsinki: Kansaneläkelaitos, pp 90-116.

Niemelä, H. and Salminen, K. (2006) *Social security in Finland*, Helsinki: Finnish Centre for Pensions, Social Insurance Institution, Ministry of Social Affairs and Health, Finnish Pension Alliance.

Nousiainen, J. (1998) *Suomen poliittinen järjestelmä (10. painos)* [*The political system in Finland*], Helsinki: WSOY.

Nousiainen, J. (2006) 'Suomalainen parlamentarismi' ['Parliamentarism in Finland'], in A. Jyränki and J. Nousiainen (eds) *Eduskunnan muuttuva asema*, Helsinki: Edita, pp 180-335.

OECD (Organisation for Economic Co-operation and Development) (2007) *Babies and bosses: Reconciling work and family life. A synthesis of findings for OECD countries*, Paris: OECD.

Pesonen, P. and Riihinen, O. (2002) *Dynamic Finland: The political system and the welfare state*, Helsinki: Finnish Literature Society, Studia Fennica, Historica 3.

Salmi, M. (2006) 'Parental choice and the passion for equality in Finland', in A.L. Ellingsæter and A. Leira (eds) *Politicising parenthood in Scandinavia. Gender relations in welfare states*, Bristol: The Policy Press, pp 145-68.

Silfverberg, A. (2006) 'Terveisiä perheestä' ['Greetings from the family'], *Helsingin Sanomat*, Nyt-liite 8/2006, pp 16-19.

Temmes, M. (2001) *Määräaikaisen valmistelun kehittäminen* [*Developing temporary law preparation*], Research Report 6/2001, Helsinki: Valtiovarainministeriö, Tutkimukset ja selvitykset.

Työministeriö (2005) *Perhevapaasäännösten toimivuus. Perhevapaasäännösten toimivuutta arvioivan työryhmän raportti* [*The functioning of parental leave schemes*], Helsinki: Työministeriö, työhallinnon julkaisuja 358.

Väänänen-Tomppo, I. (1981) *Työmarkkinajärjestöjen rooli sosiaalipolitiikan kehittämisessä Suomessa vuosina 1956–1979* [*The role of labour market organisations in developing social policy in Finland 1956–1979*], Helsinki: Helsingin yliopisto, sosiaalipolitiikan laitos, tutkimuksia 6/1981.

Waris, H. (1966) *Suomalaisen yhteiskunnan sosiaalipolitiikka. Johdatus sosiaalipolitiikkaan* [*Social policy in Finnish society: Introduction to social policy*], Helsinki: WSOY.

SEVEN

France: gender equality a pipe dream?

Jeanne Fagnani and Antoine Math

Maternity leave[1]: 16 weeks at 100% of earnings, up to a ceiling of €2,773 a month (24 weeks for third or further child).

Paternity leave: 2 weeks provided by two schemes – 3 working days at 100% of earnings, paid by the employer), and 11 consecutive days (including non-working days) at 100% of earnings, up to a ceiling of €2,773 a month, paid by the social security fund.

Parental leave: until the child is 3 years; family entitlement. A flat-rate payment (€536 per month) is paid to families with a parent not working – whether taking leave or not – whose income is below a certain level (in practice, about 90% of families are eligible). However, for parents with only one child, it is only paid until 6 months after the end of maternity leave; in other families, it is paid until the child reaches 3 years of age. Parents working part time up to 32 hours per week may receive the benefit at a reduced amount.

Leave to care for sick children: unpaid leave for parents of children under 16 years; legally, periods of leave cannot exceed 3 days (or 5 days if a child is under one year old or if there are 3 children or more), but this is a minimum and most collective agreements have special arrangements, as in the public sector where employees can take 14 days a year to care for a sick child. In cases of a serious disability or illness of a child under 20 years, every employee with at least one year of employment with an employer is entitled to paid leave to care for her/his child, or to work part time for a period of up to 3 years (the allowance is paid for a maximum of 310 working days, that is, around 14 months, within a period of 3 years). The level of the allowance depends on the duration of work for the employer and on the family structure (for example, if one parent in a couple family stops work, the amount is €39.58 per day; €47.02 for a lone parent). A similar period of leave is possible for employees who need to care for a relative at the end of life, either a child or a parent living in the same house.

Other: none.

France is a member state of the European Union. Around two thirds of eligible fathers took paternity leave in 2003. It is impossible to calculate the number of parents on parental leave because employers are not required to provide information about take-up. Research suggests that women make up 98–99% of parents taking leave.

Introduction

Since the 1970s, a concerted effort has been made by successive French governments to promote social policies designed to enable mothers to juggle both family responsibilities and full-time employment. In particular, at the beginning of the 1980s as the Socialists swept into power, there was a marked increase in the level of funds being allocated for the construction of crèches by both local authorities and the Caisse Nationale des Allocations Familiales (CNAF, the National Family Allowance Office, discussed further below). This phenomenon coincided with, indeed was stimulated by, the entry of many mothers of young children into the paid labour force. Today, along with the Nordic countries, France leads the European Union in the provision of childcare and benefits aimed at reducing childcare costs for families (Gornick and Meyers, 2003; Fine-Davis et al, 2004; Fagnani and Math, 2008). These developments have gone hand in hand with the progressive implementation of parental leave policies encouraging parents, though in reality women, to opt to stay at home after the birth of a child.

Public expenditure devoted to parental leave schemes has, therefore, increased regularly, particularly in the 1990s when a growing proportion of working mothers began to receive benefits linked to parental leave permitting them to care for their child, either full or part time, until the child's third birthday. Among the questions that will be addressed and partially answered in this chapter are: Which rationales have underpinned the periodic changes in the politics of parental leave in France? What were the primary economic and social factors influencing the decisions made by successive governments in this domain? Finally, what was the respective role played by each of the social partners during a succession of decision-making processes?

The first part of the chapter, however, will offer an overview of the institutions and social actors involved in the decision-making processes in the field of parental leave policies. In the second part, we will explore the questions outlined above. As we shall see, to better understand why successive governments have introduced reforms since the initial introduction of parental leave in 1977, it is necessary to search behind the rhetoric used to legitimate these changes and place them within their political, economic and social context.

Decision makers involved in parental leave policies and the institutional context

France's policy for families is 'explicit' insofar as it is overseen by institutions and the subject of official reports produced annually. The 'family' as such is legally recognised as an institution that plays an important role in the maintenance of social cohesion. A special branch of social security is devoted to family policy, with the principal administration carried out by the CNAF, whose programmes cover 92% of all families. The Executive Board of CNAF is made up of representatives of the social partners – trades unions and employers – and of family associations, represented by the Union Nationale des Associations Familiales (UNAF); indeed, the president of this board is traditionally a member of the tiny Confédération française des travailleurs chrétiens (CFTC, the French Confederation of Christian Workers, a Christian trade union). It is this board's responsibility to examine periodically the direction being taken by the social security system to support family policy. However, in recent decades, policy decisions have been made in practice by the government, whether or not approved by the Executive Board of the CNAF.

Where parental leave policies are concerned, the government is also a key actor in the decision-making process through numerous legal and political mechanisms. 'Family laws' are drafted and ratified through legislative channels and an agreement, known as the *convention d'objectifs et de gestion*, or COG, is made for a 4-year period between the state and the CNAF. Additionally, spending by the CNAF is tightly controlled by the Ministry of Finance and the *cour des comptes* (court of accounts). Another body, the Haut Conseil de la Population et de la Famille (the High Council for Population and Family), established in 1985, is a committee restricted to a purely consultative role, which produces reports and provides recommendations to the government on family issues and demography. Finally, the Conférence de la Famille (Conference for the Family) is a meeting held annually, since 1994, which provides an opportunity for exchange between the government, family associations and various social partners. It generally serves as a platform for the government to announce new measures. According to new plans, this conference is set to be replaced in the future by a permanent council on the family (Haut Conseil de la Famille).

The family associations are institutionally organised under the umbrella of the UNAF, a powerful lobby that gathers together several family associations or federations. This very influential actor (Chauvière, 2006) has exerted a strong influence on family policy since the establishment of the current social security system in 1945, and is mainly funded by a percentage (0.04%) of the total amount of family benefits allocated by CNAF.

Despite a certain ideological diversity among the organisations represented by the UNAF, the organisation has always promoted 'familialism' and, on the whole, has emphasised the stay-at-home option for mothers with a child less than 3 years of age. Since the 1980s, this lobby has been losing some of its influence. However, family associations have recently shown themselves to remain influential, with the government planning at the time of writing (mid-2008) to give to the UNAF half of the 28 seats on the future Haut Conseil de la Famille, in spite of stiff opposition from other social partners, and especially trades unions.

Employer groups, primarily MEDEF (Mouvement des entreprises de France), which represents large enterprises, but also CGPME (Confédération Générale des Petites et Moyennes Entreprises), which represents small to medium-sized companies, have never focused much on family issues and have demonstrated little enthusiasm for parental leave schemes. This comes as no surprise when we take into consideration that it is mainly the social contributions paid by employers that fund family benefits, an anathema to management in this age of cost cutting and efficiency. For instance, when the decision was taken in 2002 to extend paid statutory paternity leave from 3 days to 2 weeks, MEDEF strongly opposed it on the grounds that the plan was 'unfunded', that is, it was concerned that this leave was to be funded out of contributions levied on pay.

As for trades unions, their views are anything but uniform. The CFTC, the Christian trade union, is very much in favour of parental leave, while the CGT (Confédération Générale du Travail) and the CFDT (Confédération Française du Travail) strongly opposes the scheme and advocate instead a universal system of public childcare provision, staffed by well-qualified workers (Math and Meilland, 2004a). Nevertheless, because of France's traditionally low rate of union membership (only 6% of the overall workforce rising to 10% in the public sector), and the high degree of fragmentation, unions have been neither able nor very willing to exert any real influence on the outcomes of periodic reforms to parental leave policies.

Women's associations, currently represented by among others the Collectif national des droits des femmes (National Association for Women's Rights), have long been the most ardent opponents of the structure of the current parental leave scheme. They are particularly hostile to leaves of long duration, which they consider contrary to their objective of equality between the sexes, taking into account the discrimination many women face re-entering the workforce after a period of extended absence and the fact that almost exclusively mothers take up parental leave.

Two different schemes: parental leave and the childrearing benefit

It is important to understand the differences that exist between the two parts of the parental leave schemes. The first part is the *congé parental d'éducation* (CPE), the entitlement to take leave. This falls within the provisions of the *Code du Travail* (Labour Code), which sets out the regulations all employers must comply with, although they can make their own provisions if they are more favourable. The second is the *allocation parentale d'éducation* (APE), revised and updated in 2004 to become the *complément de libre choix d'activité* (supplement for the freedom of choice to work or not, CLCA). This is a flat-rate benefit paid by CNAF.

The CPE has long been provided regardless of the number of children in a family. By contrast, the APE was initially provided only to those parents having at least three children, the youngest being under 3 years of age, later extended to two-child parents in 1994 and finally to single-child parents in 2004 at the same time as the CLCA scheme was introduced. Furthermore, the eligibility conditions differ between CPE and APE or CLCA, which means that some leave takers (those on CPE) are not provided with APE or CLCA and, conversely, some recipients of the APE or CLCA are not eligible for CPE.

The CPE currently allows all employees, regardless of sex, who have worked for the same employer for at least one year preceding the birth of their child to cease employment totally or continue working on a part-time basis, in order to care for a newborn child, irrespective of number of children. This leave, which follows the end of maternity leave, may be taken until the child reaches 3 years of age, or at any time until this stage. Since 1994, all employers must provide this leave, no matter how many people they employ. According to employment legislation, the employee who is on leave is protected against dismissal. After this leave, an employee must be reinstated without a reduction in pay in the same position or a similar one, and is eligible for retraining with pay.

From 1977 to 1994: the development of parental leave policies

Leave policies: a long-standing tradition in France

At the end of the 19th century, at a time of low fertility levels compared with those of neighbouring countries such as Germany, ensuring the survival and welfare of children became a leading goal of French social policies, and continued so until the 1960s. In this context, in order to protect the health of the mother, pregnant working women became entitled to 8 weeks of leave in 1909. A law of 1913 provided low-income mothers with a benefit during the 4 weeks preceding and the 4 weeks following the birth of a child, on condition that the mother breastfed the child. An improved paid maternity leave, funded through social security contributions, was integrated into the social security system after the Second World War.

The establishment of the parental leave scheme in 1977

The *congé parental d'éducation* has its origins in employment legislation (the *Code du Travail*) and was passed into law on 12 July 1977. The official objective was to 'diversify childcare' by developing 'individualised childcare arrangements'. With continuing growth in economic activity rates for women – irrespective of numbers and ages of children – acting as a catalyst, the issue of reconciling family and professional life had begun to emerge on the policy agenda. The introduction of the CPE would, however, soon bring into conflict opposing values: of traditional state familialism on the one hand; and on the other, the rising tide of feminism brought about by women's relatively high rate of participation in the labour force in France.

The law on parental leave stated that its goal was to increase the opportunities of choice for the "woman who wishes to raise her child". As this wording suggests, the values underpinning the scheme were still very traditional and mother-oriented and, in line with France's long-standing 'maternalist' approach, only mothers were eligible. For some members of parliament on the right, the CPE could conveniently serve two purposes: it would encourage mothers, who were assumed to be the proper caregivers for their young children, to stay at home and, thereby, create job vacancies for others to fill (Jenson and Sineau, 1995). The government also paid lip service to the UNAF, which had long been urging the 'right for mothers' to care for their own children. With the abolition in 1978 of the *allocation de salaire unique* (single salary allowance) – established in 1945 in order to promote the male breadwinner model through generous assistance to families where only the man was in paid work – the demands of the UNAF became more vehement.

From its very beginnings, parental leave was perceived by the feminist movement and the proponents of 'modern' values as a means to encourage mothers to stop working. In the 1970s and 1980s, political mobilisation of women and women's organisations played a significant role in demands for public childcare services. In this context, the main political actors increasingly used their support for childcare provision as a means to attract female voters. Additionally, in an attempt to pull more women, particularly the highly skilled, into the workforce, local authorities began to set up publicly funded crèches (childcare centres) (Fagnani, 1998; Fagnani, 2000).

The creation of the childrearing benefit in 1985

Following the arrival of the Socialist Party in government in 1981, the CPE came up for reform with the law of 4 January 1984. The Socialists' more egalitarian view of gender relations showed itself (Jenson and Sineau, 1995) and fathers now became eligible: parental leave was now genuinely parental. Parents working in the private sector now gained the option to work part time after the birth of their child, seen as a way of promoting 'work sharing', which was an issue just emerging on to the political agenda at the time. Despite the gender-neutral language, however, the decision makers admitted that this scheme would affect mostly women. Additionally, an employer of fewer than 100 employees could refuse, until 1994, to grant leave if, after obtaining the opinion of the *comité d'entreprise* (a worker–management committee or works council) or the staff labour representatives, he or she believed the employee's absence could adversely effect the proper functioning of the firm.

In 1985, in the context of an increase in the unemployment rate, the Minister of Social Affairs, Georgina Dufoix, known for her sympathy to strongly Catholic elements on the left, and despite withering criticism from the members of her own governmental majority (Fagnani, 2000), created the APE. Denounced by feminist groups as a 'mother's wage' in disguise, this benefit – a low flat-rate benefit of 1,518 francs per month – was allocated to the parent, mother or father, who interrupted their employment following the birth of a child, but only in large families (with three or more children) and only if the youngest child was under 3 years of age. To appear more politically correct, legislative bodies paid lip service to a gender equal discourse when drafting the APE, but in reality the low sum of money being offered would discourage the majority of fathers from taking parental leave. The APE was paid up until the child's second birthday and was a non–means–tested benefit. In an effort to specifically target women active in the workforce, the legislation stipulated that the beneficiary must have been employed for a minimum of 2 years in the 30 months preceding the child's birth.

'L'APE Barzach' from 1986: pronatalist concern and restricting expenditure

The return of the right to power in 1986 along with a persistently low birth rate resulted in an increase in the pressures being exerted by the pronatalist lobby (Fagnani, 1998) (for a history of the natalist movement and its long and influential history in France, see Le Bras, 1995). At the same time, this was a period in which women's rights had moved to the forefront of the policy agenda following equal opportunities legislation introduced by the previous left government (Lanquetin and Letablier, 2003). Although women continued to be poorly represented in the political arena (in 1986, they occupied 5.9% of seats in the National Assembly), they were actively participating in pressure groups and numerous voices were raised to demand more high-quality childcare provision in order to realise the promise of increased access to the labour market for women.

It was within this context that Michele Barzach, the Minister of Family Affairs, developed and voiced the rhetoric of 'freedom of choice', while disingenuously declaring to the Senate, "we would like to encourage families to have more than two children" (Session of 8 December 1986, JO n°119 S). But due to the government's search for ways to limit expenditure on the family branch of the social security, the minister's initial ambitions (providing all families with a childrearing benefit) had to be restricted. The eventual reform, therefore, resulted in piecemeal measures that specifically targeted large families – defined again as having 3 or more children. They became entitled to a low, flat-rate childrearing benefit (set at half of the statutory minimum wage) for a 3-year period after the birth of a child. Smaller families were still excluded. Some requirements were later relaxed, enabling a parent to become eligible if she (or he) had worked for at least 2 years at any time in the last 10 years before the birth of the third child.

The family law of 1994: social and employment goals

In the 1990s, governments began to give priority to the development of 'individualised' childcare arrangements (such as family day care and 'nannies'), considered to be less costly than collective ones ('crèches'). In response to growing unemployment, which rose from 8.9% of the workforce in 1990 to 12.3% in 1994 and reached record highs of 14.5% for women, the right-wing government of Prime Minister Balladur decided, in 1994, to exploit the job-creating potential of the childcare sector. The result was a dramatic increase in both childcare allowances and tax concessions aimed at helping families to meet the costs of 'individualised' childcare arrangements, among which parental leave was included (Math and Renaudat, 1997; Fagnani, 1998).

At the same time, and in the face of strong criticism from the feminist movement and those supporting gender equality at the workplace (in particular, the CGT and CFDT trades unions), the government took still further measures to use childcare as a policy tool for attacking unemployment. Economically active mothers having a second child, who opted to stay at home after the birth or maternity leave, were to be provided with APE on condition that they stopped working or seeking work and had worked for at least 2 years out of the 5 years preceding the birth. (If both parents were working on a part-time basis, they could each receive APE, but the combined amount could not exceed the full rate of the APE allowance; the option of part-time work was made available from the time when APE was first taken up whereas previously it had only been available when the child was aged between 2 and 3 years.) Unemployed women were, and still are, removed from the register of those actively seeking work during the period when they receive APE, with the effect of reducing the unemployment rate.

Against the background of the unemployment crisis, the traditional model of the 'stay-at-home mother' who spends all her time caring for the family after the birth of a child made a strong reappearance (Fagnani, 2000). Simone Veil, the centre-right oriented Minister of Social Affairs in charge of family policies, took a stand and made clear her preference for promoting part-time jobs in order "to help families to reconcile family and professional life". Her position could hardly have been made clearer than when she stated before the National Assembly, during voting for family law legislation in 1994: "Our hope for the APE is that it will provide a beneficial effect on employment figures by adding what, by our own calculations, will be 50,000 new full-time jobs".

Veil had a background in promoting the advancement of women, most notably as the driving force behind the law of 1974 authorising abortion in France. Moreover, against the background of changes in the labour market and workplace organisation, research had demonstrated that leaves of long duration were likely to have an adverse impact on female employment. Nevertheless, she failed to carry the day, not being able to convince her colleagues in government of the wisdom of her views, as they were primarily concerned with placating family associations and fighting unemployment. She was, however, able to effectively block the wishes of the most conservative elements in the government who desired the creation of nothing less than what amounted to a 'mother's wage'. The conditions for receiving APE were relaxed and from this time onwards, from the moment the benefit was granted, it became possible for parents to continue working part time while still receiving the benefit, albeit at a correspondingly reduced level.

This new scheme was perceived by its opponents – in particular the two main trades unions, the CGT and the CFDT, and the women's movement – as one designed largely to address the unemployment crisis, not to meet the needs of families and children. Dissatisfaction was also expressed by those large companies that relied on a largely female workforce as well as small and medium-sized businesses that feared an increase in red tape and the effect this would have on overstretched human resources departments. But one of the most traditional family associations, Fédération des Familles de France, felt the scheme did not go far enough and should have been extended to families with only one child. According to its president at the time, the university professor Jacques Bichot, the APE should have been the main driver for change in fertility behaviour and could have encouraged families to have more children.

Later on, proposals were made by one of the committees in charge of the Conférence de la Famille held in 1997 to make parental leave more flexible and to create incentives to encourage fathers to claim for the CPE. Then, using the Swedish example as a model, a more flexible version of the CPE was formulated in 1998 by the newly appointed Délégué Interministériel à la Famille (Inter-ministerial Delegate for the Family), Pierre-Jean Rémy. He wanted to allow both parents the opportunity to spread parental leave over a much longer period, until a child's eighth birthday. Neither made any impact on policy and Rémy found little sympathy for his ideas from a government unreceptive to any measures that might contribute to the already huge public deficit.

Reforms since 2001: the decisive influence of the family associations

Official rhetoric in France on family issues began to come closer to the reality of social changes taking place. With their return to power in 1997, the Socialists placed more emphasis on the right of both parents to be present with a newborn baby. In an effort to do more than pay mere lip service to gender equality, the Minister of Family Affairs, Ségolène Royal, led the movement that resulted in the decision in 2001 to extend paternity leave from 3 working days to 2 weeks. Payment was to be made at full salary up to a certain ceiling and was to be funded from health insurance (Bauer and Penet, 2005). This measure was a clear indication that the socialist government intended to encourage 'real parental parity' and promote a less unequal division of childrearing tasks within couples.

When it came to parental leave, however, the government found itself with rather less room for manoeuvre due to the powerful interests of the family associations as represented by the UNAF. Despite numerous studies clearly indicating the detrimental effect on gender equality caused by the existence of a 3-year benefit and parental leave (Afsa, 1998; Fagnani 1998; Bonnet and Labbé, 1999; Piketty, 2003, 2005; Math and Meilland, 2004b, 2004c; Périvier, 2004), further exacerbated in the case of less skilled women (Marc, 2004), and, in spite of numerous criticisms being voiced from certain trades unions and women's organisations, the government resisted change for fear of the opposition it might provoke within these family associations.

In 2004, under the right-wing government of President Chirac, a significant change in childrearing benefit was announced. A benefit, called *complément de libre choix d'activité* or 'supplement for the freedom of choice to work or not', roughly equivalent to the former childrearing benefit (APE), was extended to working parents with only a single child (aged under 3 years) who interrupted or reduced their employment. But because of budgetary constraints, which limited the government's room for manoeuvre, the amount was set rather low (€536 per month in 2008) and the duration of the scheme was limited to 6 months after the end of maternity leave, except for parents having two or more children, in which case it continues to run until the child reaches the age of 3 years. To receive this benefit, mothers or fathers need to have worked continuously for the 2 years preceding childbirth and unemployed periods are not taken into account. This eligibility criterion has resulted in the exclusion of many women – either unemployed or in precarious or undeclared employment – from the scheme.

By 2004, the decision significantly to increase the amount of the childrearing benefit provided to parents who work part time was also taken. The rationale behind this decision was to encourage mothers to remain in the labour market on a part-time basis rather than stopping work completely. This financial incentive has proved to be very effective, with a dramatic increase in the number of recipients working part time: from 2003 to 2006, it increased by over 50% – from 139,000 to 212,000 – while the number of recipients who stopped work completely (and received the benefit at full rate) remained stable – at 374,000.

In 2006, the right-wing government introduced still further measures for the sole benefit of large families, defined as having at least three children. Following the birth of a third or further child, one of the two parents can opt to claim the *complément optionnel de libre choix d'activité* (COLCA, or optional supplement for the freedom of choice to work or not), which is provided for a total of 12 months at an increased amount (€766 per month in 2008), as an alternative to the traditional 3-year CLCA. This measure was not linked to any demographic concerns as France has, over the past two decades, outperformed other European countries when it comes to fertility rates (for example, 2.0 in 2006 compared with 1.3 in Germany). The decision to give access to COLCA to large families only was mainly driven by financial considerations.

The reasons for introducing these changes, both the COLCA and the extension of the childrearing benefit to parents of a single child, are numerous. First, right-wing governments have traditionally taken a benevolent position towards family issues and were more than happy to reap the political rewards that such announcements were sure to make. These moves had the additional effect of partly satisfying the vocal demands of family associations for *allocations familiales* – cash payments roughly equivalent to the UK's Child Benefit – to be extended to parents with only a single child who until this point had been excluded from both this entitlement and the childrearing benefit (both APE and CLCA). Second, the measures were seen as a way to reduce the high demand for places in crèches, which according to repeated surveys are viewed by parents as the most desirable form of childcare (CREDOC, 2004). Finally, the COLCA was also viewed as a means to foster gender equality within large households.

At the same time as the parental leave system was being revised, the fiscal code was also being updated through the *crédit impôt famille* (CIF or family tax credit), which was established in 2004. Provided as a financial incentive to encourage companies to develop family-friendly initiatives for their employees, the CIF stipulates that 25% of related expenses are deductible from taxes paid by the company up to a ceiling of €500,000 per year and per company (Finance Law of 2004, Art 98). Within this regulatory framework, training programmes for employees on parental leave and supplements paid to employees on maternity or paternity leave or on leave to care for sick children are included. It should be noted, however, that recent research has shown that only 35% of companies in the private sector provide a supplement for maternity or paternity leave, that is, the difference between former earnings and the benefit payment (Lefèvre et al, 2007). In the public sector, employees receive their full salary as a statutory right.

Further changes to family policy are to be expected in the future. Modernisation and reform of public institutions was a recurrent theme in the campaign promises of the current President Nicolas Sarkozy and he wasted no time convening his Council for Modernisation on 12 December 2007 to lay out his roadmap for the future. As for family policy, aside from affirming the government's objective of reducing the level of child poverty by one third in the next 5 years, there is a new level of commitment to increasing female participation in the workplace in order to achieve the employment targets agreed at the European Council meeting held in Lisbon in 2000, in particular a 60% employment rate for women by 2010.

Numerous studies in France have shown that poverty is less common in households where both adults are in employment; poverty primarily affects families with one stay-at-home parent or a single parent (Eydoux and Letablier, 2007). The evolution of the labour market has also made it necessary to encourage more women to enter the workforce. For the less qualified, jobs in the personal services sector are currently undergoing rapid expansion as a result of substantial government encouragement and subsidies. For women with higher qualifications, there are numerous sectors such as IT, financial services and tourism that are crying out for qualified staff. With this in mind, current policies that provide an incentive for parents to withdraw from the active labour force will almost certainly need to be re-evaluated. In addition, the duration of parental leave must be considered against the background of widespread research showing that returning to employment is more difficult after extended absences (Afsa, 1997; Fagnani, 2000; Piketty, 2003).

Conclusion

Since the establishment of the parental leave scheme in the 1970s and the childrearing benefit in the 1980s, successive governments and the family associations represented by the UNAF have been playing a crucial role in the decision-making processes in this policy area. 'Freedom of choice' has been the UNAF's motto, although it has turned a blind eye to the fact that a low flat-rate benefit is a disincentive for fathers to use this benefit. Despite its parallel support for the development of formal childcare provision, the UNAF has always been putting governments under pressure to extend the childrearing benefit to families with one or two children. But concern to contain costs in the family branch of the social security system has made governments reluctant to make this extension.

It was only in 1994, against the background of an increase in unemployment, that the right-wing government decided that families with two children should be entitled to childrearing benefit, an entitlement that was extended in 2004 to families with only one child, albeit for a much shorter length of leave, just 6 months. These changes were, therefore, mainly driven by employment policy considerations: the governments wanted to encourage employed mothers to stop working until their child was 3 years old. As the level of this flat-rate benefit has remained very low, the take-up rate is currently at the highest level among low-paid and/or poorly qualified mothers; most better paid and better qualified mothers resume employment after maternity leave.

In clear contrast, feminist groups have always been opposed to any measure encouraging mothers to stop working for a long period of time. Taking into consideration the negative impact of long leaves on mothers' professional careers, they argued that the Swedish parental leave scheme was less detrimental and more genuinely gender-neutral. But for them, priority should be given to services and other benefits supporting mothers' employment. In fact, emphasis has recently been put on how to devise ways to encourage women to go back to work after maternity leave, which is in line with the workfare approach adopted by the current government headed by Prime Minister Fillon. The development of formal childcare provision (registered childminders and crèches) has, therefore, been high on the social policy agenda since the election of President Nicolas Sarkozy in 2007.

France is well known for having pursued demographic objectives in its social policy until the 1970s. However, it is important to underline that changes in the politics of leave have not been linked to any demographic concerns, given the country's relatively high fertility rates. Other issues – the rise in unemployment, social inequalities in access to formal childcare services, quality of care and lack of qualified staff – are considered more important both by the trades unions and the women's associations.

Analysis of parental leave policies provides a window into the ambivalent attitudes to gender underpinning the French welfare state and shows the growing hold that employment policies have had on family policy since the beginning of the 1980s (Fine-Davis and al, 2004). Contrary to Germany (see Chapter Eight), France has not been able to adopt the Nordic model and take a more egalitarian approach to parental leave policies. In this policy field, France is a laggard country and could learn from Germany and the significant strides forward it has made through the adoption of new regulations on parental leave.

It is noteworthy that in her report about family issues given to the government in 2007, Valérie Pécresse, the current Minister of Education, proposed a decrease in the duration of the CLCA to 2 years and to offset this by increasing the amount of the benefit. By doing so, she was attempting to move gradually in the direction of the new German scheme. The UNAF, unsurprisingly, strongly opposed this reform and the idea was put to one side.

As far as the low amount of the childrearing benefit is concerned, taking into account that maternity, paternity and parental leaves have traditionally been funded through social security (payroll) contributions, employers' representatives have always been reluctant to see any change that would lead to increased labour costs. On the other hand, trades unions have never considered issues related to parental leave as a priority and have instead put emphasis on public support to working mothers.

For both economic reasons and as a result of the struggles by the women's movement, family policy has progressively integrated the 'working mother model' and there exists a whole range of measures to support working parents. Still, France falls short of the policies adopted by Nordic countries on the issue of gender equality in the field of employment and the family. Despite a gender-neutral discourse and some efforts to encourage fathers to be more involved in family life, women continue to bear the main responsibilities for work in the home (Méda et al, 2003). Most of the measures target mothers implicitly or explicitly, and childcare, both within the family and in the public sphere, remains primarily a women's issue. Consequently, gender discrimination on the labour market persists and the stakes remain considerable in the challenge to the current gender order in French society. Does this mean that real equality between men and women still largely remains a pipe dream?

Note

[1] Leave provision described here refers to statutory entitlements.

References

Afsa, C. (1997) 'L'activité féminine à l'épreuve de l'APE', *Recherches et Prévisions*, no 46, pp 1-8.

Afsa, C. (1998) 'L'allocation parentale d'éducation: entre politique familiale et politique pour l'emploi', *Insee première*, no 569.

Bauer, D. and Penet, S. (2005) 'Le congé de paternité', Etudes et Résultats 442, Paris: DREES, Ministère du Travail, des Relations Sociales, de la Famille et de la Solidarité.

Bonnet, C. and Labbé, M. (1999) 'L'activité des femmes après la naissance du deuxième enfant: l'allocation parentale d'éducation a-t-elle un effet incitatif au retrait du marché du travail?', *Recherches et Prévisions*, no 59, pp 9-23.

Chauvière, M. (ed) (2006) *Les mouvements familiaux et leur institution en France – anthologie historique et sociale*, Paris: Comité d'Histoire de la Sécurité Sociale.

CREDOC (Centre de Recherche pour l'Étude et l'Observation des Conditions de vie) (2004) *Accueil des jeunes enfants, conciliation vie professionnelle – vie familiale et opinions sur les prestations familiales*, CNAF Collection des Rapports No 191, Paris: Caisse Nationale d'Allocations Familiales.

Eydoux, A. and Letablier, M.-T. (2007) *Les familles monoparentales en France*, Rapport de Recherche No 36, Paris: Centre d'études de l'emploi.

Fagnani, J. (1998) 'Helping mothers to combine paid and unpaid work – or fighting unemployment? The ambiguities of French family policy', *Community, Work and Family*, vol 1, no 3, pp 297-312.

Fagnani, J. (2000) *Un travail et des enfants. Petits arbitrages et grands dilemmes*, Paris: Bayard.

Fagnani, J. and Math, A. (2008) 'Transfer systems and child benefit packages: a cross-national comparison', in C. Saraceno and A. Leira (eds) *Childhood: Changing contexts*, Comparative social research vol 25, Bingley: Emerald/JAI Press, pp 55-78.

Fine-Davis, M., Fagnani, J., Giovannini, D., Hojgaard, L. and Clarke, H. (2004) *Fathers and mothers: Dilemmas of the work–life balance. A comparative study in four European countries*, Social Indicators Research Series Vol 21, Dordrecht: Kluwer Academic Publishers.

Gornick, J.C. and Meyers, M.K. (2003) *Families that work: Policies for reconciling parenthood and employment*, New York, NY: Russell Sage Foundation.

Hall, P. (1993) 'Policy paradigms, social learning and the state: the case of economic policymaking in Britain', *Comparative Politics*, vol 25, no 3, pp 275-96.

Jenson, J. and Sineau, M. (1995) *Mitterand et les françaises. Un rendez-vous manqué*, Paris: Presse de la Fondation Nationale des Sciences Politiques.

Lanquetin, M.-T. and Letablier, M.-T. (2003) 'Individualisation des droits sociaux et droits fondamentaux', *Recherches et Prévisions*, no 73, pp 7-24.

Le Bras, H. (1995) *Le sol et le sang*, Paris: Ed. de l'Aube.

Lefèvre, C., Pailhé, A. and Solaz, A. (2007) 'Comment les employeurs aident-ils leurs salariés à concilier travail et famille', *Populations et Sociétés*, no 440.

Marc, C. (2004) 'L'influence des conditions d'emploi sur le recours à l'APE', *Recherches et Prévisions*, no 75, pp 21-38.

Math, A. and Meilland, C. (2004a) 'Family-related leave and industrial relations', Study for the European Industrial Relations Observatory, available at www.eiro.eurofound. ie/2004/03/study/index_2.html (accessed 21 October 2008), summary in *EIRObserver*, no 6/04, November 2004, available at www.eiro.eurofound.ie/pdf/eo04-6.pdf (accessed 21 October 2008).

Math, A. and Meilland, C. (2004b) 'Un état des lieux des congés destinés aux parents dans vingt pays européens', *Revue de l'IRES*, no 46, pp 113-36.

Math, A. and Meilland, C. (2004c) 'Les congés aux parents: contre l'égalité entre femmes et hommes?', *Revue de l'IRES*, no 46, pp 137-65.

Math, A. and Renaudat, E. (1997) 'Développer l'accueil des enfants ou créer de l'emploi?', *Recherches et Prévisions*, no 49, pp 5-17.

Méda, D., Wierink, M. and Simon, M.O. (2003) 'Pourquoi certaines femmes s'arrêtent de travailler à la naissance d'un enfant?', Premières Syntheses No 29.2, Paris: DARES, Ministère du Travail, des Relations Sociales, de la Famille et de la Solidarité.

Périvier, H. (2004) 'Débat sur le congé parental: emploi des femmes et charges familiales. Repenser le congé parental en France à la lumière des expériences étrangères', *Revue de l'OFCE*, no 90, pp 259-342.

Piketty, T. (2003) 'L'impact de l'allocation parentale d'éducation sur l'activité féminine et la fécondité, 1982-2002', Working Paper CEPREMAP No 9, Paris: Centre pour la Recherche Economique et ses Applications.

Piketty, T. (2005) 'L'impact de l'allocation parentale d'éducation sur l'activité féminine et la fécondité en France, 1982–2002', in C. Lefèvre (ed) *Histoires de familles, histoires familiales*, Les Cahiers de l'INED No 156, pp 79-109.

EIGHT

Germany: taking a Nordic turn?

Daniel Erler

Maternity leave[1]*:* 14 weeks at 100% of earnings with no ceiling; 8 weeks obligatory.

Paternity leave: none.

Parental leave: until 3 years after childbirth; family entitlement. Twelve months paid at 67% of average earnings during the 12 months preceding childbirth; if the father takes at least 2 months of leave, the overall length of benefit payment is extended to 14 months. No means test applies, but there is a ceiling of €1,800 per month. Instead of 12 (+ 2) months, the childrearing benefit may be spread over 24 (+ 4) months, but the monthly benefit level is reduced so that the overall payment remains the same. Parents receiving a childrearing benefit may work up to 30 hours a week. However, if the company they work for has less than 15 employees, they need their employer's consent.

Leave to care for sick children: up to 10 days per illness, for parents of children under 12 years at 80% of earnings with no ceiling. The maximum annual leave period that may be taken per family is 25 days.

Other: up to 6 months of unpaid leave for relatives of care-dependent persons.

Germany is a member state of the European Union (EU). It is a federal state, formed from the unification of the former Federal Republic of Germany (West Germany) and the former German Democratic Republic (East Germany) in 1990; some states (*Länder*) pay additional benefit to parents taking leave. The former leave entitlement was widely used by mothers. The new entitlement, introduced in 2007, has led to a substantial increase in fathers taking leave, up from 3.3% in 2006 to 15.4% in the first half of 2008.

Introduction

As in many European countries, German parental leave legislation has been undergoing considerable changes in recent years, culminating in the introduction of a 12-month wage replacement benefit in 2007. When parental leave was introduced in West Germany in 1986, the primary aim of policy makers was to enable and actively encourage mothers to stay at home and care for their children during the first years of their life. The new income-related childrearing benefit

(*Elterngeld*), by contrast, has the explicit purpose of reducing the length of child–related periods out of the labour market and of facilitating a stronger paternal involvement in childrearing. It thus marks a decisive move away from Germany's traditional family policy path, which, like the welfare system as a whole, had been built on the assumption of a male breadwinner family model.

The long-standing political focus on home care and the importance of mother–child relations has been partially supplanted by concerns about Germany's low fertility rates and the related need to valorise the human capital of increasingly educated women. In fact, the family policy debate of recent years has been heavily dominated by the conundrum of how to encourage young couples to have children and how to reduce the opportunity costs of childbearing for mothers. Within a broader context of family policy change and a growing attention to the expansion of childcare services, the recent parental leave reform, therefore, seems to be a clear sign of a paradigmatic shift in German family policy.

The question this chapter aims to address in the following pages is why and how such a paradigmatic policy shift has come about. At first glance, it may be tempting to simply see the current changes as a rational political reaction to mounting socioeconomic pressures. But such a rational explanation faces difficulties in explaining the timing of the current adaptations. For while German fertility rates have been extremely low since the mid–1970s, policy makers only began to tackle the issue seriously two decades later. Nor does it explain the direction of policy change, because, as Majone has aptly stated, "objective conditions are seldom so compelling and so unambiguous that they set the policy agenda or dictate the appropriate conceptualization" of policy issues (1989, p 23). In fact, German policy makers continued to privilege the expansion of cash benefits over the expansion of childcare services even when it had become evident that more cash benefits alone had little positive impact on fertility decisions.

In other words, although objective demographic pressures certainly represent important driving forces behind the family policy changes of the past decade, they are insufficient by themselves to explain the timing and direction of these changes. Any comprehensive understanding of the current paradigmatic changes of Germany's family policy path thus requires a careful look at the role of political ideas and discourses because they serve as a 'cognitive frame' (Surel, 2000) within which decisions are made. Particularly in moments of fundamental change "ideas held by actors involved in the political struggle are vital, because they become the lens through which the agents interpret the changing socio-economic environment" (Lagergren, cited in Brodin, 2005, p 3) and are thus likely to strongly influence their policy responses. As we shall see in the course of this chapter, political beliefs and discourses do indeed constitute important pieces of the complex explanatory puzzle of Germany's successive parental leave reforms.

The roots of German leave legislation

The German welfare system is often cited as an archetypical example of a male breadwinner model, providing fairly generous insurance against the risks of unemployment, sickness and old age for the breadwinner and dependent family members, while at the same time assuming that housewives will take take responsibility for the home and care work within the family. In line with a strong emphasis on subsidiarity and traditional gender role models, West German family policies for many decades focused on the expansion of family benefits and parental leave rights, whereas public childcare provision remained a political taboo. The logic was to facilitate the home care capacities of families by enabling women to stay at home and take care of young children and household chores (Bleses and Seeleib-Kaiser, 2004).

Indeed, for most of West Germany's post-war history leave entitlements were restricted to working mothers, a legacy that derived from the Bismarkian foundations of its welfare system. Already in 1878, a mandatory but unpaid 3-week leave break after birth had been introduced for the protection of working mothers and their children. Lawmakers introduced a new maternity leave law (*Mutterschutzgesetz*) in 1952. The law foresaw 12 weeks (6 before and 6 after childbirth) of paid leave for working mothers, who were also protected from unlawful dismissal. On the one hand, this measure represented a major improvement for women and an explicit financial acknowledgement of their right to care. Yet, on the other hand, it reinforced the male breadwinner rationale ingrained in West Germany's post-war social security system.

In 1979, a maternity leave reform left the basic law intact but it introduced a 6-month period of optional maternity 'vacation' (*Mutterschaftsurlaub*), during which working mothers received a monthly payment of DM750 (around €375). The new entitlement was restricted to working mothers and was heavily criticised by Christian Democratic opposition parties as a deliberate attempt to persuade mothers to work and thus limit their freedom of choice (*Wahlfreiheit*) to stay at home as housewives. In reality, however, policy continued to largely follow a male breadwinner logic, as fathers remained excluded from leave entitlements and the expansion of childcare services remained absent from the political agenda.

The situation in East Germany, under communist rule, was entirely different. From the very beginning, after the Second World War, East German policies were geared towards the active promotion of female employment, even when women had small children. The right and duty of men and women to contribute to the common good through gainful employment was, in fact, anchored in the East German Constitution and consequently young mothers could interrupt their employment for a maximum of one year after childbirth (the so-called 'baby year'). As a result of these strongly work-centric gender policy norms, which were complemented by an elaborate network of public childcare services, East German women have always had among the highest labour market participation rates in Europe and most have internalised work as a central part of their identity (Stolt, 2000).

It is, therefore, not surprising that gender and family policies featured strongly in the negotiations on German unification, as East German women feared the imposition of a West German gender role model. To overcome such fears, the bilateral unification contract (*Einigungsvertrag*) explicitly stated that a unified Germany needed "to strengthen the legal position of working mothers and fathers with regards to work–family reconciliation" and to preserve East Germany's extensive childcare network. Unification has thus been decisive for the fundamental adaptations of German family policies since the 1990s.

From maternity leave to parental leave

In West Germany, the introduction of ample parental leave rights for both parents in 1986 represented "*the* family policy innovation of the 1980s" (Bleses and Rose, 1998, p 151), because for the first time policy makers acknowledged the social and economic value of homework in concrete rather than metaphorical terms. The main novelty of the new parental leave law (*Bundeserziehungsgeldgesetz*) was that, in addition to a mandatory 6-month maternity leave period, mothers and fathers were now legally entitled to a 10-month parental leave period, with a monthly flat-rate payment of DM 600 (€307). During this period, parents were allowed to work part time, up to 19 hours per week, a measure that was aimed at facilitating the labour market attachment and re-entry of parents after their leave period.

Moreover, the new parental leave payment was no longer restricted to working mothers but now included all parents, men as well as women and irrespective of their employment status. This broadening of eligibility criteria was a major change, since it extended parental leave payments to fathers and the large group of housewives who were previously excluded. At the same time, however, the initiative also stood for continuity, because West German family policy remained heavily biased towards a home care rationale; it improved mothers' opportunities to stay at home and care for their children but deliberately shied away from expanding childcare services as a means to facilitate female labour market attachment (Bothfeld, 2005).

Following the introduction of parental leave in 1986, the coalition government led by the Christian Democratic Union and Christian Social Union Parties (CDU–CSU) gradually fulfilled its electoral promise of extending leave periods. Between 1986 and 1992, leave periods were prolonged four times, from the original 10 months in 1986 to 36 months in 1992. In the same period, the payment of leave benefits was extended from 10 months to 24 months.

The Christian Democrats portrayed these increases as 'enormous efforts' constituting a crucial step towards "the aim of a more child- and family-friendly living environment"[2]. The 1992 extension of the parental leave to 36 months and the concomitant increase of the leave allowance to 24 months were also explicitly presented as important steps towards the protection of unborn life and thus featured heavily in the post-unification debate on a new abortion law, which had to accommodate the fairly liberal abortion legislation of the former German Democratic Republic (GDR) with the more restrictive approach in the Federal Republic of Germany. Moreover, the Christian Democratic 'freedom of choice' (*Wahlfreiheit*) argument was increasingly complemented by a tenet that parental care within the family was essential for the well-being of young children. This view was clearly stated by CDU parliamentarian Walter Link:

> All teachers and psychologists concur that the foundations for people's life courses are laid during their first three years of life. Therefore it has been our goal from the very beginning, to extend parental leave time and benefits to three years. Today, parental leave and benefits enable the mother or the father to intensively educate and care for the new born child during the first years of life …[3]

The belief that children below the age of 3 years should be cared for within the family was not only dominant within the CDU-CSU. Germany's powerful confessional welfare associations – Caritas (Catholic) and Diakonie (Protestant) – as well as many confessional family associations largely shared this position and thus reinforced the conservative family policy stance of the Christian Democratic Party. And, indicating considerable political consensus, even the Social Democratic Party (SPD), the other side of the political spectrum, acknowledged the overall utility of parental leave as a family policy measure, and largely agreed with the CDU-CSU argument that a 3-year leave period "is one of the most important preconditions for a good and happy parent–child relationship"[4].

However, pointing to the lack of childcare facilities as a main obstacle for a better and more gender-equal combination of work and family responsibilities, the SPD accused the CDU-CSU of deliberately hindering women's employment opportunities:

> In the backdrop of a conservative family model it [the new parental leave proposal of 1991] continues to favour the non-employment of women and the family as the only locus of child education during infancy. The existing structural deficits of the current parental leave and benefit regulations are not tackled. If any consequences have at all been drawn from the government evaluation report, which we discussed here in the spring, then they are highly insufficient. Particularly regarding the fact that currently 53% of women do not return to their job after a parental leave period, and often drop out of the labour market entirely or at least for a prolonged period of time. I do not want to maliciously claim that parental leave in its current form is used as a deliberate means to edge women out of the labour market. But it needs to be emphasized that the current draft lacks

specific measures which could facilitate women's combination of work and family life or their labour market re-entry ...[5]

The high take-up of parental leave after 1986 had indicated a broad popular acceptance of this relatively innovative family policy measure. But a first evaluation report in 1990[6] also revealed significant problems, namely the very low number of fathers who made use of their newly acquired care opportunities and the large number of women not re-entering the labour market, a fact which lead to an actual decline of active employment rates among mothers after 1986. The SPD-led opposition, therefore, demanded the expansion of childcare facilities for children above the age of 3 years and a regular increase in parental leave payments in response to earnings growth. Some SPD parliamentarians also proposed to tie parental leave benefits to people's prior income, so making it an income replacement measure. This was to enable and encourage men, who usually earn most of the household income, to use parental leave.

Interestingly, however, the SPD had so strongly internalised the CDU's 'freedom of choice' tenet that more punitive alternatives – for example, a Swedish-style 'take it or leave it option', whereby one month of parental leave could only be taken by the father or would otherwise be lost – were categorically rejected in public, as "an excessive restriction of parents' prerogative to freely decide"[7] the intra-household division of care. The CDU-CSU coalition government, on the other hand, acknowledged that only a few fathers utilised their leave entitlements and the Family Minister Hannelore Rönsch stated that improving the conditions for parental leave and benefit utilisation was a core government concern, "because we want to especially create incentives for fathers, to partake in the care of their children"[8]. But apart from the extension of parental leave entitlements to unmarried fathers – which was a by-product of unification, as more than 40% of births in the former GDR occurred out of wedlock – and the possibility to alternate leave periods between mothers and fathers, additional incentives for fathers were not included in the 1992 parental leave reform.

More flexibility for working parents

After a period of major activism between 1986 and 1992, the issue of parental leave largely disappeared from the political agenda, despite a declared bipartisan intention to introduce further measures aimed at increasing the utilisation of parental leave among fathers and at smoothing female labour market re-entry. To some degree, this may be explained by a growing political focus (in West Germany) on the expansion of childcare services in the aftermath of unification and a related rise in child allowances, necessitated by consecutive Constitutional Court judgments (Gerlach, 2000). But there also appeared to be a lack of political will to tackle the complex issue of intra-household role models through active political intervention. Thus it was only in the year 2000, 2 years after coming into power, that a SPD–Green coalition government introduced its own parental leave reform proposals, which followed and in many ways exceeded the requirements of the EU's parental leave directive (see Chapter Fifteen).

The 2001 parental leave reform represented an elaboration of existing legislation rather than a fundamental shift. On one side, the utilisation of leave was rendered more flexible, as parents were now allowed – in agreement with their employer – to spread the last 12 months of their combined leave entitlements over a period of 8 years after the birth of their child. Moreover, it was possible for parents to take leave simultaneously, whereas previously they had had to alternate. On the other side, the part-time dimension of parental leave was decisively strengthened by the introduction of a legal entitlement to part-time work and an increase in the maximum number of weekly part-time hours per parent from 19 to 30. Even though the right to part-time employment was restricted to companies with more than 15 employees and depended on their economic situation, the introduction of this entitlement proved to be a contentious issue.

The red–green government defined the extension of the maximum weekly part-time hours in combination with a legal right to part-time work as a crucial "structural change", serving as "an important catalyst"[9] for the growing acceptance (particularly among men and employers) of part-time employment as a viable means for the better combination of work and private life. The measures were also widely supported among family associations and unions, while opposition parties as well as the key national employer organisations were far more sceptical (Erler, 2005). Even though the CDU-CSU was not principally opposed to the legal right to part-time employment, it wanted to restrict such claims to people with care responsibilities for children or elderly relatives. In the words of Markus Grübl from the CDU:

> The fundamental difference between SPD and CDU on part time is the following: we perceive a part-time employment option as a concrete obligation of employers, but only in the presence of children or care-dependent relatives. We oppose an unconditional right to part time because we also understand the needs of companies.[10]

Ina Lenke from the Free Democratic Party went even further by arguing that the new legislation was a 'boomerang law'. In her eyes, the "legal right to part-time employment further undermines women's possibility to compete with men"[11], because companies may be less likely to employ women if they run the risk of them opting for part-time work. Similar arguments were also put forward by employer organisations, which were concerned about additional bureaucracy, less flexibility and less planning security.

Despite such political skirmishes, all major political parties acknowledged the need for more flexible leave entitlements that were better able to satisfy the diversifying needs of families. Much more contentious was the introduction of a so-called 'budget option' (*Budgetregelung*): this allowed parents to reduce their paid leave period to one year at a higher monthly benefit rate of €450, instead of the standard 2-year leave period at €300 per month. Both the SPD and Greens had long declared their intention to reduce the opportunity costs to parents of taking leave by facilitating their earlier return to the labour market. But once in government both parties were afraid of offering their political opponents fertile ground for making accusations about limiting parental freedom of choice. Hence the 'budget option' was an attempt to square the circle: it offered parents the possibility to take shorter leave at a higher compensation rate but did not touch the parental right to 2 years of paid leave and an additional year of unpaid leave.

Notwithstanding the cautiousness of its attempt to tackle the tricky issue of Germany's long period of parental leave (WSI, 2005, p 322) and its well-documented opportunity costs (Bollé, 2001; Del Boca and Pasqua, 2005; Schönberg and Ludsteck, 2007), the red–green government was immediately accused of undue meddling in intra-household affairs. In fact, conservative champions of the traditional male breadwinner family were critical of the 'budget option', because they perceived it as a veiled attempt to reduce the time parents stayed at home with their children. Renate Diemers (CDU), for example, argued that:

> The 12-month budget option of parental leave will render child care by other persons than the parents a norm. Which is not a mere side effect but is explicitly desired by you [the government]. It simply does not fit into your world view, that mothers or fathers can dedicate themselves entirely to the family.[12]

The problem for opponents of the new budget option was that it could be freely chosen by parents, which made it difficult to maintain that the measure was an undue restriction of parents' freedom of choice. In fact, the most important conservative family organisations – the Family Association of German Catholics (Familienbund Deutscher Katholiken) and the Protestant Association for Families (Evangelische Aktionsgemeinschaft für Familien) – focused their criticism on the fact that the budget option involved financial losses for families, as €5,400 over 12 months (12 × €450) was substantially less than the €7,200 over a 2-year time span (24 × €300).

Far more critical than such largely partisan-inspired complaints, however, was the widespread societal criticism of the red–green government's unwillingness to increase the payment rates and income ceilings of parental leave. As a matter of fact, in 2004 the government actually reduced the income ceiling for the first 6 months of paid leave (that is, the level of net family income above which no benefit payment was made) from €51,130 to €30,000. This cost-saving measure led to a significant drop in the number of families receiving the full benefit level and thus undermined the scheme's universality (Dingeldey, 2004). Of course, an SPD-led government was particularly susceptible to criticisms about social injustice, because during their years of opposition, the Social Democrats had repeatedly demanded higher benefits and more generous income ceilings. The red–green coalition tried to defend its choice of not raising benefit levels and reducing income ceilings by shifting the blame on the fiscal irresponsibility of its predecessor government and the need to consolidate public finances. Yet for a coalition that had partly won the elections by invoking a need for more social justice and family policy reform, these criticisms were difficult to deflect.

The new *Elterngeld*: a tale of compromise and policy learning

After the passage of the 2001 parental leave reform, the red–green government's political attention largely turned towards the expansion of childcare services and all-day schools in West Germany, an issue that had always been dearer to the SPD than to the CDU. But, during the run-up to the national election campaign of 2005, the red–green government took up the proposals of a white paper on sustainable family policies, which argued for the introduction of a one-year wage replacement benefit similar to "successful" schemes in Scandinavian countries (Rürup and Gruescu, 2003, p 54). As in earlier circumstances, the CDU and particularly its more conservative regional sister party the Christian Social Union derided the initiative as too strong an infringement of family autonomy that compromised families' freedom to care for their infants at home. Instead, the CDU-CSU proposed the introduction of a so-called '*Familiengeld*'[13], which was to offer parents a €600 monthly benefit for each child under 3 years and €300 per month for children between 4 and 17 years.

Throughout the 2005 election campaign, the differences between Social and Christian Democratic parental leave objectives appeared to be irreconcilable, not so unusual an occurrence in political election campaigns. In reality, however, policy makers across the political spectrum agreed on the need to tackle Germany's demographic problems through a reorientation of the country's family policy settings. In the light of Germany's stubbornly low fertility rates – total fertility rates have been hovering around the 1.4 mark since the early 1980s – policy makers were increasingly worried about the potential socioeconomic consequences of population ageing. Concerns about the future sustainability of Germany's health and pension systems as well as the spectre of severe labour shortages of highly qualified workers helped both to raise the strategic importance attributed to family policies and erode the traditional ideological divide in this policy field.

Within this context of political convergence, the traditionalist circles in the CDU-CSU were increasingly marginalised and no longer able to block a move away from Germany's home care logic. Women, who today outperform men in terms of educational attainment, were increasingly seen as a crucial human capital source, too valuable to lose from the labour market. The fact that almost one third of the female population between the age of 35 and 39 remains childless, a proportion that reaches 38% among women with an academic degree (BIB, 2004), was of particular concern, because it revealed that 'high potential' women in particular faced difficulties combining family and professional aspirations. Hence, when the SPD and the CDU-CSU formed a 'grand coalition' government in 2005, the earlier Christian Democrat's *Familiengeld* proposal was quickly dropped in favour of an '*Elterngeld*' proposal, which had the explicit intention of reducing the length of child-related absence from the labour market, because "from a societal perspective any withdrawal from gainful employment constitutes a loss of professional capabilities for the labour market"[14].

In line with this statement of intent, the new parental leave legislation, which replaced the previous *Erziehungsgeld* regulations in 2007, included a number of important innovations that clearly moved the incentive structure away from a male breadwinner logic. Yet inevitably it also contained a number of compromise solutions, which had been necessary to overcome the lingering resistance of socially conservative factions.

To start with, the newly dubbed *Elterngeld* no longer constitutes a flat-rate benefit, as it now provides parents with 67% of their previous earnings, rendering it more similar to an income maintenance scheme. While virtually all political and social actors supported the introduction of such a scheme, political representatives from the left criticised it as effectively constituting "a redistribution from the poor to the rich"[15] as the law proposal "basically subsidizes those who need it least [that is, higher income earners] with the most"[16]. To dispel such criticisms, the government introduced a minimum benefit level of €300, irrespective of prior employment status, a maximum benefit ceiling of €1,800, and a supplementary low-income component (*Geringverdiener Komponente*).

A second innovation concerns the length of leave payments, which are now paid for a period of 12 rather than 24 months. When the idea of shorter leave periods at higher compensation rates was first publicly raised by a red–green government in 2003, social conservatives immediately condemned it as an infringement of families' freedom to choose the right care solution for their children. To avoid such allegations, the grand coalition's Minister for Family, Senior Citizens, Youth and Women, Ursula von der Leyen, decided, from the very beginning, to complement the standard one-year paid leave period with an option to spread the payment over 24 months at a replacement rate of 33.5%.

This was an evident concession to strong socially conservative currents within the CDU-CSU. But overall, the compromise represented a major success for the minister, whose declared aim was "to encourage parents to an early return to the labour market", because "with every year out of employment parents permanently lose around 5 per cent of their income compared to childless employees and they are prevented from acquiring new know-how and professional capabilities"[17]. By reducing the standard length of paid leave without closing off to parents the possibility to opt for longer leave periods, the minister managed to significantly increase the incentives for a faster return to employment without offering the champions of the traditional home care model much scope for attack. In the end, the measure received broad support from social and economic actors across the political band.

Interestingly, representatives of German industry were among the most enthusiastic supporters of shorter leave periods, because they hoped for a reduction in the drain on human capital associated with long leave periods. Moreover, some believed that the prospect of shorter leave periods would "increase the pressure on all actors to tackle the issue of childcare", offering the national government – which has little influence on social services, due to Germany's federal structure – "a lever to activate regional and local administrations"[18] on the issue of care. Others, such as the Free Democratic Party, warned that without a prior expansion of childcare services the reduction of leave periods would inevitably cause tensions as it increased the demand for childcare for young children without augmenting supply, thereby harming the ability of parents to reconcile their work and family life[19]. To a large extent, the government seems to share these concerns and has therefore accelerated the expansion of childcare services for children under 3 years that the red–green predecessor government had commenced.

The third *Elterngeld* innovation is the introduction of 2 'daddy months', which are exclusively for fathers. Originally, the government had planned to reserve two of the 12 months of paid leave for fathers, meaning that, similar to Sweden, fathers had to 'use or lose' at least 2 months of leave. But, once again, the government faced stiff opposition from conservative circles, which decried the state interference in private family matters. And, once again, the government came up with a compromise, by inventing a daddy bonus that simply adds – instead of deducting – 2 months of leave to the standard leave period (12 + 2).

While this solution entails considerably higher costs than a more punitive 'use it or lose it' option, it was of strategic importance because it enabled the government to overcome resistance – particularly within the CSU – against a measure that was seen as crucial for any successful attempt to raise the paternal take-up of leave. And, the latest parental leave statistics seem to confirm the utility of the new feature, as the number of fathers taking leave has more than quadrupled, from 3.3% in 2006 to 15.4% in the first half of 2008 (Statistisches Bundesamt, 2008). The political efforts of the last decade to facilitate a more active involvement of fathers in childrearing thus appear to be finally bearing some fruit, and these developments may be further reinforced by changes in the overall family policy framework.

The wider policy context: signs of changing paradigms

The 2007 parental leave reform represents a milestone for the German family policy context: for the first time a family policy measure unambiguously aims at reducing female career interruptions and increasing men's involvement in the childrearing domain. These parental leave changes are a clear sign of changing rationales shaping family policy, but by themselves these changes are insufficient proof of a general paradigm shift. It is the fact that a number of other policy reforms point in a similar direction that underpins this chapter's contention that we are currently witnessing a decisive departure from West Germany's historical male breadwinner model.

Throughout the 1990s, Germany's intensifying family policy efforts primarily focused on the expansion of family tax benefits and transfer payments, in line with the traditional (West) German preference for family subsidiarity. Required to act by a number of Constitutional Court rulings, which had judged the level of public transfers insufficient to guarantee the minimum living standard of families with children, policy makers raised financial support levels for families while largely sidestepping the crucial issue of childcare (Erler, 2005). However, some early signs of change had already surfaced during the early 1990s.

In the aftermath of German unification, the CDU-CSU-FDP coalition government of the time reluctantly instituted a legal right to part-time childcare for the 3- to 6-year age group. This step was largely necessitated by the enormous differences in the supply of childcare services between East and West Germany and the insistence of East German women on maintaining their long-established network of public childcare services. For West Germany, the introduction of a legal right to childcare – albeit limited to children over 3 years and to part-time attendance – represented an important step away from its cash-based family policy legacy. Care responsibilities were no longer left exclusively to the family, but began to be gradually accepted as an issue of social solidarity and equality.

When, in 1998, a red-green coalition government came into power after 16 years of Christian Democratic dominance, it began to move family policies further away from a focus on the male breadwinner model towards a more gender-neutral focus on work–family reconciliation. Reforming parental leave legislation in 2001 was a first step by government in this direction. More important, however, was the institution of a national all-day school fund in 2003 (4 billion euros spread over 4 years) and the passage of a national law on the expansion of childcare services (*Tagesbetreuungsausbaugesetz*), which, since 2005, has provided an annual 1.5 billion euros to local authorities for the expansion of nurseries in West Germany, the availability of which lags far behind East Germany – in 2007 just 8.1% of West German children under 3 years of age had a place in a nursery, against 37.4% in East Germany (Statistisches Bundesamt, 2007).

In spite of the precarious state of Germany's public finances and the very limited competence of the federal government in the area of social services, a carefully guarded domain of the *Länder*, national governments have been the main driving force behind the recent efforts to expand childcare services. Indeed, the current grand coalition government has continued and intensified the push for this expansion. Between 2007 and 2013, the national (federal) government will provide local authorities with an additional 4 billion euros as a contribution to the operating and investment costs for newly created childcare services. The declared aim of the new Child Support Law (*Kinderförderungsgesetz*[20]) is to ensure by the year 2013 a childcare place for 35% of all children under 3 years and a legal right to services for this age group, bringing Germany into line with the EU's Barcelona childcare targets.

When the current Family Minister Ursula von der Leyen initially launched these ambitious goals she met with substantial resistance from the regional and local authorities – which feared that they would have to bear the brunt of the costs – as well as heavy obstructionism from socially conservative factions within the CDU-CSU, decrying the discrimination of home care solutions. In order to overcome these objections, the national government committed itself to an unusual national–*Länder* co-financing model, while it also agreed to introduce, by 2013, a monthly care allowance for parents who opt to care for their young children at home. Through such compromises, the government has thus prepared the ground for a significant expansion of childcare services, an achievement that, in combination with the new *Elterngeld*, will fundamentally alter the German family policy landscape.

Conclusion

The developments of German parental leave legislation are, in many ways, a useful proxy for changes of the country's family policy setting in general. In fact, when parental leave was introduced in West Germany, in 1986, the new entitlement embodied a major advancement, because it offered concrete financial support and legal rights to parents. At the same time, however, the law continued to follow a home care logic and was designed in a way that encouraged long absences by mothers from the labour market. Things began to change during 1990s, when policy makers gradually began to realise that their family policy objectives where increasingly out of sync with Germany's socioeconomic realities. The parental leave overhaul described in this chapter is just one clear sign that the objectives and instruments of German family policies are undergoing fundamental changes and no longer have the perpetuation of the male breadwinner model at their core. But what have been the main driving forces behind such fundamental transformations?

German unification represents without doubt the starting point for any explanation of the current policy changes because it forced a divided political class to confront and reconcile two diametrically opposed family and gender policy approaches. The systemic shock of unification set in motion a cumulative policy learning process that led to a gradual rapprochement of different political positions between the CDU-CSU, which, like centre-right governments across Europe, have always tended to prefer cash-for-care benefits (van Kersbergen, 1995; Morgan and Zippel, 2003), and the SPD, which had insisted on the need for the expansion of public childcare services, in line with the traditional Social Democratic preference for public services in kind (Huber and Stephens, 2001).

During the course of the bilateral unification negations, West Germany's Christian Democratic coalition government had only grudgingly accepted the maintenance of the highly developed childcare system that underpinned East Germany's work-centred gender policy approach. But, confronted with the different experiences and expectations of East German women, policy makers within all political parties gradually began to discuss the potential merits of a system that offered women better opportunities to combine work and family life.

The tentative family policy reorientation catalysed by unification was reinforced by a growing concern among all political parties about Germany's chronically low fertility rates and the related issue of population ageing. Faced with the reality that neither the provision of ever longer parental leave nor the repeated increase of family allowances had had any tangible effect in terms of higher birth rates, policy makers began to look to their European neighbours for possible policy solutions. While the EU's direct impact on German work–family policy initiatives has been 'rather slight' (Falkner et al, 2002), the process of peer learning has been crucial for recent policy reforms. The introduction of a wage-related leave benefit as well as dedicated daddy months, for example, has been clearly inspired by the Swedish parental leave system, while the current push for childcare expansion has taken many cues from the French system, which has successfully combined institutional childcare solutions with a more flexible system of registered childminders.

The EU-induced intensification of mutual policy learning has thus been important because it has provided German policy makers with new ideas about possible policy solutions. Yet, it is the change of government in 1998 that represents the second crucial tipping point for the current reorientation of German family policy. For at a time when policy makers across the political spectrum were already questioning the effectiveness of Germany's family policy legacy and converging on the possible policy solutions, a red–green coalition government was offered a window of opportunity for change.

By successfully linking the issues of paternal involvement in childrearing and childcare expansion with the CDU's long-standing freedom-of-choice tenet, the new government managed to muster support for a cautious readjustment of Germany's cash-based family support system, preparing the ground for the relatively incisive changes currently under way. It may be a historic irony, but in many ways West German policy makers are currently busy catching up with the gender policy legacy of their East German brethren.

Notes

[1] Leave provision described here refers to statutory entitlements.

[2] Hannelore Rönsch (Minister for the Family and the Elderly), Bundestag, Stenographisches Protokoll 12/19: 1235, 22.03.1991.

[3] Bundestag, Stenographisches Protokoll 12/50: 4104, 17.10.1991.

[4] Ulrich Böhme (SPD), Bundestag, Stenographisches Protokoll 12/50: 4101, 17.10.1991.

[5] Erika Simm (SPD), second reading of a parental leave proposal, Bundestag, Stenographisches Protokoll 12/54: 4503, 07.11.1991.

[6] Bundestagsdrucksache 11/8517.

[7] Rose Götte (SPD), first reading of a parental leave proposal, Bundestag, Stenographisches Protokoll 12/19: 1247–1248, 22.03.1991.

[8] Hannelore Rönsch (CDU), Bundestag, Stenographisches Protokoll 12/50: 4100, 17.10.1991.

[9] Interview with Kerstin Griese (SPD), cited in Erler (2005), Berlin, 09.09.2004.

[10] Interview with Markus Grübl (CDU), cited in Erler (2005), Berlin, 30.06.2004.

[11] Interview with Ina Lenke (FDP), cited in Erler (2005), Berlin 01.07.2004.

[12] Renate Diemers (CDU), second reading of a parental leave proposal, Bundestag, Stenographisches Protokoll 14/115: 10957, 07.07.2000.

[13] See CDU–CSU Party Position Paper *Nachhaltige Politik für Familien ist ein Markenzeichen der Union*, Berlin: CDU/CSU Bundestagsfraktion, February 2001.

[14] Bundestagsdrucksache 16/1889, p 14.

[15] Bundestagsdrucksache 16/1877, p 1.

[16] Prof. Butterwege (University of Cologne), first reading of the *Elterngeld* proposal, Bundestag, Stenographisches Protokoll 16/16, p 21, 03.07.2006.

[17] Bundestagsdrucksache 16/1889, pp 14–16.

[18] Dr. Achim Dercks (German Chamber of Industry and Commerce), first reading of the *Elterngeld* proposal, Bundestag, Stenographisches Protokoll 16/16, p 19, 03.07.2006.

[19] Miriam Gruß (FDP), first reading of the *Elterngeld* proposal, Bundestag, Stenographisches Protokoll 16/40: 3730, 22.06.2006

[20] Bundestagsdrucksache 16/9299: law proposal.

References

BIB (Bundesinstitut für Bevölkerungsforschung) (2004) *Bevölkerung. Fakten – Trends – Ursachen – Erwartungen – Die wichtigsten Fragen*, Wiesbaden: Statistisches Bundesamt.

Bleses, P. and Rose, E. (1998) *Deutungswandel der Sozialpolitik. Die Arbeitsmarkt- und Familienpolitik im parlamentarischen Diskurs*, Frankfurt: Campus Verlag.

Bleses, P. and Seeleib-Kaiser, M. (2004) *The dual transformation of the German welfare state*, Houndmills: Palgrave Macmillan.

Bollé, P. (2001) 'Parental leave', in Martha F. Loutfi (ed) *Women, gender and work. What is equality and how do we get there?*, Geneva: International Labour Organization.

Bothfeld, S. (2005) *Vom Erziehungsurlaub zur Elternzeit. Politisches Lernen im Reformprozess*, Frankfurt: Campus Verlag.

Brodin, H. (2005) 'Does anybody care? Public and private responsibilities in Swedish eldercare 1940-2000', Doctoral thesis, Umeå University.

Del Boca, D. and Pasqua, S. (2005) 'Labour supply and fertility in Europe and the U.S.', in T. Boeri, D. Del Boca and C. Pissarides (eds) *Women at work: An economic perspective*, Oxford: Oxford University Press, pp 125-53.

Dingeldey, I. (2004) 'Holistic governance: Zur Notwendigkeit reflexiver Gestaltung von Familien- und Arbeitsmarkpolitik. UK, Frankreich & Deutschland', Unpublished position paper for the German Family Report.

Erler, D. (2005) 'Public work–family reconciliation policies in Germany and Italy', Doctoral thesis, Università di Siena.

Falkner, G. et al (2002) *Transforming social policy in Europe? The EC's parental leave directive and misfit in the 15 member states*, MPIfG Working Paper 02/11, Cologne: Max Planck Institute for the Study of Societies.

Gerlach, I. (2000) 'Politikgestaltung durch das Bundesverfassungsgericht am Beispiel der Familienpolitik', *Politik und Zeitgeschichte*, B 3-4/2000, pp 21-31.

Huber, E. and Stephens, J.D. (2001) 'Welfare state in the era of retrenchment', in P. Pierson (ed) *The new politics of the welfare state*, Oxford: Oxford University Press, pp 107-45.

Majone, G. (1989) *Evidence, argument and persuasion in the policy process*, New Haven, CT: Yale University Press.

Morgan, K.J and Zippel, K. (2003) 'Paid to care: the origins and effects of care leave policies in Western Europe', *Social Politics*, vol 10, no 2, pp 49-85.

Rürup, B. and Gruescu, S. (2003) *Nachhaltige Familienpolitik im Interesse einer aktiven Bevölkerungsentwicklung*, Report for the Bundesministeriums für Familie, Senioren, Frauen und Jugend, Berlin: Bundesministeriums für Familie, Senioren, Frauen und Jugend.

Schönberg, U. and Ludsteck, J. (2007) *Maternity leave legislation, female labor supply, and the family wage gap*, IZA Discussion Paper No 2699, Bonn: IZA.

Statistisches Bundesamt (2007) *Kindertagesbetreuung regional 2007. Ein Vergleich aller 439 Kreise in Deutschland*, Wiesbaden.

Statistisches Bundesamt (2008) *Öffentliche Sozialleistungen – Statistik zum Elterngeld. Anträge von Januar 2007 bis Juni 2008*, Wiesbaden.

Stolt, S. (2000) 'Grenzen der Emanzipation durch Arbeit. Anerkennungskämpfe ostdeutscher Frauen in Paarbeziehungen vor und nach der Wende', *Feministische Studien extra*, vol 18, pp 81–92.

Surel, Y. (2000) 'The role of cognitive and normative frames in policy-making', *Journal of European Public Policy*, vol 7, no 4, pp 495-512.

van Kersbergen, K. (1995) *Social capitalism: A study of Christian Democracy and the welfare state*, London: Routledge.

WSI (Wirtschafts- und Sozialwissenschaftliches Institut) (2005) *FrauenDatenReport 2005. Handbuch zur wirtschaftlichen und sozialen Situation von Frauen*, Hans Böckler Stiftung, Berlin: Edition Sigma.

NINE

Hungary and Slovenia:
long leave or short?

Marta Korintus[1] and Nada Stropnik

Hungary

Maternity leave[2]: 24 weeks at 70% of earnings, with no ceiling.

Paternity leave: 5 days at 100% with no ceiling.

Parental leave: until child is 3 years; a family entitlement. Paid at 70% of earnings until child is 2 years up to a ceiling of HUF96,600 (€320) per month, then a flat-rate payment of HUF28,500 (€95)[3] per month. For uninsured parents, paid at flat rate for the whole period.

Leave to care for children: varies according to age of child from unlimited (for children under one year) to 14 days per family per year (6–12 years) at 70% of earnings.

Other: if there are 3 or more children, either parent may take leave between the third and eighth birthday of the youngest child, with a flat-rate payment of HUF28,500 (€95) per month. Paid breastfeeding breaks for mothers until child is 9 months.

Slovenia

Maternity leave: 105 calendar days (15 weeks) at 100% with no ceiling.

Paternity leave: 90 calendar days (13 weeks) at 100% of earnings for 15 days up to a ceiling of 2½ times national average earnings (approximately €3,430 per month); social security contributions paid for remaining period.

Parental leave: 260 calendar days (37 weeks) per family at 100% of earnings up to a ceiling of 2½ times national average earnings (approximately €3,431 per month). Extended by 30 days if there are already two children in the family under 8 years, by 60 days if three children, and by 90 days if four or more children of this age.

Leave to care for dependants: 7 working days per person per episode of illness (or 15 working days for a child under 7 years or with a disability) at 80% of earnings.

Other: paid breastfeeding breaks for mothers.

Hungary and **Slovenia** are member states of the European Union (EU). Slovenia gained independence in 1991 after being part of Yugoslavia. **Hungary** has a low level of employment among women with children under 3 years and a low level of part-time employment among women workers. It was a pioneer in the introduction of parental leave. There is no information on take-up, although it is estimated that most children under 3 years have a parent taking leave and that very few of these parents are fathers. There is a low level of formal childcare provision for children under 3 years.

Slovenia has a high level of maternal employment and a low level of part-time employment among women workers. About three quarters of fathers took the fully paid 15 days of paternity leave in 2008, but the great majority took no more. All mothers take some parental leave; in 2008, only 6% of fathers took any part of this leave.

Introduction

Communist parties ruled in Hungary and Slovenia after the Second World War. Their ideology put women alongside men in the labour force, and mothers of young children were not exempt. Economic necessity and the desire for a decent standard of living also kept mothers in employment. Consequently, parental leave was regulated earlier and better than in many capitalist countries. This was also due to a shortage of childcare services, while, at the same time, migration to urban areas and small apartments contributed to less care by extended families.

During the socialist years before 1989, there were rather high levels of female employment in Hungary, and it was often said that women's employment had reached the maximum level possible not only socially but also demographically. *Bölcsőde* (nurseries) were initially developed extensively, but since 1984, nursery places have dropped by about 60%. Today, female labour force participation rates are low compared with the EU average (Frey, 2008), although it should be noted that, unlike some other countries, women on parental leave in Hungary are categorised as economically inactive, which can affect cross-national comparisons. The majority of children under 3 years are cared for by mothers taking leave or by relatives (mainly grandmothers), and only 8–10% attend nurseries.

Developments have been rather different in Slovenia. For decades, women have accounted for over 45% of the workforce; virtually every adult woman in Slovenia has been employed. As many as 85% of women with children below 12 years of age are employed for more than 30 hours a week (SORS, 2006). In 1990, about 30% of children below 3 years of age were in subsidised childcare facilities (Stropnik, 1997, p 101), and this had risen to 44% by 2007/08 (SORS, 2008) when the supply of childcare places almost completely met the demand.

This chapter offers, first, a historical overview of the development of parental leave policies in these neighbouring countries, both formerly socialist but today with very different leave systems. An attempt is made to explain why their systems have become so different – in spite of an apparently similar approach to women's labour market participation during the socialist years – by looking at how they have been shaped by political processes and relevant actors, with particular attention to the debates that preceded reforms. In the second section, we look at Hungary and in the third Slovenia. In the fourth section, we draw comparisons, focusing on the very differing lengths of leave in the two countries, a subject of considerable significance to women's position in the labour market and their general economic status. This raises the arguments for and against a long period of leave and comparison of the two countries' experiences with their differing policy regimes.

Leave policies in Hungary

Until 1966: maternity leave only

Maternity leave originated in 1884 with an Act that allowed women 4 weeks of leave after the birth of a child. Further legislation in 1927 provided a benefit for 6 weeks before and 6 weeks after birth, at 100% of earnings. This system was substantially changed in 1953, under the communist regime; but whereas earlier regulations addressed health-related concerns, the 1953 reforms were a response to concerns about a declining birth rate and were intended to create favourable conditions for having children. The period of paid postnatal leave was extended to 12 weeks, and employed mothers were allowed breastfeeding breaks until their child was 9 months old. Employers could not refuse to employ pregnant women, and could only dismiss mothers with babies younger than 3 months old for some serious offence. The intention to increase the number of available childcare places was also stated.

Apart from some small measures on eligibility and employment protection, the situation did not basically change again until 1967.

From 1967 to 1989: maternity and parental leave

The first form of extended maternity leave – *gyermekgondozasi segely* (GYES) – was introduced in 1967, followed by the second one – *Gyermekgondozasi dij* (GYED) – in 1985. GYES was designed to address two problems: the need to balance work and childrearing, and the possibility of emerging unemployment related to economic reforms. Maternity leave was extended until a child was 2½, with a flat-rate payment for the whole period, then in 1969 to the child's third birthday. In 1982, fathers were allowed to take up the leave instead of the mother after the child became one year old and part-time work was also allowed when the child was one-and-a-half years old.

These changes had a sizeable but temporary effect on the number of births, since they only replaced the earnings of low-income women. To promote births among other women GYED was introduced. Initially, it was paid for one year, and eligibility was the same as for maternity leave. But payments were similar to sick leave, providing 65-75% compensation, compared with approximately 30% for GYES. In 1987, leave was extended to the child's second birthday, and the goal seemed to be to replace GYES with GYED, which was more favourable for women even if more costly for the state. This shift stopped at the end of the 1980s, as the economy ran into difficulties (Tárkányi, 1998).

During and after the transition, there have been several changes closely related to the politics of the governing parties. The following discussion, therefore, is organised around the successive governments since the beginning of transition. However, despite all these changes, it is not really known what the public think. Do they think it better to have long periods of leave or a comprehensive system of childcare services?

Antall government (1990–94): 'social economy'

This first democratically elected (right-wing) government separated family and social policy in its programme, and sought to create a so-called 'social economy', compensating for the negative effects of economic change on society. The declared aims of family policy were to stop the decline in the population and to achieve effective protection for all unborn babies. The idea of a stable family emerged as one of the government's answers to social problems, and changes in the leave system reflected the value attached to the traditional role of women in the family.

Abortion was more tightly circumscribed, fully paid maternity benefit was extended and GYET (*Gyermeknevelési támogatás*) introduced, to enable the mother in a family with three or more children to take leave and receive benefits between the third and eighth birthday of the youngest child. Ever since, GYET has been considered an acknowledgement of motherhood as paid work. At the same time, many nursery places closed when responsibility for providing these services devolved to local government, without earmarked state support, militating against women with young children returning to employment.

From the government's perspective, these changes seemed to suit the child-centred mentality of Hungarians, and to address emerging unemployment. Opposition parties voiced several criticisms: the system was too generous given the state of the economy, it encouraged families to live off child benefits, it promoted an obsolete view of women's role and it was not capable of halting the decline in births. While it had little effect on women's labour force participation, women's use of GYED slightly decreased while use of GYES increased, due to discretional ministerial decisions that allowed women to access this leave/benefit without any previous work record; GYES, therefore, appeared to begin functioning as a universal benefit, rather than a form of childcare leave. Meanwhile, the decline in the population continued, and spending on family support reached a peak in 1991, then began to fall back.

Horn government (1994–98):'economic stability'

The 1994 elections brought changes. The new (left–wing) government's programme prioritised economic stability, and social and family policies were subordinated to this goal. The Finance Minister considered the size and structure of redistribution as the root of the country's economic problems. The subsequent changes created the strictest family support policy in post-transition Hungary.

Because family policy was considered a major expenditure and source of redistribution, the changes had two goals: less expenditure and better targeting. GYED and tax credit for families with children were abolished; family allowance, GYES and GYET were no longer conditional on previous employment but were tied to income level. The real losers were parents with previous employment; if their income was high enough before having a baby, they were not eligible for the means-tested provisions, like family allowance or GYES following the period of maternity leave. With limited nursery places, returning to work was not a real alternative for them either.

Criticism from the opposition parties concerned the disappearance of demographic goals, the abolition of GYED being unjust for women active in the labour market, the short implementation period for the new legislation (giving no possibility of choice to those families whose children were already conceived) and the injustice of the means-test criteria for families with more than three children. Expenditure on family support fell, although administrative costs rose. Even though targeting became better, abolishing GYED had an adverse effect on child poverty, and the real value of benefits decreased. About 9% of families and 7% of children dropped out of the financial support system for families. With the loss of benefits previously taken for granted, the financial situation of families with children became uncertain for the first time.

Orban government (1998–2002): 'supporting families'

Elections brought fresh changes. The family policy of the new (right-wing) government aimed at restoring the security of family life, improving the conditions for having children and stopping the decrease in population. The means tests for family allowance, GYES and GYET were abolished, and GYED and the tax credit for families with children were restored. This was the first time that GYES became really universal, no longer tied to previous employment or income. In 2002, fathers became eligible for 5 days of paid leave at the time of the birth of their child.

The emerging rhetoric was again about the value and recognition of motherhood. Support was targeted not only at those citizens and families who were in need, but also at those identified as willing to do something to improve their situation. In line with EU guidelines, creating part-time work opportunities got on to the agenda as a means to balance work and family life. The opposition's recommendations for modifications mainly referred to increasing family allowance payments, at least in line with inflation. It also suggested increasing GYES and GYED payments, and lengthening GYED to 3 years; increased demand for nursery places at the age of 2 coupled with limited availability were cited as justification.

The impacts were mixed. The fertility rate grew, but so too did child poverty and social inequalities, since family allowance was not increased and many families were not able to claim the tax credit. Part-time employment opportunities did not spread, and the number of nursery places fell again; only about 6% of the age group could access childcare.

Medgyessy government (2002–04) and Gyurcsany government (2004–06): 'social transition'; Gyurcsany government (2006–10): 'fighting child poverty'

A left-wing coalition won the 2002 elections, and from the perspective of family and leave policies, there have been no subsequent major changes in approach between 2002 and 2004. The first government programme – 'social transition' – was supposed to be based on the growing economy. The so-called '100 days programme' outlined plans to implement general welfare and social policy goals. The target group was the whole society, the emphasis on the need for a complex system of measures to protect families, including income, labour, housing and education policies. At the same time, the government was bound, by signing the European Joint Inclusion Memorandum in 2003 and the priorities of the related National Action Plan, to support women's labour market participation, balancing work and family life, and the (broadly defined) welfare of children. These were to be achieved by increasing financial support and services for families, by developing child welfare and childcare services, and by providing free meals and books for children in need. Government rhetoric set increased births and reduced child poverty as criteria of success.

The resulting measures were seen more as corrections to previous legislation, for example, increasing the amount of GYES in case of twins and making grandmothers eligible for GYES. These were populist actions, introducing no new elements into the family support system. The main criticism from the opposition parties was about increased dependence on benefits and the limited support for women returning to the labour market after having taken up GYES or GYED (see Figure 9.1 for the current system of leave, including GYES, and GYED).

A new '100 steps programme' followed the new Prime Minister taking office in 2004. Eight of these steps were related to setting up a 'just family support system'. There were two targets: to improve the chances of those returning to the labour market after having taken up GYES or GYED, and to limit eligibility to tax credits for those with high incomes. Employers of young mothers returning after leave could get a reduction in their social security and health contributions; mothers on GYES could return to work and still receive the GYES payment after their child became one year old. Allowing mothers to work while taking up GYES was in line with supporting women's return to the labour market, but this

Figure 9.1: Types of leave available for insured and uninsured parents

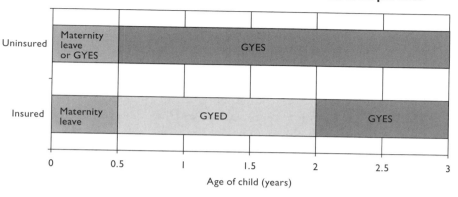

change made GYES payment into a form of social allowance, therefore losing its original function.

The opposition's main criticism centred on the value system, arguing for longer GYES and GYED, up to 5 years, supporting a conservative family model with the mother staying at home as long as possible.

In 2006, the coalition government was re-elected, ensuring a continuation of policies. Today, the main strategic goal is to fight child poverty, and family policy seems to have been transformed into child policy. In 2007, the parliament passed the National Strategy *Legyen jobb a gyermekeknek* ('Making things better for our children') for the years 2007–32, whose goals include reduced child poverty and improved chances for children. It requires the government to prepare an action programme every 3 years, based on the National Strategy. Supporting parents' labour market participation and developing services for children, including childcare, are seen as the main means of reducing poverty.

Conclusion

Overall, the extent of financial support for families has not changed during the transition years. No government developed childcare services as much as it could have. Demographic goals seemed to override other considerations; these, it has been thought, are best achieved by supporting women to stay home to bring up children. Over the years, the only non-profit organisation that has had influence on leave policy in particular and family policy in general is NOE (Nagycsaládosok Országos Egyesülete, or National Association of Large Families), representing families that have more than three children. Its goals have always been to support mothers to stay home with children.

Until recently, gender equality has not entered the debates about leave policy and achieving a balance between work and family life. Organisations calling for equal rights for women in the 1990s and the early 2000s focused on reducing domestic abuse, 'equal pay for equal work' and women's representation among decision makers. Within government, there has always been some agency or unit with a remit for gender equality, but none has ever dealt with leave or childcare.

The rhetoric of right- and left-wing coalitions seems to intermingle. Often, the same goals are set but in different contexts. The parliamentary documents illustrate the growing dominance of the language and values of EU directives and guidelines on both sides.

Today, demographic goals have less importance and there is growing emphasis placed on women's labour force participation and the evaluation of family policy from the perspective of employment policy. Benefit payments mainly came from the insurance fund before 1989, but there is a slow transformation going on, towards financing from the state budget, linking the funding of social and family policy to the condition of the economy.

Leave policies in Slovenia

From 1927 to 1974: maternity leave only

The 1919 International Labour Organization Convention Concerning the Employment of Women before and after Childbirth was ratified by the Kingdom of Serbs, Croats and Slovenians in 1927, and 12 weeks' paid maternity leave was introduced. In 1945, the Federal People's Republic of Yugoslavia, of which Slovenia formed a part, was founded, and maternity leave was defined by the Decree on Leave for Women before and after Childbirth (1946) and various other Acts regulating employment relationships. Employed women were entitled to 6 weeks of paid leave before and 6 weeks after childbirth. A 1949 Decree extended maternity leave to 90 calendar days with full earnings compensation; women employed by farm cooperatives were included. Breastfeeding mothers could work half time until their child was 6 months, receiving about 75% of full pay.

The first Employment Relationships Act was adopted by the federal parliament in December 1957. This introduced employment protection for pregnant women and extended maternity leave to 105 calendar days. Subsequently, in 1966, individual Socialist Republics within the Federal Republic could grant more rights in their territories. Up to 1974, therefore, the main issue was enabling women to combine their right to employment with motherhood.

From 1975 to 1985: maternity and parental leave

Workers' self-management was enacted in Yugoslavia in 1950, but it was the 1976 United Labour Act that had the greatest influence on decision-making processes in the country. From 1975 to 1986, the right to leave for childbirth and childcare was regulated by both the Employment Relationships Act and self-management agreements. Earnings compensation during *maternity* leave was part of healthcare insurance, while compensation during *parental* leave was regulated by self-management agreements concluded by each of the 60 municipal childcare associations. These were conceptualised as forums where the interests of working people, parents and employees in childcare services were expressed and coordinated by their representatives, in other words, self-managed by all interested parties.

The Childcare Association of Slovenia became the main actor in shaping parental leave policy. In 1974, the parliament of the Socialist Republic of Slovenia unanimously enacted an extension of leave, as proposed by the association. Although called childcare leave and lasting 141 days (in addition to the existing 105 days of maternity leave), it was in fact the mother's right – but with the possibility for her to transfer it to the father.

One year's leave from 1986

The idea of one year of maternity and parental leave had already appeared in all Yugoslav Socialist Republics in 1979. At that time, experts had already alarmed the public by pointing to the ageing population in Slovenia. However, more important for further developments in Slovenia was the introduction of a year's leave in some of the other Socialist Republics of Yugoslavia.

Between 1982 and 1986, there were initiatives and discussions by a wide range of actors in Slovenia, particularly the Childcare Association, the Social Care Association, the Association of Socialist Youth, the Association of Labour Unions and the Socialist Association of Working People. Politicians, experts and journalists were highly engaged in this public debate. In 1985, the focus of debate was the possibility of increasing leave in order to reverse the fertility trend, and the father's role in the family was also discussed. The government was positive to the idea of one year's leave, to promote children's health and development, but there were no funds to finance the extended leave prior to 1986.

Research was called for and initiated by the Childcare Association of Slovenia, and the study – *Parental leave as an element of bio-social reproduction* – was completed in 1985 (Jogan and Malačič, 1985). The socio-medical (Krajnc-Simoneti and Bregar-Fuss, 1985) and psychological view (Horvat et al, 1985) was that extending leave until the child was one or 2 years old would benefit the child's development. The legal view (Zupančič and Končar, 1985), on the other hand, was that it was not necessarily beneficial for the child to have the mother at home; if she were unhappy, she could not fulfil her role in a satisfactory way. To achieve its purpose of benefiting the child, extended leave should be shared by the parents. Furthermore, if fathers did not take leave, the extension might undermine women's employment and economic independence, and therefore their position in the family and equal opportunities in general. A similar concern was expressed in the sociological analysis (Jogan, 1985), while a demographic and economic analysis (Malačič, 1985) raised doubts about whether an extended parental leave would enhance the birth rate.

Legislation was eventually adopted in February 1986. The leave period was extended by 119 days, to give 365 calendar days of leave altogether: 105 days' maternity leave and 260 days' parental leave (in order to encourage full-time use, the leave was relatively shorter if taken half time). The research study (Jogan and Malačič, 1985) provided justification: long-term economic impact, healthy development of children and population growth. In the short run, cost savings were expected from decreasing use of childcare and absence from work to care for sick children.

Political transformation (from 1990) and the Resolution on the Foundations of Family Policy (1993)

Slovenia's first democratic (multi-party) elections took place in spring 1990; the government was formed by a coalition of centre-right parties. Independence was proclaimed in June 1991 following a referendum, with the first parliamentary elections in the independent country taking place in 1992. A coalition government was formed by the centre-left Liberal Democratic Party (LDS) and United List of Social Democrats (ZLSD); the centre-right Slovenian Christian Democrats (SKD), Social Democratic Party of Slovenia and Democratic Party; and the Greens of Slovenia.

   The new government engaged numerous experts in the drafting of a Resolution on the Foundations of Family Policy (referred to below as 'the Resolution'), a professional and political document presenting a comprehensive view of the middle-term development of family policy in Slovenia. The discussion and voting on amendments in the National Assembly reflected the political and ideological differences within that body. As stated by a Member of the Assembly, "the government coalition consisted of two, in their essence, mutually exclusive blocks or value systems: one of them following the ethical basis of the European enlightenment, and the other one following a Christian ethos as the basis of European civilisation" (Janez Podobnik, 10th session of the National Assembly, 1993). On the one hand, there was a demand that women should not lose out in their professional lives due to motherhood; on the other hand, the state was requested to support parents wanting to devote more time to their families, with cash and other means.

   The Resolution was approved, almost unanimously, in July 1993. It says:

> Gradually and in accordance with material conditions of the society we shall look for possibilities to eventually extend the childbirth and childcare related leave (to two or three years). In doing so, we shall strictly respect the principle of equal opportunities and rights of both parents. In order to achieve this, we shall draw up legislation and solutions that:
>
> – will not act as a disincentive for employment;
> – will not decrease possibilities for female employment;

- will assist enterprises with female or male employees taking parental leave, so that motherhood, in particular, will (no more) be a reason for lower employment opportunities. (Chapter III, point 3.3.1)

The right to vary working time for parents with children below 3 years of age, already held by parents of disabled children:

... will be extended gradually and in accordance with material conditions of the society. Working part time after parental leave (as an option) should become the right of both parents, and namely so that they take weekly or monthly turns working part time. In pension insurance, the period of working part time will be considered as full time. (Chapter III, point 3.3.2)

The 1990s: attempts to prolong leave to 2 or 3 years

This was the most exciting period in the politics of leave in Slovenia. There were intense public debates on three major interrelated Acts – the Family Benefits Act, the Employment Relationships Act and the Personal Income Tax Act – during which the country considered and eventually decided against a long leave policy. It merits, therefore, particular attention.

A wide range of actors were engaged in shaping leave policy in the 1990s: the Ministry of Labour, Family and Social Affairs, political parties, the governmental Office for Equal Opportunities, various experts, non-governmental organisations, pressure groups, media and the general public. The main issues discussed in relation to the possible extension of maternity and parental leave to 2 or 3 years were its impact on women's employment opportunities and equal opportunities for men and women in general. During the debate, paternity leave arose as an issue because of the provisions of the EU parental leave directive and Slovenia's accession to the EU, along with a need to encourage and enable fathers to take their share of parental leave. Research again contributed to the debate, albeit mostly referred to by the opponents of extended leave rather than its supporters.

The Family Benefits Act was proposed in 1992. Formally, it could not include the amendment submitted by the SKD and the Slovenian National Right Wing to extend the leave to 3 years (with 100% earnings compensation in the first year, 70% in the second and 50% in the third), since leave of absence from work was regulated by the Employment Relationships Act; the Family Benefits Act dealt only with financial compensation. Consequently, in December 1994, at the end of the International Year of the Family, three SKD members proposed revisions to both Acts, to extend leave to 3 years with an alternative option of part-time leave until a child was 65 months.

The proposers disagreed with the objection that their reform would discriminate against women, arguing that they were talking about parents and not mothers taking the extended leave, and that the use of this leave was not obligatory but rather a right that parents could opt for. They further argued that their proposal realised the goals set by the Resolution and that, in the context of a low fertility rate, 3 years of leave would stimulate births.

The issue was highly politicised and provoked wide debate. Public opinion surveys were conducted in the hope that they could be used to support one view or another. The 1995 survey financed by the Office for Female Policy showed 62% support for extending parental leave (MDDSZ, 1995), with highest support for 3 years' leave in the 25- to 30-year age group, despite many believing that it would have negative consequences for women's employment. In another survey, 41% supported leave lasting 3 years, although 77% believed that it would reduce female employment and career opportunities (MDDSZ, 1995). A survey for the main Slovenian daily newspaper *Delo* showed slightly more against the 3-year leave than in favour; equal proportions (41%) thought longer leave would increase or make no difference to fertility (Partlič, 1994).

The critics warned of many negative consequences of long parental leave: unequal opportunities for both sexes in the labour market, organisational problems for employers, budgetary constraints, worsening of the financial situation of young families and so on. On one hand, it was argued that only the well-off would be able to take 3 years of leave, forgoing part of their earnings; on the other hand, well-educated women were not expected to take it, since they would not accept the consequent loss of human capital and opportunities for career progression. This would leave only a small proportion of women (nobody was seriously thinking of fathers) likely to take 3 years of leave.

Some political parties, seeing no way of rejecting the proposal since it was in line with the Resolution goals, came up with arguments proving its harmful consequences. The LDS argued that account should have been taken of expert opinion that births would increase only if other necessary conditions for childrearing were fulfilled. It was ready to discuss the extension of parental leave as an option, but only within a comprehensive set of measures aimed at achieving a more equal gender division of childcare responsibilities, a higher standard of living and a better quality of life. In its view, motherhood was not a profession that should be paid, but a woman's choice.

The ZLSD and its Female Forum argued that none of the goals defined for extending leave would be achieved. Indeed, the experts' arguments indicated quite the opposite effect: female employment opportunities and earnings would decrease, young families' budgets would shrink and fewer children would be born. As a rule, an economically dependent woman is not satisfied nor can her child be happy. The problems identified by the SKD required different solutions. The ZLSD, therefore, would only support revisions to parental leave that included incentives for fathers to assume more care or to decrease the long hours that young children spent in childcare centres. For them, it was not the length of leave that was the urgent issue; rather, it was the lack of possibilities to reconcile work and family through part-time employment and achieving greater participation by fathers in childcare.

Both the LDS and the ZLSD came up with their own ideas of how to improve leave: introducing paid paternity leave to be used during maternity leave, extending parental leave by 3 to 6 months with incentives for fathers to take some of that leave, various options for taking part-time leave and so on.

The government Office for Female Policy warned of the worsening position of women both in the labour market and in the family if they took 3 years' leave. The government, too, was opposed to the proposals, because, it said, the conditions in the Resolution were not fulfilled. It thought the advocates of reform were wrong when they argued that their proposals would ensure gender equality. The proposal took no account of labour market consequences, particularly lower employment opportunities for women, while the expectation that more fathers would be involved in childcare did not square with current use of fathers' entitlement to leave (only 0.5% of fathers were taking any parental leave in spite of full earnings compensation).

The financial consequences of the proposal were uncertain. Extended parental leave would increase employer costs and employers would probably not be ready to bear the costs arising from long absences from work. According to the government's evaluation, the savings on unemployment benefits would be far lower than assumed by the supporters of extended leave, and the financial consequences for the state budget would be significant. The extension of parental leave would disrupt the childcare system, which in 1994 provided for 29% of one- and 2-year-olds; if all parents took 3 years of leave, fewer staff would be needed and many would become unemployed.

The trades unions did not have a common position; some were in favour, others against. Supporters perceived longer leave as offering improved social security for women employed in industries undergoing restructuring. Opponents warned of the impact of 3 years' leave on female employment and particularly for first job seekers; labour costs might increase with adverse consequences for the competitiveness of the Slovenian economy.

Entrepreneurship – the association representing industry and trade – pointed out that women's role was not just to be mothers but also to be fully and equally engaged with men in society. The country's economy could not afford the loss of an important part of the labour force for two additional years. Female managers warned of great damage to the economy, in particular in industries with high proportions of female employees. Even female entrepreneurs would employ men rather than women, since there is no place for emotions in business.

The proposal by the SKD was, however, actively supported by the Catholic Church through the Slovenian Caritas, the Movement for Life and the Council for Family. Priests encouraged the faithful to sign a petition supporting the proposal to extend parental leave (Zvonar-Predan, 1995). This was sent, with about 30,000 signatures, to the National Assembly.

Researchers tried their best to remain independent and objective in this heated atmosphere. According to Kukar (1995), the debate on the 3-year leave should have taken into account that women accounted for more than half of post-secondary graduates; that more educated people had higher professional aspirations; that low earnings in Slovenia required two earners to maintain a family; and that gainful employment was a source of financial independence and security, status in society, and social relations and networks. One should not, therefore, expect women to give up employment, even though most women want to have children.

Šušteršič (1995) argued that it was a mistake to assume that female employment opportunities would not deteriorate because women would not have to take all 3 years of leave. Since human behaviour depends not only on previous experience but also on expectations, employers would adapt their decision making immediately new leave regulations were adopted or even before. They would not invest in training employees who might take parental leave and would tend to give them jobs where they could be more easily substituted. They would prefer male employees to female. Because some women preferred to care for their children for several years, all women would face worse employment opportunities. Consequently, the proposal would not increase choice; through its impact on employers' expectations, it would promote one choice and decrease the possibility of the other.

Stropnik (1996) researched the economic consequences of the proposed extension. Concerns about the feasibility of financing full earnings compensation during extended leave from the state budget proved justified. Stropnik also doubted that most parents would take unpaid leave or leave with low earnings compensation. Two earnings were needed to guarantee a decent (sometimes only minimum) standard of living. She also pointed to the proven negative consequences – on future earnings, human capital, career progression, and job security – of long leave taken (almost) exclusively by mothers.

The discussion in the National Assembly was long and polemical, at times emotional and intolerant (Jakopec, 1995). The SKD's proposal to revise the Employment Relationships Act (to extend the maternity and parental leave to 3 years) was rejected in June 1995; consequently, the proposed complementary revisions to the Family Benefits Act were rejected as well. Besides the SKD, the proposal for extended leave was supported by the Social Democrats and (with some reservations) the Slovenian People's Party. Other political parties considered the measure inadequate for increasing births and decreasing unemployment, and feared it would limit women's role to that of housewife (Taškar, 1995).

The National Assembly called on the government to draft revisions to both Acts, taking account of the proposals made in the public debate. Asked to do so within one month, the government had not done so more than a year later, due to a long procedure for getting agreement to a new Employment Relationships Act. In December 1995, the anniversary of its former proposal, and encouraged by the petition in favour of extending parental leave, the SKD submitted a new proposal: a gradual extension of leave to 2 years, with 90% earnings compensation for the second year of leave. One parent could remain on leave until a child's third birthday, without earnings compensation but with social security contributions paid from the state budget. Fathers would be additionally granted an individual right to 14 days of leave to be taken during maternity leave.

Concerned about financial consequences, the government suggested waiting until the draft 1997 budget was ready. In the autumn of 1996, a new National Assembly took office and three SKD members resubmitted the proposals. Nothing significant happened until May 1998 when the government proposed they be rejected, since it was itself going to submit a new Parenthood and Family Benefits Act that would comprehensively regulate maternity and parental leave and other family benefits. The EU parental leave directive would be taken into account, as would the Resolution guidelines about more equal division of responsibilities between the parents, creating conditions for reconciliation of work and family responsibilities, supporting psycho–social and material security of the family and so on.

Introduction of paternity leave in 2002

In July 1998, the government proposed new legislation, the Parental Protection and Family Benefits Act. Organisations and individuals submitted over 100 amendments, and in January 1999, the competent National Assembly Committee organised a public hearing that resulted in proposals to the National Assembly. Then in June 2000, shortly before new elections due in October, the government changed from a centre-left to a centre-right coalition and submitted amendments to the proposed Act, but elections came before the National Assembly had completed the second reading of the proposed legislation. The new centre-left government – taking office in November – proposed new amendments in May 2001, and the new Act was finally unanimously approved in November.

The Parental Protection and Family Benefits Act is a compromise between the positions of the centre-right and centre-left. Parental leave was extended for large families and more options were implemented for part-time leave up to a child's third birthday. Several political parties and the Office for Female Policy interpreted the EU directive on parental leave as requiring paternity leave of 90 days; this was accepted. Fathers are entitled to full earnings compensation for 15 days, up to a ceiling of 2½ times national average earnings, with social security contributions (based on the minimum wage) paid from the state budget for the remaining 75 days. (In February 2006, the centre-right government proposed further revisions to paternity leave. Fathers are now obliged to use at least 15 days of paternity leave during the child's first 6 months, which was expected to enable more fathers to take paid leave, for instance, in the case of pre-term-born children. The remaining leave can be used until the child is 3 years old, aimed at encouraging fathers to spend more time with their young children.)

The 2001 Act introduced other changes. Either parent can take leave, although both must sign a written agreement setting out how they plan to use the entitlement. Seventy-five days of leave may be taken until the child's eighth birthday. Leave may also be taken on a half-time basis until a child's third birthday, with social security contributions (based on the minimum wage) paid from the state budget for the difference from full time. From January 2007, this right can be used until the youngest child reaches 6 years of age if the parent is taking care of two children (the LDS was against this change, arguing that it would increase the discrimination of women in the labour market). In addition:

- The father of the child or the child's grandparent is entitled to use maternity leave (up to 77 days following the birth of the child) and parental leave if the mother is a student below 18 years of age.
- Parental leave is extended by 30 days if parents are already bringing up at least two children below the age of 8 years; by 60 days if they are bringing up three children; and by 90 days if they are bringing up four or more children.
- Parents may take full-time parental leave simultaneously not only in the case of multiple births but also if, at the birth of a third child, they are already bringing up two children below the age of 8.
- There is no ceiling for the earnings compensation during maternity leave.

In 2000, the centre-right parties proposed the introduction of a childcare supplement to be paid to parents whose pre-school children do not attend publicly funded childcare services. The supplement would have been equal to half the cost of a subsidised place and would have been paid from one year of age up to the start of schooling. This proposal was not accepted. But since 1994, a monthly lump-sum allowance has been granted for one year to all parents who are not eligible for the insurance-based benefit during parental leave (about 14% of parents on parental leave).

A comparative perspective

Today, despite a common history of communist regimes, Hungary has a 3-year leave system with limited childcare provision for children under 3 years, while Slovenia has a leave system of around one year, with extensive childcare provision for one- and 2-year-olds. There are several reasons for these considerable differences. The first is the political regime. The faces of socialism were different in the two countries, as post-war Yugoslavia, of which Slovenia was part until 1991, fell outside of the Soviet sphere of influence in 1948. This enabled Yugoslavia to shape its policies more freely and to allow individual federal units to grant more rights and benefits in their territories if they could finance them. By contrast, Soviet control over Hungary only relaxed somewhat towards the end of the 1960s, opening the way for the introduction of economic reforms (and leave reforms).

In the 1970s and 1980s, Sweden was a model for Yugoslavia, and particularly for Slovenia, for parental leave and childcare policies. From the 1970s, in these two policy areas, Slovenia has more resembled Sweden than other former socialist countries. For instance, Sweden introduced the father's right to take a part of the parental leave in 1974, the first country in the world to do so; in the same year, Slovenia enacted the possibility for the mother to transfer her entitlement to parental leave to the father, which became effective in 1975.

Developments during the transition period (from the end of the 1980s) have also been different in Hungary and Slovenia. Transition had no impact on parental leave policy in Slovenia; mostly the decision-making process changed. In Hungary, the transition brought changes that removed the obligation to have a job, making it possible for women to stay home as housewives, whether or not they had children. The revival of religion seemed to strengthen more conservative views of women's roles. The first (right-wing, conservative) government's rhetoric and policy making reflected these developments, especially by emphasising the importance of mothers staying home for the development of young children.

Parental leave policy is closely related to childcare policy and female labour force participation. If parental leave lasts until a child is 3 years old and if parents (mothers) tend to take it, less childcare is needed than if the leave lasts only one year. The opposite, too, is true: if there is subsidised and good-quality childcare available for very young children, it is not necessary to have long parental leave. The final balance is usually strongly influenced by the employment rate of women and the values and attitudes in the society.

In Hungary, the majority of children under the age of 3 are cared for at home by mothers on leave. While there are no data available on the proportion of parents taking leave, an estimate can be made on the basis that 8–10% of children below 3 years of age were in nurseries in 2006 (KSH, 2007); the remainder probably had a parent (predominantly mothers) taking up one of the parental leave options. It is thought that mothers with higher education and better-paid jobs take shorter periods of leave because of the implications of prolonged absence from work for careers. By contrast, parents in Slovenia have only around 14 months of leave, except in cases of multiple births or the birth of a handicapped child, or if they are already bringing up at least two children below the age of 8 years. About a third of one-year-old children are admitted to childcare centres, and more than a half of 2-year-olds. Childcare services are of relatively high quality, and are available and affordable for families.

While maternity leave has been generally perceived as a health and welfare measure for women and newborn children, the rationale for parental leave has been somewhat different in Hungary and Slovenia. In both countries, the benefits for young children have been important, but in Slovenia the interest of mothers has been considered to a much greater extent than in Hungary. Strong concern about the consequences for equal opportunities of a long – 2 or 3 years – leave was expressed throughout the discussions on such proposals, and this is reflected in the regulation of parental leave. In Hungary, the 1997 Act on the protection of children and guardianship, and the 1998 Act on family support, emphasise the rights of children, which were used as one of the arguments for both pieces of legislation, while the issue of equal opportunities for women has not been present so strongly in the debate about parental leave.

Those in favour of extending leave in Slovenia believed that it would stimulate births. However, the length of parental leave has not been the reason for low fertility rates in Slovenia, nor did previous extensions increase the number of births (Stropnik and Šircelj, 2008). There is also empirical evidence that parental leave extensions have had only a temporary effect on a basically downward trend in fertility in Hungary (Spéder and Kamarás, 2008).

The Hungarian case proves that fears about the impact of long leave periods on women's employment – clearly expressed by the centre-left political parties in Slovenia during the debate on extending leave to 2 or 3 years – were well founded. The proportion of women taking leave who want to return to their job and have an employer who would employ them has increased over the years. But a large portion still cannot or do not want to go back to their previous job, and the chance of returning to a former job is strongly correlated with the length of leave taken (Frey, 2008).

Other research (Koncz, 2006) into the characteristics of female employment in Hungary between 2000 and 2004 confirms that women have difficulties of reintegration into the labour market, labour market segregation is being reproduced, and promotion opportunities and earnings are unequal. Positive employment-related measures for women are quite limited, and those that have been introduced, such as new legislation to prioritise pregnant women and women with young children, have not had good results.

Quite recently, the issue of child poverty entered the debate in Hungary. There are arguments (Ignits and Kapitány, 2006) that during the transition years, the emergence of unemployment and the growing social inequality forced the support system of family policy to take over more and more the tasks of social policy. The effects of this support system on alleviating poverty are sizable. Data from the Hungarian Central Statistical Office show how transfers – including payments to leave takers – decrease child poverty, from 48% to 20%. Even though supporting parents' labour market participation and developing services for children – including childcare – have been identified in the government programme as the main means of reducing poverty, the effects of cutting back on leave periods (and therefore the benefits tied to them) might worsen the situation of those families whose income relies on this form of support.

In Hungary, GYET (whereby the mother in a family with three or more children may take leave and receive benefits between the third and eighth birthday of the youngest child) was introduced in 1992. It has been considered an acknowledgement of motherhood as paid work ever since. The Slovenian centre-right political parties also proposed a benefit to be paid to mothers staying home to care for young children. However, the centre-left parties did not support the idea of 'pay for maternity'. The centre-right political parties had some success on this issue in 2006, but only to the extent that the state pays the social security contributions of one parent leaving the labour market to care for four or more children until the youngest child reaches 10 years (and since 2007, also until the youngest of two children reaches 6 years).

In Hungary, while policies have changed quite often and quite a lot during the transition years, perceptions of women's role in society and within the family have changed far less. An international comparative study (Pongracz, 2008) of expectations concerning paid work and family responsibilities indicates that the changes in Hungarian society had no influence on the nostalgia felt for traditional gender values and divisions of family responsibilities, even though others (Brayfield and Korintus, 2008) found that support for women's employment has increased over time among both men and women. This confirms the argument (Blaskó, 2005) that the acceptance of the male breadwinner model after 1989 was mostly due to massive unemployment in the early 1990s. The overall picture emerging from a survey of the National Institute for Family and Social Policy indicates that the respondents favour the option of the mother staying home with a young child; think that nurseries are used mainly because the mother needs to have a job to ensure enough income for the family; and are of the view that a wife would rather work part time, or not work at all, if the husband earned enough for the family to live on (Korintus, 2008). But the responses have to be interpreted carefully, considering the widespread lack of childcare services. It is not known what percentage of parents have a real choice between taking up leave or using childcare.

But in Slovenia it is widely believed that good-quality childcare is not a bad option for children after their first birthday. This does not necessarily mean that Slovenian women do not share the view of Hungarian women (Frey, 2008; Korintus, 2008) – namely, that it would be best for children if their mothers stayed at home and cared for them. Quite the opposite is the case: a great majority (64%) of the Slovenian respondents (aged 20 to 64 years) in the Population Policy Acceptance survey agreed that the best childcare is by parents (Stropnik, 2001). However, about a half (56%) of the respondents aged 20 to 49 years considered that parental leave lasting one year was long enough, compared with 43% who considered it too short (Stropnik et al, 2008); this reflects the polarisation between the advocates of longer parental leave and those who warn against its pitfalls. The same survey identified one year of full-time leave followed by 2 years of part-time leave combined with part-time employment as the most favoured hypothetical way of taking parental leave (Stropnik et al, 2008).

Conclusion

Looking at the political decision-making process for family and leave policies in Hungary over the transition period, two major features are evident: the absence of consensus about underlying principles, values, aims and means; and the emphasis laid on financial support (Czibere, 2006). The lack of even minimum agreement can clearly be seen in the sharp changes in the direction of policy making under different governments and the resulting complicated, piecemeal character of the system. Providing financial support, rather than developing childcare services for children under 3, seemed to be the only common ground for successive governments.

Recently, however, this approach has been changing somewhat, due to the influence of EU policy and recommendations by the Organisation for Economic Co-operation and Development for further work to identify and remove barriers to the creation of jobs, including hours and flexibility that suit working parents, and to reduce the length of parental leave, channelling savings into childcare services (OECD, 2007). In line with these slight changes in policy, Hungarians' perception of the role of women has also been changing. However, it remains to be seen what the near future will bring in terms of family and leave policies, and whether a comprehensive approach can be agreed on and realised.

Generally, in Slovenia, mothers' rights to work were never seriously questioned. The Slovenian Public Opinion Surveys conducted in the 1990s show a continuous decrease in the proportion of those who agreed with the statement that the husband should earn money while the wife should take care of the household and family, from 40% in 1991 to 30% in 1998 (Toš, 1999). Since almost all women of relevant age are today included in higher secondary education, and half continue education at the post-secondary level, it may be expected that women will remain highly attached to the labour market. Children are a high priority in Slovenia, but people will decide to have (more) children only in an environment offering them, particularly women, free choice in managing family and professional life. As stressed by Kukar (1995), one can only speak of a free choice if all of the following conditions are fulfilled: appropriate earnings compensation during parental leave, counting leave in the contribution years for pension insurance; the right to work part time with full pension contributions; the guarantee of returning to the same or an equal job; and good-quality, affordable and full-time childcare (if both parents opt for full-time employment). If any of these conditions go unfulfilled, free choice is constrained.

What appears clear is that parental leave will not be extended in Slovenia unless it seems certain that the possible extension will be taken equally by both parents. Otherwise employers would presume that women would take the whole of the leave, which would undermine women's labour market opportunities. Slovenia and Hungary are likely to be poles apart on leave policy for some time to come.

Notes

[1] Andrea Gyarmati researched parliamentary documents for the Hungarian part of the chapter.

[2] Leave provision described here refers to statutory entitlements.

[3] Converted into euros at exchange rate on 23 February 2009, rounded up to the nearest 5 euros.

References

Blaskó, Zs. (2005) 'Dolgozzanak-e a nők? A magyar lakosság nemi szerepekkel kapcsolatos véleményének változásai 1988, 1994, 2002' ['Should women work? Changes in the Hungarian population's opinions related to gender roles, 1988, 1994, 2002'], *Demográfia*, vol XLVIII, no 2-3, pp 159-86.

Brayfield, A. and Korintus, M. (2008) 'Changes in public support for maternal employment in Hungary and the USA, 1988–2002', Paper presented at the 38th World Congress of the International Institute of Sociology, 26-30 June, Central European University, Budapest.

Czibere, K. (2006) 'Szociálpolitika' ['Social policy'], in M. Szabó (ed) *Szakpolitikák a rendszerváltás utáni Magyarországon, 1990–2006* [*Transition-years policies in Hungary, 1990–2006*], Budapest: Rejtjel kiadó.

Frey, M. (2008) 'Hungary: possibilities of and barriers to the employment of women on child care leave', in P. Moss and M. Korintus (eds) *International review of leave policies and related research 2008*, Employment Relations Research Series No 100, London: Department for Business Enterprise and Regulatory Reform, pp 30-4.

Horvat, L., Zupančič, M. and Winter, M. (1985) 'Psihološki argumenti za in proti podaljšanju porodniškega dopusta' ['Psychological arguments for and against the extension of parental leave'], in M. Jogan and J. Malačič (eds) *Porodniški dopust kot sestavina biosocialne reprodukcije* [*Parental leave as a constituent part of a bio-social reproduction*], Ljubljana: Skupnost otroškega varstva Slovenije, pp 221-57.

Ignits, Gy. and Kapitány, B. (2006) 'A családtámogatások alakulása: célok és eszközök' ['The changes in family assistance: aims and means'], *Demográfia*, vol XLIX, no 4, pp 383-401.

Jakopec, M. (1995) 'Strinjali so se, da je za več otrok treba kaj storiti' ['They agreed that something should be done if we are to have more children'], *Delo*, 3 June, p 2.

Jogan, M. (1985) 'Sociološki del' ['Sociological part'], in M. Jogan and J. Malačič (eds) *Porodniški dopust kot sestavina biosocialne reprodukcije* [*Parental leave as a constituent part of a bio-social reproduction*], Ljubljana: Skupnost otroškega varstva Slovenije, pp 127-88.

Jogan, M. and Malačič, J. (eds) (1985) *Porodniški dopust kot sestavina biosocialne reprodukcije* [*Parental leave as a constituent part of a bio-social reproduction*], Ljubljana: Skupnost otroškega varstva Slovenije.

Koncz, K. (2006) 'A felzárkózás elmaradása: a magyar nők munkaerő–piaci helyzete' ['Missing out on catching up: the labour market position of Hungarian women'], *Statisztikai Szemle* [*Statistical Review*], vol 84, no 7, pp 651-74.

Korintus, M. (2008) 'Hungary: views of the 22-35 year old population concerning parental leave and childcare', in P. Moss and M. Korintus (eds) *International review of leave policies and related research 2008*, Employment Relations Research Series No 100, London: Department for Business Enterprise and Regulatory Reform, pp 15-22.

Krajnc-Simoneti, S. and Bregar-Fuss, N. (1985) 'Socialno medicinski vidiki' ['Socio-medical aspects], in M. Jogan and J. Malačič (eds) *Porodniški dopust kot sestavina biosocialne reprodukcije* [*Parental leave as a constituent part of a bio-social reproduction*], Ljubljana: Skupnost otroškega varstva Slovenije, pp 189-220.

KSH (Kozponti Statisztikai Hivatal) (2007) *Szocialis statisztikai evkonyv, 2006* [*Yearbook of Welfare Statistics, 2006*] Budapest: KSH.

Kukar, S. (1995) 'Ugodnosti za starše, ko so otroci majhni' ['Benefits for parents while the children are small'], *Delo*, 11 March, p 31.

Malačič, J. (1985) 'Demografski in ekonomski del' ['Demographic and economic part'], in M. Jogan and J. Malačič (eds) *Porodniški dopust kot sestavina biosocialne reprodukcije* [*Parental leave as a constituent part of a bio-social reproduction*], Ljubljana: Skupnost otroškega varstva Slovenije, pp 1-126.

MDDSZ (Ministry of Labour, Family and Social Affairs) (1995) *Analiza izvajanja ukrepov Resolucije o temeljih oblikovanja družinske politike v Republiki Sloveniji* [*Analysis of the implementation of the Resolution on the Foundations of Family Policy measures*], Ljubljana: Ministrstvo za delo, družino in socialne zadeve.

OECD (Organisation for Economic Co-operation and Development) (2007) *Economic survey of Hungary 2007: Improving reconciliation between work and family*, Paris: OECD.

Partlič, S. (1994) 'Različna mnenja o tem, ali bi daljši porodniški dopust povečal rodnost' ['Different opinions on whether a longer parental leave would increase fertility'], *Delo*, 4 February, p 4.

Pongracz, M. (2008) 'Hungary: mother's role – employment versus family', in P. Moss and M. Korintus (eds) *International review of leave policies and related research 2008*, Employment Relations Research Series No 100, London: Department for Business Enterprise and Regulatory Reform, pp 22-30.

SORS (Statistical Office of the Republic of Slovenia) (2006) *Materinski dan* [*Mothers' Day*] First Release, Population, 23 March, Ljubljana: SORS.

SORS (2008) *Kindergartens, Slovenia, school year 2007/2008*, First Release, 18 April, Ljubljana: Statistical Office of the Republic of Slovenia.

Spéder, Z. and Kamarás, F. (2008) 'Hungary: secular fertility decline with distinct period fluctuations', in T. Freyka, T. Sobotka, J.M. Hoem and L. Toulemon (eds) *Childbearing trends and policies in Europe*, Demographic Research Vol 19, Special Collection 7, pp 599-644.

Stropnik, N. (1996) 'Porodniški dopust – pogoji, oblike in posledice podaljšanja' ['Parental leave - conditions, forms and consequences of its extension'], in T. Stanovnik and N. Stropnik (eds) *Medgeneracijski transferji dohodka v Sloveniji* [*Inter-generational income transfers in Slovenia*], Ljubljana: Inštitut za ekonomska raziskovanja.

Stropnik, N. (1997) *Ekonomski vidiki starševstva* [*Economic aspects of parenthood*] Ljubljana: Znanstveno in publicistično središče.

Stropnik, N. (2001) 'Prebivalstvo Slovenije in družinska politika' ['Population of Slovenia and family policy'], in N. Stropnik and M. Černič Istenič (eds) *Prebivalstvo, družina, blaginja: Stališča do politike in ukrepov* [*Population, family, welfare: Attitudes towards policy and measures*], Ljubljana: Inštitut za ekonomska raziskovanja, pp 7-55.

Stropnik, N. and Šircelj, V. (2008) 'Slovenia: generous family policy without evidence of any fertility impact', in T. Freyka, T. Sobotka, J.M. Hoem and L. Toulemon (eds) *Childbearing trends and policies in Europe*, Demographic Research Vol 19, Special Collection 7, pp 1019-58.

Stropnik, N., Sambt, J. and Kocourková, J. (2008) 'Preferences versus actual family policy measures. The case of parental leave and child allowance', in C. Höhn, D. Avramov and I. Kotowska (eds) *People, population change and policies: Lessons from the Population Policy Acceptance Study, Volume 1*, Dordrecht: Springer, pp 391-410.

Šušteršič, J. (1995) 'Nomija in logija', *Razgledi*, 17 February, p 11.

Tárkányi, Á. (1998) 'Európai családpolitikák: a magyar családpolitika története' ['European family policies: the history of Hungarian family policy'], *Demográfia*, vol XVI, no 2-3, pp 233-68.

Taškar, J. (1995) 'Porodniški dopust bo še naprej le eno leto' ['Parental leave will remain only one year long'], *Delo*, 3 June, p 1.

Toš, N. (ed) (1999) *Vrednote v prehodu II. Slovensko javno mnenje 1990–1998* [Values in transition II. Slovenian Public Opinion 1990–1998], Dokumenti SJM 6, Ljubljana: Fakulteta za družbene vede, IDV – CJMMK.

Zupančič, K. and Končar, P. (1985) 'Pravni del' ['Legal part'], in M. Jogan and J. Malačič (eds) *Porodniški dopust kot sestavina biosocialne reprodukcije* [*Parental leave as a constituent part of a bio-social reproduction*], Ljubljana: Skupnost otroškega varstva Slovenije, pp 259-302.

Zvonar-Predan, D. (1995) 'Politika in dojenčki' ['Politics and infants'], *Večer*, 14 March, p 4.

TEN

Iceland: from reluctance to fast-track engineering

Thorgerdur Einarsdóttir and Gyda Margrét Pétursdóttir

Maternity leave[1]: there is no separate maternity leave. Part of parental leave is reserved for women and women must take 2 weeks of this leave following birth.

Paternity leave: there is no separate paternity leave. Part of parental leave is reserved for men.

Parental leave: 9 months at 80% of earnings up to a ceiling on payment of ISK535,700 a month[2]. Leave can be taken on a part-time (50%) basis and extended in length. Three months are reserved for mothers and 3 months for fathers. The remaining period is a family entitlement and may be taken by either mother or father.

Leave to care for sick children: none

Other: each parent has the right to 13 weeks' unpaid leave until the child is 8 years old.

Iceland is a Nordic country, but not a member state of the European Union (EU). It does not have separate maternity, paternity and parental leaves, but a single system of 'birth leave', the period of leave divided equally between mothers, fathers and a family portion to be divided as parents choose. Prior to the recent introduction of the father's quota, few fathers took any leave. But the latest figures (for 2006) show that now most take leave; 88 fathers take leave for every 100 mothers taking leave, using on average 100 days compared with 185 days for mothers. This means that most fathers take the part of parental leave reserved for fathers, but only a small minority (19% in 2005) took any of the period that parents can share; 90% of mothers took some or all of this period.

Introduction

Parental leave in Iceland has been developing since the Second World War. Until recently it was a highly complex, patchwork system that distinguished between different groups of women and men, with various entitlements and payments. The rights of women depended on whether they worked in the public or private sector of the labour market; while the system provided certain groups of men with limited entitlements and totally excluded others. The parental leave reforms from the year 2000 brought revolutionary changes with 3 months' leave for each parent, in addition to 3 months to share – a total of 9 months. As a result, men in Iceland have the longest non-transferable father's leave quota in the world. These Icelandic reforms of the parental leave system have gained wide attention, and have moved the country from a minimal system to a fast-track engineering of parental roles. The Nordic model of parental leave with a special father's quota today has its most radical expression in Iceland.

Following a brief historical background, this chapter explores the politics behind the Icelandic leave legislation. We suggest that several factors were influential in the emergence of the new radical system. First, the limitations of the previous system meant that implementing the new system took nothing away *from* anyone; there was no reduction of existing rights. Second, court rulings had stated that it was illegal to discriminate between men and women concerning parental leave. It was apparent that the exclusion of men under the previous system violated the constitution of Iceland. Third, the new reform was situated within the prevalent emphasis on men in the Nordic gender equality discourse.

The fourth and most important point is the specific context of national politics in Iceland. The liberal/right-wing government in office in 2000 responded to strong pressure for gender equality measures with the parental leave reform. This reform was not launched as a family policy or welfare issue but primarily as a measure to explicitly address the gender pay gap. The broad political consensus reflects support for a fast-track social engineering approach and state intervention, exceptional in the liberal Icelandic political context that is, typically, characterised by a resentment of central authority and government (Ólafsson, 2003).

A short historical overview

The first legislation on birth leave for women in the Nordic countries dates back to the end of the 19th and the start of the 20th centuries. The legal framework initially aimed at the protection of working mothers and their newborns, evolving in the period after the Second World War into a system covering women in paid work, establishing their rights and entitlement to payments (Valdimarsdóttir, 2006, pp 4-7). The social protection system of Iceland at the time was in its infancy. In 1954, women in the civil service became entitled to 90 days of paid maternity leave, putting them in a much better position than other women. Their rights continued to be assured by special legislation, which gradually improved the length, flexibility and payment of maternity leave. Women in the civil service maintained their advantages over other women until the reforms of 2000.

In 1975, mothers in the private employment sector who were "unable to work due to childbirth" received unemployment benefit for 90 days (Gíslason, 2007, pp 6-7; see also Eydal, 2000). Next, the 1980 Act on Birth Leave (No 97) gave parents working in the private sector 3 months' leave. Dismissal of women on maternity leave was now forbidden and their payments were no longer unemployment benefits but covered by social insurance; however, they were low, flat-rate amounts dependent on the previous extent of the mother's labour market participation (Gíslason, 2007, p 7). A Bill proposing the same rights and payments to all women regardless of their labour market position was repeatedly put forward in the Icelandic parliament during the 1980s, but without success. Hence, this somewhat arbitrary system persisted until the reform in 2000.

While the Icelandic system was arbitrary enough for women, it was even more so for men. Not only did their rights depend on their own employment sector (public or private), but also on the labour market situation of their spouse. Men employed in the public sector had no rights. Men married to or cohabiting with women who were civil servants had very limited rights, amounting either to unpaid leave or paid leave based on their spouse's income. Men working in the private labour market, and men married to or cohabiting with women working in the private market, had limited rights, which were again dependent on the entitlement and leave usage of their spouse. A clause in the 1980 Act gave these fathers a right to the last month of leave if the mother gave her permission (Gíslason, 2007, p 7). Hence, men's rights to leave were initially conditional on the situation and agreement of mothers.

The idea of some form of leave for fathers had been proposed in different quarters for decades. It was first mentioned publicly in Iceland at a conference held in 1975 to mark the United Nations (UN) Year of the Woman, where one or 2 weeks of leave for fathers was suggested by a group of women. The justifications were both the mother's need for rest and the importance of strengthening the relationship between father and child (Skýrsla Kvennaársnefndar, 1977, p 44; Gíslason, 2007, p 7). The Women's Alliance, active from 1983 to 1999, put forward numerous Bills for maternity/paternity leave, but without success (Eydal, 2000; Jónsdóttir, 2007). In 1993, the so-called 'men's committee', a working group on behalf of the Minister of Social Affairs, put forward the demand for a separate leave for fathers (Félagsmálaráduneytid, 1993, p 9). In 1998, the Icelandic Federation of Labour, Iceland's largest trade union, called for paid paternity leave, and the same demand came from other labour unions as well as the employers' associations (Gíslason, 2007, p 8).

The first serious attempts to introduce paternity leave in practice were taken by the City of Reykjavík in 1996–98 with a pilot project co-funded by the EU (Einarsdóttir, 1998). Soon after, the municipality of Reykjanesbaer introduced 2 weeks' birth leave for their male employees. In 1997, a 2-week right was granted to all men in the civil service, that is, those employed by the state and the City of Reykjavík. With an Act on paternity leave in 1998, these 2 weeks of paternity leave were extended to all men in Iceland, although payments differed according to employment sector.

Hence, the gradually evolving leave rights of men were no less arbitrary than the system of maternity leave had been for women. The structural discrepancies between men and women, and the exclusion of men from parental leave, was heavily contested in the late 1990s. The parental leave system was far behind that of the other Nordic countries and changes in the system were overdue. Having outlined the historical background, we turn now to explore why the reformed system took the form it did, why a father's quota was implemented, and why this leave period exclusively for fathers was longer than any introduced in the other Nordic countries.

Changes overdue – but why these changes?

The long-standing reluctance by the state to equalise the leave rights of women and expand the limited rights of men was suddenly reversed by the Act on maternity/paternity and parental leave passed in 2000. Leave was extended from 6 months to 9 in three phases from 2001 to 2003, linking 3 non-transferable months to each of the parents and leaving 3 months for the parents to divide at their own discretion. The leave can be taken part time, until the child is 18 months, with a reduction in payments. Payments to leave takers amount to 80% of gross earnings, with a fixed minimum amount and, since 2004, a ceiling on payments set at ISK535,700 a month. Those who are not active in the labour market, or work less than quarter time, receive some financial compensation from the state.

The lengthening of parental leave and the equalisation of the rights of men and women formed part of the policy statement of the coalition government of the liberal/right-wing Independence Party and the centre Progressive Party that came to office in the spring of 1999. When the Bill on parental leave was introduced in the spring of 2000, it was not preceded by long discussions or investigations. In some ways, this is characteristic of Iceland, but unlike other Nordic countries. Compared with them, the state administration of Iceland is small and weak, and there is also a less significant public sector and a lower level of domestic consensus. Expert knowledge in the state administration has, therefore, always been limited, with fewer resources and less emphasis on long-term policy making. In the Icelandic context, with coalition governments typical, this has led to individual politicians and political parties having a strong influence (Kristinsson, 1993). The Bill on parental leave, put forward by the Minister of Social Affairs, reflects this clearly.

There are several reasons behind the specific path taken in the 2000 Icelandic reform, with its sudden change of direction. The first reason is that the existing system was a poorly functioning patchwork of measures; it was a parsimonious system with rather limited rights even for those groups of women who were best covered. Hence, when the new reform was introduced it benefited all concerned. In some European countries the parental leave system has developed along the housewife/breadwinner model with relatively long maternity leave and low compensation for leave takers. Such a system can be transformed into a universal and formally gender-neutral system of parental leave, as in the case of Germany and Spain (before 2005) but without much effect. The legacy of traditional gender relations is institutionalised and there is not much potential for change (Einarsdóttir and Pétursdóttir, 2004).

While attempts to transform a traditional maternity leave system into a seemingly gender-neutral system tend to be ineffective, it is also politically controversial to shorten previously shared rights by turning some part into a father's quota, not least since the shared rights are often perceived as women's rights. In this respect, the path taken by Iceland is different from the other Nordic countries. In Sweden and Norway, the (shared) parental leave was already relatively long, up to one year, when the specific father's quota was introduced (Valdimarsdóttir, 2006). In Norway, there is no political will to extend parental leave in total, and the introduction of a longer father's quota has been hindered by a reluctance to transform part of the shared leave into a period for the exclusive use of fathers (Fréttabladid, 2008).

But in Iceland, with its relatively complicated and limited entitlements by Nordic standards, nothing was 'taken from women' in this sense; there was no shared right that the parents perceived as the mother's right. All changes, therefore, were additions welcomed by all political players. However, qualitative research does reveal that some mothers did feel that fathers' rights had been improved while their rights had been overlooked (Pétursdóttir, 2004). In addition, before the reform women working in the public sector had the 80% benefit payment made up to their full salary, while men working in the public sector did not receive such payments. This was contested on the grounds of sex discrimination and is expected to be changed (Gíslason, 2007, pp 11-12).

A second reason for the specific Icelandic path was the need to react to challenges from the judicial system. In 1998, the Supreme Court of Iceland ruled that it was a violation of the law and the Constitution to exclude men from parental leave (judgment 208/1997, pronounced 5 February 1998). Following this, the state recognised the right to parental leave for men in public service who were married to or cohabiting with women also employed in the public service, while other men continued to be excluded. In addition, the Complaints Committee on Equal Status came to similar conclusions on three occasions in 1999[3], but without any reaction from the state. When the Minister of Social Affairs put forward the Bill on parental leave, he mentioned that it was a response to pressure from the UN and the EU, which will be discussed later. But although he did not mention the challenges from the judicial system, these had become a burdensome concern for the government.

The third reason why Icelanc took its particular stance was the Nordic emphasis on men in the gender discourse. The inclusion of men in work on equality had been increasing in the Nordic context since the 1980s, resulting in a plethora of publications, events and conferences (see, for example, Nordic Council of Ministers, 1987, 1995a). While the Nordic Council of Ministers' cooperation programme for gender equality for 1995–2000 did not address men explicitly (Nordic Council of Ministers, 1995b), there was a shift in the 2000–05 cooperation programme, where the inclusion of men is one of three main areas of priority (Nordic Council of Ministers, 2000).

This emphasis on men is clearly reflected in national policy documents in Iceland as well as in general discourse. The 'boys' discourse' has been prominent in Iceland (Jóhannesson, 2004), and the shift is clearly visible in the Act on the equal status and equal rights of women and men from 2000 (Flóvenz, 2007). The new parental leave reform, therefore, was very much in line with the prevailing emphasis on men in the Nordic gender equality discourse. Moreover, it gave Iceland the opportunity to take the lead in the matter, as will be discussed more thoroughly in the next section.

Fast-track engineering of gender equality

This section analyses the new reform from the perspective of the parliamentary debate around the Bill in 2000. The data used in this analysis consist of the explanatory statement accompanying the Bill (law on birth and parental leave 95/2000) and the debates that followed its presentation to parliament (Althingistidindi, 2000 125 löggjafarthing). The Bill on parental leave was introduced in the spring of 2000 by Páll Pétursson, Minister of Social Affairs and member of the centre-oriented Progressive Party (previously the Farmers' Party). In the first reading of the Bill, 10 members of parliament (MPs) discussed it in 18 separate speeches. Then the Bill went to the Committee on Social Affairs, which did not make or suggest any revisions. Back again in the full Parliament, 7 MPs discussed the Bill for the second reading in 25 separate speeches. The Bill was passed in the spring of 2000; at this point, 4 MPs discussed their vote. Interventions during these different stages amount to approximately 109 pages of written text, 82 of these being parliamentary debate.

The data was read and coded for recurring themes or discursive strands; the process was then repeated to validate their weight in the analysis. Discourse analysis was used to explore the underlying meaning of certain words and statements and how they reflect a particular system of knowledge or ideas. Discourse analysis is based on the notion of knowledge as socially constructed and needing, therefore, to be historically and culturally contextualised. According to Gill (2000), discourse analysis provides us with a critical awareness of our taken-for-granted everyday knowledge. It recognises that our language has formative powers; as individuals, we are shaped by existing discourses while taking part in their shaping and reproduction.

Paternity leave as a gender equality issue

The explanatory statement accompanying the Bill cites an attitude survey carried out 5 years previously: "A survey carried out by the Social Science Institute at the University of Iceland in 1995 showed that most of the male participants thought that there was a *general interest* among men to balance work and upbringing of children" (emphasis added). It is worth noting that the participation of fathers in Iceland in the year 2000 is framed, as this quotation illustrates, in terms of *interest* and *free will*. This is similar to the Swedish discourse when shared parental leave was introduced in 1974; the unifying idea at that time in Sweden was that parental leave was a *free choice* for men in order to make it attractive (Klinth, 2005, p 212).

Aside from the survey, no scholarly resources, inquiries or research are cited in the explanatory statement. Furthermore, the parliamentary discussion reflects a limited understanding of the issue of gender equality with one noteworthy exception – Bryndís Hlodversdóttir, a member of the Social Democratic party, who spoke during the first reading:

> In my opinion fathers should, by all means available, be encouraged to participate more fully in the caring of children from early on to enable them to bond with their children from the beginning. Not only does it lay an important foundation in the emotional communication between father and child but it will also allow for men in larger numbers to care for their children and that is certainly to the benefit of the whole family.

In essence, what Hlodversdóttir is saying is that 'fathers sharing means fathers caring', and vice versa. By being on leave, fathers will gain valuable insight into their children's needs and will therefore contribute their fair share to caring in the future. But fathers' emotional gain is for the most part absent from the discussions in parliament and the focus is on equality matters.

Members of parliament were for the most part very enthusiastic about the legal reform. This included members of the two ruling parties, the liberal/right-wing Independence Party and the centre Progressive Party, as well as the two opposition parties, the Socialist Party and the Social Democratic Party. The Bill was supported by 50 MPs out of 63, an almost unanimous vote, as 12 MPs were absent on the day of voting and one MP was present but did not vote. Some of them talked about "a milestone" or "a turning point" in gender equality matters, aimed at fixing the inequality between men and women, with the 'daddy months' seen as a means to that end. In the words of a member of the Socialist Party, Steingrímur J. Sigfússon:

> I think that everyone is clear about what is most important when it comes to equal status between men and women in the labour market and ways to mitigate the gendered inequality and the gender pay gap which exists in the labour market disadvantaging women. What is needed is a way to make the status of men and women equal regarding parental leave, children's sick leave, caring in the home etc. The way towards this goal is through increased and independent rights for fathers *or men*. In the light of the nature of the matter that is the *only way*. (Emphasis added)

A subtle reference to gender equality is indicated by mentioning both fathers and men. Men do not go on paternity leave without being fathers, but the formulation opens up the issue by framing it as a men's issue. In the eyes of Sigfússon, a certain period tied to men is the only way to move forward. The gender equality dimension is also visible in the words of Páll Pétursson, the Minister of Social Affairs and a member of the Progressive Party. In introducing the Bill to the parliament, he pointed to the status of gender equality issues in Iceland by referring to the UN Committee on the Elimination of Discrimination against Women. Pétursson mentioned the gender pay gap "which is believed to exist here" and argued that the Bill was a significant step in its elimination. He indicated that the Bill was a response to external pressure from the UN to eliminate the gender pay gap; although he did not mention rulings and challenges from the judical system, it was implicit.

Other equality matters were also mentioned frequently, such as the unequal division of caring and household tasks, for example in these words of Arnbjörg Sveinsdóttir, a member of the Independence Party:

> It is my belief that this matter will bring us by giant steps towards increased equality between women and men…. Fathers going into their homes to equally care for and bring up their children in the first months of the children's lives will transform companies' attitudes towards their employees…. Gender equality requires realistic solutions which ensure that men and women have the same work opportunities both inside and outside the home. This has been acknowledged. One of the most important issues in that respect concerns justice, that fathers and mothers will have equal rights to parental leave. The system we are familiar with now and existing discrimination, together with prevailing views on gender division on work, hinders individual freedom of choice in respect to a career and a platform within the family…. The improvements we will achieve by this Bill are that we will attain more equal status between women and men in the labour market, more equal status between men and women in the home, the employers' costs concerning children will be more equally distributed, there will be more people paying taxes to support the welfare system and we will have improved economic rationalisation because women's manpower will be utilised.

Sveinsdóttir's speech concisely illustrates the liberal view. Legislation is used to create equal opportunities in the labour market and in the home, to equalise societal costs and to utilise women's labour power to the fullest. It is, as Sveinsdóttir puts it, "first and foremost an equality matter". These critical issues of gender equality do not arise very frequently – once every hundred years – as Drífa Hjartardóttir, also a member of the Independence Party, suggested: "The Bill is one of the biggest and most important steps taken towards gender equality since women's right to vote".

As these passages suggest, the Bill was explicitly framed as a gender equality measure. Moreover, numerous gender equality issues were mentioned suggesting a 'one-size-fits-all' approach; in other words, it is possible to achieve equality by passing into law a Bill on parental leave, the assumption being that other gender-related issues will then fall into place. This suggests a 'quick-fix solution'. We look now at the neoliberal concerns and the more traditional views within the Independence Party.

Correcting a market failure

In 2000, the economy in Iceland was booming. Unemployment rates were at an all-time low, so the Unemployment Insurance Fund was able to meet existing needs as well as to build a surplus. It was decided that a certain percentage of that fund would be used to finance parental leave payments. Members of the Independence Party went to great lengths to show that implementing the law on parental leave would not require cuts elsewhere to finance the programme. Some would even profit or at least public spending would be minimised, as argued by Pétur Blöndal, an Independence Party MP:

> ... if this Bill has the effect it could have, that is people will be working part time for 2½ years, the need for childcare centres which are run by the municipalities will lessen. It will soon become apparent how much will be saved in that area. For parents it will also be economically sound as I pointed out earlier because they won't have to spend money on childcare.

So the argument for parental leave has been reduced to a matter of profit – inequality is costly, women's labour is not used sufficiently, and parents will use their leave to ensure that their children can stay at home for 2½ years because economically that is the most rational thing to do. Hence, everyone will profit including the employer because from a productivity perspective it is better to have people working part time, as Pétur Blöndal also pointed out.

Blöndal had long been outspoken on his neoliberal convictions. He was in favour of the legislation for more reasons than the savings to be made in public spending. He saw it as a way to correct a market failure, which would also save costs:

> For a long time I have fought for the implementation of parental leave, for numerous reasons. If individual abilities are to be fully utilised there has to be equality on the labour market to ensure that the most talented individual is hired for the job. This is not the case today. Inequality between people, which manifests itself in inequality between men and women, is screaming out and has to be fixed by

all means available. The legislation has been cleared of all inequality except when it comes to parental leave. That is the only law which still discriminates between men and women.... When this Bill has been passed, which will even out the difference between women and men in 3 years, nothing will be left but prejudice and nepotism ... men's and women's prejudice against women and particularly women's prejudice against themselves. They don't have the guts to stand in the line of fire. This needs to be fixed but that is presumably something we can't fix with legislation. Inequality is expensive; therefore it is societally viable to eliminate inequality.

As can be seen from Blöndal's highly neoliberal speech, the new legislation was meant to correct 'market failures'; there is no understanding of structural discrimination in Blöndal's view, only prejudice and nepotism.

While Blöndal justifies the social engineering of the new reform as a positive way to correct market failures, others see it as a necessary evil, a temporary measure aimed at bridging the gender pay gap. This is because the state intervention, which is built into the Bill, goes against the neoliberal convictions of some members of the Independence Party, especially the younger ones, as exemplified in the words of Thorgerdur Katrín Gunnarsdóttir:

> [The Act] will be revised after a certain time to evaluate it and then we can see if we haven't attained what is very important, to increase the equality in the labour market, among other things to try to decrease the gender pay gap which exists and many surveys have confirmed. My vision for the future is actually such that some day we need to let go of the state intervention, which manifests itself in the Bill in the form of 3 months being preserved for women and 3 months for men, it is non-transferable and that is a key issue in the equality debate.... But I hope in the future we will be fortunate enough to not have to put such a clause in the law and we can say: Here you have 12 months of parental leave and you can divide it at your own discretion. That is my vision for the future ... that parents can chose.

What Gunnarsdóttir is suggesting is that the law is a temporary rectifying strategy, a form of affirmative action. But at the same time, as pointed out by Kristján L. Möller, a member of the Social Democratic Party, Gunnarsdóttir is eager to show her allegiance to the neoliberal arm of her party, by talking about abandoning the state intervention that is built into the legislation. The quote also illustrates the general lack of insight into the issue of gender equality. The gender pay gap has proved to be a persistent problem and a recent survey shows that it has not decreased in the 12 years between 1994 and 2006 (Capacent Gallup, 2006). In the neoliberal view, a social engineering measure is justified as a temporary means to eliminate the gender pay gap, but the Act could soon be revised. It is a temporary measure because the problem can be solved quickly; a quick-fix solution, as suggested earlier, to a quick-fix problem.

Some members of parliament suggested that the law could be amended in as little as 3 years. By that time the law would be fully implemented and, therefore, revisions would be needed, as Arnbjörg Sveinsdóttir, member of the Independence Party and head of the Social Affairs Committee, suggested. Sveinsdóttir said that the clear-cut division between men and women, with a leave quota specified for each, should be temporary but was necessary now "to pin down and secure men's rights". The phrase being used to illustrate men's position and why it needs "to be pinned down and secured" (*festa í sessi*) is the same phrase used by the Minister of Social Affairs in his speeches on the matter; the phrase is also present in the explanatory statement accompanying the law.

A quick analysis of the Icelandic language reveals that the phrase refers to power, and the reign of the ruler and how secure his position is. The main burden of the phrase is power (Jónsson, 2002). The one whose power is intact is not at risk of being overthrown (Árnason, 2002). Why this choice of phrase to refer to men's position, one may ask. It might have been more appropriate to talk about creating a tradition, for example. The phrase 'pinning down and securing' suggests that men have been kept from their children and that their powers need to be pinned down and secured to enable them to utilise their legal rights.

Not all were as optimistic about the law's effect on men's behaviour as the Independence Party MPs. Steingrímur J. Sigfússon, a member of the Socialist Party, noted that there was a long way to go before independent non-transferable rights for the father could be abolished. It was only in the year 2003, when some had proposed that the law might be revised, that fathers' rights were eventually and for the first time ever extended to 3 months. If the law is supposed to be evaluated, such as the use made by fathers of their allotted parental leave time, its full effects will not be felt for some time to come. It was, for example, impossible to estimate initial use until mid-2005, since parents have 18 months after their child is born to utilise their rights and further time is needed to allow for adaptation by parents to the new policy.

The parliamentary discussion reveals knowledge of the legislation that is being passed, not least the Social Affairs Committee that handled detailed scrutiny in the parliament. The committee concluded that savings would be made for the muncipalities, as parents would be staying home for longer periods and therefore making less use of ECEC services. Pétur Blöndal, a member of the committee, suggested that parents would share the leave by both working part time alongside part-time leave.

One MP, Einar Oddur Kristjánsson from the Independence Party, did oppose the Bill, claiming that it would jeopardise societal stability. He had long been known in Icelandic politics as 'the saviour' because of his particular political views as a former spokesperson for the Confederation of Icelandic Employers. In the parliamentary discussion, he is a supporter of 'stability' in terms of both economic and gender relations. He uses phrases such as "extremely dangerous", "not threaten the state of competition" and "keep balance, not burden". He states:

> Nobody reads the writing on the wall. For months it has been written on the wall that facing us economically are some dangers, great dangers and therefore we need to move carefully but unfortunately no one seems to notice this.... People are all ready to pass this Bill even though in the Bill the financial aspect is not well thought out.... I can agree and say that it is a good thing to increase the parental leave; it is a very good thing that fathers participate, young fathers.... [But] how are we going to finance this? Who is supposed to pay?... The condition of the State Treasury is such, I declare, that it can't increase its expenditure.... Why is the Parliament in such a hurry to pass this Bill?... Don't we have enough time to make up our minds then and then use our manhood and say who is going to pay for all this?... There is no compelling reason why this Bill needs to be made into a law at this moment.

There are some obvious gendered implications of Kristjánsson's choice of words in the passage quoted above, for example "manhood". He talks about paternity leave for "young fathers"; does that indicate that paternity leave is not for mature men? There is also a subtle reference to irresponsibility in the phrase "Who is supposed to pay?". He sees the proposed Act as threatening for the economic stability; the symbolic connotations suggestive of female irresponsibility are not hard to miss.

Kristjánsson's fellow party member, Pétur Blöndal, is quick to point out that he is in the dark about the costs:

> I think with the utmost planning the municipalities, because the need for day care centres will decrease, could save 1.5 up to 2 billion [Icelandic Krona] a year. This is not present in the explanatory statement accompanying the law. The parents themselves will save 20,000 [Icelandic Krona] each month; this has not been established either. Therefore the 80% being paid is quite ample if you take this into account. When everything is taken together it might well be the case that this Bill is not costing very much. It saves a lot elsewhere.... If the companies will focus on implementing flexible working hours and work environment, teleworking and working from home and other such measures, so the parents could of course stay at home and work but at the same time stay with their children, then this could possibly benefit the economy.

Blöndal's focus is on the labour market. His ideas about caring for an infant are also of interest, in particular how he sees the possibility of working from home and caring for a child at the same time in such a way that it will contribute to economic growth, all in harmony with his neoliberal beliefs.

What is of interest is how the issue of parental leave becomes an issue about money. Blöndal's and Kristjánsson's contributions to the debate went on for some time. In Iceland it is more common for people of different political groups to fight over money, so we interpret these events as intra-party conflicts between Blöndal and Kristjánsson, as well as Arnbjörg Sveinsdóttir, who trivialises Kristjánsson and uses patronising irony to get her point across and to calm him down: "I applaud the distinguished MP Einar Oddur Kristjánsson over this Bill. He said in the beginning that he welcomed this Bill fondly. That's what I like to hear". Kristjánsson is quick to answer back: "Unfortunately the distinguished MP did not notice correctly. I did not applaud the Bill.... I have nothing against this Bill in itself. I have nothing against increasing parental leave but people have to be aware of how they are going to pay for it".

During the debate, Kristjánsson switches his wording from 'welcoming' the proposed Act to 'having nothing against' it, implying an understatement or downgrading. What the discussion reveals is an underlying resistance. Not only is Kristjánsson the watchdog of economic stability, but he is also watching out for the status quo, guarding the gender system and traditional roles, and he uses his knowledge and expertise in economic affairs to do so. He also uses an approach known in discourse analysis as agreeing with a 'but', also known as 'managing issues of stake and interest and disclaiming' (Willig, 2001).

National spirit

It has been suggested that a women's faction within the Independence Party used its leverage to lobby for the parental leave legislation. To get a fuller understanding of how the changes in 2000 were implemented, it is important to provide the reader with a quick insight into the national spirit of Icelanders. There is a desire, possibly also a need, for a small nation to excel, and to be seen or noticed in the global context, as a speech from Drífa Hjartardóttir, an Independence Party MP, illustrates. She referred to an article in *Morgunbladid* (a daily newspaper tied to the Independence Party) by social scientist Ingólfur V. Gíslason, prior to speaking at a Nordic conference:

> Then Ingólfur says, with the permission of the Speaker of the House: "When this was decided a few weeks ago I expected to be able to use for the most part old grief laden numbers which illustrate the vile status of family affairs in Iceland and in particular the vile status of Icelandic fathers. Then Geir Haarde [then Minister of Finance, currently Prime Minister], Ingibjörg Pálmadóttir [Minister of Health] and Páll Pétursson [Minister of Social Affairs] held a press conference and announced big changes.... I immediately sent emails to my colleagues and others interested abroad and told them of this important news. Then a new

concept was born in the Nordic discourse. I received a notification
of changes in the workgroup I am supposed to participate in. Now I
am supposed to talk about the 'Icelandic model' of parental leave and
I receive a longer period of time than other speakers. And what is of
more importance, the other speakers are asked to adjust their speeches
so that they can discuss how the other Nordic countries can adapt their
schemes to the 'Icelandic model'. The thought behind the Bill that the
Ministers presented is therefore becoming a precedent, setting the tone
in the Nordic discussion." I think it is very important that this came
through today because it is very enjoyable, but unfortunately not every
day, that Iceland is in the forefront of the equality debate among the
Nordic countries.

And not only in the Nordic context is it unusual for Iceland to be at the forefront,
but also in a wider European context. For in the words of the Minister of Social
Affairs, "this matter will put us in the forefront among states in the European
Economic Area".

Conclusion

The 'Icelandic model' in parental leave schemes, with a 3-month non-transferable
'father's quota', has gained wide attention. This chapter has attempted to
contextualise the parental leave reform of 2000, examining its background,
contributing factors, main players and main rationales. It is remarkable in many
respects that Iceland has initiated the longest father's quota that now exists. It
was introduced as a fast-track social engineering measure by a liberal/right-wing
government, and in a country with long-standing liberal traditions, characterised by
a deep resentment of central authority and suspicion to governmental intervention.
While it was a part of the policy declaration of the liberal/right-wing coalition
government that came into power in 1999, it was not a very well-prepared project,
based neither on research nor on long-term policy making. In short, the reform
and the Bill that brought it about were not well informed.

Several factors were at play in the emergence of the new radical system. First,
the existing system was rather parsimonious and hence, when the new system was
introduced, very little was taken from anyone; in a manner of speaking 'nobody
loses and everyone gains'. Second, court rulings had stated that it was illegal to
discriminate between men and women in parental leave, and that the exclusion of
men violated the constitution of Iceland. In addition, the reform was a response
to external pressure, from the UN and EU, as well as a response to national
demands for more actions to be taken in gender equality issues. Third, the new
reform sat well with the prevalent emphasis on men in the Nordic gender equality
discourse. Fourth, and most importantly, specific features of national politics in
Iceland allowed this legislation to develop in an interesting way. The reform was
primarily framed as a gender equality issue and the broad political consensus

around it raises questions, since it reflects support for social engineering and state intervention that is exceptional in the liberal Icelandic political context, not least when it comes to gender issues.

Analysing the parliamentary debates reveals that even the most neoliberal factions of the liberal/right-wing Independence Party supported the reform and managed to justify it within the neoliberal ideological framework, primarily as a 'correction of market failures'. Interestingly, tension was found within the Independence Party between neoliberals supporting the reform and more conservative individuals warning about the cost of the reform and supporting economic and gender stability. The analysis shows that the making of policy in this case was more complex, creative and dynamic than a traditional left–right perspective might suggest.

Notes

[1] Leave provision described in this box refers to statutory entitlements.

[2] Due to the financial crisis at the time of publication, no euro exchange rate is given for the Icelandic krona.

[3] Complaints Committee on Equal Status Conclusion Nos. 7/1999, 9/1999 and 10/1999, available at www.rettarheimild.is/Felagsmala/KaerunefndJafnrettismala/1999 (accessed 21 October 2008).

References

Althingistidindi 2000 125 löggjafarthing (2000) Reykjavik: Althingi (Parliament of Iceland).

Árnason, M. (ed) (2002) *Íslensk ordabók* (3rd edn), Reykjavík: Edda.

Capacent Gallup (2006) *Launamyndun og kynbundinn launamunur*, Reykjavik: Capacent rannsóknir and Félagsmálaráduneytid, available at http://felagsmalaraduneyti.is/media/ acrobat-skjol/Launamunur_og_kynbundinn_launamunur_2006.pdf (accessed 21 October 2008).

Einarsdóttir, T. (1998) *Through thick and thin: Icelandic men on paternity leave*, Reykjavik: Committee on Gender Equality, City of Reykjavik.

Einarsdóttir, T. and Pétursdóttir, G.M. (2004) *Culture, custom and caring: Men's and women's possibilities for parental leave*, Akureyri and Reykjavík: Centre for Gender Equality and Centre for Women's and Gender Research.

Eydal, G.B. (2000) 'Nordic child-care policies and the case of Iceland', in P. Lang (ed) *Families and family policies in Europe*, Frankfurt am Main: Peter Land Europäischer Verlag der Wissenschaften, pp 104-26.

Félagsmálaráduneyti (1993) *Skýrsla nefndar félagsmálaráduneytis og erindi flutt á málthingi í maí 1992 um breytta stodu karla og leidir til ad auka ábyrgd theirra á fjolskyldulífi og bornum*, Reykjavík: Félagsmálaráduneyti.

Flóvenz, B.G. (2007) 'Jafnréttislog í thrjátíu ár', *Úlfljótur*, vol 60, no 1, pp 5-23.

Fréttabladid (2008) 'Vilja fedraorlof ad íslenskum haetti', 13 March, p 16.

Gill, R. (2000) 'Discourse analysis', in M.W. Bauer and G. Gaskell (eds) *Qualitative researching with text, image and sound: A practical handbook*, London: Sage Publications, pp 172–90.

Gíslason, I.V. (2007) *Parental leave in Iceland. Bringing the fathers in: Developments in the wake of new legislation in 2000*, Akureyri and Reykjavík: Centre for Gender Equality and Ministry of Social Affairs.

Jóhannesson, I.Á. (2004) *Karlmennska og jafnréttisuppeldi*, Reykjavík: Centre for Women's and Gender Research.

Jónsson, J.H. (2002) *Ordaheimur. Íslensk hugtakaordabók med orda- og ordasambandaskrá*, Reykjavík: JPV útgáfa.

Jónsdóttir, K. (2007) *"Hlustadu á thína innri rodd": Kvennaframbod í Reykjavík og Kvennalisti 1982–1987*, Reykjavík: Sögufélag.

Klinth, R. (2005) *Pappaledighet som jamstalldhetsprojekt*, Stockholm: SOU, Statens Offentliga Utredingar (No 66), available at www.regeringen.se/content/1/c6/04/79/13/7c37d086.pdf (accessed 21 October 2008).

Kristinsson, G.H. (1993) 'Valdakerfid fram til vidreisnar 1900–1959', in G. Halfdanarson and S. Kristjansson (eds) *Íslensk thjódfélagsthróun 1980-1990*, Reykjavík: Félagsvisindastofnun and Sagnfraedistofnun Háskóla Islands, pp 321-54.

Nordic Council of Ministers (1987) *The men and gender equality*, Copenhagen: Nordic Council of Ministers (Nord 1987:017).

Nordic Council of Ministers (1995a) *Towards new masculinities: Report from a Nordic conference on men and gender equality*, Copenhagen: Nordic Council of Ministers (Nord 1995:026).

Nordic Council of Ministers (1995b) *Co-operation programme for gender equality for 1995--2000* [*Nordiskt samarbetsprogram på jämställdhetsområdet 1995-2000*]. Available at: www.norden.org/pub/velfaerd/jamstalldhet/sk/US1995403/US1995403.asp (accessed 15 April 2009).

Nordic Council of Ministers (2000) *Co-operation programme for gender equality for 2000-2005* [*Ministerrådsforslag om Samarbeidsprogram: Nordisk likestillingssamarbeide 2001-2005*] Available at: www.norden.org/sagsarkiv/docs/Bet_b195.pdf (accessed 15 April 2009).

Nordic Council of Ministers (2006) *Focus on gender – Working towards an equal society: Co-operation programme for gender equality for 2006–2010*. Available at: www.norden.org/pub/velfaerd/jamstalldhet/sk/ANP2006777.pdf (accessed 15 April 2009).

Ólafsson, S. (2003) 'Contemporary Icelanders – Scandinavian or American?', *Scandinavian Review*, vol 91, no 1, pp 6-14.

Pétursdóttir, G.M. (2004) '"Ég er tilbúin ad gefa svo mikid". Sjálfraedi, karllaeg vidmid og mótsagnir í lífi útivinnandi maedra og ordraedum um ólíkt edli, getu og hlutverk', Unpublished MA thesis, University of Iceland.

Valdimarsdóttir, F.R. (2006) 'Nordic experiences with parental leave and its impact on equality between women and men', *TemaNord*, No 531, Copenhagen: Nordic Council of Ministers.

Willig, C. (2001) *Introducing qualitative research in psychology: Adventures in theory and method*, Buckingham: Open University Press.

ELEVEN

The Netherlands: bridging labour and care

Janneke Plantenga and Chantal Remery[1]

Maternity leave[2]: 16 weeks, 6 weeks before the birth and 10 weeks after at 100% of earnings, up to a ceiling equivalent to the maximum daily payment for sickness benefit (€180).

Paternity leave: 2 working days at 100% of earnings, with no ceiling, paid by the employer.

Parental leave: from 1 January 2009, 26 times the number of working hours per week per parent per child; for example, a full-time job of 38 hours a week gives a leave entitlement of 988 hours. Paid, via a fiscal benefit, at 50% of the minimum wage (€1,356.60 per month for a full-time employee).

Leave to care for a sick child: twice the number of weekly working hours per year for parents of children living at home at 70% of earnings, paid by employer.

Other: the same conditions as leave to care for a sick child apply in the case of a sick partner or parent. There is also long-term compassionate leave for employees with a child, partner or parent with a life-threatening illness, which entitles employees to unpaid leave of up to 6 times their working hours per week, to be taken on a part-time basis. An employer can refuse short-term care leave (for a sick child, parent or partner) and long-term compassionate leave if the organisation's interests might be seriously harmed. In addition, for these leaves and paternity leave employers are permitted to deviate from the statutory entitlements by collective labour agreement or (under certain conditions) by written agreement with the works council or staff representatives. In these cases, employees can be offered more or less than the statutory entitlement (for example, less payment, a shorter leave or no right at all).

All employees who have completed one year's continuous employment with their present employer have the right to increase or decrease their working hours; this does not apply to employers with less than 10 employees, and an employer can refuse to grant the request if the interests of the organisation might be seriously harmed.

The Netherlands is a member state of the European Union (EU). It has the highest level of part-time employment among men and women of any member state in the EU or Organisation for Economic Co-operation and Development (OECD). In 2006, 44% of women and 21% of men entitled to parental leave took leave, averaging 9 months and 10 hours a week (mothers) and 11 months and 8 hours a week (fathers). During their period of leave, mothers worked on average 60% of their working hours, fathers 80%.

Introduction

Until recently, Dutch leave policies were very limited. The only policy was a 12-week pregnancy and maternity leave for married women, which was introduced by the Sickness Benefit Act of 1930. Yet by the end of the 20th century, as a result of changing family forms and labour market patterns, leave arrangements had become a major policy issue, with debates focusing on entitlement, length of leave and income support. The first important change was the extension of maternity leave from 12 to 16 weeks in 1990. In 1991, parental leave was introduced, allowing for leave being taken on a part-time and unpaid basis for a maximum of 6 months. Paternity leave and emergency leave followed in 1997. In 2001, legislation on different types of leave to care for children and other relatives was integrated into one encompassing framework: the Work and Care Act. In 2005, after years of debate, a long-term compassionate leave was introduced, to assist a partner, child or parent with a life-threatening disease. The latest development is the life-course scheme, which was implemented in 2006, and which created the possibility of saving part of earnings in order to fund a subsequent period of non-employment including parental leave.

This chapter will address the development of leave policies, in particular parental leave, in the Netherlands. This development has involved different interpretations of the purpose of leave and the division of responsibilities between the government, social partners and parents. Starting from a position in which parental leave was interpreted as a way to facilitate part-time employment, the Parental Leave Act provided a basic entitlement to take part-time, unpaid leave for a relatively short period of time. It was left to the social partners to supplement this minimum, for example in terms of length or payment. Over time, however, public responsibility for leave has increased. This is apparent not only in the increasing number of leave policies, but also in a growing public involvement in the provision of income support. During this process, the interpretation of parental leave seems to have changed from a labour market instrument pure and simple into a more complex instrument also intended to facilitate parenthood and the well-being of children.

First debates: the introduction of the Parental Leave Act in 1991

In the Netherlands, the early debates around parental leave mainly focused on the costs and benefits in terms of the (female) employment rate. Only rarely were leave policies discussed as part of the care system with young children as the primary beneficiaries; rather the design of parental leave was inspired by practical feasibility and labour market effects. An important consideration was to increase the relatively low rates of employment among women, and it was assumed that part-time working hours were important in achieving this goal. Parental leave policy, therefore, should enable young parents to work part time during a period of heavy care responsibilities. A second important consideration in these early debates was that leave policy should favour the equal division of paid and unpaid work between men and women. Consequently, there was a strong emphasis on introducing an individual right and making the leave arrangement attractive for men.

An important early initiative on parental leave was the request to the government in 1980 by the parliament's Permanent Commission for Emancipation Policy to provide a note on parental leave (TK, 1985-1986). One of the immediate causes of this request was the EU draft directive on parental leave that was being prepared at that time (Boswijk, 1992) (see Chapter Fifteen). The government's response came about a year later. In line with the Dutch tradition of consultation, the Minister of Social Affairs and Employment and the State Secretary of Culture, Recreation and Social Work sought advice from the Equal Opportunities Board (Emancipatieraad) and the Social and Economic Council of the Netherlands (Sociaal-Economische Raad SER). The Equal Opportunities Board was an independent advisory body on equal opportunities, which was active between 1981 and 1997. The SER, established in 1950, is the main advisory body to the Dutch government and parliament on national and international social and economic policy. It represents the interests of trades unions and industry, with the aim of helping to create consensus on national and international socioeconomic issues.

In its request for advice, the government specified two important considerations for any legal provision on parental leave. A first consideration referred to the fact that the overall labour force participation rate of women was increasing but at the same time many women left their job after the birth of a child. According to the government, there should be more opportunities enabling parents to reduce their working hours and not have to leave the labour market altogether. Second, as part of a general emancipation policy, the government had committed itself to a fairer distribution of paid and unpaid work. In order to reach this goal, the responsibilities for raising children should be shared more equally between men and women, so the introduction of parental leave was supposed to be helpful in this respect (SER, 1983, p 70). The government's starting point was "that supporting the combination of parenthood and paid employment is the shared responsibility of parents (employees), society as whole and employers" (SER, 1983, p 69). It was emphasised that parental leave is one means to support the combination of paid work and parenthood, alongside part-time employment, childcare facilities and flexibility of working hours (SER, 1983, p 68). Moreover, the government considered a part-time leave preferable so that the leave taker might remain attached to the labour market.

The government remained rather cautious about income support for leave takers. Although it recognised that the responsibility of society could be expressed through payment made to parental leave takers, a paid leave financed by the public purse was not considered feasible, given the socioeconomic situation of that time. A statutory paid parental leave was also not considered to be an option as this would disadvantage the labour market position of newly weds and persons with young children, in particular women. In summary, the right to parental leave as such was considered an important first step, but payment of the leave should be left to the social partners (SER, 1983, p 71).

The advice of the Equal Opportunities Board

The Equal Opportunities Board argued that the government should strive for an emancipated society in which each individual is engaged in paid and unpaid (care) activities (Emancipatieraad, 1983). This implied a substantial reduction of working hours per day or per week in order to have sufficient time to care for dependents. In addition, there should be an adequate system of childcare services. From this perspective, parental leave was considered as a temporary measure until the emancipated society was fully realised.

In its advice, the Equal Opportunities Board also recommended that each parent with a child younger than 4 years should have a right to take part-time leave by reducing their working hours to (a minimum of) 20 hours per week. The threshold of 20 working hours was chosen because it would maintain sufficient commitment to employment and limit depreciation of human capital. It was further suggested that the leave should be paid during the first year at the level of 50% of previous earnings. Such support would smooth the transition of family income towards an ideal situation in which both parents would work on a less-than-full-time basis. The board also advised that the leave should be an individual right in order to avoid only women taking it up.

The advice of the SER

Not surprisingly, the SER advice on parental leave differed significantly from the advice of the Equal Opportunities Board. While the Equal Opportunities Board emphasised the responsibility of the government for the relationship between work and family life, the SER placed the primary responsibility on the parents. It was considered as incorrect "to shift responsibilities that result from private choices to society and employers" (SER, 1983, p 31). Society and employers should, however, cooperate in finding solutions for the 'problem' of combining work and care. Was there a need for legal regulation? SER did not have a unanimous answer to this key question. The members representing employers and the majority (7 out of 13) of the independent experts were against legislation, referring to both principal and practical objections. But the members representing employees and 3 (out of 13) independent members (3 independent members abstained) were in favour. They emphasised the social importance of parental leave for "executing the right to employment" (SER, 1983, p 34).

As such, this part of the council supported an unpaid, part-time leave, with a minimum of 20 working hours, during the first 3 years after birth. During the first 8 months, the non-working hours should be regarded as (unpaid) leave; after this period, there should be a right to work part time. When the child reached primary school age, employees could request employers to increase the number of working hours to the original level.

The introduction of the Parental Leave Act

After some years of debate, in 1985 the government decided in favour of legislation. A proposal was presented in the policy note *Combination parenthood-paid employment* (*Combinatie ouderschap-betaalde arbeid*) (TK, 1985-1986). An important reason for taking this step was that social partners were taking no initiatives on parental leave, for example not including it in collective agreements. The proposal emphasised that the legal entitlement should be kept to a minimum, presenting employers with as few problems as possible (TK, 1985-1986, p 23). It provided for an unpaid leave of up to 6 months for employees with at least one year's service with their current employer. The proposals of the Equal Opportunities Board and part of the SER for a leave period of 4 years were considered incompatible with the aim of a minimum standard and would result in too many organisational problems (see also TK, 1987-1988, p 4). In addition, the government did not follow the advice that the leave should be taken immediately after the birth as both parents taking up leave at the same time would result in the loss of too much income. Instead, the government proposed that parental leave could be taken within 2 years after the birth of the child. This would enable both parents to use their individual right to leave (TK, 1985-1986, p 30).

The proposed leave was unpaid, as parents were considered primarily responsible for raising their children. In addition, it was argued that a paid leave would result in an undesirable increase in the tax burden for both the private and public sectors. Members of two Social Democratic parties, who were not part of the government, proposed a motion to investigate the possibility of a (partially) paid leave, but this motion was rejected by the parliamentary majority.

In line with the earlier advice, the proposed leave was on a part-time basis: there was no right to full-time leave and the employee should remain active in the labour market for at least 20 hours per week. In addition, parental leave was defined as an individual, non-transferable right, not a family right. Defining parental leave as a family right would increase the risk that the take-up rate among women would be much higher than among men. On pragmatic grounds, an individual right is easier to implement as most parents work for different employers (TK 1985-1986, p 24). Variations from the standard legal provision were allowed by way of collective labour agreements, as long as the total number of leave hours was at least equal to the legal entitlement.

It took another 2 years before the Bill was brought before parliament (TK, 1987-1988). With a few exceptions, this Bill was similar to the earlier proposal. One exception referred to the time period within which the leave should be taken. In the final Bill, this was extended from 2 to 4 years. Four years would cover the period until children started primary school (admission at 4 years is voluntary but nearly universal; compulsory school age is 5 years) and would as such provide more flexibility for parents. It took another 2 years to get the Bill adopted. So, finally, in 1991 Parental Leave Act came into force.

Developments between 1991 and 2001: increasing flexibility and transparency

Although the parental leave legislation was welcomed as a first important step towards a more gender-equal society, there were several problems with the actual design of the leave policy. A first evaluation of the Parental Leave Act, in 1994, indicated low take-up; approximately 27% of the female and 11% of the male employees who were entitled to take parental leave actually did so (Spaans and van der Werf, 1994). The evaluation also indicated that the parental leave legislation only played a minor role in the introduction of part-time working hours for young parents. Indeed, the proportion of women who decided to work part time immediately after the birth of a child was higher than the proportion who took up parental leave, reflecting in part the effect of the spread of part-time working hours that had been taking place since the mid-1980s (Plantenga, 2002). Rather – and perhaps not surprisingly – it appeared that both female and male leave takers indicated that they took up leave in order to spend more time caring for their children. Yet the stipulations of the Act – especially the 20 hours threshold – excluded quite a number of (part-time) working mothers from taking leave.

Another problem was that the actual design of the leave policy did not favour an equal sharing of paid and unpaid work. It was presumed that a more flexible approach, especially the possibility to spread the leave hours over a longer period of time, would increase the take-up among men. A final argument against the rather rigid part-time orientation of the parental leave legislation was that this approach was not in line with the EU's draft directive on parental leave, which (either implicitly or explicitly) favoured a full-time leave.

The perceived remedy to solve these problems was to adopt a different orientation towards parental leave. While the 1991 Act could be interpreted as introducing a statutory right to reduce working hours against the background of a rather standard working time regime, the new proposal brought parental leave in line with the growing reality of rather diverse and individualised working hours. In new draft proposals (TK, 1995-1996), parents still had the legal right to lower their working hours by 50% over a period of 26 weeks. But the total amount of leave was related to actual working time, being set at 13 times the number of contracted weekly working hours. Moreover, employees may ask to spread the leave hours over a longer period than 6 months or to take more hours per week, and employers can only refuse if their business interests would be severely damaged as a result. It was also suggested that the period until which the leave could be taken should be extended from 4 to 6 years, to facilitate the transition from childcare facilities to primary school. As a result of this proposal, the flexibility of the leave policy was increased and was also extended to part-time workers.

Despite these major changes, the leave would remain unpaid. The proposal to introduce a certain level of payment, as suggested for example by Arachne, the Women's Lobby Group, and the Equal Opportunities Board, was not adopted. The government persisted in its original view that income support during leave is an issue to be settled by the social partners in industrial agreements. The evaluation of the Act in 1994 gave no reason to change this view; the argument that leave was only accessible for the happy few was undermined by the fact that the average income of leave takers did not differ substantially from the overall average income (TK, 1993-1994).

The amendments proposed by the government were passed, but so too was an additional amendment, tabled by a member of a Social Democratic party. This proposed that the period until which the leave can be taken should be extended until the child is 8 years old, in line with the EU directive on parental leave that had been adopted in 1996 (TK, 1997). The revised Parental Leave Act came into force on 1 July 1997.

2001 Work and Care Act

Between 1991 and 2001 the policies regarding working parents also started to change. By the end of the 1990s, the government had explicitly recognised that it was no longer feasible to treat the relationship between work and family life as mainly the private responsibility of employees (TK 1998-1999, p 6); rather, it should be the shared responsibility of employees, employers and the government. Against this changed political background, the Work and Care Act was proposed, taking this shared responsibility as an explicit point of departure. The Act's goal was to streamline the different leave provisions, while also introducing some new ones. Further flexibilisation of parental leave was proposed, so that it could be divided up and taken in several parts. In order to prevent too much fragmentation (with the risk that the leave might be used for other than care purposes), a maximum of three parts was proposed (TK 1998-1999, p 29).

The Work and Care Act came into force on 1 December 2001. Consolidating previous legislation, the Act included the right to paid maternity leave (16 weeks), paid paternity leave (2 days), unpaid parental leave (for a maximum of 6 months on a part-time basis) and provisions in case of adoption and multiple births. In addition to the specifically child-related leave benefits, provisions for care for family or household members included paid emergency leave, paid short-term carers' leave and a regulation to finance a career break in order to care or to study. Since June 2005, the Work and Care Act has been extended, with an entitlement available to all employees to take (unpaid) long-term leave to care for a terminally ill child, partner or parent. The design of the long-term compassionate leave follows to some extent the logic of the parental leave legislation. The maximum duration of this leave is six times the weekly number of working hours, to be taken in a period of 12 successive months. In contrast to parental leave, however, compassionate leave is not a statutory right; employers may refuse on grounds of causing serious harm to business.

Employers' involvement

From the very beginning, employers have been given an important role in the introduction of leave policies within the Dutch working time regime. By way of collective labour agreements, the social partners are supposed to top up public policy, which is mainly concerned with guaranteeing the minimum right. In order to create some flexibility and to allow for tailor-made solutions, the leave legislation is also of a so-called three quarter mandatory legal nature. This means that deviation from the standard legal provision is allowed by way of collective agreements or by a decision of the employees' council. In the case of parental leave, such deviating agreements are, for example, possible with regard to the splitting up of the leave and/or the spreading of the leave over the year. Moreover, the age stipulation (the fact that the leave has to be taken up before the eighth birthday of the child) may be changed.

The particular role of employers in the development of leave policy reflects the overall system of industrial relations with consultation and involvement at the central level. At the same time, it is a system that emphasises the importance of decentralisation and tailor-made solutions, and yet the division of responsibilities is rather fluid. As the OECD puts it: "The government specifies issues that it thinks should be the topics under discussion in industrial bargaining. If the outcomes are – as they have been over leave, working time flexibility and childcare, to some extent – it may then consider imposing legislation" (OECD, 2002, p 16). An interesting illustration of this search for the optimal division of responsibilities is offered by the issue of payment for leave.

Within the context of the Parental Leave Act, the matter of payment was left to the employees and the employers; collective agreements should have made provision for income support. However, several studies indicated that the majority of employers did not offer any payment during the period of parental leave and this majority proved to be fairly stable. The unpaid character of the leave had a negative impact on the take-up rate, an evaluation in 1999 indicating that only one in five eligible parents actually made use of this right (Grootscholte et al, 2000). Yet in workplaces with paid leave, the take-up rates were five times higher than in those without paid leave. Two thirds of the parents who were entitled to the leave but did not use it said that they would have taken it if there had been a payment at the level of 70% of their normal earnings.

The rather reluctant attitude of the employers and the effects of this attitude on take-up rates created a growing public support for additional measures. A more positive approach from the side of the employers was also favoured because of the presumption that higher take-up rates would contribute to a more equal sharing of unpaid care work, which was still an important goal of Dutch emancipation policy. Finally, arrangements for paid leave would fit with developments in Europe, where an increasing number of EU member states offered paid parental leave (TK 2000-2001, p 5).

But making paid leave mandatory was still considered a bridge too far, given the primary role employers were supposed to play in matters concerning labour conditions. The solution was found in changing the fiscal incentive structure. By 2001, employers could deduct 50% of the costs of providing paid leave to their employees from their tax bill, on condition that the payment during parental leave was at least 70% of the minimum wage. In addition, payment should be included in the collective agreement or the payment should be available to at least three quarters of the company's employees. With this tax deduction, the actual cost of taking leave became the shared responsibility of the employee, the employer and the government.

Employers, however, have never been overly enthusiastic about the Work and Care Act, nor have they been very eager to supplement the legal provisions for parental leave. Research carried out in 2004 indicated than only half of employers were familiar with the Act; see Table 11.1 for more details. In fact, the largest group of employers could be categorised as 'not familiar and having a neutral to negative attitude' (41%); small companies in particular did not have a positive view on these matters. A second group is not familiar with the Act either, but is less negative. These employers offer the minimum legal leave provisions, although they are not exactly aware of all the details of the legislation. A third group is familiar with the Act, but view it negatively; to their mind, the employee should be primarily responsible. This attitude is particularly strong among firms in agriculture and financial services. A fourth group is also rather reluctant. These companies understand the importance of leave facilities, but think that the employer should not bear all the risk; if there is a need for leave, the employee can take some days off. Finally, a fifth group is familiar with the law and these employers have a rather positive attitude; they offer their employees at least the legal requirements and even encourage the use of leave by providing information.

In sum, the employer is an important player in Dutch leave policy. At the same time, however, the employer is a rather reluctant player and not very familiar with all the details. There is a sense that the employer is overburdened by the details of the measures. The research also indicates that – more than 10 years after the introduction of the Parental Leave Act – only a minority of the potential leave takers are entitled to paid parental leave (van der Linden and van der Werf, 2004).

Table 11.1: Typology of employers with regard to the Work and Care Act

Typology	%	Most typical sector / firm
Not familiar with the Act; neutral to negative attitude and offering few if any possibilities	41	Employers with less than 50 employees; construction; other services
Not familiar with the Act; positive attitude and offering legal possibilities	13	
Familiar with the Act; neutral to negative attitude and offering few if any possibilities	18	Agriculture; financial services
Familiar with the Act; in principle positive attitude but offering only limited possibilities	14	
Familiar with the Act; positive attitude and offering at least legal possibilities	14	Employers with more than 50 employees; education, health; welfare,
Total	100	

Source: Van der Linden and Van der Werf, 2004, pp 76-7

Parental leave: take-up rates

The fact that young parents in the Netherlands are not entitled to paid parental leave presumably explains why take-up is still far from universal; see Table 11.2 for further details. In 2006, the take-up among women amounted to 44% in contrast to 21% among men. Although men's take-up rate is considerably lower, it is fairly high compared with that of other European countries (Plantenga and Remery, 2005).

Table 11.2 indicates that there are also slight differences in the average length of the leave taken by men or women. Men on average take 8 hours of leave per week and spread their leave hours over 11 months. Women take more hours of leave per week, as a result of which the duration of the leave period is, on average, somewhat shorter. The data seem to indicate that, in a typical case, both parents use the possibility to spread the leave hours over a longer period of time.

Table 11.2: Take-up of parental leave among employees entitled to the leave, 2000–06

	Take up of parental leave		Average length of leave, in hours per week		Average length of leave, in months	
	Female	Male	Female	Male	Female	Male
2000	39.0	15.8	12	9	8	11
2001	45.3	15.7	12	8	8	10
2002	37.3	15.9	12	9	8	11
2003	42.1	15.9	12	8	8	10
2004	39.6	18.0	11	9	9	10
2005	44.1	18.9	11	8	8	11
2006	43.8	21.0	10	8	9	11

Source: CBS Statline

Part-time parental leave is thus still the usual option, despite the possibility to organise leave on a full-time basis.

This is in line with the overall emphasis on part-time working within Dutch society. Whereas in some of the other European countries leave is taken before the parents start to use childcare facilities, in the Netherlands a more parallel approach is advocated. To balance work and family life, parents use part-time working hours, partly facilitated by parental leave legislation, in combination with part-time use of childcare provision. One consequence of this is that childcare services take children at a very young age, as soon as the 16 weeks of maternity leave has finished.

More detailed research indicates that the take-up rate of parents is related to both personal and organisational characteristics (van Luijn and Keuzenkamp, 2004, pp 167-8). An important variable is educational attainment: the higher the level of education, the higher the take-up rate. Another important factor is the orientation to paid work. Perhaps surprisingly, employees who are more oriented to paid work have a higher take-up rate of parental leave. This can be explained by the fact that employees less oriented to paid work either drop out of the labour market completely for a period of time, or choose to work part time immediately after maternity leave. Orientation to paid work should not, however, be mixed up with ambition, as ambitious employees have a lower take-up rate. Take-up is also lower when employees presume that it will be difficult to combine work and family. Another factor is the number of reconciliation measures offered by the employer; there is a positive connection between the number of measures offered by the employer, which may be a proxy for a modern organisational culture, and parental leave take-up.

Finally, the culture of presence has an impact: the more an employee feels that is unacceptable to be absent from the workplace, the lower the take-up rate. Surprisingly, when controlling for other variables, gender is not significantly related to take-up of parental leave. At a more general level, it appears that employees entitled to leave do not take it because of work-related reasons ('the job does not allow it'; 'colleagues have to take over', 'the continuity of the work may be endangered'). The loss of income also plays an important role in not taking leave.

To sum up the current state of affairs, it seems that parental leave has become quite acceptable to young parents and that the spread of leave over a longer period of time has become a particularly useful option for balancing work and care. In a typical case, well-educated young parents with an orientation to paid work will opt for parental leave for one or 2 days a week. If they both worked full time before the birth of the child, the mother will probably reduce her working hours to 3 or 4 days a week, while the father reduces his full-time working week by one day. A childcare service will be used on a part-time basis in order to cover the 2 or 3 days when both parents are at work. After the leave period, the mother will most probably keep her working hours at 3 or 4 days a week, but the father is more likely to go back to full-time work.

Recent developments: towards a more public responsibility?

Although the Work and Care Act was considered as a final piece of legislation, the debate around this subject has never completely stopped. Important issues that have been raised include the need to increase the labour force participation rate of women, the well-being of young families, the growing individualisation of working times and the modernisation of the social security system. At the same time, there has been a growing reluctance to add just another piece of legislation to an already complex dossier. Rather, the emphasis has been on finding an innovative and flexible approach that would solve several problems and would fit into a more mature and individualistic approach towards social security. In this context, the life-course perspective has become an important frame of references for both policy makers and academics, on the grounds that it would benefit young families who suffer from the stresses of combining employment and childrearing, would favour individualisation and diversification, and would result in a more sustainable participation rate (Plantenga, 2005).

The first initiative to move to a life-course scheme was made in 2002 but it took until 2006 before the actual Dutch life-course scheme came into effect. According to this scheme employees may save up to 12% of their gross annual income tax-free for a 'life-course product'. Employees may use it to finance a period of non-participation in the labour force. In principle, this period of leave may be for all kinds of different purposes, like going on holiday, care obligations or taking a sabbatical. A maximum sum equivalent to 210% of the previous year's earnings may be saved, which amounts to 3 years of leave at 70% of earnings; the deferred tax principle is applicable, so that taxes are not paid on the savings account, but solely on money withdrawn. In addition, there is a bonus for each participating year, so that the life-course scheme can be described as a fiscally facilitated private saving scheme.

In theory, the introduction of the life-course scheme seems to indicate a shift towards more individualised systems of social security – that is a shift from public to private responsibility. Yet the scheme is flexible enough to create a mixture of savings and insurances, and private and public responsibilities. By granting an extra fiscal benefit if the leave period is used for certain purposes, defined as socially beneficial, the scheme offers possibilities to introduce public funding into an otherwise private scheme.

This is exactly what happened with parental leave. Parents who take up parental leave and participate in the life-course scheme have access to an extra fiscal benefit equivalent to 50% of the minimum wage (€1,356.60 per month for a full-time employee) for the statutory period of parental leave. By granting this tax credit, the public responsibility for parental leave is underlined. Personal savings within the context of the life-course scheme may be used to fund a longer period of leave or to increase the level of payment. The tax credit is, however, not linked to drawing down private funds; it is available for simply participating in the life-course scheme. As a result, although the statutory right for parental leave is still unpaid, young parents have access to some financial support while taking leave as long as they participate in the life-course scheme.

This particular organisation of income support for leave takers may not be a very elegant or transparent solution, as the time component of parental leave is now part of the Work and Care Act, while the payment is organised within the context of the life-course scheme. Yet, it indicates a shift in how leave is interpreted, from being seen primarily as a scheme enabling part-time working hours for parents to one in which the well-being of young parents and children also plays a role. The introduction of a tax credit also indicates the difficulty of generating full coverage for paid leave by collective labour agreements. The reluctance of employers to provide income support is acknowledged and the government has taken over responsibility for this. Within this context, it is only logical that following the introduction of the parental credit within the life-course scheme, the fiscal facility for employers who provide paid parental leave has been terminated.

The latest development in parental leave legislation concerns the length of the leave period. At the start of the fourth cabinet of Jan Peter Balkenende in 2007, the Coalition Agreement stated that parents should be able to combine labour and care, working and raising children. "In the rush hour of life it should be possible to organize some time out. The life-course scheme also serves that purpose. The statutory right to parental leave will be lengthened from 13 to 26 weeks per employee and will not be transferable. The life-course scheme will be reorganised accordingly" (Coalition Agreement, 2007, p 29).

As of 1 January 2009, this extension of the parental leave period has come into effect. Moreover, the condition of participation to the life-course scheme in order to have access to the fiscal benefit equivalent of 50% of the minimum wage for the period of leave has been abolished; this is now available to all parents (SZW, 2008). In addition, parental leave will become more flexible, although further details in this respect are not yet available (JG, 2008). Again, this is an indication of a slightly different interpretation of the leave policy. It is likely that this somewhat broader perspective has been inspired by the involvement of a right-wing Christian Democrat Party with a high profile on family policy.

The slight reorientation also seems to imply a shift from a concurrent towards a more consecutive relationship between leave arrangements and childcare provision. In the latest Emancipation Policy Note, for example, it is said that the 26 weeks per parent has been chosen so that working parents, when taking up parental leave, can care for their child during his/her first year (OCW, 2007, p 31). This implies a clear break from the early considerations, in which the leave taker was supposed to remain attached to the labour market and in which the parental leave scheme should only facilitate part-time working hours.

Conclusion

For a long time, the Dutch policies on parental leave have been rather limited compared with those in some other European countries. The Parental Leave Act complied only to the minimum requirements of the EU directive on parental leave. In fact, it seems fair to say that Dutch policy makers have always had some ambivalence towards the instrument of leave. It is likely that this ambivalence is partly related to the dominance of Christian Democratic parties on social issues and the ensuing emphasis on individual responsibility. Rather than the state being directly involved in family matters, the emphasis has been more on enabling parents to assume their own responsibilities.

Another factor that has contributed to the rather ambivalent attitude is the Dutch working time regime that is characterised by relatively short full-time working hours and a high rate of part-time employment. As a result, the pressure for extended leave policies has never been strong. Rather, parental leave policy has been regarded as something that should facilitate attachment to the labour market during a period in which care responsibilities are rather heavy. As such, parental leave legislation has always entitled parents to work part time. In line with this, the payment issue has only been of secondary importance.

Another characteristic element of the Dutch legislation is the emphasis on flexibility. In principle, the standard regulation (as valid until 1 January 2009) set out in legislation provides a 6-month entitlement to part-time leave. If the employer agrees, however, the hours of leave may be taken on a full-time basis (covering a period of 3 months) or may be spread over the year. It is presumed that this flexible design is one of the reasons why the take-up rate of men is relatively high in the Netherlands.

The development of parental leave legislation also demonstrates the search for the proper design of policy. On the whole, this search seems rather 'incremental' and problem-oriented; there has been no particular, goal-oriented plan. As such, the specific details of the parental leave legislation seem to illustrate the typical Dutch problem-solving style of decision making (see, for example, Hemerijck and Visser, 1999). This particular style and the heavy reliance on party political compromises may not always translate into very transparent regulations. This is illustrated in the case of parental leave by the entitlement to leave and the entitlement to income support being covered by different legislation. This is not a very carefully considered design and it is quite conceivable that this complexity reduces take-up of parental leave (de Haan and Plantenga, 2007).

Apparently, this complexity has been recognised by the policy makers, as the link between payment of parental leave and the life-course scheme has been disconnected. As of 1 January 2009 all (new) parents taking parental leave are entitled to a fiscal benefit equivalent to 50% of the minimum wage during the statutory period of leave. As such, the inclusion of payment within the life-course scheme may be assessed as a slight detour, which has made financial support for leave takers from public funds more acceptable. Within a European perspective, the extension of the period of parental leave to 26 weeks is certainly an improvement. The level of payment, however, remains rather low, which raises serious concerns on the affordability and, related to this, the take-up of parental leave.

Notes

[1] The authors wish to thank Ivy Koopmans for her helpful comments on an earlier draft.

[2] Leave provision described here refers to statutory entitlements.

References

Boswijk, L. (1992) *Ouderschapsverlof in Nederland. Literatuuroverzicht januari 1980–juli 1991*, Amsterdam: Discom.

Coalition Agreement (2007) *Coalition agreement between the parliamentary parties of the Christian Democratic Alliance, Labour Party and Christian Union*, Publisher unknown.

de Haan, P. and Plantenga, J. (2007) 'Ouderschapsverlof in de levensloop', *Economisch Statistische Berichten*, 5 oktober, pp 598-9.

Emancipatieraad (1983) *Zorg en arbeid. Advies over verlofregelingen voor de zorg van kinderen en anderen, kinderopvang en arbeidstijdverkorting*, Den Haag: Emancipatieraad.

Grootscholte, M., Bouwmeester, J.A.and de Klaver, P. (2000) *Evaluatie Wet op het ouderschapsverlof*, 's-Gravenhage: Ministerie van Sociale Zaken en Werkgelegenheid.

Hemerijck, A. and Visser, J. (1999) 'Beleidsleren in de Nederlandse verzorgingsstaat', *Beleid en Maatschappij*, vol 26, no 1, pp 13-26.

JG (2008) *Beleidsagenda 2009*, Den Haag: Programmaministerie Jeud en Gezin.

Plantenga, J. (2002) 'Combining work and care in the older model: an assessment of the Dutch part-time strategy', *Critical Social Policy*, vol 22, no 1, pp 53-72.

Plantenga, J. (2005) 'Dutch debates: modernising social security by introducing the life-course as a frame of reference', in P. de Gijsel and H. Schenk (eds) *Multidisciplinary economics: The birth of a new economics faculty in the Netherlands*, Dordrecht: Springer, pp 53-64.

Plantenga, J. and Remery, C., w.a.o. Helming, P. (2005) *Reconciliation of work and private life: A comparative review of thirty European countries*, Luxembourg: Office for the Official Publications of the European Communities.

OCW (2007) *Meer kansen voor vrouwen. Emancipatiebeleid 2008–2011*, Den Haag: Ministerie van OCW.

OECD (Organisation for Economic Co-operation and Development) (2002) *Babies and bosses. Reconciling work and familiy life. Volume 1: Australia, Denmark and the Netherlands*, Paris: OECD.

SER (Sociaal-Economische Raad) (1983) *Advies combinatie ouderschaps- en beroepstaken*, Den Haag: Sociaal-Economische Raad.

Spaans, J. and van der Werf, C. (1994) *Evaluatie van de Wet op het ouderschapsverlof*, 's-Gravenhage: VUGA.

SZW (2008) *Plan van aanpak vervolg advies Commissie Arbeidsparticipatie*, Den Haag: Ministerie van Sociale Zaken en Werkgelegenheid.

TK (1985-1986) *Combinatie ouderschap-betaalde arbeid*, Den Haag: Tweede Kamer vergaderjaar 1985-1986, 19 368, nos 1-2.

TK (1987–1988) *Regelen betreffende de aanspraak op ouderschapsverlof (Wet op het ouderschapsverlof)*, Den Haag: Tweede Kamer vergaderjaar 1987-1988, 20 528, no 3.

TK (1993–1994) *Voortgangsrapportage inzake de positie van vrouwen in de arbeid*, Den Haag: Tweede Kamer vergaderjaar 1993-1994, 22 913, no 15.

TK (1995–1996) *Wijzging van titel 7.10 (arbeidsovereenkomst) van het Burgerlijk Wetboek met betrekking tot ouderschapsverlof*, Den Haag: Tweede Kamer vergaderjaar 1995-1996, 24 869, no 3.

TK (1997) *Handelingen Tweede Kamer over het wetsvoorstel Wijziging van titel 7.10 (arbeidsovereenkomst) van het Burgerlijk Wetboek met betrekking tot het ouderschapsverlof (24869)*, Den Haag: Tweede Kamer 45e vergadering, 28 januari 1997, pp 3577-87.

TK (1998–1999) *Arbeid en zorg*, Den Haag: Tweede Kamer vergaderjaar 1998-1999, 26 447, no 2.

TK (2000–2001) *Wijziging van belastingwetten c.a. (Belastingplan 2001)*, Den Haag: Tweede Kamer vergaderjaar 2000-2001, 27 431, no 3.

van der Linden, L. and van der Werf, C. (2004) *Ervaringen van werkgevers met de Wet arbeid en zorg*, Leiden: Research voor Beleid.

van Luijn, H. and Keuzenkamp, S. (2004) *Werkt verlof?*, Den Haag: Sociaal en Cultureel Planbureau.

TWELVE

Norway: the making of the father's quota

Berit Brandth and Elin Kvande

Maternity leave[1]: there is no separate maternity leave except for pregnant women who must stop work because of chemical, biological or physical hazards ('pregnancy leave'). Part of parental leave is reserved for women.

Paternity leave: 2 weeks. Any payment is made by employers and depends on collective bargaining.

Parental leave: 44 weeks at 100% of earnings or 54 weeks at 80% up to a ceiling of 6 times the basic national insurance benefit payment, NOK421,536 (€48,455)[2]. Nine weeks are reserved for mothers and 6 weeks are for fathers (*fedrekvoten* or 'father's quota'). The remaining period is a family entitlement and may be taken by either mother or father.

Leave to care for sick children: up to 10 days per year per parent with one or two children under 12 years at 100% of earnings up to a ceiling of NOK421,536; 15 days if more than two children.

Other: each parent has the right to one year of unpaid leave after parental leave.

Parents with a child aged 12–36 months are entitled to receive a cash benefit on condition that they do not use a full-time place in a publicly funded childcare centre. In 2008, the benefit was NOK3,303 (€380) per child per month.

Norway is a Nordic country, but not a member state of the European Union. It does not have a separate system of maternity leave; part of parental leave is reserved for mothers and a shorter period for fathers. Prior to the introduction of the father's quota, less than 4% of fathers took some parental leave; latest figures show that 89% now take leave, with 70% taking more than 5 weeks. It is most common for parents to choose the option of longer leave with reduced payment.

There is an entitlement to early childhood education and care (ECEC) for children from 12 months of age.

Introduction

Norway was the first country to reserve part of paid parental leave for fathers, making it a leader in parental leave policies and fathers' rights. Gender-neutral parental leave had been available for fathers from the 1970s, but few had taken up this opportunity to share parental leave with the mother. The father's quota, introduced in 1993, gave fathers an exclusive right to 4 weeks of parental leave, which in principle could not be transferred to the mother. From its very start, the father's quota proved to be a success judging by its high take-up rate.

Several other countries have since followed Norway's lead. But the Norwegian case is interesting because Norway had long been regarded as the most conservative of the Nordic countries with respect to employment for women and ECEC services for children (Leira, 1992). The aim of this chapter is to contribute to understanding what Diane Sainsbury (2001) has called 'the Norwegian puzzle'. It will explore how the construction of statutory parental leave rights for fathers can be explained in the Norwegian context by looking at the debates prior to their introduction. The point of departure is the characteristics of the Norwegian welfare state, which strongly influence family policies. The chapter will also consider how the political parties in Norway managed to achieve political consensus on this issue, and the influence of the men's movement, particularly the Committee on Men's Role that was active in the late 1980s.

Dualism in Norwegian family policy

Family policies are part of general welfare state policies in Norway. Generally speaking, there has been political consensus about the development of the Norwegian welfare state, most political parties identifying with its stable ideological basis. The Scandinavian welfare state model has been identified by Esping-Andersen as a social democratic regime distinct from the liberal and conservative regimes (Esping-Andersen, 1990; Esping-Andersen et al, 2002). One important characteristic is that it builds on egalitarianism as a core value in policy making. The political scientist Helga Hernes has described it as 'woman friendly' because of the way the state takes responsibility for reproduction, thus facilitating changes in women's lives (Hernes, 1987). The concept has been critically examined in later literature, and the relationship between gender equality and woman friendliness questioned (Borchorst and Siim, 2002). Nevertheless, it identifies another important characteristic, with much in common with what Esping-Andersen (1990) later termed 'defamilialisation'.

Despite gender equality being a central aim, much research has described ambivalence and dualism as a distinct characteristic of the intent and content of Norwegian family policies (Leira, 1992, 2006; Ellingsæter, 2003, 2006; Brandth et al, 2005; Ellingsæter and Leira, 2006; Borchorst, 2008). This dualism can be seen in all the three main policy approaches to caregiving: parental leave, 'cash for care' and ECEC services.

The Norwegian parental leave period amounts to 54 weeks mostly at 80% of earnings or 44 weeks at 100% throughout (the benefit is termed 'parental money'). In 2000, 79% chose to use the longest alternative (Danielsen and Lappegård, 2003). There is also an unpaid leave of one year for each parent. The parental leave system consists of several parts. There are individual parts of the leave reserved for the mother and for the father, but the longest part of the leave can be shared. There is great room for parental choice as to how the leave may be taken.

Parental leave policy is based on what has been labelled the 'work line' or earnings–related social insurance programme. Parents 'earn' the right to services from society through participation in working life. Generally speaking, the work line has been a principle of Norwegian welfare state policy since the early 1990s, and it is meant to encourage people to choose employment rather than social security benefits. In this way, family policies are closely connected to employment policies.

The parental leave system is a typical example of the work line. Parents qualify by being in the workforce for 6 of the 10 months prior to birth. It rewards employment achievement, as the amount of parental money is, to some extent, based on working hours and level of earnings. This provides strong encouragement for both parents to establish themselves in the labour market before having children and for both parents to combine work and family obligations: the ideal is that both mothers and fathers should be employed, a dual earner/dual carer model.

It was a Labour government that introduced a father's quota into the parental leave system. This move represented the gender equality model in Norwegian family policies, promoting the sharing of paid and unpaid care work. The debate on the father's quota in the early 1990s took place before neoliberal ideas had obtained a strong hold on public policy making.

In 1998, a conservative coalition government came into power. It introduced the 'cash-for-care' system, a home care allowance, arguing strongly for free choice for parents between home care and ECEC services. Parents with children from 12 to 36 months receive a cash grant if they do not use publicly subsidised ECEC; the measure is also intended to give parents more choice in deciding between private and public services. The cash-for-care reform was very controversial in the 1990s. Before its introduction, there was a heated and polarised debate, and the 1998 election has been called the 'cash-for-care election'. Supporters claimed that it would help solve the time squeeze felt by working parents and give parents increased freedom of choice, particularly between using publicly funded ECEC and providing care at home. Opponents argued that it was a setback for gender equality, as it would encourage mothers to reduce their employment. Moreover, it was feared that it would reduce the need for publicly funded ECEC services, and that an anticipated cutback in these services would make it difficult for mothers to choose employment.

The cash-for-care reform represents a different track in Norwegian family policy. It introduces a policy not dependent on parents' participation in working life; valorises unpaid work and care; and strengthens the family as a care producer by providing cash benefits irrespective of parental employment. This track supports a traditional division of work in the family, the male breadwinner family model, facilitating one of the parents (in practice, the mother) staying home. Both tracks, therefore, have been expected to influence the work–family relationship, but in different ways: "the models point to conflicting social and cultural values and political interests when it comes to politicising fatherhood and especially motherhood.' (Leira, 2006, p 29).

Dualism can also be observed in the political attitude towards publicly funded ECEC services (kindergartens or *barnehager*). Norway has had the lowest coverage rate for these services among the Scandinavian countries, especially for children under 3 years old. The main reason for these differences between Norway on the one hand and Sweden and Denmark on the other has been ambivalence about mothers' participation in the workforce and about ECEC services for children (Ellingsæter, 2006). This ambivalence has made it difficult to gain full support for the political aim of securing full kindergarten coverage in Norway. Only in 2003 did all the political parties join together and sign what was called the 'day care guarantee', which said that all Norwegian children between one and 6 years of age would be guaranteed a place in a publicly funded kindergarten.

Denmark and Sweden have for longer and to a greater extent stressed in their policy making the need for supporting working mothers and the idea of equal opportunities. The politics in these countries have also had a clear focus on the rights of children. In Norway, however, there has been greater tension between those who have supported working mothers and kindergartens and those who have seen home care as best for children. Yet many mothers of young children are in the workforce. The result has been widespread use of the 'grey' market in private family day carers, and more children in the 1970s and 1980s cared for in private arrangements than in publicly funded ECEC (Ellingsæter and Gulbrandsen, 2005). A substantial number of parents used the cash-for-care allowance to pay private carers because they lacked access to kindergartens.

Many surveys have shown that ECEC services are most commonly demanded by parents, and that private solutions are least preferred. The majority of Norwegian parents support public ECEC services, but this has been underestimated by government; the supply of public ECEC services, therefore, has never met demand (Ellingsæter and Gulbrandsen, 2005). In these circumstances, the cash-for-care system has been a brake on the development of a public ECEC system (Ellingsæter and Gulbrandsen, 2005).

In sum, the policies described above demonstrate distinctly different approaches to mothers and fathers as carers and breadwinners. Cash for care stimulates parental care in the home; ECEC services favour dual earners. Parental leave liberates employed parents from paid work to be carers for their children during the first year; one may say that it stimulates home care for dual earners. Inspired by Pateman (1992) and Fraser (1997), Borchorst (2008) generates three visions of gender equality represented by these care policies: the *caregiver parity model* aims to keep care work in the home, supported by public funding; the *universal breadwinner model* is based on moving care work from the home to ECEC services; and the *universal caregiver model* aims to make women's life patterns the norm for both women and men. The father's quota is clearly embedded in this third vision.

Parental leave – shifting objectives

Parental leave policies have stressed changing objectives over the years. During the early decades motherhood was in focus. Norwegian mothers in 1909 were the first in Scandinavia to gain maternity leave, 6 paid weeks as part of the Health Insurance Act (NOU 1996:13). The aim was to *protect working mothers* from the hazards of industrial work, in their own interest as well as the children's. Leave was extended in 1947 to 12 weeks, the first 6 remaining mandatory. Thus, the nature of the earliest leave schemes was to provide special health protection for women.

The debates on maternity leave at the start of the 1900s coincided with other protective measures for women workers, such as night work. Working-class women favoured such protective rights, while professional women favoured equal rights for women and men in the labour market and feared that special protection for women would weaken their position. The conflict between employment for women and motherhood was also visible in these early debates. Subsequently women's role in the family was more strongly emphasised in social policy reforms, and Norway was known as the 'country of housewives' (Frønes, 1994). We see two contrasting principles: women's right to paid work on the one hand and motherhood as the principal duty and responsibility of women on the other.

In the 1970s, the idea of equal rights was behind the extension of leave, one year in total with 18 weeks paid. One rationale was to give parents more time with their children. Mothers were to be ensured the opportunity to combine participation in the labour market with giving birth and providing care. What was totally new, in the reform of 1977, was that 12 of the 18 weeks could be shared between the parents, moving away from the idea of leave being a right only for women. However, the new policy sent a mixed message: the eligibility of the father was derived from the mother and her participation in working life, implying that the mother was the main carer. Nonetheless, by granting fathers the right to share the leave, this legislation signalled a new political view about men's responsibilities and participation in childcare. Moreover, the 1977 Work Environment Act granted fathers a right to take 2 weeks of unpaid leave at the time of the child's birth, the so-called 'daddy days', enabling fathers to spend time with the mother and child on their return from hospital. Both parents now had access to individual and shareable rights.

Leave schemes were gradually extended in the late 1980s and early 1990s. The idea of equal rights continued to be a strong rationale for developing parental leave. However, the shared portion of parental leave was little used by fathers, and to stimulate fathers to take leave, the father's quota was introduced, reserving part of parental leave as an individual right for fathers. At this point, an additional rationale emerged – the child's need for a caring father. In order to strengthen the father's place in the child's life, it was considered important that he should take part in caregiving during the child's first year. The purpose of a special quota was so that the child would have better contact with the father, its aim being to bolster not only equal rights but also fatherhood.

The point of departure for introducing the father's quota, and later its extension by 2 weeks in 2005 and 2006, was an explicit political aim to strengthen the father–child relationship, but also as a consequence of this, to change the gendered division of care work. To accomplish this, the principle of special rights for fathers was chosen. The father's quota moved the decision of who would take leave out of the family and on to the structural level to apply to 'all' fathers. It is a right that has been negotiated for men as employed fathers. It is thus no longer completely up to each individual father or parental couple to choose who stays at home with the baby.

In addition to the three main aims of motherhood, equality and fatherhood, the idea of choice has increasingly been stressed in political debates since the late 1990s. The formerly gender-neutral, totally shareable parental leave scheme contrasted with the gendered, non-shareable father's quota raises the question of freedom to choose. Even if the freedom to choose has always been a factor in the debate on leave schemes, it has increasingly grown into an aim in itself in care policies. In the latest changes to the parental leave scheme, emphasis has been put on increased flexibility and freedom of choice for families, while equal rights and father–child contact have been relegated to the background.

In sum, one may say that parental leave builds on a broad set of values and objectives. In the following section, we consider how this came to influence the political debate on the father's quota.

Political disagreement and consensus

The family policy dualism or ambivalence described above is reflected in a split among Norwegian political parties concerning the family and the care of children. In contrast to the stormy debate surrounding the cash-for-care scheme that highlighted differences between socialist and non-socialist parties in Norway, the development of the parental leave system was much more peaceful and could be accepted by most of the political parties. With two exceptions (the Conservative and Progress Parties), all parties were in favour of the father's quota. But although both sides of right–left political divide could agree on the quota, their reasons for doing so were quite different.

Seven parties represented in parliament took part in the debates on the expansion of the parental leave system including the father's quota: the Progress Party and the Conservative Party on the right; the Christian Democratic Party, the Liberal Party and the Centre Party representing the non-socialist centre; and the Labour Party and Socialist Party on the left. The father's quota and the extension of parental leave period from 35 to 52 weeks took place at the same time in 1993, making it difficult to distinguish arguments about the father's quota from the wider parental leave debate. Despite this and the relative consensus, several conflict lines between the parties can be detected.

The following account builds on Kari Håland's Master's thesis (2001, pp 51–63). She analyses the political debate from the mid-1980s to the mid-1990s, as it was in this period that the major changes in the leave system took place. Most of the changes were made by Labour governments, but all parties were basically in favour of parental leave. What separates them is the priority put on it.

The 1985 parliamentary debate followed a Green Paper that proposed a gradual extension of parental leave to one year (NOU 1984:26). The arguments were not for or against extending leave, but the timing of it. The Labour and Socialist Parties wanted immediate expansion, while the centre-right parties wished to postpone it for economic reasons.

In this debate, the Labour Party argued that an extended leave would improve the situation of working *women*. The Conservative Party argued for initiatives that would give *families* better conditions, and defined parental leave as a family measure. The Progress Party criticised parental leave for favouring employed women over home-working women and was the only party in this debate to oppose the work line. The difference between the Socialist and Progress Parties continued: the former found the tempo of expansion too slow, while the latter was more concerned with home-working women and wanted family policies that provided more equal support to the two groups.

From 1987 to 1993, parental leave was expanded every year until it reached 52 weeks with 80% pay, without much disagreement between the parties. Håland points out that the differences between them only appeared from time to time when parties wanted to demonstrate disagreement in their reasons for supporting the initiative (Håland, 2001, p 55). The agreement on the length of the parental leave reflected a long-term goal that most of the parties had accepted.

The father's quota was introduced in a White Paper on gender equality (St.meld., 1991-92: 70) and debated in parliament in 1992. All parties were in favour of the quota except the Conservative and the Progress Parties. Their main argument was that it would hinder families' freedom of choice, families themselves being best able to decide which of the parents should take parental leave. One of the representatives from the Conservative Party put it like this: "For us conservatives, freedom of choice and responsibility are the guiding principles for family policy.... Personally, I strongly decline coercive solutions in politics" (Bernander, St.tid., 1992-93, p 3661). This is not an unexpected argument, as freedom of choice is an important aspect of the ideology of right-wing parties; similarly, in the Swedish debate, the extreme right-wing party was the only one to define the father's quota as coercion. The majority of the Norwegian parties, however, saw it as an acceptable exercise of mild pressure on fathers to participate more in childcare, and held that it would represent an important signal of men's responsibility.

So, one dimension of disagreement between the parties in the father's quota debate concerned the question of choice, with an incipient conflict between a neoliberal ideology propounding freedom from state control and legislation that has been described as more 'paternalistic'. This conflict was to become much stronger.

Second, the parliamentary debates about the father's quota illustrate different perspectives on gender equality between the parties. For instance, the father's quota was supported by both Labour and Christian Democratic Parties, but on different grounds. The Labour Party saw the father's quota as an important step towards equal responsibility for work and home between mothers and fathers. The Christian Democratic Party on the other hand, saw it as positive that the quota would give fathers greater insight into women's care work in the home and thus come to value it more highly. As Håland points out (2001, p 59), this argument mirrors a maternalistic perspective on gender equality rather than a dual earner/dual carer view. The example illustrates that the father's quota is interpretatively flexible; it can be seen as a means to valorise women's work in the home or to stimulate equal sharing.

A third dimension of difference between the parties in this debate concerned the work line, or more generally speaking, women's employment. The political parties on the left have advocated the work line, wanting to reward families where both parents are employed outside the home. The centre-right, on the other hand, has on several occasions opposed employment-based rights in family policy, and argued for measures that support the traditional one breadwinner family. As stated by one of the Christian Democratic Party representatives, "the difference between economic contribution to homeworking and employed women in connection with childbirth is still too large.... We wish to put priority to parents who stay at home' (Bjartvedt, St.tid., 1992-93, p 971).

Håland (2001, p 97) points out that, generally speaking, no parties are actually opposed to the ideology represented by the work line. When the centre-right opposes policies that are based on parental employment, this may indicate that it regards care work as a necessity for society. Consequently, it wants to reward it by increasing cash benefits for home carers. All three topics – freedom of choice, gender equality and eligibility based on the work line – demonstrate a difference between the parties about the preferred family model.

The interesting question is how to explain the predominant consensus in the political treatment of the father's quota in spite of the political cleavages described above. The main answer is that parental leave including the father's quota was able to satisfy aims on both sides of the dualism in Norwegian family policy. In the context of the shareable part of the leave being extended considerably at the same time as the father's quota was adopted, the parties that favoured home-based care were satisfied, as parental leave in fact means a familialisation of care. Parental leave represents an arrangement where the ideal is parental care during the first year of the child's life without having to use any external care. The relatively long period of paid leave thus allows for the family to have a mother at home and a father at work. All parties agreed that it is important to give parents more time with their children, and extended parental leave allowed for this. Moreover, all parties were in favour of supporting stronger father involvement and gender equality; and in 1993 reserving 4 weeks for fathers did not represent any competition with motherhood. As we have seen, the quota could also be defined to fit different models of gender equality.

The Committee on Men's Role

The influence of the men's movement, particularly the Committee on Men's Role that was active in Norway in the late 1980s, was important for preparing the ground for the father's quota. The committee was appointed by the Ministry of Consumer Affairs in 1986 (now named the Ministry of Children and Equality). The objective was to speed up the work on equal opportunities by focusing on men and their possible contribution (NOU 1991:3). The first leader of this committee was Jens Stoltenberg, then the leader of the youth organisation of the Norwegian Labour Party. Jens Stoltenberg is currently Prime Minister (at least until elections in Autumn 2009). The rest of the committee included representatives from the trades unions, the employers' organisation and the Labour and the Conservative Parties, two researchers, one each from psychology and medicine, a well-known actor and a journalist working in the national broadcasting corporation. The committee was given the following mandate: "The goal of the group should be to encourage a debate on changes in the role of men. The focus should especially be on questions connected to men, children and care responsibilities. The work should build on the experiences that the Swedish Committee on Men's Role had made, but be adjusted to the Norwegian context" (NOU 1991:3, p 6).

We see from this that men and care for children was expected to be the main focus for this group. It is also interesting that the inspiration and the model for their work was another Nordic country.

The committee was very active in taking the initiative to start a public debate on men's roles. In the report on its work, the committee says that the media was very interested in its activities and that its high profile on the public scene contributed greatly to promoting public interest in equal opportunities and men (NOU 1991:3, p 7). In addition to men and caring responsibilities, the committee focused on men and divorce, and men and violence. It is, however, interesting to observe that while the topic of men and care covered 14 pages in its final report to the Ministry of Family Affairs (NOU 1991:3), the two other topics were only given 5 pages each. The question of men and caring had a very central position in the committee's output.

The committee argued that men ought to participate far more in care work for three reasons. First, greater involvement by fathers might result in a stronger relationship between fathers and children. If father spent more time with their children on an everyday basis, it would benefit children's identity development. The committee pointed to research that showed that both the intellectual and emotional development of a child improved through a close relationship with its father. It focused especially on the positive effects this would have for sons in preventing aggressive behaviour, but also considered it important for confirming the gender identity of daughters.

Second, greater involvement in childcare would benefit men themselves and their development as human beings (Mannifest, 1989). Men's relations with children would give their lives new dimensions, and not just emotional ones. For example, it would give them experience of coping with trivialities and chaos. The love that a child gives can "thaw even a Rambo" (Mannifest, 1989, p 22). Participation in childcare was thus considered the most appropriate way of changing the traditional role of men.

The third argument included the relationship with the mother. If fathers got more involved in childcare, it would contribute to more democratic relationships between women and men and a more equal distribution of duties and rights both at work and in family life. The committee pointed to the fact that in spite of the changing role of mothers in Norwegian society, men had not taken an equal part in care work. Mothers therefore worked a double shift. The committee added that encouraging men to care more for small children would probably also have a positive effect on caring for elderly relatives. This third argument, however, is not given much place in the two reports from the committee (Mannifest, 1989; NOU 1991:3). The main focus is on what the child might gain from a closer relationship with the father. The argumentation is therefore mainly *child-oriented*.

One reason advanced by the committee for men's limited participation in childcare was the parental leave arrangement at that time. Total leave was 24 weeks in 1989. Although 18 of these weeks could be shared by mothers and fathers, the period was regarded as too short to be shareable in practice. Mothers needed the time to recover after giving birth and to breastfeed. Moreover, it was argued that fathers would feel more confident in caring when children had got a bit bigger (Mannifest, 1989, p 29).

The committee proposed a much more extensive leave period – 18 months. To ensure that fathers took a considerable share of this leave, they suggested that 6 months be reserved for each of the parents, leaving 6 months to be shared. The leave period should be gradually extended over 10 years. Another important proposal was that the parents should be given flexibility by having a choice between reduced working hours or not working. Payment while taking leave, they added, should be based on the income of each of the parents and be made dependent on the mother or the father taking over the care of the child; until then, eligibility for parental money had been dependent on the income of the mother.

An interesting point in the committee's report to the Minister of Family Affairs was a proposal to start a discussion on whether compulsory military service should be connected to parental leave. Compulsory service, the argument ran, could then be partly done either in the military or as care work in the society (NOU 1991:3, p 15).

The proposal to extend the leave period to 18 months, reserving 6 months for the father, was much more radical than today's policy (although the principle of reserving one third of the leave period for the father has become the foundation of the parental leave system in Iceland; see Chapter Ten). The proposal, as well as discussions in the committee that were extensively covered by the press, may have prepared the ground for acceptance and use of this type of leave among Norwegian men. It may also have influenced a discursive change from equal rights to men's (fathers') rights.

It is interesting to use the subsequent research on fathers' experiences with the quota to discuss the proposals put forward by the committee. More than 90% of the fathers who have used the father's quota say they have taken it because they wanted to be together with their child, and almost 90% believed that the child needed the presence of the father (Brandth and Kvande, 2003). Thus the relation with the child was the great motivational factor for the fathers – it is the child that draws the father home. In the words of one father, an industrial worker: "That the dad gets a month's leave, I really think that is great so that the father also has contact with the baby and not just the mother. We both thought this was a great idea".

We also see how important the child is in fathers' thinking about what the leave is for when we consider how they assign priorities while on leave. They take care of the child, change nappies, play with and feed the child; they focus on the child's upbringing, giving the child challenges and protection. Although many fathers recognise the equal rights dimension, it is the relationship with the child, not the mother, that is most important, as this father clearly indicates when asked what the father's quota meant:

> "What was most positive was that I had contact with my boy – I could be together with him and he also got to know me, you know. I really think so. Because even if he saw me on a daily basis at other times too, I think it was special then … and if you spend a lot of time with your child and care for it and all that, then I think the child gets more familiar with the father and feels more safe and trusting."

It is quite clear that fathers primarily use the quota to deepen their relationship with and orientation towards their child, not to achieve equal rights with the mother. Bekkengen (2002) has similar findings in a study in Sweden, pointing out that such a focus on the child is particular to the Nordic countries. Child-oriented masculinity is a different matter from equal rights orientation. For the 'new man', the child is at the centre (Brandth and Kvande, 1998). This is also a masculinity that appears to be appreciated by the mothers.

In 2007, the Minister of Children and Equality appointed a new group – the 'Men's Panel' – to discuss the roles of men. This time there were 32 men in the group who all held a high profile in their respective areas: representatives from political parties, trades unions, the employers' organisation, sports organisations, the gay movement and various organisations fighting for men's rights. In addition, there were two authors and a high-profile editor of a tabloid newspaper. The new committee included a much wider range of members than the earlier one, the main difference being the inclusion of a large number of representatives from private companies. The panel's mandate was to give recommendations to the minister on parental leave, fathers' rights in divorce negotiations, men and violence. We see here similar topics to those the first committee worked on.

The Men's Panel handed over its recommendations to the ministry in March 2008. The majority of the panel proposed extending leave at 100% pay from 44 to 52 weeks and dividing the parental leave into equal parts; with the current leave of 44 weeks, this would mean four parts each of 11 weeks, one part reserved for the mother, one for the father and two parts for the parents to decide how to share. But if the total length of the leave period was increased to 52 weeks, it should be divided into three equal parts, similar to the recommendation of the first committee. The representative from the Conservative Party did not agree with this recommendation on the grounds that parents should be able to decide themselves how to share the parental leave.

The earlier Committee on the Role of Men recommended encouraging further research on men and masculinities. It pointed out in its report (NOU 1991:3) that there was a lack of research on men's experiences and lives. Although there has not been any special programme for research on men and masculinities in Norway, research in this field has been undertaken since the end of the 1980s with a focus on fathers and their possible contributions to childcare (for example, Brandth and Kvande 1989a, 1989b; Ellingsæter, 1989; Holter, 1989). This research field has gradually increased and a network for researchers on men and masculinities has been established. Members of the network have produced research that has been used by the legislators and policy makers. Overall, we can say that the parental leave and father's quota discussion has made an important contribution to work on equal rights, which has been shaped by women working in government ministries. The equal rights debate has helped change previous gender-specific family legislation that was seen to discriminate against men.

In sum, the work of the Committee on Men's Role and the research focusing on fathers have quite clearly played an important role in the making of the father's quota in Norway. They have stimulated public discourse on the topic and legitimated the quite radical regulations that were to come. In the White Paper leading up to the new law on parental leave in 1993, which introduced the father's quota, we find the same arguments as are made in the reports of the Committee on Men's Role. The fact that the committee included representatives from both the trades unions and the employers' organisation, as well as the two main political parties at the time, prepared the ground for consensus on the introduction of the first father's quota system in the world.

Conclusion

The aim of this chapter has been to understand some of the forces behind the introduction of the father's quota in Norway. Maternity leave was considered radical in the context of the 1900s, but by the last quarter of the 20th century it was deemed conservative, even if protecting mothers as employees has been continually seen as important. Since what is radical in one historical period may be conservative politics in the next, it is important to consider policies in their context, whether that context be historical or national.

Norwegian family policies must be understood in the context of gender and family values. Taken together, the three different care policies that we have described above all reveal the varying ideologies of gender equality, parenthood and what are the best ways to care for one's children. The conflicting relationships between ideologies are played out in party politics resulting in compromises that have formed the dualism so characteristic of Norwegian policy, the 'two-track system'.

The idea of the father's quota originated in the 1980s. It is seen in governmental and other reports as an important means to reduce gender inequality and strengthen the father–child relationship, bearing in mind that the right to share the parental leave period on a voluntary basis had not been successful in bringing fathers into the home. The government-appointed Committee on the Men's Role supplied important inputs to the debate from 1986. Its recommendation of a special period reserved for fathers was rapidly transformed into politics, albeit in a less ambitious way. The father's quota was popularly accepted, and later research has documented that fathers do not object to being 'gently forced' into taking leave.

As the father's quota was presented as a win–win solution for child, father and mother, its introduction was not very controversial. It satisfied many views, and so obtained broad political consensus. The neoliberal arguments concerning free choice were not strong enough to stop it at the time. Moreover, the quota was introduced together with a general expansion of the parental leave period, so did not require taking time from the mother.

The question of how to get more fathers to take longer leave than the 6 weeks of the father's quota is a recurrent theme in the public debate and has been a hotly debated topic recently (in 2008). On the one side, it is contended that fathers' rights to leave should remain voluntary, in keeping with the current situation. On the other side, it is argued that the compulsory part of the leave (that is, the 'use it or lose it' principle) should be extended to a third of the total period, since earmarking part of the leave for fathers has proved successful.

The debate about earmarking more leave for fathers has produced conflicting issues. One is the question of free choice, which has featured more strongly in recent years than in the late 1980s and early 1990s. Another is a conflict between motherhood and fatherhood. It has been customary practice that mothers have used the longer, shareable part of the leave. Therefore, earmarking parts of it as recommended by the recent Men's Panel and also by the government-appointed

Committee on Equal Pay (NOU 2008:6) has provoked arguments such as "fathers wanting to take leave from the mothers" and "forcing mothers to return to work early".

In the general debate today, motherhood is brought more into the picture by the strong emphasis on breastfeeding. Since 2002, mothers have been recommended by the government to fully breastfeed until the baby is 6 months old and to prolong breastfeeding until it is one year old, in the interests of the baby's health. The current length of the leave, its flexibility and mothers' rights to reduced working hours during the breastfeeding period allow for this. Nevertheless, the breastfeeding policy has brought the medical profession into the debate about parental leave for fathers, emphasising women's superior biological care abilities. Thus, in the current debate, breastfeeding has become a main argument against extending the father's quota. The well-known Norwegian gender traditionalism and ambivalence towards employed mothers is again making its mark in family policy debates. In Norway, family policy dualism seems to remain latent, ready to emerge again and again.

Research has suggested that reserving/earmarking part of the parental leave for fathers has made a change when it comes to influencing the norm of good fathering and improving men's position as fathers. However, when it comes to obtaining gender equality, the results seem more doubtful. Although parental leave has been motivated by gender equality, the outcome may not be so. Rather, gender equality may come to mean gender segregation. As long as the father's quota is what defines good fathering and what fathers are expected to take, it contributes to cementing the traditional division of care work, but in a slightly different way than in the traditional one breadwinner family. Now it is in the form of long leave for mother, short leave for dad. Thus the quota has not changed the gendered character of childcare in a fundamental way; it has only modified it.

Notes

[1] Leave provision described here refers to statutory entitlements.

[2] Converted into euros at exchange rate on 23 February 2009, rounded up to the nearest 5 euros.

References

Bekkengen, L. (2002) *Man får välja – om föräldraskap och föräldraledighet i arbetsliv och familjeliv*, Stockholm: Liber.

Borchorst, A (2008) 'Woman-friendly policy paradoxes? Childcare policies and gender equality visions in Scandinavia', in K. Melby, A.B. Ravn and C.C. Wetterberg (eds) *Gender equality and welfare politics in Scandinavia: The limits of political ambition?*, Bristol: The Policy Press.

Borchorst, A. and Siim, B. (2002) 'The women-friendly welfare states revisited', *Nordic Journal of Women's Studies*, vol 10, pp 90-8.

Brandth, B. and Kvande, E. (1989a) 'Når likhet blir ulikhet', in R. Haukaa (ed) *Nye Kvinner. Nye Menn*, Oslo: Ad Notam, pp 117-42.

Brandth B. and Kvande, E. (1989b) 'Like barn deler best', *Nytt om Kvinneforskning*, vol 13, no 3, pp 8-18.

Brandth, B. and Kvande, E. (1998) 'Masculinity and child care – the reconstruction of fathering', *The Sociological Review*, vol 46, no 2, pp 293-314.

Brandth, B. and Kvande, E. (2003) *Fleksible fedre*, Oslo: Universitetsforlaget.

Brandth, B., Bungum, B. and Kvande, E. (2005) 'Innledning: valgfrihet i omsorgspolitikken', in B. Brandth, B. Bungum and E. Kvande (eds) *Valgfrihetens tid. Omsorgspolitikk for barn møter det fleksible arbeidslivet*, Oslo: Gyldendal akademisk, pp 11-25.

Danielsen, K. and Lappegård, T. (2003) 'Tid er viktig når barn blir født', *Samfunnsspeilet*, vol 17, no 5, pp 34-8.

Ellingsæter, A.L. (1989) 'Hvorfor jobber pappa overtid?', in R. Haukaa (ed) *Nye Kvinner. Nye Menn*, Oslo: Ad Notam, pp 143-65.

Ellingsæter, A.L (2003) 'The complexity of family policy reform: the case of Norway', *European Societies*, vol 4, no 4, pp 419-43.

Ellingsæter, A.L. (2006) 'The Norwegian childcare regime and its paradoxes', in A.L. Ellingsæter and A. Leira (eds) (2006) *Politicising parenthood in Scandinavia. Gender relations in welfare states*, Bristol: The Policy Press, pp 121-44.

Ellingsæter, A.L. and Leira, A. (eds) (2006) *Politicising parenthood in Scandinavia. Gender relations in welfare states*, Bristol: The Policy Press.

Ellingsæter, A.L. and Gulbrandsen, L. (2005) 'Den lange veien. Barnehage som reell valgmulighet', in B. Brandth, B. Bungum and E. Kvande (eds) *Valgfrihetens tid. Omsorgspolitikk for barn møter det fleksible arbeidslivet*, Oslo: Gyldendal akademisk, pp 159-82.

Esping-Andersen, G. (1990) *The three worlds of welfare capitalism*, Cambridge: Polity Press.

Esping-Andersen, G., with Gallie, D., Hemerijck, A. and Myles, J. (2002) *Why we need a new welfare state*, Oxford: Oxford University Press.

Fraser, N. (1997) *Justice interruptus. Critical reflections on the 'postsocialist' condition*, London: Routledge.

Frønes, I. (1994) 'Dimensions of childhood', in J. Qvortrup, M. Bardy, G. Sgritta and H. Wintersberger (eds) *Childhood matters. Social theory, practice and policies*, Aldershot: Avebury, pp 145-64.

Håland, K. (2001) 'Kontantstøtten – et veiskille i norsk familiepolitikk?', Master's thesis, Trondheim: NTNU.

Håland, K. (2005) 'Fra enighet til strid i familiepolitikken', in B. Brandth, B. Bungum and E. Kvande (eds) *Valgfrihetens tid*, Oslo: Gyldendal akademisk.

Hernes, H. (1987) *Welfare state and women power. Essays in state feminism*, Oslo: Norwegian University Press.

Holter, Ø.G. (1989) *Menn*, Oslo: Aschehoug.

Leira, A. (1992) *Welfare states and working mothers: The Scandinavian experience*, Cambridge: Cambridge University Press.

Leira, A. (2006) 'Parenthood change and policy reform in Scandinavia, 1970s–2000s', in A.L. Ellingsæter and A. Leira (eds) *Politicising parenthood in Scandinavia: Gender relations in welfare states*, Bristol: The Policy Press, pp 27-52.

Mannifest (1989) *Førebels statusrapport frå Mannsrolleutvalget* (Preliminary report from the Committee on Men's Role), Oslo.

NOU 1984:26 (Green Paper), *Befolkningsutviklingen*, Oslo: Norges Offentlige Utredninger.

NOU 1991:3, *Mannsrolleutvalgets sluttrapport*, Oslo: Norges Offentlige Utredninger.

NOU 1996:13, *Offentlige overføringer til barnefamilier*, Oslo: Norges Offentlige Utredninger.

NOU 2008:6, *Kjønn og Lønn*, Oslo: Norges Offentlige Utredninger.

Pateman, C. (1992) 'Equality, difference, subordination: the politics of motherhood and women's citizenship', in G. Bock and S. James (eds) *Beyond equality and difference*, New York, NY: Routledge, pp 17-31.

Sainsbury, D. (2001) 'Gender and the making of welfare states: Norway and Sweden', *Social Politics*, vol 8, pp 113-43.

St.meld. (White Paper) 1991-92: 70, *Likestillingspolitikk for 1990-åra*, Oslo.

Stortingstidende (St.tid.), 1992-93.

THIRTEEN

Portugal and Spain: two pathways in Southern Europe

Karin Wall and Anna Escobedo

Portugal

Maternity leave[1]: 120 calendar days (17 weeks) at 100% of earnings or 150 days at 80%, with no ceiling. Mothers have to take 6 weeks after the birth of a child; the rest may be transferred to the father.

Paternity leave: 5 working days at 100% with no ceiling; obligatory.

Parental leave: 3 months per parent until child is 6 years. No payment except for 15 calendar days at 100% with no ceiling if taken by the father immediately after maternity or paternity leave.

Leave to care for children: 30 days a year per family for sick children under 10 years at 65% of average earnings; no time limit if a child is in hospital.

Other: 2 hours' absence per working day per family for 12 months after a child's birth, without loss of earnings (paid by employer).

Spain

Maternity leave: 16 weeks at 100% up to a ceiling of €3.074 per month. Mothers can transfer up to 10 weeks to fathers or choose to take them part time over 20 weeks.

Paternity leave: 15 calendar days, 2 days to be taken after birth, the rest during/at the end of maternity leave, at 100%. May be taken part time with employer's agreement.

Parental leave: until child is 3 years; an individual entitlement. No payment, but some regional governments offer low flat-rate benefits.

Leave to care for dependants: 2 days per worker for a 'seriously ill' child or other family reasons, without loss of earnings (paid by employer).

Other: one hour's absence per working day per family for 9 months after a child's birth (paid by employer). Reduced hours may be consolidated to allow a 2–4 week extension of maternity leave. Working parents may reduce their working hours (from one eighth to half of working time) until a child is 8 years, without payment; some regional governments offer benefits for the working time reduction.

Portugal and **Spain** are member states of the European Union (EU). **Portugal** has a high level of maternal employment and a low level of female part-time employment. It is estimated that about three quarters of mothers are eligible for maternity leave. Although obligatory, in 2006 only 61% of fathers took paternity leave and 49% the 15 days of paid parental leave (however, take-up is underestimated as statistics exclude employees with special social protection regimes, for example, in the civil service and banks). There is no information on take-up for the remainder of parental leave, but it is thought to be low because it is unpaid.

Spain is not a federal state, but has strong devolution to regions. It has a relatively low level of maternal employment. Paternity leave, introduced in 2007, had an estimated take-up of 45% during the first year, while 65% of women having a child benefited from maternity leave. Take-up of parental leave is low, equivalent to 6% of births in 2005; fathers accounted for 4.5% of users.

Introduction

Much about the welfare state and family policy in Southern Europe has been analysed and reported on, but there has been no systematic effort to look in historical context at the evolution of policies and to understand the paths taken in some countries but not in others. As in other European countries, Spain and Portugal have moved away from policies focusing on the 'traditional' male breadwinner model (Crompton, 1999; Pfau-Effinger et al, 2009). However, reconciliation policies, and leave policies in particular, have not necessarily shifted at the same pace in both countries or in the same direction.

The main aim of this chapter will be to compare the particular routes taken by parental leave policies in Spain and Portugal since their transitions to democracy. Understanding the politics of leave policy in these countries involves analysis along three main lines: identifying the main aims, policy measures and turning points in leave policies since the 1960s; focusing on the actors, constraints or political processes that sustained or influenced these policies; and analysing the linkages between leave policy and major shifts in other related policies. For parental leave is but one element in policy packages intended to support the reconciliation of work and care for young children. Analysis of the connections of leave policy to the development of early childhood education and care (ECEC) services and to other gender, family and employment practices and policies is essential to capturing the overall meanings and rationales of leave policy in a particular country.

Against a historical backdrop, the chapter will compare current leave policy models in the two countries and discuss commonalities and differences. In Southern European welfare regimes, emphasis has largely been placed on a 'male breadwinner' leave scheme model where women do not work outside the home when they have young children (Flaquer, 2000; Wall, 2002). But this model may be being superseded, to a greater or lesser extent, by another: 'early return to full-time work', where some women return to full-time work after a short period of well-compensated leave (Wall, 2007). In a comparative European perspective, the main challenge here is to see to what extent parental leave policies in Portugal and Spain are diverging or whether both are moving in the direction of the 'early return' model.

Leave policies in Portugal

The Salazar dictatorship

After a military coup in 1926, which overthrew the first Republic (1910–26), Salazar took over the government as Prime Minister in 1932. Based on radical right-wing and anti-liberal Catholicism, the Salazar dictatorship emphasised the 4-part doctrine of God, fatherland, family and work. The concept of the family as the smallest unit in an organic and corporatist society, churchgoing and organised hierarchically (male breadwinner 'head of family', subordinate homemaker wife, obedient children), dominated daily lives and legislation. Civil rights relating to marriage and divorce (first introduced in 1910) were changed, the 'concordat' established with the Vatican forbidding divorce for Catholic marriages. Other rights that women had gained were restricted or annulled. In the new Civil Code, husbands were entitled to revoke work contracts signed by their wives without their consent, and married women were considered to be legally responsible for managing the household. Care for young children was in the hands of families, mostly women who, even if never barred from economic activity with the aim of contributing to the *family's* economic well-being, were always expected to put their domestic and caring duties first. For the care of the very needy or those with no family, the state relied on private, mostly church-related, charities (Wall, 2002).

Within this context, the state recognised that women had a minimum right to leave from work in order to recover physically from childbirth. According to the 1937 law, working women "may be dispensed from working for 30 days, on the occasion of childbirth, without the employer being able to dismiss them.... If they have been providing good services for more than a year, they may be entitled to a benefit of one third of previous earnings". In other words, entitlement to compensation depended on the employer's goodwill.

Legislation to protect women workers was passed in the 1950s and again in the late 1960s, with the aim of regulating women's work according to the demands of "domestic life, morality and social well-being". It forbade night work for women and punished acts that "went against the dignity of women in work". In 1969, for the first time, the law forbade dismissal during pregnancy and for one year after birth and entitled mothers to a daily one-hour period for breastfeeding. This emerging state protection of women's work is an important indicator of changes in the labour market and in society at this time. During the 1960s, female activity rates almost doubled, rising to nearly one third of the female population aged 15–64 by 1970, clearly indicating that women were moving rapidly into the labour market. This was due to a diversity of factors: the depletion of the male labour force due to emigration and the colonial wars; massive recruitment of women into the manufacturing sector, especially labour-intensive industries; the development of a feminised service sector in the cities; and investment among urban elites in women's higher education – by 1970, 44% of students were women.

The first years after the revolution

Preceded and anticipated by many of these societal changes, the 1974 revolution marked a major turning point in family policy, with the political–juridical framework governing families and women's rights undergoing radical change (Almeida and Wall, 2001). Divorce and working women's rights were among the earliest and most demanded changes. Only a few months after the April revolution, the concordat was changed and divorce between Catholic spouses permitted once again. In early 1976, 90 days of fully compensated maternity leave were introduced. Other rights for working women, such as equal pay for equal work and the protection of pregnant women in the workplace, were also granted.

The family still occupied an important place in the new democratic regime's 1976 Constitution, but the constitutional principles were profoundly changed. Emphasis was placed on equality between partners, and democracy and diversity in family relationships. This led to major reforms of family law, such as abolishing the concept of the male 'head of family'. To support families with children, the Constitution recognised the state's obligations to give information on family planning, to impose equality in all domains, to develop a public network of childcare services, and to cooperate with parents in the education of children.

Legal changes concerning women's and workers' rights were introduced during the 1970s and with the support of all major political parties as well as of other actors such as trades unions, women's movements and the Catholic Church. As one author puts it, the mere 'shame' of a 50-year dictatorship, which interfered explicitly in private lives, seemed sufficient to give lawmakers freedom (Ferreira, 1998), allowing for the emergence of a certain state feminism. At any rate, it gave the political elite ample leverage to introduce the principles of gender equality as a natural part of the democratisation process. The politics of equality also led to the institutionalisation of gender policy, with the setting up in the 1970s of the Commission for the Condition of Women as well as the Commission for Equality in Work and Employment (CITE).

The 1980s and early 1990s

The 1980s and early 1990s brought a shift in the politics of leave policy. During the 1970s, the focus was on the importance of work for women's emancipation and on the linkage between leave and the protection of women in the labour market. It is only in the early 1980s that an additional family focus, on the issue of 'parental' care rather than maternal care, emerges more strongly. Building on to the issue of the importance of women's work, this family perspective had a crucial role in opening up the policy agenda to the problem of work–life balance, already under discussion in many European countries.

The first landmark in this process was the 1984 law on 'maternity and paternity', prepared in the context of a coalition government by the Socialist (PS) and Social Democrat (PSD) Parties (1983–85). However, it was the Communist Party (PC) members of parliament who gave the initial impulse to this legislative change by proposing, in 1982, a 'package' of laws on abortion, family planning and the protection of maternity. Divisions were deep on the first issue, but there was more consensus about the leave scheme model proposed: a 4-month fully paid maternity leave, an unpaid parental leave, other care-related leave entitlements and the building up of childcare services with opening hours adapted to families' needs.

With a few changes, the proposal was integrated into a law presented jointly by PS and PSD members of parliament and approved in 1984. It established new and quite ambitious leave arrangements, explicitly emphasising the need for 'parental' provisions, and services 'compatible with parents' working life', and also underlining the rights of both parents, *on an equal basis*, to professional self-fulfilment and participation in civic life. It entitled either parent to miss work for up to 30 days per year to care for a sick child under the age of 10, mothers with children under one year to a reduction of 2 working hours per day, and fathers to take up maternity leave in the case of the mother's death, illness or training.

In the 1980s, the leave arrangements had a limited impact on families caring for sick children as they provided replacement pay for a minority of families (low-income families, lone parents and civil servants). Nevertheless, they granted a new legitimacy for leave to care for dependants and for gender sharing of such leave. Over the next decade, the leave scheme was gradually reinforced and provided with more state funding. In 1988, during a PSD government (1985–95) that placed emphasis on the protection of maternity and paternity, access to maternity leave was made easier (6 months of insurance contributions) and replacement pay for lone parents caring for sick children was increased. After this and until the late 1990s, there were no further major changes in leave legislation, except for the transposition of the 1992 EU maternity directive (see Chapter Fifteen), which extended maternity leave to 98 days. The same law (1995) established the right of fathers to miss work for 2 days (without compensation) and to share maternity leave (after the 6 weeks that must be taken by the mother). In the same year, too, replacement pay (65% of average earnings) was introduced for all workers caring for a sick child below the age of 10. In summary, although the PSD in government between 1985 and 1995 did not put reconciliation high on the policy agenda, at the end of its term it had consolidated and even extended, largely prompted by the EU directive, some of the principles of the existing leave scheme.

From the outset, the first leave scheme set out in the 1980s reflected the notion of a dual breadwinner model based on a symmetrical integration of both sexes into the employment system. As for the care of children, although the basic idea of the state as carer was emphasised in the 1976 Constitution, in the early 1980s a mixed welfare model began to emerge, based on the state subsidising non-profit institutions. It was implemented through legislation (1983) on the status of non-profit institutions or *instituições particulares de solidariedade social* (private institutions of social solidarity, IPSS) and the formalisation of yearly agreements on the flat-rate subsidy to be paid by the state for each child provided for by IPSS. Expansion of services was slow but steady; nevertheless, provision remained low and unevenly distributed, with many low-income families in large urban areas finding it difficult to access subsidised services.

However, the development of childcare facilities during this period did have a considerable impact on families' care strategies. Data from a national survey show that whereas in the 1970s almost half of all mothers stayed at home to care for a child aged 12 to 24 months, in the 1990s only one in every four mothers did so and 18% (7% in the 1970s) used full-time childcare services (Wall, 2005); the other mothers used paid childminders or family care (mostly grandparents).

The past ten years

A second major shift in leave policy took place in the late 1990s (Wall, 1997, 2004), under a PS government in power between 1995 and 2002. Compared with the previous decade, there was a stronger and more explicit emphasis on gender equality, on the need to involve fathers, and on the setting of precise goals for the expansion of childcare services. Reflecting the priority given in the party programme to gender equality and work–family balance, but also encouraged by the 1996 EU directive on parental leave, the recent PS governments (1995–2002; 2005–08) have highlighted two major objectives: the promotion of gender sharing in leave arrangements; and the expansion of childcare services to support dual earner parents.

The linkage being made between family and gender equality policies was reflected in the setting up of a High Commission for Family and Gender Equality. Influenced by the European debates on reconciliation, the High Commissioner organised several awareness-raising campaigns on the need for gender equality in the household division of work. Particular stress was laid on the involvement of fathers in the care of young children, with references to the 'father's quota' introduced earlier in the Nordic countries.

However, the driving force for alterations in leave policy in the late 1990s was, as usual in Portuguese family policy, the ministry responsible for social affairs, called the Ministry of Labour and Solidarity at that time. Taking advantage of a favourable budgetary context, the Secretary of State for Social Security prepared the new law on maternity and paternity with briefings not only from the High Commission but also from CITE, the main advisory body on work and equality within the ministry and headed at the time by a feminist and strong advocate of gender equality.

Proposals to emphasise the gender sharing of leave were prepared through public debate and hearings, discussion of a study commissioned by CITE on expectations and the costs of leave for fathers (Perista and Chagas Lopes, 1999), and negotiation both with employers, generally more reluctant to make changes in leave arrangements, and trades unions (CITE is a tripartite institution). The issue was also taken up in civil society, for example by Graal, a Catholic feminist movement that in 1996–98 organised an important debate on reconciliation. The Graal project – 'Promoting an active society' – prepared recommendations on the promotion of work–life balance for men and women and passed them on to policy makers. In public debate, the increased involvement of fathers was advocated from a family perspective (to promote father–child bonding and family cohesion), from a gender perspective (to promote equal opportunities and gender sharing of care) and from a labour market perspective (to reduce employer discrimination against women).

In summary, a considerable constituency was built up during the late 1990s to promote reconciliation policy, in particular from the perspective of gender equality, providing support from different sectors of society and practically the whole of the political spectrum. In its final form, the 1999 law brought in some significant entitlements, especially for fathers. Maternity leave was increased to 120 days and paternity leave (now with full compensation) to 5 days; fathers were also granted an individual right to 2 weeks' fully compensated parental leave and became entitled to take up or share the 2-hour reduction in working time. Campaigns were launched to raise awareness of these three rights for fathers and take-up increased steadily but slowly, indicating that social norms would take some time to change. To boost take-up, the 5-day paternity leave was made obligatory in 2004.

Other major trends in family policy during the first period of Socialist government included a debate on the liberalisation of abortion, leading to a referendum that rejected abortion on demand during the first 10 weeks of pregnancy; changes in the regulation of cohabiting partnerships and divorce; and expansion of service provision to support families. As women's employment continued to rise steadily (from 53% in 1991, to 65% in 2001), there was mounting dissatisfaction with poor access to low-cost services, in particular in large urban areas. Driven by reconciliation policy objectives as well as by educational and child development goals, priority was given to expanding pre-school education for 3- to 6-year-olds and coverage increased from 55% in 1995 to 78% in 2002.

Family policy discourse and objectives changed for a short period (2003–05), when a centre–right-wing coalition came to power. For the first time since the

1970s, there was some questioning of the leave scheme based on a full-time dual breadwinner model. The Minister for Social Affairs (a member of the Christian Democrat Party) advocated longer leave periods or part-time work for mothers. The focus on pronatalist, pro-life and familialist objectives put the spotlight on support for large families, more leave and work flexibility for mothers, and the development of services to support life rather than working parents. However, strong budgetary constraints, as well as other factors such as the traditionally low levels of part-time work, led to the introduction of some flexibility in the leave scheme rather than major changes: choice between maternity leave for 120 days at 100% or 150 days at 80% was introduced, as well as unpaid part-time parental leave for 12, instead of 6, months.

Re-elected in 2005, the Socialist Party took up its former commitments to work–life balance and gender equality. Other issues, such as abortion, poverty, domestic violence and the protection of children, were also high on the policy agenda (a second referendum led to the approval of a new law on abortion in 2007). However, in the context of continuing budgetary constraints, falling standards of living and the sharpest drop ever in fertility rates (1.36 in 2006, down from 1.56 in 2000), family policy goals tended to focus on three major objectives: reconciling work and family life; financial support for families, especially the most vulnerable; and the promotion of fertility.

The major goal on the 'reconciliation' agenda is to increase childcare services for children under 3 years, to meet the 33% Barcelona target[2] by 2009. Expansion of pre-school education, extension of school opening hours and the need to involve fathers in leave taking have also been high on the agenda. Changes in the leave scheme have recently been approved. As from February 2009, paternity leave taken during the first month after birth will be increased to 20 working days and the 'initial parental leave' (formerly 'maternity leave') will be increased to 5 months with full earnings compensation (or 6 months at 83% of earnings) on condition that the father (alone) takes one whole month of the leave. In other words, the extension of paid leave has been linked more strongly to the principle of gender sharing of leave. Parental leave (3 months) will be paid at 25% of earnings if taken immediately after the 5 months of 'initial parental leave'.

An overview of developments in Portugal

In summary, developments in parental leave policies in Portugal over the past few decades are closely associated with changing trends in families and gender roles and with two contrasting social and political contexts (before and after the 1974 Revolution). Over the past three decades, the basic framework of public response to the challenges posed by full-time work and family life has consistently stressed a short, fully compensated leave, complemented by a system of publicly subsidised services to care for young children and by a variety of partially compensated, gender-neutral entitlements to take time off work (for example, 30 days to care for sick children).

Two main policy perspectives have underpinned this 'early return to full-time work', gender equality-orientated leave policy model: first, the endorsement of a full-time dual earner model and of gender equity in employment, a perspective sustained by social norms and practices as Portuguese women made a large-scale entry into employment from the 1960s onwards; second, the endorsement of a connection between leave policy and the expansion of state-subsidised childcare services. A third perspective, endorsing gender equity in caring and the need for fathers' involvement in leave taking, has also been emphasised, but it is more recent and less firmly embedded in social norms and practices (Crompton et al, 2007).

The political context post-1974 seems to be an important factor in explaining the common endorsement, over time, of these three perspectives: three main parties – PC, PS and PSD – and in particular the latter two, which have alternated in power during the past 25 years, have built up a fairly strong consensus regarding the link between reconciliation policy and gender equality policy as well as a shared vision of the importance of subsidised services to support families; they also share a vision of the state's role in shouldering the costs of leave in order to make it effective. This relative consensus in the politics of leave policy, also associated with policies made and implemented at a national level (rather than also at a regional level, as in Spain), has made for considerable continuity in the politics of leave. In spite of this continuity, however, implementation of the leave policy model has not been easy. Budgetary constraints, the slow expansion of services, the need to provide other types of support for low-income families (such as cash benefits) and the large number of families that need affordable non-profit services – all these factors have made for a leave policy model built slowly even if quite coherently.

Leave policies in Spain

The pre-democratic period (up to 1975)

In 1900, a law regulating working conditions for women and children introduced a working time reduction for breastfeeding and prohibited maternal work for 3 weeks after delivery. After the Spanish government ratified the 1919 ILO Maternity Protection Convention, the first maternity insurance providing pay for 12 weeks was enacted in 1929 and extended by the Second Republic (1931–39).

During Franco's dictatorship (1939–75), formal employment of mothers declined as labour legislation allowed the dismissal of women on marriage and discouraged the employment of married women. A male breadwinner model was imposed by means of political regulations, even though the economy was unable to sustain such a model. The authoritarian family policy was based on supplements to male wages for dependent wives and children, as well as on state intervention in housing. However, to make ends meet, second jobs for men and informal work for women were widespread.

In this context, leave for working mothers was not an issue. Maternity leave was consolidated into the social security system (Alonso Olea and Tortuero, 2002). Twelve weeks' maternity leave was extended to all affiliated employees at 75% of wages in 1966, within the sickness benefit scheme, but covered few mothers. This low proportion of formally employed mothers had well-defined entitlements and the support of economically inactive female relatives to care for their children within extended family networks.

The Spanish democratic transition (1976–82)

The Spanish Constitution of 1978 established the principle of equality among all Spaniards, men, women and children, culminating in the reform of the Civil Code in 1981. Compared with Portugal, the democratic transition was more liberal and reformist. The Spanish feminist movement focused on the rights of women to have an independent life with or without children, and this demand was not linked to family or reconciliation policies. As a reaction to the pronatalist and antifeminist family policies formulated during the dictatorship, groups that in other countries supported egalitarian family policies avoided policy making in the area of the family in Spain (Valiente, 1996). The focus was on new formal rights (to formal work, to political participation, to divorce, to abortion), while motherhood was perceived as a traditional issue. Furthermore, it was easier to campaign for civil rights than for more expensive social rights in the context of a rudimentary welfare state and economic restructuring, while middle-class women could cope by making private arrangements.

Labour relations were transformed by the 1980 Workers' Statute (Estatuto de los Trabajadores), the main law regulating work in Spain. It extended maternity leave to 14 weeks, retained the one-hour 'breastfeeding' working time reduction (paid by employers), provided for 2 days of birth leave for fathers or in case of acute illness of relatives (paid by employers) and brought in unpaid parental leave for a maximum of 3 years and the possibility of an unpaid reduction of working hours for mothers and fathers with children under 6 years or handicapped children. The law extended rights to employees in the private sector that already existed in the public sector, in particular the provision governing parental leave, which established the right to return to a previous job as soon as a vacancy was available.

The socialist (PSOE) government (1982–96)

This was a period of developing universal social rights in a context of economic restructuring and membership of the EU. Social policy priorities were health, education, pensions and promoting employment. In 1983 the Instituto de la Mujer (Institute for Women) was created as the government body commissioned to promote gender equality in state policies. In 1984, the socialist government carried out a major labour reform in order to deal with widespread unemployment and non-declared work. It liberalised fixed-term working contracts and introduced a low-cost, part-time work contract. Casual work subsequently became one of the structural features of the Spanish labour market.

In a major education reform in 1990, compulsory education was extended and all ECEC was integrated into the educational system. The political goal was to ensure universal coverage of early education for children aged 3 years upwards, a target reached at the end of the 1990s. The birth to 3 years age group was to be provided for according to demand, in cooperation between state, regional and local administrations and with no clear funding commitment.

Following EU accession in 1986, as part of the reforms to adapt to European policies, maternity leave was extended to 16 weeks in 1989, allowing mothers to transfer the last 4 weeks to the father. Breastfeeding leave could also be transferred to the father, and an adoption leave of 8 weeks was introduced (subsequently equalised with maternity leave). In 1994, as part of a reform of social security, maternity leave was detached from the sickness scheme, where it was paid at 75% of earnings usually supplemented by employers, and payment was increased to 100% of earnings. Arrangements were made for partial social security provision for employees (covering healthcare and pension rights) during the first year of the unpaid parental leave.

Overall, however, leave policy had low priority in a context of high unemployment (female unemployment peaked at 32% in 1994) and growth in temporary work (up to one third of employees from 1990 onwards). It was seen as a threat to women's opportunities in the labour market. Research showed how mothers in temporary positions did not feel entitled even to use maternity leave (Escobedo, 1999).

The conservative government (1996–2004)

The conservative Popular Party (PP) in government promoted a liberal expansion of the economy, accompanied by a significant flow of illegal immigration and rising house prices. Family policy was on the agenda, with a National Family Policy Plan. But measures focused on tax deductions, large families and family-friendly provision by employers, with no increase in public spending on families and children.

Maternal employment based on an early return to work was promoted by means of tax incentives, improvements to part-time contracts and a policy oriented to the expansion of the private market in childcare, including a tax deduction compensating for around one third of private full-time childcare costs. The government deregulated services for children under 3 years, excluding them from an education law in 2003, to encourage the development of more diversified and cheaper nurseries oriented to providing opening hours needed by working parents rather than educational goals.

In 1999 a law "to promote the reconciliation of work and family life of employed persons" was approved and presented as completing the transposition of the EU directives on maternity protection and parental leave. It made maternity leave flexible, allowing mothers to take it on a part-time basis (20 weeks part time after the compulsory 6 weeks), extended to 10 weeks the mother's right to transfer maternity leave to the father, and allowed leave to be interrupted if the baby was in hospital. It created an unpaid leave to care for dependent relatives for up to one year. However, no measures were taken to cover the specific situation of employees in temporary or other forms of atypical work or the self-employed, who constitute half the workforce.

The 1999 law was accompanied by a strong information campaign and helped to place the topic of reconciliation on the policy agenda. It was followed by some regional diversification of leave policies. While labour regulation and social security were very centralised, other policies (such as education, health, social and care services, and labour market activation) have been decentralised: *comunidades autónomas* (autonomous communities) and their parliaments play a leading role. Some of these 17 autonomous communities started to develop additional leave entitlements.

Navarre (2000), the Basque Country (2003) and Castilla-León (2004), all governed by conservative parties with noticeable Christian Democratic or Catholic influence, introduced flat-rate benefits for parents taking either parental leave or a reduction in working time to care for children. The Basque Country offers a monthly €200 flat-rate benefit for mothers (€250 for fathers) on parental leave; Navarre €330 monthly for one year of parental leave for a second child, and until the child is 3 for third and subsequent children; Castilla-León a means-tested benefit equivalent to 12 months of minimum wage, paid in a lump sum at the end. Even though the Basque Country has introduced a slightly higher benefit as an incentive for fathers, from a gender equality perspective the final result is that users of these low flat-rate benefits are overwhelmingly women.

Meanwhile, in 2002, the Catalan government introduced earnings-related measures to support reconciliation of work and family life, but these were confined to the public sector, the government acting in effect as a family-friendly employer. These included a month's full pay for the father after maternity leave, a one third working time reduction on full pay for one year from the end of maternity or paternity leave, and a one third working time reduction at 80% of earnings or half time at 60% until the child is 6. The working time reduction on full pay has been very popular with fathers and mothers, resulting in equal use in some professional groups. Take-up rates for the other non-fully compensated working time reductions were initially low, but increased strongly between 2003 and 2006, particularly among mothers, widening gender differentials (Escobedo, 2008).

Some lower supplementary entitlements were also introduced by other autonomous communities, contributing to growing diversity in this policy field. This is also apparent in services for children under 3 years. Here the highest coverage is to be found in the Basque Country (46%) and Catalonia (31%), the lowest in Castilla-León (3%), while Navarre is on a par with the national average (22%). In the Basque Country, Catalonia and Navarre, payments for parental leave and ECEC services are both being pursued, while the more conservative

Castilla-León seems to be developing the leave option as an alternative to publicly supported services.

Around the turn of the century, the dual earner family model extended to families with small children, encouraged by higher female educational attainment, low wages and unstable temporary employment for both men and women, and an escalation of house prices. Women are increasingly likely to stay in the labour market after their first child, with a 65% employment rate among women with one child under 3 years. For most young mothers, this means full-time working. Although recent policy changes may stimulate good-quality, part-time work in the future, for the present part-time work tends to be unstable and is mainly found in low-status occupations, which explains why the rate of voluntary part-time employment is so low. In 2006, only 2.7% of Spanish female employees stated they were working part time in order to care for children or other dependants, compared with an EU average of 11.3% (European Commission, 2008).

An important footnote to this period is that it saw the start of a strong influx of female immigration, which has continued over the past decade. The proportion of non-nationals in the workforce rose from 2% in 1999, to 14% in 2007. This has provided a new labour supply for care and household services and thus contributed to diversifying work–family arrangements, as some workers have employed migrant women as carers and cleaners (Flaquer and Escobedo, 2009).

The current situation (2004–08)

When the PSOE returned to power in 2004, one of its first measures was to revoke the PP's 2003 education law, reintegrating services for children under 3 years into the education system, while allowing for a great deal of regional autonomy. This has led to a decentralised, diversified and rapid development of childcare provision, partly within the education system, partly outside it, with low quality assurance. This is a controversial issue, with experts demanding greater public intervention and investment (Balaguer and Arderiu, 2007). In 2006, however, the government agreed to raise public funding to improve coverage of services for children under 3 years.

In 2005, major reforms modernised family law, permitting same-sex marriage and facilitating divorce and joint custody. For the first time, the left wing has produced an innovative family policy discourse. In the same year, the central government improved leave and working time reduction policies for its own employees. These improvements were extended in 2007 to the whole public sector, and some to all employees.

While there have been initiatives on leave and childcare services, there is a lack of coordination between them. A 2006 law on dependency has opened up the possibility of tying unpaid leave to care for severe dependants to a new €487 monthly social security payment for family carers. The logic is to 'activate' adult housewives with low employment opportunities (on average in their fifties), integrating them into this type of employment scheme. The law, however, excludes children under 3 years of age from its definition of dependants, except for those with severe disability or chronic illnesses.

The most recent reform of leave arrangements in Spain took place in 2007, in the framework of a general law on gender equality, introducing principles such as the balanced representation of women and men in politics, gender equality plans at company level, and a generic right to work–life balance. For the first time, fathers receive an individual and non-transferable entitlement, paid at 100% of earnings: a 2-week paternity leave to be taken during or after maternity leave. Coverage of maternity leave benefit has been improved to include more marginalised groups. Unpaid working time reductions have been extended and made more flexible for families: from one eighth to a half of working time until a child is 8 years (or 12 in the public sector) or to care for a dependent relative. This reform paves the way for a new development of the leave system, where maternity leave is no longer the only generally available paid entitlement. The programme of the Socialist Party re-elected in 2008 includes doubling regulated places for children under 3 and extending paid paternity leave up to one month.

An overview of developments in Spain

Spain is heterogeneous: there is territorial diversity, expressed in social behaviour and political decentralisation, affecting many fields relevant to leave policy. So generalisations are difficult. But we can say that Spain made a late transition to the dual earner family around the year 2000, and has also left behind the 'short leave male breadwinner model', although it remains unclear which leave model is emerging. Some features of the 'early return to full-time work leave model' are still present, but maternal full-time work is not as dominant as in Portugal. Features of the 'parental choice-oriented policy model' are also found; even though parental leave is basically unpaid, it is available full or part time until the child is 8 years old, with some social security protection, and with recently introduced payments in some autonomous communities or for some occupational groups.

The whole political spectrum agrees on promoting maternal employment and services all over the country, although there is less agreement on conditions. ECEC policies in Spain have emphasised pre-school education but shown less concern for the needs of working parents, many of whom must rely on unregulated, non-subsidised services for children under 3 years. On the other hand, there is a lack of agreement about parental leave at the national level, although some consensus on promoting the option to reduce working hours in a protected, very flexible and reversible way. This option may favour different work–care combinations among partners, facilitating diversity in family life.

Finally, the reform providing universal care guarantees for adult dependants opens up new possibilities for coordination between care services and home care payments. Full or part-time leave arrangements will be taken up by more and more male and female employees at different stages of their lives.

Beyond the male breadwinner model: a comparative perspective

Portugal and Spain have shared many social and demographic similarities over the past 50 years and both have experienced the transition from a right-wing dictatorship to democracy. Nonetheless, as one looks closely at these two countries, their individual histories and characteristics are visible not only in family and gender role patterns but also in the political processes, debates and turning points that have led to specific pathways for leave policy.

If we compare leave arrangements in Spain and in Portugal, we find important commonalities and differences. In 2007, both countries had a short, fully compensated maternity leave of 4 months where mothers have to take 6 weeks, the rest being transferable to fathers. Spain started earlier, introducing 12 weeks' leave (at 75% of earnings) as early as 1966, while Portugal introduced 12 weeks in 1975 (at 100%); on the other hand, Portugal is slightly more generous at present, with no ceiling on earnings compensation.

Both countries have introduced some flexibility in use: in Portugal leave may be taken for 4 months at 100% or 5 months at 80%, while in Spain flexibility is between full- and part-time leave. Paternity leave is also similar: in 2007, both countries have a short paid leave to be taken after birth (2 days in Spain, 5 in Portugal) and paid parental leave for fathers (13 and 15 days, respectively). In this case, Portugal started out almost a decade earlier (1999) and state funding at 100% for all 20 calendar days is more generous. A third similarity is that both countries have maintained and transformed the old 'breastfeeding leave', consolidating it as a working time reduction that can be used by either parent during the first year after the birth of the child.

The two other similarities identified are related to the countries' economic difficulties during recent decades and to the late development of the welfare state in Southern Europe. In both cases, the transition to democracy and 'catching up' with other European countries took place in a context of budgetary limitations, leading to low levels of social expenditure. Central state funding of leave arrangements and care services was in competition with other priorities such as education and health. The setting up of a well-paid leave scheme was therefore gradual and highly dependent on economic and political fluctuations. Finally, in this context, it is also important to underline the influence of EU initiatives and debates. In both countries, these have been policy drivers; not only have they given national policy makers a hand in prioritising the issue of reconciliation, but they have also served as a 'model' for the structuring of certain types of leave arrangement. However, this does not mean that the direction of change is necessarily the same. The transposition of the 1996 directive, for example, stimulated debate and change in both countries, but very much in line with the policy priorities adopted at the time in each country (more centred on flexibility for working mothers in Spain, more centred on gender sharing in Portugal).

There are at least three significant differences in current leave arrangements, first with regard to the length of parental leave introduced in both countries in the early 1980s. Whereas in Spain it may be taken for 3 years and the unpaid reduction in working hours (up to half of total working hours) may be taken until children are 8, in Portugal leave may only be taken for 3 months until the child is 6 years and there is no scope for a reduction in working hours. In both countries, parental leave has traditionally been unpaid, and take-up is estimated to be low. However, whereas in Portugal there has been no move towards enabling reductions in working time, in Spain several autonomous communities have introduced some payment for working time reduction (which may be conceptualised as 'part-time parental leave'), so opening up the leave scheme to greater choice.

The second difference relates to parents' entitlement to take time off work to care for sick children. This is much more generous in Portugal: 30 days per year to care for sick children below age 10 (compensated at 65%), compared with only 2 days paid by the employer in Spain.

The third difference lies in the relationship between working hours, leave arrangements and services. Although formal childcare provision for children below age 3 years is similar, it is probably more important to note that the relationship with leave – the complementarity – is different. In Spain, there has been little state commitment to subsidising services for children under 3 years and opening hours of services in the public sector are similar to school hours so do not easily fit in with working parents' schedules. In Portugal, commitment to the public funding of services was established in the early 1980s; although expansion of subsidised third sector services has been slow, these services have responded to the needs of parents with long working hours.

Looking at policy developments over time and in the context of different political, social and economic conditions is another way to draw comparisons. Both countries have experienced an authoritarian government and the subsequent transition to democracy. Both right-wing dictatorships upheld male breadwinning and women's subordinate status, even if, in both countries, women's participation in the informal economy was always quite significant. However, when we look at the years of transition (1970s and 1980s), we find that the concept of 'transition' is used to describe political and social changes that, in practice, followed distinct pathways.

In Portugal, the concept of transition is used to describe a revolution introducing sudden and profound changes in society, including strong advocacy for social rights by the whole political spectrum, in particular the rights of women and men to (full-time) symmetrical integration in the employment system. In the 1980s and 1990s, in a context of high female employment, this placed pressure on state policy makers to build up services and paid leave entitlements, in spite of budgetary limitations. In Spain, the concept of transition describes a process of change that also rejected former labour and family policies, but that took place gradually and under different types of pressure and advocacy. Pressure arising from a dominant 'female full-time work ethic' and high levels of maternal employment was largely absent. Women's groups focused on gaining formal rights to autonomy and emancipation rather than the protection of working mothers. In a context of high unemployment and low female employment, the main parties in government in the 1980s and 1990s prioritised health, education and the promotion of employment; to combat unemployment and non-declared work, they introduced low-cost temporary or part-time working contracts.

A second dimension of difference may be found in the connections over time between leave policy, reconciliation policy and gender equality policy. In Spain, gender equality policy emerges strongly during the transition to democracy, but it does so largely detached, at least during the 1980s and 1990s, from the politics of leave policy. Political consensus and pressure from society and families were rather weak: female participation in the labour market was growing but still low and the governing parties failed to put family issues, including reconciliation, high on the agenda or build up a shared view of public support and expenditure regarding leave and service provision.

Moreover, in contrast with the two main parties in Portugal, those in Spain (PSOE and PP) have developed contrasting leave policy perspectives rather than a common endorsement of a particular leave scheme. The conservative government (PP) neither located its 1999 law in the framework of gender equality policy nor developed new and effective leave measures; as mentioned above, it focused on liberalisation, part-time work, tax deductions and family-friendly measures by employers. It is only later, in 2007, with the PSOE in power (and with rising female employment rates), that leave arrangements were located within the framework of gender equality policy and that the question of public expenditure on service provision for children below 3 years were brought into the debate.

In other words, different political, economic and social contexts have made for different policy perspectives and different outcomes. In Portugal, there has been a stronger and more continuous linkage between leave and gender equality policies, between the leave system and public support for ECEC provision adjusted to long working hours, between the latter and a full-time dual earner model that emerged in the 1970s and is incorporated into social norms and labour market traditions. Political consensus emerging from the two main centrist parties has also contributed to continuity and coherence in leave policy. At the same time, however, it has made for some lack of diversity and innovation (no regional differences, no other forms of leave such as long leave for home-based care or working time reductions over longer periods of time), for low emphasis on employer friendliness, and for more emphasis on state regulation and expenditure on leave and services.

In Spain, leave policy has until recently evolved separately from, rather than enmeshed in, the gender equality agenda, and strongly linked to the devolution of funding and management of ECEC services to regional governments and to families. As a result, compared with Portugal, there has been more emphasis on a variety of care solutions and types of leave to support reconciliation, and more emphasis too on the benefits of longer leaves, part-time work and unpaid reductions in work. Overall, then, there is a more liberal and decentralised view of the state's role.

As a result, the move away from male breadwinning and female caring is undoubtedly strong in both countries, but parental leave policies have developed in different directions over the past few decades. Whereas in Portugal there seems to be one fairly stable and consensual leave policy model – based on an *early return to full-time work*, with strong linkages to gender equality and service provision policies – in Spain the leave policy model is more diverse, certainly more *choice-orientated* than Portugal: it is based on the promotion of some early return to work after a short well-paid leave, while also emphasising the advantages of longer leaves and part-time options. Low government commitment to service provision with long opening hours and strong devolution of funding and services to employers and regional or local governments have also built up loose and varied linkages between service provision and the leave system, with higher expectations on families to organise their own care arrangements (for example, through employing domestic workers).

More dependent on changes in party politics and on regional governments, less vulnerable in economic terms (current standards of living are higher in Spain than in Portugal), dual earner families in Spain can therefore choose from a variety of leave policy principles, entitlements and arrangements. These characteristics have led to a specific type of choice-orientated leave policy model rather than to a predominant early return to full-time work model. However, compared with the French or Finnish 'choice-orientated' model (Wall, 2007, 2008), the Spanish model is more weakly linked to subsidised services and to gender equality policy (even if over the last years it is catching up fast on the latter issue). 'Choice' in leave to care, be it in Finland or France, has been strongly based on the central state building up childcare services in the 1970s or 1980s, as well as the possibility, introduced in the 1990s, of longer leaves to care or part-time options. This Southern European choice-orientated solution has therefore followed a different pathway, leading to an emphasis on varied and territorially diverse leave arrangements, lower complementarity with service provision and linkages to informal as well as formal services.

Notes

[1] Leave provision described here refers to statutory entitlements.

[2] EU member states agreed in 2002 at a meeting in Barcelona "[to strive] to provide childcare by 2010 to at least 90% of children between 3 years old and mandatory school age and at least 33% of children under 3 years of age".

References

Alonso Olea, M. and Tortuero, J.L. (2002) *Instituciones de seguridad social*, Madrid: Civitas.

Almeida, A.N. and Wall, K. (2001) 'Família e quotidiano. Movimentos e Sinais de Mudança', in J.M. Brandão de Brito (ed) *O país em revolução*, Lisbon: Círculo de Leitores, pp 277-307.

Balaguer, I. and Arderiu, E. (2007) *Calidad de los servicios para la primera infancia y estimación de la demanda. Colección: Estudios, 53*, Madrid: Ministerio de Trabajo y Asuntos Sociales.

Crompton, R (ed) (1999) *Restructuring gender relations and employment: The decline of the male breadwinner*, Oxford: Oxford University Press.

Crompton, R., Lyonette, C. and Wall, K. (2007) 'Family, gender and work–life articulation: Britain and Portugal compared', *Community, Work and Family*, vol 10, no 3, pp 283-308.

Escobedo, A. (1999) 'Work–family arrangements in Spain', in A. van Doorne-Huiskes, L. den Dulk and J. Schippers (eds) *Work–family arrangements in Europe: The role of employers*, Amsterdam: Thesis Publishers, pp 103-29.

Escobedo, A. (2008) 'Políticas de licencias parentales y de atención infantil para los menores de tres años y sus familias: el caso español en el contexto internacional', in M. Pazos (ed) *Economía e igualdad de género: Retos de la Hacienda Pública en el siglo XXI*, Madrid: Instituto de Estudios Fiscales, pp 161-83.

European Commission (2008) 'Indicators for monitoring the Employment Guidelines including indicators for additional employment analysis. 2008 Compendium', available at http://ec.europa.eu/employment_social/employment_strategy/pdf/2008compendium_en.pdf (accessed 21 October 2008).

Ferreira, V. (1998) 'Engendering Portugal: social change, state policies and women's social mobilization', in A. Costa Pinto (ed) *Modern Portugal*, Palo Alto, CA: Society for the Promotion of Science and Scholarship, pp 162-88.

Flaquer, L. (2000) 'Is there a Southern European model of family policy?', in A.A. Pfenning and T. Bahle (eds) *Families and family policies in Europe*, Frankfurt and New York, NY: P. Lang, pp 15-33.

Flaquer L. and Escobedo, A. (2009) 'The metamorphosis of informal work in Spain: family solidarity, female immigration and development of social rights', in B. Pfau-Effinger, L. Flaquer and P. Jensen (eds) *Formal and informal work: The hidden work regime in Europe*, New York, NY: Routledge, pp 143-68.

Perista, H. and Chagas Lopes, M. (1999) *A licença de paternidade – Um direito novo para a promoção da igualdade (Colecção Estudos 14)*, Lisbon: CESIS – Ministry of Labour and Solidarity.

Pfau-Effinger, B., Flaquer, L. and Jensen, P. (eds) (2009) *Formal and informal work: The hidden work regime in Europe*, New York, NY: Routledge.

Valiente, C. (1996) 'The rejection of authoritarian policy legacies: family policy in Spain (1975–1995)', *South European Society & Politics*, vol 1, no 1, pp 95-114.

Wall, K. (1997) 'Portugal: issues concerning the family in 1996', in J. Ditch et al (eds) *Developments in national family policies*, Brussels and York: European Observatory on Family Policies and University of York, pp 213-49.

Wall, K. (2002) *Family change and family policy in Portugal*, ICS Working Paper, Lisbon: Instituto de Ciências Sociais da Universidade de Lisboa.

Wall, K. (2004) 'Portugal: policies, challenges, opportunities', in B. Cizek and R. Richter (eds) *Families in EU 15: Policies, challenges and opportunities*, Vienna: European Observatory on Family Policies, OIF, pp 195-207.

Wall, K. (2005) *Famílias em Portugal*, Lisbon: Imprensa de Ciências Sociais.

Wall, K. (2007) 'Leave policy models and the articulation of work and family in Europe: a comparative perspective', in P. Moss and K. Wall (eds) *International review of leave policies and related research 2007*, Employment Relations Research Series No 80, London: Department for Business, Enterprise and Regulatory Reform, pp 25-43.

Wall, K. (2008) 'I modelli di politiche relative ai congedi e l'articolazione lavoro/famiglia in Europa: una prospettiva comparativa', *Sociologia e Politiche Sociali*, vol 11, no 1, pp 59-86.

FOURTEEN

Sweden: individualisation or free choice in parental leave?

Anders Chronholm

Maternity leave[1]: there is no general entitlement to statutory maternity leave. But pregnant women are eligible for 50 days of leave paid at 80% of income if they work in jobs considered injurious or involving risk to the foetus.

Paternity leave: 10 working days at 80% of earnings with a ceiling of SEK410,000 per year (€36,815)[2].

Parental leave: 480 days of leave at 80% of earnings for 390 days up to a ceiling of SEK410,000 per year (€36,815); the remaining 90 days at a flat-rate payment of SEK180 a day (€15). Sixty days are only for the mother and 60 days only for the father. The remaining 360 days are a family entitlement. In addition, each parent is entitled to take unpaid leave until a child is 18 months.

Leave to care for sick children: 120 days of leave per year per family for each child under the age of 12, and for children aged 12 to 15 with a doctor's certificate, at 80% of earnings. Sixty of these days also can be used to stay home with young children if the regular caregiver is sick.

Other: parents can take a 25% reduction of normal working hours until a child reaches the age of 8 years or completes the first grade of school; there is no payment for working reduced hours.

Sweden is a Nordic country and a member state of the European Union. It has a high level of maternal employment. It was the first country in the world to introduce parental leave, in 1974. In 2004, about 80% of fathers took paternity leave, for an average of 9.7 days out of the 10 days available. Almost all families use paid parental leave. Although mothers still take most parental leave, the proportion of total days used by men has been increasing – from 7% in 1987 to 21% in 2007. Mothers use just under two thirds of leave days taken to care for sick children (64% in 2004).

There is an entitlement to early childhood education and care for children from 12 months of age.

Introduction

The development of Swedish parental leave policy, first introduced in 1974, can be seen as an example of strategic actions from different political institutions. They starting point for this chapter is that political institutions not only act but also create cultural norms that influence public opinion (Rothstein, 2002). The development of Swedish parental leave policy also shows how an academic elite can produce a theoretical basis for political decisions (Klinth, 2002).

That Sweden was the first country to introduce parental leave, instead of confining leave policy only to leave for mothers, could be explained as a result of the academic and political debates in Sweden during the 1960s. These debates led to the adoption of new ideas among leading politicians. To develop such new political ideas, the introduction of new words is often of central importance (Hirdman, 1998). Until the 1960s, the Swedish debate over gender equality was limited to different 'women's questions' because the term 'gender equality' itself was not yet introduced. The first step towards a new way to discuss equality between women and men was the introduction of role theory into the political debates, making men a part of the 'problem'. Two new words, introduced in both academic and political publications at the beginning of the 1960s, were '*könsroll*' (gender role) and '*jämställdhet*' (gender equality).

But to give a broader historic background to the development of Swedish parental leave policy, three other main terms should be mentioned that show the changing political focus during the first half of the 20th century. From the beginning of the century, the focus was 'maternal policy'. During the 1930s, 'population policy' became dominant. Then, from the 1950s, the term 'family policy' began to appear in official contexts (Ohlander, 1992).

The population crisis and the vision of a welfare state

One of the first Swedish laws to address maternal policy was introduced in 1900 and stated that mothers with industrial occupations were not to be employed during the first month after the birth of a child (Ohlander, 1992). At this time, many Swedish women worked under very bad conditions, sometimes for only half the wages paid to men, and this was particularly the case in the textile industry (Schmitz, 2002). Maternity insurance, to pay women on maternity leave, became an important subject for the women's association of the Social Democratic Party, from 1907; however, it met with very little understanding among the male members of the parliament. Not until 1931 was the first maternal insurance introduced, providing working mothers with newborn children with compensation for one month's loss of income.

In these early years of the century, the conflict between parenthood and earning a living was an important political question mainly for women, also resulting in different views and priorities inside the political parties (Ohlander, 1992). There was, however, a broader understanding of the importance of human reproduction for maintaining the industrial workforce and military manpower (Plantin, 2001). Already in the late 19th and early 20th centuries, child welfare had become an important matter in the Scandinavian countries. Norway was the first country in the world to introduce a Children and Young Persons Act in 1896, followed by Sweden in 1902. This law was developed in 1924 when municipal child custody boards became obligatory, the legislation remaining largely unchanged until it was replaced with the Social Services Act in 1980 (Andersson, 2006).

The interest in child welfare at the turn of the century can also be regarded as connected to the hard living conditions of many families, which resulted in high levels of emigration and infant mortality and a declining birth rate. In order to increase the birth rate, a law was introduced in 1910 forbidding the sale of contraceptives (Plantin, 2001). However, the birth rate continued to decline, the number of births falling from 130,000 in 1911 to 87,000 in 1931 (Elmér, 1975).

One of the recommendations from Alva and Gunnar Myrdal in their book *Kris i befolkningsfrågan* [*Crisis in the population question*], published in 1934, was the abolition of the 1910 law. They argued that birth control should be regarded as a right, and that in order to increase the birth rate it was necessary to understand the fundamental reasons why many couples were not willing to accept having children as a public responsibility. A majority of families had become aware of the connection between living standards and numbers of children, and were choosing a higher standard of living instead of more children. The responsibility for the declining birth rate should not, therefore, be thrown at poor families but should rather be seen as a socio-political problem, including the distribution of resources between the social classes. The Myrdals argued that "the problem for us is: depopulation or social reforms. And the programme will be: a new society characterised by social solidarity, where the whole nation to a greater extent will feel responsible for the children who will become their next generation" (Myrdal and Myrdal, 1934, p 16, author's translation).

Among the proposals they put forward to realise these goals were universal child allowances, housing allowances for families with many children, free healthcare for all children, free education with free school books and a free meal at school, and free day care centres. Alva Myrdal was a social psychologist and Gunnar Myrdal was a professor in economics, but both had been members of the Social Democratic Party since the beginning of the 1930s and had close relations with members of the Social Democratic government that came to power in 1932. Their book had a great influence and convinced many about the importance of developing an active social welfare policy.

The Prime Minister, Per Albin Hansson, himself brought up by a lone mother in materially poor conditions, created the vision of a 'people's home' (*folkhemmet*), a society where everyone cares for others as if in a family (Hirdman, 2006). To be able to realise the new goals and raise the country's living standards, the Minister for Finance, Ernst Wigforss, together with Gunnar Myrdal, introduced a new planned economy, becoming the first to use a Keynesian economy model (Therborn, 1992).

Gunnar Myrdal also became leader of the 1935 Population Commission (Plantin, 2001). Even if most of the proposals from the commission were rejected, some results were implemented during the 1930s. In 1937, housing loans were established to encourage earlier marriages. In 1938, the law against the sale of contraceptives was scrapped and employers were forbidden to dismiss women because they were pregnant (Ohlander, 1992). In that year, also, a general maternity benefit was introduced, together with the possibility for lone mothers to get an extra benefit subjected to a means test. A universal child allowance paid to the mother was introduced in 1948 and in 1955 maternity provision was extended to 6 months' leave, 3 months paid and 3 unpaid (Plantin, 2001).

A century of social democracy

During the first half of the 20th century, social reforms became a major theme, not only for the Social Democratic Party but also for the other political parties. However, the Social Democrats, being the largest party, dominated Swedish policy during this time, with two or more equally strong bourgeois parties in permanent opposition. From 1921 to 1985, the Social Democrats attracted an average of 45% of the voters, receiving more than half of the total votes cast in five elections (Therborn, 1992).

The election victory in 1932 was the beginning of a period of 44 years with a Social Democratic government. In 1976, a 3-party coalition consisting of the Conservative, Liberal and Centre Parties formed the first bourgeois government for almost half a century. After two periods of these bourgeois governments, the Social Democratic were returned to power in 1982. In 1986, the Prime Minister, Olof Palme, leader of the Social Democratic Party since 1969, was murdered in the street on his way home in Stockholm, an event that for many marked the end of the vision introduced in the 1930s of Sweden as a secure 'people's home' (Molin, 1992). In 1991, the Social Democrats lost another election and a bourgeois government was formed by the three parties from the 1976 coalition together with a fourth party, the Christian Democrats. The Social Democratic Party again won the elections in 1994, retaining power another 12 years until the elections in 2006.

The realisation of emancipation

In 1962, the report *Kvinnors liv och arbete* (*Women's life and work*) was published, based on an investigation led by the sociology professor Edmund Dahlström. The study, starting in 1958, was financed by SNS, a Swedish educational association supported by Swedish commerce and industry. In 1960, Norwegian academics were invited to join the study and they are represented in the final report writing in their own language and including Norwegian research (SNS, 1962). Through this report, a wider public was introduced to new concepts – gender equality and gender roles – related to social structures and socialisation, concepts that would be central to the coming political debate during the 1960s and 1970s.

Among the political parties it was the Liberals that first engaged in the gender equality questions. Already in a 1961 essay, Eva Moberg, a journalist and feminist, had started an intensive debate over the emancipation of women, discussing the issue in relation to the emancipation of men. She developed her ideas further in a book *Kvinnor och människor* [*Women and human beings*] (Moberg, 1962). She argued that economic independence for women was related to the sharing of housework and childcare, focusing on the importance of changing the male gender role. Compared with earlier debates where the problems arising from combining responsibility for childcare and housework with employment were regarded as specifically 'women's questions', Moberg's focus on men's responsibilities inside the family was a radical change.

Also during the 1960s, lobbying groups formed by young academics, mainly from the Liberal and Social Democratic Parties, were stimulating the gender equality debate by their attempts to influence journalists, members of the Swedish parliament and policy makers in government departments. One of the most important was Group 22, whose membership included Professor Edmund Dahlström, from the women's life and work inquiry. Another active member was Lisbeth Palme, and her husband, Olof Palme, who became Prime Minister in the Social Democratic government in 1969, was invited to participate in discussions with the group (Florin and Nilsson, 2000, pp 50-1).

At the beginning of the 1970s, Olof Palme made a speech in Washington about the importance of men's emancipation, a concept first brought into Swedish debates by Eva Moberg 10 years earlier. In 1972, he introduced gender equality as a main political subject at the Social Democratic Party congress, resulting in the setting up of a special government gender equality unit, the Jämställdhetsdelegationen. The term *jämställdhet* (gender equality) was now firmly established, not only in political debates but also as an important concept for future state policies. By including the new gender equality ideology in its own policies, the Social Democratic Party could gain a more radical identity and attract more female voters in its competition with the Liberal Party and other left parties (Florin and Nilsson, 2000, pp 11-12).

According to the Swedish historical researcher Yvonne Hirdman, the political debates leading to the parental leave reform drew on different arguments. While politicians from the Liberal Party were arguing for more equal gender roles in the family, the Social Democrats paid more attention to increasing women's participation in the labour market as a way of improving the economic position of poorer families. The dual earner family was seen as one way to reduce inequalities between families, thereby giving children a more equal standard of living (Hirdman, 2001).

The parental leave reform was proposed in 1972 in the final report of the Family Policy Committee, formed in 1965 by the Social Democrats. The committee recommended that maternity leave for women should be transformed into parental leave for women and men. An account of its discussions shows that parental leave was mainly intended to be a complement to public childcare for working parents. The National Board of Health and Welfare, by this time responsible for the quality of the Swedish public childcare system, was asked if 6 months of age could be regarded as an appropriate age for children to enter nurseries or family day care. Its answer was that the 6-month age limit for entry was common even if psychological research had shown that infants relating to new carers and environments during the second half of their first year are usually anxious and stressed by the experience. However, the board concluded, public childcare was still the best solution for many children because "many families today, as before, do not have the possibility to provide for the young child's need of security and adequate care. These families need support from the society in some form, and a place in public day care could be one of several possible supporting measures" (SOU 1972:34, p 222, author's translation).

The Family Policy Committee accordingly proposed a parental leave whose length was adapted to the 6-month age limit for entry to public childcare services. To make the parental leave too long, they also argued, would hamper the career prospects of women. The possibility for men to use the proposed leave was regarded as important both for the child and for a more equal sharing of caring responsibilities between parents, but also because the mother then could get back to her work or studies earlier. However, the committee surmised, even if fathers were to get the same entitlement to use parental leave, "it is probable that for a long time forward it will be the mother who will stay at home during the whole or the main part of the parental leave" (SOU 1972:34, p 223, author's translation).

The committee made some other significant proposals. It regarded it as important for fathers to have the possibility to take leave for 10 days after the birth of the child, to be together with the mother. And it also proposed a 'temporary parental leave' to care for sick children. This had been a demand since 1969 from LO, the Swedish Trades Union Confederation (*Landsorganisationen i Sverige*), an umbrella body for trades unions that organise mainly blue-collar workers; it had called for working parents to be able to use health insurance when their children were sick. LO's response to the committee's proposals, when circulated for consideration, was positive, but it did not comment on the possibility of fathers taking parental leave. Instead, LO emphasised the importance of a fast development of the public childcare system (Klinth, 2002).

Parental leave was introduced in 1974, and extended during the 1970s from an initial 6 months to 7 months (1975), then 9 months (1978). The 1970s was a decade when the number of dual earner families was increasing, and when children's well-being became an issue, for example in discussions about public childcare and new ideas about parenting. An intense debate about the rights of the child preceded a Swedish law against child abuse in 1979, which made corporal punishment and humiliating treatment of children illegal.

So during this time, when parental leave came on to the public and policy agenda, the raising of children became an official political issue rather than merely a private family matter. Public childcare was presented as the best alternative for children, a statement that was also supported by research showing that children attending public childcare services showed better results when they started at school (Andersson, 1990). The increasing use of public childcare could be seen as a step towards public socialisation of children, making parents' responsibilities more complementary. For many employed parents, parental leave was the main opportunity open to them to allow them to stay at home for a longer period with their child. As the first year can be regarded as crucial for children's well-being, parental leave became fundamental to enabling parents to give their child a good start in life. However, the statistics on the usage of parental leave during the first decades after its introduction showed that, even if fathers had the same rights, it was mainly mothers who were using it.

Fathers' use of parental leave

In 1980, fathers' share of the total amount of paid parental leave days taken stood at just 5% and 10 years later it was still only 7% (SCB, 2006). Fathers had the right to use half of the parental leave days available to a family, but they could also transfer their own share of leave days to their partner. As the parental leave benefit based on income was only 3 months for each parent in the beginning, and mothers were recommended to breastfeed their child for at least 6 months, it became natural for most fathers to hand over their part of the leave entitlement (Chronholm, 2004, 2007). In 1978, paid parental leave was extended to 9 months and in 1980 to 12 months (RFV, 1998), doubling in length in just 6 years.

However, there were more explanations as to why parental leave was mainly used by women during these early years of the new benefit. Even if the number of paid parental leave days was being regularly increased, until 1986 men could not get a benefit based on their own salary if the mother of the child was not herself entitled to income-related benefit (Bekkengen, 1996). That the parental leave benefit for both parents was related to the woman's income clearly illustrates how the introduction of Swedish parental leave was intended more to stimulate women to work than to encourage men to care for children.

Two years after the introduction of parental leave, in 1976, the Social Democrats lost a general election for the first time after 44 years in the government. During their years in opposition, between 1976 and 1982, they became more radical in their equality debates, arguing for a father's quota in parental leave (that is, a period of non-transferable leave only for fathers) as a way to raise the share used by fathers. The bourgeois government rejected this proposition as being part of a socialist ambition to get family life more centrally controlled (Klinth, 2002, p 271). But when the Social Democratic Party regained power in 1982, the father's quota formed no part of its policy; gender equality within families was now treated as a private matter for parents themselves to decide.

In 1991, Sweden again elected a bourgeois government and during the following years the father's quota was again introduced as a means of stimulating gender equality. But this time, it was the Liberal Party, part of the governing coalition, that advocated this radical proposal, leading to the introduction of the first 'father's month' in 1995. A second father's month was introduced in 2002, this time by the Social Democratic government.

Gender equality discussions about parental leave in Sweden show two main ideological influences that cross formal party political borders. Both can be regarded as important for the development of parental leave in Sweden. The first influence is feminism, both as an academic discipline and as a political movement; the second is the movement for fathers' rights, with its roots in a role theory that claims the importance of fathers as role models for children. The introduction into parental leave of the first father's month was in part a result of both of these influences (Klinth, 2002).

From a feminist point of view, an equal distribution of the parental leave days has been regarded as important for improving women's opportunities in the labour market. From the fathers' rights perspective, the focus has been men's equal opportunities to develop relationships with their children. These two interests seem to lead to the same goal – the equal distribution of parental leave days between mothers and fathers. However, they are not representative of all Swedish couples. Research results have shown that many mothers and fathers are satisfied with an unequal distribution of the parental leave days (RFV, 2003). Earlier research also showed that many mothers want to take the main part of the leave themselves (Haas, 1992).

The feminist case for a father's quota can be regarded as most attractive for women who value their careers as much as parenthood. As the possibility of sharing the parental leave days equally between mothers and fathers was included from the start in 1974, it could be argued that those couples where the father wants to take his share of leave would not need special father's months. Research during the 1990s on equal distribution of parental leave when the first father's month was introduced showed that couples sharing leave did exist, even if the official statistics for the same period reported fathers' usage of parental leave days to be, on average, only around 10% (Chronholm, 2004, 2007).

It is notable that this way of presenting only the average use of all paid parental leave days in a year, for all fathers and all mothers together, has rendered the statistics unable to describe the complexity and variations in Swedish family life. As a further example of these statistical inadequacies, single parents have been included in the same statistics as two-parent families. Yet the public debates concerning parental leave in Sweden have mainly been influenced by these general statistics, leading to the conclusion that most fathers have been unwilling to take their share of parental leave if not forced to.

This brings us back to the Swedish 'fatherhood movement' and more especially the 'daddy group' that was formed by the liberal–conservative coalition government at the beginning of the 1990s. This group was meant to discuss the possible introduction of a father's quota into parental leave, but it also used its influence to start a discussion about joint custody, stressing the importance of the child's right to both parents (DS 1995:2). Three years later, a new law on joint custody was introduced. As joint custody also guarantees the right to use parental leave, this law made it more possible for fathers to use parental leave after a divorce. Where only one of the parents, most often the mother, gets custody of the child, that parent gets the right to use all of the father's share of the parental leave (Sundström and Duvander, 1998).

After the so-called 'father's month' was introduced in 1995, the proportion of fathers who used the leave did increase. Among fathers of children born in 1993, 51% used some leave days before their child was 4 years old; but among fathers of children born in 1996, the figure increased to 77% (RFV, 2002). However, the average number of days used by fathers taking leave decreased during the same period. Consequently, the 'father's month' did not increase fathers' share of the total amount of paid parental leave days taken during the course of a year. Indeed, the share was even lower after introducing the father's month; 11.4% in 1994 compared with around 10% in the following years (RFV, 1998).

One reason for this declining usage could have been the new rules introduced in 1995. The parental leave benefit had been set at 90% of previous earnings, but was reduced to 80% in 1995. In addition, the regulations about when parental leave benefit could be drawn were tightened. Before 1995, it was possible to claim benefit without taking time off from work, for example for weekends or vacation (Chronholm, 2004); this was no longer possible after 1995.

With the introduction of a second non-transferable month in 2002, the father's share of paid parental leave days reached 15.5% and had increased to 20.8% by 2007. This extension of fathers'-only leave was introduced by the Social Democratic government, showing that it had again adopted the idea of individualisation of parental leave that it had dropped in the 1980s. In 2004, it also decided to set up an inquiry about how to develop parental leave in the future. The government's investigator, Karl-Petter Thorwaldsson, reporting in 2005, proposed new rules on Swedish parental leave. The proposal was influenced by the Icelandic parental leave model (see the Chapter Ten), with one third of the parental leave days only for the mother, one third for the father and one third to be shared as the parents wanted. However, the proposal went further than the original Icelandic model by increasing the non-transferable period for each parent to 5 months (in Iceland the period is 3 months), expanding the parental leave based on income replacement from 13 to 15 months (SOU 2005:73).

Thorwaldsson thought that the changes were needed to improve women's position in the labour market. Employers, he argued, are often wary of employing women because of the risk that they will stay away from their jobs to care for children. He also stressed that women staying at home more than men could be a reason for the gender gap in earnings. For similar reasons, he also wanted to reduce the period during which parental leave could be used: today, leave can be taken until a child has reached 8 years of age; he proposed bringing that down to 4 years.

The main focus in this Social Democratic proposal was the improvement of women's opportunities in the labour market (SOU 2005:73). Not everyone in the Social Democratic Party supported the proposals for changes in the leave system, but in any case, there was no possibility of realising any of them; as the Swedish elections in 2006 showed, the Social Democrats had run out of time in government. Before these elections, one of the government's last decisions about parental leave was to raise the ceiling on the parental leave benefit by 25% from 1 July 2006, another change, alongside the second father's month, aimed at getting fathers to use more parental leave.

Studies show that one of the most influential predictors of the division of leave is the father's earnings (Sundström and Duvander, 2000). The father's share of leave increases as earnings increase, up to the ceiling on the benefit payment (that is, the maximum amount paid in benefit). By raising the ceiling more, fathers with high incomes would be able to take parental leave without losing more than 20% of their earnings.

A 'new' family policy

A four-party coalition consisting of the Conservative, Liberal, Centre and Christian Democrat Parties formed a bourgeois government in 2006. This government presented a new family policy reform to be introduced during the coming parliament. The reform included the introduction of a municipal childcare allowance and a gender equality bonus. Both these proposals were agreed and were introduced from 1 July 2008.

The purpose of the childcare allowance is to increase the possibility for parents to stay at home when children are under 3 years of age. Local authorities (*comunes*) can decide whether or not to introduce the reform in their area. The allowance will be set at a maximum of SEK3,000 (€270) per month for each child under 3 years of age, and will be treated as tax-free and non-pensionable income. To be entitled to the maximum benefit, parents should not use the public childcare system, although each comune will have to decide if it will pay a reduced allowance to families whose children use the system only part time. It will also be possible to get the allowance if the parent is working full time; the only condition is that the public childcare system is not used, so the money could be used to pay for private childcare. However, it is not possible for parents to get the allowance if they already receive other social benefits such as parental leave benefit, sickness benefit, unemployment compensation and so on (Socialdepartementet, 2008a).

At the same time, the new government has introduced a gender equality bonus, with the aim of stimulating more equal sharing of parental leave. The parent using most parental leave days will get a tax reduction, up to SEK100 per working day, during the time the other parent uses parental leave, or about SEK3,000 (€270) per month. The first 60 days will not be included in the bonus, as these represent the individualised part of the paid parental leave days that is not transferable to the other parent. The more equally the parents share the parental leave, the more bonus they will get, up to the maximum of SEK13,500 (€1,210) per child. If the parents use the same amount of parental leave days, splitting the entitlement down the middle, the bonus will be paid to the youngest of the parents. Only parents with joint custody qualify and the bonus will be paid only for children born after 30 June 2008 (Socialdepartementet, 2008b).

The bourgeois majority of the Swedish parliament has presented these reforms as a modern and flexible family policy. The opposition parties, however, have been critical on several points. They find the childcare allowance old-fashioned and argue that it could make the labour market situation worse for many women. The evaluation of a similar childcare allowance in Norway has been brought into the political debates and resolutions in the Swedish parliament (see Chapter Twelve). The Norwegian evaluation has shown, *inter alia*, that the childcare allowance impedes the integration of minority ethnic women into the labour market and the linguistic development of their children, as it means that they are missing out on the stimulation they could get by attending childcare centres (Ernkrans and Malmström, 2007). The opposition parties have also been critical of the gender equality bonus, arguing that the rules could be hard for many parents to understand and that the reform will probably not have much effect.

Conclusion

The most important changes in the Swedish parental leave since its introduction in 1974 have been the individualisation of one month in 1995 and a second month in 2002. As the 6 months of leave initially introduced corresponded with the recommended time for breastfeeding, individualisation of any of this period (for example, one or 2 months for the mother and the same period for the father) would probably have caused problems for and protests from many families. The Family Policy Committee formed by the Social Democrats in the 1960s and responsible for the proposal to change maternal leave into parental leave accordingly regarded gender equality in the use of this measure as a long-term process that should be based on free choice and negotiations inside the families. However, it is important to realise that both parents had the same rights from the start; each had their own portion of parental leave, so a father could decide not to transfer his entitlement to the mother, thereby gaining the opportunity of taking 3 months' leave, albeit with payment based on his own salary *only* if the mother of the child was also entitled to an income-related benefit. However, statistics from the early years of parental leave show that most fathers did transfer their portion.

The report from the Family Policy Committee also shows that the length of parental leave was adjusted to the age at which children could enter public childcare. Parental leave during the 1970s was, therefore, mainly regarded as a complement to public childcare services, both together forming the necessary structure to make it possible for women to join the workforce. Public childcare has, from the large expansion during the 1970s and 1980s until now, been a political issue: Social Democrat governments have had a more positive attitude than bourgeois governments, the former supporting an early return by women to the labour market, while the latter have been more focused on the possibilities for caring for children at home, at least while they are under 3 years old.

The development of parental leave during the period of bourgeois government between 1976 and 1982 includes two extensions of parental leave, to 9 months in 1978 and 12 months in 1980 (RFV, 1998). During the same period, the Social Democrats in opposition proposed a father's quota. This was, however, rejected by the bourgeois government (Klinth, 2002).

That the individualisation of parental leave has been a controversial question, sometimes regarded as a reduction of parental freedom of choice, becomes obvious when studying the ambivalent attitudes both in the Social Democrat and bourgeois parties. Returned to power in 1982, the Social Democrats did not raise this question again. Instead, the first father's quota was introduced by the bourgeois government in 1995, although the second month, in 2002, was introduced by a Social Democrat government. These varying policy responses under different governments reflect divided views within the parties, presumably also connected to differing intra-party attitudes to feminist arguments.

From a feminist point of view, it is men who have had the opportunity to choose whether or not to take parental leave; women do not have the same opportunity (Bekkengen, 2002). The result in practice is clear. Men can, and do, give priority to their careers while women have to take the main responsibility for the children. From this point of view, gender equality necessitates putting some pressure on men to take parental leave by an individualisation of parental leave days – a father's quota. The first father's month was introduced with mainly this kind of feminist rationale, although arguments from the 'daddy group' also supported the reform (Klinth, 2002).

The split inside the Social Democratic Party over further individualisation became obvious when the results from their inquiry into the future development of parental leave were presented in 2005, proposing a non-transferable period of 5 months for each parent. When the proposal was discussed inside the party, it turned out to be too radical and no more individual months were added to the parental leave. Instead of advocating further individualisation, the bourgeois government formed in 2006 has come up with another possible solution to encourage couples to share parental leave more equally – a gender equality bonus.

The bonus is based on financial incentives, in this case tax reductions, which are a feature of the politics of the Conservative Party. Even if the gender equality bonus has been criticised by the opposition parties for being too complicated to have any effect, it still can be seen as a kind of declaration from the bourgeois government that it supports gender equality. In fact, gender equality has been a long-term part of the politics of one bourgeois party, the Liberal Party, which took the initiative to introduce the first father's month in the 1990s.

The ideology of the Christian Democrat Party supports the other reform introduced 2008 – the childcare allowance. This could mainly be seen as an alternative to public childcare, giving parents the opportunity to stay at home with their children for a longer period than is possible using only parental leave. However, the allowance can also be used to pay for private childcare if both parents prefer to work, in theory again widening parental choice.

Focusing on the development of Swedish parental leave in recent decades, it becomes clear that it is a result of both Social Democrat and bourgeois governments. The Social Democrats introduced the policy in the 1970s, mainly as a way to encourage women to combine having children with labour force participation. But it was bourgeois governments that extended parental leave and introduced the first individualised month to stimulate more men to take parental leave (although, as noted, different parties making up bourgeois coalition governments have somewhat different views about details of leave policy).

With cross-party backing, Swedish parental leave can be regarded as a stable system that will probably remain and develop in the future, irrespective of which government is in power. Further individualisation of leave, with more father's months, is not apparently on the agenda of the bourgeois government for the moment. But it might reappear if the Social Democrats win the next elections. From the introduction of the second individualised month in 2002 to the radical proposals in the inquiry of 2005, the Social Democrats have shown that individualisation of parental leave has become part of Social Democrat family policy.

Notes

[1] Leave provision described here refers to statutory entitlements.

[2] Converted into euros at exchange rate on 23 February 2009, rounded up to the nearest 5 euros.

References

Andersson, B.-E. (1990) 'Familjen och barnomsorgen', in B.-E. Andersson and L.Gunnarsson (eds) *Svenska småbarnsfamiljer*, Lund: Studentlitteratur, pp 91–108.

Andersson, G. (2006) 'Social barnavård då och nu', in H. Swärd and M. Egerö (eds) (2006) *Ligga till last. Fattigdom och utsatthet – socialpolitik och socialt arbete under 100 år*, Malmö: Gleerups, pp 99–112.

Bekkengen, L. (1996) *Mäns föräldraledighet – en kunskapsöversikt*, Arbetsrapport 96:12, Karlstad: Högskolan Karlstad.

Bekkengen, L. (2002) *Man får välja – om föräldraskap och föräldraledighet i arbetsliv och familjeliv*, Malmö: Liber.

Chronholm, A. (2004) *Föräldraledig pappa. Mäns erfarenheter av delad föräldraledighet*, Göteborg: Department of Sociology, Göteborg University.

Chronholm, A. (2007) 'Fathers' experience of shared parental leave in Sweden', in *Articuler vie familiale et vie professionelle: une entrée par les pères. Recherches sociologiques et anthropologiques, No 2*, Louvain-la-Neuve: Université Catholique de Louvain.

DS 1995:2 *Pappagruppens slutrapport/Arbetsgruppen (S 1993:C) om papporna, barnen och arbetslivet*, Stockholm: Fritze.

Elmér, Å (1975) *Från fattigsverige till välfärdsstaten. Sociala förhållanden och socialpolitik i Sverige under nittonhundratalet*, Stockholm: Aldus/Bonniers.

Ernkrans, M. and Malmström, L. (2007) *Verklig jämställdhet kräver jämställt arbetsliv och jämställt familjeliv*, Sveriges Riksdag Motion 2007/08:A279, Stockholm: Sveriges Riksdag.

Florin, C. and Nilsson, B. (2000) *'Något som liknar en oblodig revolution…'. Jämställdhetens politisering under 1960- och 70-talen*, Umeå: Umeå University.

Haas, L. (1992) *Equal parenthood and social policy: A study of parental leave in Sweden*, New York, NY: State University of New York Press.

Hirdman, Y. (1998) *Med kluven tunga. LO och genusordningen*, Stockholm: Atlas.

Hirdman, Y. (2001) *Genus – om det stabilas föränderliga former*, Malmö: Liber.

Hirdman, Y. (2006) *Det tänkande hjärtat. Boken om Alva Myrdal*, Stockholm: Ordfront.

Klinth, R. (2002) *Göra pappa med barn. Den svenska pappapolitiken 1960–1995*, Umeå: Borea.

Moberg, E. (1962) *Kvinnor och människor*, Stockholm: Bonniers.

Molin, K. (1992) 'Historical orientation', in K. Misgeld, K. Molin and K. Åmark (eds) *Creating social democracy: A century of the Social Democratic Labor Party in Sweden*, University Park, PA: The Pennsylvania State University Press, pp xvii–xxix.

Myrdal, A. and Myrdal, G. (1934) *Kris I befolkningsfrågan*, Stockholm: Albert Bonniers Förlag.

Ohlander, A. (1992) 'The invisible child? The struggle over social democratic family policy', in K. Misgeld, K. Molin and K. Åmark (eds) *Creating social democracy: A century of the Social Democratic Labor Party in Sweden*, University Park, PA: The Pennsylvania State University Press, pp 213-36.

Plantin, L. (2001) *Mäns Föräldraskap. Om mäns upplevelser och erfarenheter av faderskapet*, Göteborg: Institutionen för socialt arbete, Göteborg: Göteborg University.

RFV (Riksförsäkringsverket) (1998) *Statistikinformation Is-I 1998:009*, Stockholm: RFV.

RFV (2002) *Spelade pappamånaden någon roll? Pappornas uttag av föräldrapenning. RFV analyserar 2002:14*, Stockholm: RFV.

RFV (2003) *Mamma, pappa, barn – tid och pengar*, Socialförsäkringsboken 2003, Stockholm: RFV.

Rothstein, B. (2002) *Vad bör staten göra? Om välfärdsstatens moraliska och politiska logik*, Andra upplagan, Stockholm: SNS Förlag.

SCB (Statistiska Centralbyrån) (2006) *Uttag av föräldrapenning och tillfällig föräldrapenning 1974–2005*, Örebro: SCB.

Schmitz, E. (2002) 'Kvinnors fackliga kamp. Från textilarbetarstrejken 1890 till textilarbetarstrejken 1931', in J. Askegård, K. Bosdotter and K. Misgeld (eds) *Kvinnor tar plats. Arbetsmarknad och industriarbete på 1900-talet*, Stockholm: Arbetarrörelsens arkiv och bibliotek, pp 33-51.

SNS (Studieförbundet Näringsliv och Samhälle) (1962) *Kvinnors liv och arbete*, Stockholm: SNS.

Socialdepartementet (2008a) *Lag (2008:307) om kommunalt vårdnadsbidrag*, Svensk författningssamling.

Socialdepartementet (2008b) *Lag (2008:313) om jämställdhetsbonus*, Svensk författningssamling.

SOU 1972:34 *Familjestöd. Betänkande avgivet av familjepolitiska kommittén*, Stockholm: Statens Offentliga Utredningar.

SOU 2005:73 *Reformerad föräldraförsäkring. Kärlek Omvårdnad Trygghet. Betänkande av Föräldraförsäkringsutredningen*, Stockholm: Statens Offentliga Utredningar.

Sundström, M. and Duvander, A.-Z. (1998) 'Föräldraförsäkringen och jämställdheten mellan kvinnor och män', in I. Persson and E. Wadensjö (eds) *Välfärdens genusansikte*, SOU 1998:3, Stockholm: Statens Offentliga Utredningar, pp 69-91.

Sundström, M and Duvander, A.-Z. (2000) 'Family division of childcare and the sharing of parental leave among new parents in Sweden', in A.-Z. Duvander (ed) *Couples in Sweden: Studies on family and work*, Stockholm: Swedish Institute for Social Research, Stockholm University.

Therborn, G. (1992) 'A unique chapter in the history of democracy: the Social Democrats in Sweden', in K. Misgeld, K. Molin and K. Åmark (eds) *Creating social democracy: A century of the Social Democratic Labor Party in Sweden*, University Park, PA: The Pennsylvania State University Press, pp 1-34.

FIFTEEN

The European directive: making supra-national parental leave policy

Bernard Fusulier[1]

Introduction

Both maternity leave and parental leave are the subjects of European Union (EU) legislation. In both cases, minimum standards are defined by law, not just nationally but cross-nationally. While there are some international standards on leave, for example the International Labour Organization's Maternity Protection Convention, only the European Union sets legally enforceable supra-national standards that have been agreed by its member states, originally (in 1957) just six countries, today 27 with a combined population of half a billion people. Europe, therefore, brings us to an international politics of leave, where countries with very different welfare regimes have to try for a common ground.

The EU's directive on parental leave was adopted in 1996 (Council Directive 96/34/CE of 3 June 1996), 13 years after the European Commission first proposed this measure, in 1983, and following many disagreements between member states. Today, it is institutionalised in so far as it is implemented in national law and is thus an integral part of the leave policy of member states; the 12 member states that have joined the EU since 1996 have all had to adopt the directive and the standards it sets. We could even forget that it took 13 years to create it! During this time, it proved impossible for the member states to agree on this legislation.

This directive was not the first dealing with leave for family reasons. Four years earlier, the directive on maternity leave (Council Directive 92/85/CEE), or more specifically 'on the introduction of measures to encourage improvements in the health and safety at work of pregnant workers and workers who have recently given birth or are breastfeeding', was adopted on 19 October 1992. It was the tenth individual directive to be adopted under the 1989 Framework Directive (89/391/EEC), which set common standards for occupational safety and health at work; other directives dealing with specific issues introduced within this legislative framework covered such subjects as manual handling of loads and display screen equipment.

The directive setting standards for maternity leave also has its roots in the Charter of Fundamental Social Rights for Workers (known as the Social Charter), adopted in 1989 by all member states with the exception of the United Kingdom, whose Conservative government under Margaret Thatcher was strongly opposed; it was not, in fact, adopted by the UK until 1998, under a newly elected Labour government. The charter is a political declaration containing "moral obligations" whose object is to guarantee that member states respect certain social rights mainly relating to the labour market, vocational training, social protection, equal opportunities and health and safety at work. It also contains an explicit request to the European Commission – the EU's executive branch, responsible for proposing legislation, implementing decisions, upholding the EU's treaties, and its general day-to-day running – to put forward proposals for translating the content of the Social Charter into legislation.

The charter and the subsequent history of directives on maternity leave and parental leave illustrate very clearly the politics of policy making in a multinational system such as the EU. The charter included the proposal for a 'maternity directive', and based this on Article 118A of the 1957 Treaty of Rome, the agreement that founded the European Economic Community, the precursor of the European Union. This article allowed the European Council – comprising the heads of state or government of the member states – to intervene in the field of health and security at work through a qualified majority. In other words, a maternity directive introduced as a health and safety measure could be adopted even if some member states were opposed. This strategic choice avoided the unanimity rule, necessary for many other types of directive, and sidestepped the opposition of the UK government. So when the maternity directive was agreed in October 1992, the UK (and Italy) abstained, but they were unable to veto the measure and were bound to implement it; in the case of the UK, this meant introducing new eligibility conditions that extended access to maternity leave, enabling more women to benefit than under previous purely national legislation.

As we will see, this story of UK opposition and finding a way to get round was a recurrent theme in the long-running saga of getting a directive on parental leave. However, this time there was another logic and another institutional procedure. The parental leave directive was the first agreement obtained in the framework of the European social dialogue between social partners.

This chapter examines the history of the directive on parental leave, from 1983 to 1996, and in particular the changing political context and how and why this directive was proposed, obstructed and eventually adopted, including the procedures and process for securing agreement. The chapter does not analyse the implementation of the directive in the different member states and its effects. Based mainly on official texts, it aims to show how and why, at the European institutional level, the directive was proposed, then blocked, and finally adopted. Particular attention is paid to the institutional mechanisms that enabled an agreement between social partners, and specifically the role of the European Commission in the promotion and launching of negotiations within the framework of the European social dialogue. The chapter finishes by saying something about the content of the framework agreement and draws attention to some of the major criticisms about it. But first, an introduction to the social dialogue and what it means in a European context.

The European social dialogue

Social dialogue is the term used to describe the consultation procedures involving the European social partners: the Union of Industrial and Employers' Confederations of Europe (UNICE), the European Centre of Enterprises with Public Participation (CEEP) and the European Trade Union Confederation (ETUC). It encompasses discussions, joint action and sometimes negotiations between the European social partners, and discussions between the social partners and the EU's institutions. The dialogue was started by the European Commission in 1985, and Article 138 of the EC Treaty (as amended by the Single European Act) formally requires the Commission to develop it (http://europa.eu/scadplus/glossary/social_dialogue_en.htm).

The European social dialogue emerged from the mid-1980s in the so-called Val Duchesse process. This was the result of an initiative taken by Jacques Delors, the incoming President of the European Commission in January 1985, to invite the chairs and general secretaries of all the national organisations affiliated to the EU-level organisations of employers and workers (UNICE, CEEP and the ETUC) to a meeting at the castle of Val Duchesse outside Brussels on 31 January 1985. At this historic meeting, the social partners agreed to engage in furthering the social dialogue. The aim of this initiative was to encourage cooperation between European organisations of social partners to improve growth and employment. However, it was only with the 1992 Maastricht Treaty on European Union that the social partners became officially associated in all new initiatives of the European Commission on social policy matters (European Commission, 2003).

This incorporation of social partners into European policy-making processes was original, but built on a strong tradition of collective industrial relations in many European countries. Several European directives, policy guidelines and recommendations aim to enhance social dialogue between the social partners at national, local and company level. But the European social dialogue embeds these relationships into the institutions of the European Union and goes well beyond simply consulting with social partners; it gives a place for social partners to enter into negotiations that could lead to intersectoral or sectoral European agreements. The European Commission calls this process *independent social dialogue*, "that is to negotiate independently agreements which become law. It is that ability to negotiate agreements which sets the social dialogue apart" (COM/2002/341 final). In concrete terms, it brings together organisations representing labour and management to consider various aspects of the world of work, for instance, working conditions, the definition of wage standards, continuing training particularly in new technologies, and the organisation of work and working time to reconcile flexibility and security (COM/2002/341 final). This takes account of the limits of EU competence (or legal powers); for example, salaries are excluded from the social dialogue (Kirton-Darling and Clauwaert, 2003).

The institutionalisation of social dialogue is part of a growing EU concern for transparency and democratic governance. Following the rejection of the Maastricht Treaty by the Danish population in a referendum in June 1992, the European Commission and other European institutions were accused of being a bureaucratic, even technocratic, machine that neglected active participation from the main actors of organised civil society. Faced by these accusations of a 'democratic deficit' in Europe, in the early 1990s the European Commission was given the mission to systematically enlarge participation in decision-making processes by interested socioeconomic parties. The European Commission also recognised a social subsidiarity principle: "it is for the social players to make the first move to arrive at appropriate solutions coming within their area of responsibility; the Community institutions intervene, at the Commission's initiative, only where negotiations fail" (COM/2002/341 final). In 1998, a new dimension was introduced to the social dialogue: the setting up of sectoral social dialogue committees, representing different areas of economic activity (such as agriculture, banking and construction). For the European Commission, this held out the prospect of getting closer to the grassroots: "the sectoral approach promotes listening to players in the field at all levels, and enables problems specific to the various sectors to be dealt with" (European Commission, 2003, p 7).

The results of social dialogue negotiations between social partners vary and can take different forms:

- general recommendations;
- precise obligations or actions, accompanied by monitoring mechanisms at national and European levels;
- joint opinions;
- agreements with legal effect because they are transposed into national law by a directive or national laws.

The parental leave directive was the first cross-industry framework agreement. Agreed in 1995, it has been followed by four other agreements of the same sort, covering part-time work (1997), temporary workers (1999), teleworking (2002) and work-related stress (2004).

The aborted 1983 directive proposal

In 1983, the European Commission first proposed a directive on parental leave and leave for family reasons (COM/83/686 final). This was done as part of its action programme on the promotion of equal opportunity for women 1982–85 (COM/81/758 final, action A7), which had been the subject of a Council resolution in 1982 (OJ No C 186/3, 23 July 1982). It was decided that the European Commission would carry out research on experiences in the field of parental and family leave in the then 10 member states (Belgium, Denmark, France, Greece, Ireland, Italy, Luxembourg, the Netherlands, the United Kingdom, West Germany) and prepare a legal instrument aiming at promoting this type of leave. This action had been recommended by the European Parliament as early as 1981, in the Resolution on the situation of women (OJ No C 50,11 February 1981, point 22) and in the opinion of 12 May 1982 for a new Community action programme on the promotion of equal opportunity for women (at that date, the term used was the 'European Economic Community', to be replaced by 'European Union' after the Treaty of Maastricht in 1993). In 1983, the European Parliament went further and insisted, in a Resolution on family policy adopted on 9 June, on a family policy that would give priority to the implementation of parental leave (OJ No C 184, 11 July 1983).

Last but not least, the Commission also had the support of another of the European institutions: the European Economic and Social Committee (CES 385/82 D/AC/JJ of 28 April 1982).

The EESC is a consultative body that gives representatives of Europe's socio-occupational interest groups, and others, a formal platform to express their points of views on EU issues. Its opinions are forwarded to the larger institutions – the Council, the Commission and the European Parliament. It thus has a key role to play in the Union's decision-making process (http://eesc.europa.eu/organisation/how/index_en.asp).

Studies carried out by the Commission showed that parental leave and leave for family reasons were increasingly found among member states, in national legislation as well as in collective agreements on working conditions. Leave for family reasons, of short duration but allowing the worker to take time off work in case of an emergency or some other exceptional family situation, was already in practice in most member states. But parental leave, allowing working parents to dedicate time to the care of very young children after the maternity leave, was a more recent concept and was applied in a variety of ways (COM/83/686 final). It was, therefore, deemed necessary to decide on common legal measures governing these working conditions; in other words, measures that would be applicable throughout the Community.

In its 1983 proposal, the Commission explains that the sharing of family responsibility between parents is an essential part of the strategies aimed at increasing equality between men and women in the labour market. The 1976 directive on equal treatment for men and women had stipulated circumstances involving the protection of women when gender equality rules might not apply, for example in the case of pregnancy or maternity (OJ No L 39, 14 February 1976, Article 2); but the existence in some member states of 'extra' leave to take care of young children available only for mothers was considered to be a discriminatory measure that could be corrected by introducing the concept of parental leave, which by definition should be equally available to men and women (COM/83/686 final). This proposal was also situated in a wider international context, as part of the follow-up to international conventions on equal opportunities, adopted by the United Nations (UN Convention on the Elimination of All Forms of Discrimination against Women, adopted in 1979 by the UN General Assembly) and by the International Labour Organization (ILO Convention no 156 and Recommendation no 165 concerning equal opportunity and equal treatment for men and women: workers with family responsibilities), as well as declarations and communications from the Organisation for Economic Co-operation and Development (OECD) (OECD Declaration adopted at the High Level Conference on Employment for Women, Paris, 16-17 April 1980) and the Council of Europe (Council of Europe Conference of European Ministers in Charge of Family Affairs, Rome, 22-29 May 1981).

Furthermore, parental leave was considered to be a type of absence from work that could favour the creation of more flexibility in organising working time and the reduction of working time. It was even suggested that parental leave could help put young unemployed workers to work by enabling them to replace workers on leave. However, the proposal went on to warn that there could be an adverse effect of permanent removal of mothers from the labour market, or a negative impact on recruitment of young workers, more specifically mothers (COM/83/686 final).

For the definition of parental leave, the proposal referred to that provided by the International Labour Organization. Parental leave meant:

> ... leave given to the father or the mother in a period after the end of the maternity leave, in order to allow the working parents to take care of their newly born child for a certain time, while maintaining a certain number of guarantees in matters of employment, social security and salary. As is the case for maternity leave, the birth of twins, triplets, etc does not open a right to a supplementary period of leave and no specific provision has been planned for those cases. It must be clear, however, that parental leave, as maternity leave, can be granted again when other children are born. (COM/83/686 final, p 6)

Parental leave provided for families where both parents were working and for single-parent families, whether the children were adopted or not. It would be optional rather than mandatory, granted for a minimum period of 3 months per worker, and would operate as an individual rather than a family entitlement: "a worker's right to parental leave should not be transferable" (COM/83/686 final). The legislative proposal included the private as well as the public sectors, and full-time as well as part-time workers. It was to be applicable to working parents of young children under 2 years old, or 5 years old in the case of adopted or disabled children. It left the member states free to decide if the leave period would be paid or not, although it believed an allowance to be desirable. The Commission also called attention to "the positive contribution it makes to the overall charge to society of the care and early education of young children" (COM/83/686 final).

The Commission placed its proposal in the wider context of European policy: this proposal of a directive on parental leave was "a real component part of the total strategy on economic, social and family policy, and on [sic] an adequate demographic evolution" (COM/83/686 final, p 5). Furthermore, it was a necessary step towards building a functioning common market based on a level playing field: "the differences from Member States to Member States in the working conditions relating to leave for parents risk hindering the establishment and disrupting the functioning of the common market". Lastly, a common legal entitlement would contribute to the objective set out in Article 117 of the Treaty of the European Community, the continuous improvement of living and working conditions.

Legislative deadlock to the proposal

The Commission's proposal received a favourable opinion, subject to a few amendments, from the European Parliament and the Economic and Social Committee (Opinion of the European Parliament of 30 March 1984, and Opinion of the CES of 24 May 1984, Factiva, European Information Service of 3/02/1995). The Commission submitted a modified proposal, including these amendments, on 15 November 1984 (COM/84/631 final). However, this proposal for a directive remained deadlocked for almost 10 years because of the implacable opposition of the Conservative government in the United Kingdom, first under Margaret Thatcher and then under her successor, John Major. Eurosceptical and resistant to any attempts to re-regulate the UK labour market, the UK government refused to allow legal competence in this area to be consigned to Europe; it believed that these measures had to remain a prerogative of the member states.

Despite numerous efforts by the European Council of Ministers to find a compromise, under the rotating presidency of different member states, the draft directive remained only a draft. As long as a unanimous vote by all the member states was required for the adoption of this initiative, efforts were doomed to failure by the implacable opposition of the United Kingdom (see Paes, 2004).

An opportunity for unblocking the situation arose with the adoption in 1992 of the Treaty on the European Union, also called the Maastricht Treaty, and of its annex: the Social Policy Protocol, including a Social Policy Agreement concluded by the social partners in October 1991. While preparation for the Maastricht Treaty was under way, the social partners, with the support of the European Commission, requested to be given an official and structural role in the EU's decision-making processes. Then faced by the United Kingdom's opposition to any adoption of more advanced social measures at the European level, the other governments found a solution by adding to the Treaty a protocol that legally bound 11 of the 12 member states. This protocol allowed these states to use European institutions and procedures to take action in the social field, allowing decisions to be made with a qualified majority (Article 137) so no one country could exert a veto:

> Noting that eleven Member States ... wish to continue along the path laid down in the 1989 Social Charter; that they have adopted among themselves an Agreement to this end; that this Agreement is annexed to this Protocol; that this Protocol and the said Agreement are without prejudice to the provisions of this Treaty, particularly those relating to social policy which constitute an integral part of the 'acquis communautaire'. (Treaty on European Union, OJ No C 191, 29 July 1992)

The qualified majority in the Social Protocol allowed participating countries to adopt a series of social measures. Its objectives were:

- promotion of employment;
- improvement of living and working conditions;
- adequate social protection;
- social dialogue;
- the development of human resources to ensure a high and sustainable level of employment;
- the integration of persons excluded from the labour market (http://europa. eu/scadplus/treaties/maastricht_fr.htm#SOCIAL).

The United Kingdom remained outside this procedure until 1997, when the new Labour government in the UK came to power and a new treaty, the Amsterdam Treaty, was adopted (signed on 2 October 1997, and coming into force on 1 May 1999).

With these new conditions in place creating a new policy-making context, the proposal for a parental leave directive was brought back to the negotiation table under the Belgian presidency of the Council of Ministers in 1993. Since the United Kingdom announced yet again its objection to the measure and threatened to use its veto, the Commission decided to launch an initiative within the framework of the newly agreed Social Protocol (COS/1996/0033:01/10/ 1995). At the same time, the Commission published its White Paper, *European social policy – A way forward for the Union*, in which it underlined the importance it attached to progress in the field of the reconciliation of family and working lives, as a fundamental part of its strategy to promote employment and growth (European Commission, 1994).

Second Directive proposal: removing the impasse, negotiation and agreement

On 1 January 1995, Austria, Finland and Sweden joined the EU. In February 1995, Commissioner Padraig Flynn, in charge of social policy in the European Commission, invited the European social partners to consider parental leave measures at the European level. UNICE, ETUC and CEEP were represented

(Agence Europe, 31/05/1995; Agence Europe is the European Union press agency).

Originally, UNICE, mainly representing large business companies, was very reticent and sceptical about this use of the new route opened up by the European social dialogue. It was hesitant to enter into negotiations directly with ETUC. UNICE considered that national legislation – or even collective agreements concluded at sectoral or at individual employer level – were the most adequate instruments; in its view, there should be no European-level agreement on parental leave. However, in July 1995, UNICE changed its mind. Although it could refuse negotiations on parental leave in the framework of the European social dialogue, it concluded that it could not prevent the European Commission from moving ahead and proposing a new directive. In that case, it was strategically preferable to be a participant rather than a spectator (Arnold, 1999).

It should be added here that the Social Protocol contains two steps in the consultation process. The first step, which cannot last more than 6 weeks, is to identify what orientations a European policy can take. In the second step, the Commission sends a letter with the possible content of an initiative in a specific field. At this stage, the social partners can send the Commission either an opinion or a recommendation, or else they can decide to open negotiations themselves. In the latter case, they have 9 months to reach an agreement, although that time period can be extended if necessary; during this time, the traditional legislative process in the European Council and Parliament is suspended. If an agreement is reached by the social partners at the end of that period, they may request that it become a Council directive, thus making the agreement mandatory. Otherwise, the European institutions again take over the policy-making process.

At the beginning of July 1995, the general secretaries of ETUC, UNICE and CEEP wrote a letter to Commissioner Padraig Flynn, asking the Commission to suspend its legislative initiative concerning "conciliation of professional life and family life" (parental leave), because they were to begin a negotiation on the theme, following the procedures set out in the Social Agreement of the Maastricht Treaty (Agence Europe, 7/07/95).

On 12 July 1995, they held their first meeting, chaired by Mrs Johanna Walgrave, President of the National Labour Council in Belgium (Agence Europe, 13/07/95). The aim was to reach an agreement before the end of the year.

The General Secretary of the ETUC, Mr Emilio Gabaglio, considered that an agreement must meet three conditions: to guarantee an income and a minimum duration of parental leave of at least 3 months; to extend the measure to dependent elderly parents (that is, it should not concern only children); and to include leave covering unexpected or emergency reasons (Agence Europe, 7/09/95). Employers wanted small and medium-sized enterprises to be excluded from the agreement, with a threshold of 50 employees before any agreement was applicable.

On 6 November 1995, UNICE, CEEP and ETUC agreed on a proposal for a framework agreement on parental leave. Employers did not win the case on the size of undertakings; there were no exemptions. But while the ETUC obtained an agreement that included provisions for illness or emergency reasons, it was not extended to include dependent elderly parents. Moreover, the agreement said nothing about financial compensation to workers taking leave; that was left to member states to decide. It did suggest, however, that parental leave should be an individual right of at least 3 months, not transferable, although the exact duration would be determined at national level. The period of leave could be taken at any time by any worker, male or female, before a child reached 8 years of age (the 8 years threshold comes from the existing Swedish system, considered to be the best example of leave policy). A worker would have the right to return to his or her previous job or to an equivalent job, and he or she would be protected from redundancy. Workers on leave should continue to receive social security coverage for all risks (pension, social security, illness, redundancy and so on).

The agreement stipulates minimum standards, but member states may adopt more favourable terms. They retain discretionary power in a number of important areas, for example in determining the conditions for access to parental leave; remuneration while on leave; whether to allow full-time or part-time parental leave; and notification periods. This flexibility ensured the continuation of a great variety of parental leave systems from one member state to another.

This agreement still had to be formally ratified by the social partners. On 14 December 1995, the UNICE, CEEP and ETUC sealed the framework agreement on parental leave and forwarded it to the European Commission, asking that it be implemented by a Council of Ministers decision through a Commission proposal; this meant the Commission turning the framework agreement into a directive. The Council adopted the Commission's proposal for a directive on parental leave on 3 June 1996 (Directive 96/34/CE).

This directive contained the agreement as negotiated by the social partners and applied it throughout the European Union, except for the United Kingdom. Following a change of government in the UK and the signing of the Amsterdam Treaty, Council Directive 97/75/CE of 15 December 1997 extended Directive 96/34/CE to include the United Kingdom (OJEC L 010 of 16/01/1998). After 14 years, all member states were covered by legislation setting common standards for parental leave.

The contents of the directive

The directive on parental leave provides a common framework for parental leave, to be transposed into national law. Let us see what this European framework consists of.

Field of application

The conditions set out in the framework agreement on parental leave apply to all workers, male or female, having a contract or a working relationship defined by legislation, collective agreements, or usual practice in each member state (clause 1, paragraph 2).

Maximum age of the child

Clause 2, paragraph 1 stipulates that workers must have the right to parental leave to take care of a child after birth or adoption, and that the leave must be available up to a certain age that can be up to 8 years, but which is to be defined by member states and/or the social partners.

Duration

Clause 2, paragraph 1 sets a minimum duration for the leave of 3 months per parent. Member states and/or social partners may decide on aspects of flexibility, for example if the parental leave can be taken full time or part time, as one block of time or several shorter blocks, or in the form of a time–credit system (clause 2, paragraph 3, point a).

An individual and non-transferable right

Clause 2, paragraph 1 provides that working men and women must benefit from an individual right to parental leave. Clause 2, paragraph 2 states that in order to promote equal opportunity and equal treatment between men and women, the right to parental leave should, *in principle*, be non-transferable (thus allowing a potential loophole for countries that insist on a family entitlement).

Access conditions and modes of application

Clause 2, paragraph 3 stipulates that the access conditions and modes of application of parental leave are defined by law and/or by collective agreements in member states, in keeping with the minimal standards of the agreement. Member states and/or social partners may: make the right to parental leave conditional on a period of work qualification and/or a length of service qualification that should not exceed one year; adjust the access conditions and modes of application of the parental leave to the specific circumstances of adoption; and set notice limits.

Exceptions

Clause 2, paragraph 3 (e and f) allows employers to delay granting parental leave for justifiable reasons (for example, in the case of seasonal work) and allows specific arrangements to cover functional and organisational requirements in small enterprises.

Protection of the worker against dismissal and right to return

Clause 2, paragraph 4 underlines that, in order to ensure that workers can benefit from their right to parental leave, the member states and/or the social partners will take all necessary measures to protect workers from redundancy because of their request for or taking of parental leave, according to legislation, collective agreements or national practice. Clause 2, paragraph 5 also adds that, after parental leave, the worker has the right to get his or her job back or, if this is impossible, an equivalent or similar job in conformity with his or her contract or work relationship.

Preservation of worker's rights

Clause 2, paragraph 6 stipulates that pre-existing rights or rights in the process of being acquired by the worker at the beginning of the parental leave must be maintained as such until the end of the parental leave. At the end of the parental leave, these rights are applicable, including changes that may have occurred in legislation, collective agreements or practice. Clause 2, paragraph 7 states that member states and/or social partners define the contract or working relationship scheme for the duration of the parental leave. Clause 2, paragraph 8 notes that all social security questions must be examined and determined by the member states, according to national law, taking into account the importance of continuing rights to social security benefits for the various risks, more specifically for healthcare.

Time off from work on grounds of force majeure

Clause 3, paragraph 1 states that member states and/or social partners must take the necessary measures to allow workers to be absent from work, in accordance with legislation, collective agreements and/or national practice, for '*force majeure*' reasons linked to emergency family situations in case of illness or accident, making the immediate presence of the worker essential. Member states and/or social partners can specify the access conditions and application methods, and limit this right to a certain duration per year and/or per situation (clause 3, paragraph 2).

Transposition of parental leave

Member states were invited to transpose the directive into national law by 3 June 1998 and, for the United Kingdom, by 15 December 1999. It was not an enormous challenge for most of the member states because only four countries (Belgium, Ireland, the UK and Luxembourg) did not already offer this kind of leave and the implementation of the directive did not really conflict with any national legislation.

An analysis of this transposition process was made in a Commission Communication in June 2003 (COM/2003/358 final). It observed that of the

15 member states concerned at the time, most had a right to parental leave that was in line with the directive. However, a few violations were observed. For example, Greece was considered to be in violation because maritime workers were excluded from the application of the directive. Luxembourg was also in violation because of a rule that if pregnancy or adoption occurs during a period of parental leave, the leave terminates and is superseded by maternity or adoption leave. The Commission considered this to be incompatible with the directive, and requested the European Court of Justice to establish whether the Grand Duchy of Luxembourg had correctly transposed the framework agreement on parental leave into national law. In April 2005, the court declared that the Grand Duchy had failed to fulfil its obligations under Council Directive 96/34/EC.

The Commission's 2003 report underlines the great variety of ways in which member states have chosen to transpose the directive. For example, the time period within which parental leave can be taken varies enormously from one country to the other: in Austria, it can be taken up until the child (natural or adopted) is 2 years old, if the leave is taken in one go; in France, Finland and Germany, until the child is 3 years old; in Ireland, Luxembourg and the United Kingdom, until the child is 5 years old; and in Denmark, Italy, the Netherlands and Sweden, until the child is 8 years old. Moreover, variations can exist within an individual country, according to the sector (public or private) and to specific situations such as a disability or the type of leave taken (full time or part time).

In a report for the Council of Europe, Eileen Drew (2005) shows, among others, the great diversity concerning payment of parental leave. Some states such as Cyprus, Spain, Greece, Ireland and the United Kingdom do not give any payment whereas states such as Estonia, Finland, Norway, Slovenia and Sweden give an earnings-related payment, varying between 70% and 100% of usual earnings. Other countries give a flat-rate payment, creating a greater or lesser incentive to take leave (for example, €1,600 a month in Luxembourg, but far less in Austria, Belgium and France).

Eugenia Caracciolo (2001) argues that the fact that member states are not obliged to ensure a payment to parents on leave is one of the weak points of the directive. According to this analyst, the directive also implies that it is mainly women who are responsible for taking care of children. Stephen Hardy and Nick Adnett (2002) argue that the directive is inadequate for meeting its objectives of work–life balance and equality between men and women: the participation rate of fathers remains low, thus maintaining or even reinforcing gender inequality in the labour market.

So, progress or pitfall? Recognising this fundamental ambiguity, Peter Moss and Fred Deven (1999) consider the EU directive on parental leave to be less a conclusion than a potential starting point for the redesign of an European social model more able to respond to contemporary social changes, including enabling a better equilibrium between work and family as well as between modern motherhood and fatherhood.

Conclusion

Because of the unanimity rule for decision taking and because of the United Kingdom's opposition, the first proposal for a directive on parental leave could not be adopted despite the commitment of the European Commission and broad support in the Council of Ministers. The inclusion, in an annex to the Maastricht Treaty, of the Social Protocol and the recognition of qualified majority decision making enabled the institutional deadlock to be broken and opened the way to a new initiative from the Commission. In a context of promoting social dialogue, in response to an accusation of a democratic deficit in Europe, and given the desire of the social partners to be recognised as the best way to find solutions capable of meeting the needs of both employers and workers, it was possible to begin a collective negotiation.

The trades unions, represented by ETUC, were at once interested, while UNICE, the main employer representative, was uncertain about entering the social dialogue mechanism on this question. But negotiation began through indirect pressure from the European Commission, which was ready to push the matter forward and to take action by itself if the employers' representative did not accept the social dialogue. The social partners were then able to negotiate an agreement, each having agreed to drop part of its original claims.

Despite the great latitude given to member states by the directive, it was interpreted by some analysts as an advance in the promotion of a society where professional life and family life could be reconciled (Schmidt, 1998). Today, leave entitlements are an accepted and central part of European policy: Article 33 of the Charter of Fundamental Rights of the European Union, signed in Nice (2000) and adapted in Lisbon in 2007, recognises that "to reconcile family and professional life, everyone shall have the right to protection from dismissal for a reason connected with maternity and the right to paid maternity leave and to parental leave following the birth or adoption of a child" (Official Journal of the European Union, 2007). The European Employment Strategy and the Community action programme on equal opportunities for women and men refer to the reconciliation of family and working life in various policy documents. The social partners' agenda also includes this subject through, for instance, better provision of care services, gender equality, lifelong learning, structures of work and working conditions. We need, also, to take into account a broader context where other international organisations define (but cannot enact) guidelines for policy, through conventions and resolutions (for example, International Labour Office) or through international studies (see the recent OECD reports *Babies and bosses* and *Starting strong: Early childhood education and care policy*; OECD, 2001, 2002, 2003, 2004, 2005, 2006). Moreover, other stakeholders such as the women's movement and family activists as well as scholars play an important role in the public debate, for instance creating expectations, showing the adverse effects of some policy developments and opening new perspectives. Thomas A. Kochan's book *Restoring the American dream: A working families' agenda for America* (2006) is one example among many.

Certainly, these developments and contributions constitute a statement of public commitment and central values on the symbolic level. Of course, it is fundamental to produce institutional supports, legislation and collective agreements. Nevertheless, legislation weakly backed up with resources is insufficient to equalise the 'capabilities' of individuals to take advantage of entitlements (Sen, 2004). As we have seen, some analysts criticised the EU directive on parental leave, mainly on the basis that it reproduced inequality between men and women, but also because it does not specify levels of parental leave payment and leaves too many important subjects, such the time period within which leave must be taken, to the discretion of member states. That could mean that it is necessary to dare to defy the principle of subsidiarity in order to imagine a deeper and more effective integration of EU social policy. Utopian or a natural progression?

Postscript

As this book was going to press, in October 2008, the European Commission announced 'a work–life balance package', including measures on leave policy, stating that "work–life balance is at the core of Europe's strategy for growth and jobs". It proposed to "strengthen women's entitlement to ... maternity leave" through revising the existing maternity leave directive to extend the duration of leave from 14 to 18 weeks; introducing the principle of full pay during this period (albeit with "a possibility for Member States to introduce a ceiling that must not be below sickness pay"); and giving "the right for women coming back from maternity leave to ask for flexible work arrangements". On other forms of leave, including parental leave, following the Commission's consultation with European employers' and trades union representatives on possible work–life balance measures in 2006–07, "the social partners decided in July 2008 to launch formal negotiations on updating the existing EU rules on parental leave ... the social partners have a period of nine months to carry out their negotiations" (European Commission, 2008).

Note
[1] The author thanks Daniel Rochat for his help.

References

Arnold, C. (1999) *The politics behind the social protocol of the Maastricht Treaty – does the Maastricht Treaty have a strong social dimension?*, Working Paper, Amherst, MA: University of Massachusetts.

Caracciolo, E. (2001) 'The family-friendly workplace the EC position', *International Journal of Comparative Labour Law and Industrial Relations*, vol 17, no 3, pp 325-44.

Drew, E. (2005) *Parental leave in Council of Europe Member States*, Strasbourg: Directorate General of Human Rights, Council of Europe.

European Commission (1994) *European social policy: A way forward for the Union*, Brussels: Commission of the European Communities.

European Commission (2003) *The European sectoral social dialogue*, Brussels: Employment and Social Affairs, Commission of the European Communities.

European Commission (2008) 'Work–life balance package (memo/08/603)', available at http://europa.eu/rapid/pressReleasesAction.do?reference=MEMO/08/603&format=HTML&aged=0&language=EN&guiLanguage=en (accessed 21 October 2008).

Hardy, S. and Adnett, N. (2002), 'The parental leave directive: towards a "family-friendly" social Europe?', *European Journal of Industrial Relations*, vol 8, no 2, pp 157-72.

Kirton-Darling, J. and Clauwaert, S. (2003) 'European social dialogue, an instrument in the Europeanisation of industrial relations', *Transfer*, vol 9, no 2, pp 247-64.

Kochan, T.A. (2006) *Restoring the American dream: A working families' agenda for America*, Cambridge, MA: MIT Press.

Moss, P. and Deven, F. (eds) (1999) *Parental leave: Progress or pitfall? Research and policy issues in Europe*, The Hague/Brussels: NIDI/CBGS Publications.

OECD (Organisation for Economic Co-operation and Development) (2001) *Starting strong I*, Paris: OECD.

OECD (2002) *Babies and bosses: Reconciling work and family life, Vol 1: Australia, Denmark and the Netherlands*, Paris: OECD.

OECD (2003) *Babies and bosses: Reconciling work and family life, Vol 2: Austria, Ireland and Japan*, Paris: OECD.

OECD (2004) *Babies and bosses: Reconciling work and family life, Vol 3: New Zealand, Portugal and Switzerland*, Paris: OECD.

OECD (2005) *Babies and bosses: Reconciling work and family life, Vol 4: Canada, Finland, Sweden and the United Kingdom*, Paris: OECD.

OECD (2006) *Starting Strong II: Early childhood education and care*, Paris: OECD.

Official Journal of the European Union (2007) 'Charter of Fundamental Rights of the European Union', available at http://eur-lex.europa.eu/LexUriServ/LexUriServ.do?uri=OJ:C:2007:303:0001:0016:EN:PDF (accessed 21 October 2008).

Paes, B. (2004) *Vers un dialogue social européen. L'exemple de la directive sur le congé parental'*, *Rapport de fin d'études*, Louvain-la-Neuve: Institut des Sciences du Travail, Université Catholique de Louvain.

Schmidt, M. (1998) 'The EC directive on parental leave', *Bulletin of Comparative Labour Relations*, vol 32, pp 181-92.

Sen, A.K. (2004) 'Elements of a theory of human rights', *Philosophy and Public Affairs*, vol 32, no 4, pp 315-56.

SIXTEEN

Conclusion

Sheila B. Kamerman and Peter Moss

Why a focus on parental leave policies?

This is a book about public policies targeted at young children, mainly but not exclusively under 3 years of age, and their families, and that treat parenting as a core issue for child, family and employment policies. Parental leave policies incorporate responses to multiple concerns, including economic support of families with very young children; protection of maternal and child health, pregnancy and childbirth; promotion of maternal employment; gender equality in the labour market and home; support for parental time with children (both fathers and mothers); involvement of parents in infants' care; and efforts to ensure that babies start their growth and development in decent circumstances.

Leading child development experts continuously and unambiguously stress the importance of the first few years of life (Shonkoff and Phillips, 2000). But only recently have policies targeted at children under 3 years of age and their families become an important focus of public policy. The increased attention to this age group and their care is due to the efforts of scholars (such as Kamerman and Kahn, 1991; Ruhm, 1998; Moss and Deven, 1999; Shonkoff and Phillips, 2000; Tanaka, 2005), national and international organisations (such as the influential US national organisation Zero To Three, the International Labour Organization (ILO) and the Organisation for Economic Co-operation and Development (OECD)) and European Union (EU) policy initiatives, including those announced at the European Council and Commission meetings in Lisbon in 2000 and Barcelona in 2002 .

The EU has shown a consistent policy interest in both leave and early childhood education and care, driven by employment and gender equality goals. But this has gained new impetus in the 21st century. At the Lisbon summit in March 2000, EU leaders set out a new strategy, based on a consensus among member states, to modernise Europe. This became known as the 'Lisbon Strategy' and was simplified and relaunched in 2005. A major focus of the Lisbon Strategy was on increasing employment, including an explicit target of raising the rate of female employment from an EU average of 51% in 2000 to 60% by 2010 (Plantenga and Siegel, 2004). When the European Council and Commission met in Barcelona in 2002, participants identified several priority actions for the achievement of these employment targets and for achieving greater gender equity. These included the removal of barriers to and disincentives for female labour force participation, in particular, the provision of accessible childcare for all. Member states adopted further targets: to provide childcare by 2010 to at least 90% of children between the age of 3 and mandatory school age (5, 6, or 7, depending on the country) and at least 33% of children under age 3 (Plantenga and Siegel, 2004, p 5).

Most recently, and ongoing at the time of writing, the European Commission has instigated a further policy initiative, "exploring what further action might be taken at European level in relation to reconciliation [between professional, private and family life]" (European Commission, 2006, p 10). The Commission has concluded that to achieve more equal sharing of family responsibilities between men and women, "incentives for fathers to take parental leave, the payment of parental leave, paternity leave, and possibilities for leave to care for the elderly and other dependent family members seem to be priorities" (European Commission, 2007, p 14). It remains to be seen where this may lead in terms of policy proposals.

The 'reconciliation of work and family life' (the term used by the EU) or 'work–life balance' is now one of the major topics on the European social and economic agenda, as it is for many member states. According to a European Commission press release (European Commission, 2008), from October 2008, policies designed to help people balance employment, personal and family life improve the quality of life for both women and men and increase labour force participation, especially among women. Reconciliation, it is widely agreed, requires support for a package of policies: early childhood education and care (ECEC) services, flexible work schedules and, especially important for a good beginning to parenthood, job-protected parental leaves following childbirth or adoption (or when children are ill): "taking the birth of a child as a starting point, the leave system is the first relevant aspect of the care system" (Plantenga and Siegel, 2004, p 109).

It is in this context of the importance of the early years for many policy fields that we have looked in this book at developments in 15 advanced industrialised countries and the EU with regard to parental leave policies. Our focus has been on the formation of policy, not their outcomes. In particular, we have looked not only at the 'what' of leave policies, but also at the 'why', 'who', 'when' and 'how'. What are the major components of these policies? Why have these policies taken the diverse forms that they have? Why have some policy choices been made and others not? Who have been the influential actors in policy formation? When have major policy changes been introduced and why then? How have policy decisions been made?

The policy-making process

As Hayes (1982) states, public policy making takes place over time and rarely can be explained by only one event or one decision. The process is complex and involves multiple actors and stakeholders. Policy making is not a coldly rational process, but rather an incremental series of decisions, beginning with the definition of the problem to be addressed, and involving many actors and influences, including government decision makers, scholars and advocates, as well as employers, trades union leaders and international organisations. According to Pierson (2005) and Derthick (1975), it is a combination of exciting and innovative events, such as, for example, the enactment of parental leave policy in Sweden in 1974, the father's parental leave quota in Norway in 1995, the transition from socialism and authoritarian governments to capitalism and democracy in Spain, Portugal and Central and Eastern European countries, and less dramatic or conflictual developments such as the early 20th century movement from unpaid to paid maternity leaves.

Our case studies of the politics of parental leave policies illustrate these general conclusions very well, as well as the sheer diversity of policy making between countries, accounting for the sheer diversity of policies that exist today. What we can point to are some of the main influences on policy making, even while recognising that these influences vary in their effect between countries and configure in different ways.

History matters

Before turning to current politics, it is important to consider the history of leave policies. Recent scholarship has underscored the importance of history in understanding the development of political processes and policy developments (Pierson, 2004). As Charles Tilly writes:

> At least for large-scale political processes, explanations always make implicit or explicit assumptions concerning historical origins of the phenomenon and time-place scope conditions for the claimed explanations ... every significant political phenomenon lives in history, and requires historically grounded analysis for its explanation. (Tilly, 2005, pp 5, 20)

We would agree, with Tilly, that policy makers and policy researchers "ignore historical context at their peril" (Tilly, 2005, p 20). A brief historical overview suggests the following developmental stages of parental leave policies in the advanced industrialised countries. Our focus is on the broad macro patterns; the country specifics have been described in the country chapters.

- 1883 to the 1960s: the emergence of brief maternity leave policies, paid and/or unpaid, largely under health policy auspices.
- 1970s to the 1990s: two parallel developments: (1) childcare/childrearing leaves, first in Hungary in 1967 and then in other former Soviet bloc countries; and (2) parental leave policies, first in Sweden in 1974, then in the other Nordic countries, and subsequently in other European countries (and later, some other countries such as Canada).

- 1990s to the present: longer leaves, and the growing attention to fathers' participation in parenting and parental leaves.

These stages of leave development have been influenced by different factors, some of which we consider here.

Maternal and infant health

Paid maternity leaves were established as part of the invention and enactment of social insurance by Bismarck in the Germany of the 1880s. Bismarck turned to social insurance as a device for binding workers and other groups to the state. The first national social insurance law was introduced to Germany in 1883, providing for health insurance, paid sick leave and paid maternity leave. Belgium and France (1893 and 1894) followed soon after. These leaves were established on the assumption that relieving women of workplace pressures before and after childbirth for a few weeks, while protecting their economic situation, would protect and promote their own and their babies' physical well-being. By the First World War, 21 countries had established maternity leave covering 4 to 12 weeks, and of these 13 were paid (Gauthier, 1996). By the Second World War, almost all Western European countries had established such paid leave policies, with a focus on promoting and protecting maternal and child health.

The later movement from maternity to parental leave policies is not because the health factor is now redundant; indeed, with current debates about the optimal period of breastfeeding, the health factor in leave determination may be due renewed attention. Rather, it indicates a transition from a focus on health to a broader concern with child, family, gender equality and employment goals.

Fertility and population policies

A second factor that has, historically, shaped leave policies is demography, in particular concern with low and declining fertility rates. The early academic and political debates in the 1930s focused first on fertility issues, in France and Sweden, and population policy in Finland, and later, in the 1950s, on family policy in France and the Nordic countries. In Chapter Fourteen of this volume, Anders Chronholm quotes the Myrdals' conclusion on 1930s Sweden: "The problem for us is depopulation or social reforms" (p 229, this volume). The Myrdals recommended a universal child allowance paid to the mother and a longer maternity leave, thus helping to launch the beginning of a 44-year history of Social Democratic leadership in which the political agenda consistently included paid maternity leaves initially and parental leave policies (and ECEC services) subsequently. France has a long history of concern with low fertility rates and pronatalist policies enacted in response. As recently as 2006, the government introduced additional measures for the sole benefit of large families, those having at least three children (see Chapter Seven in this volume).

From another perspective, the relationship between policy and fertility is not so clear-cut. A comparison between Sweden and Finland shows that "labour market developments and women's opportunities for employment may be more important determinants of fertility than specific family-policy regulations" (Neyer, 2006, p 16). Neyer's conclusion is that any investigations of the impact of family policies on fertility and female labour force participation need to take the welfare state, gender relations and labour market context into account. Nonetheless, concern with low fertility rates remains a factor in the political debates, as can be seen in Chapters Four and Eight.

Labour market trends and policies

In reviewing the history of maternity, paternity and parental leave policies, the third important factor driving European developments, after health protection and fertility, has been labour market policy, often linked with concern about gender equity and family change. During the 1960s and 1970s, labour force participation rates of women, in particular women with young children and married women, began to rise dramatically in many of the industrialised Western countries. At the same time, the ideology of the Soviet bloc countries led to increased efforts at implementing a full employment policy and, therefore, policies that would support such a pattern. The policy response to support longer leaves emerged, with benefits replacing all or most of prior wages or a modest, flat-rate cash benefit.

Gender equity

The movement from maternity leave policies to parental leave policies shows some shift of policy focus and rationale. From the 1960s, and starting in Scandinavia, especially Sweden, gender equity became part of the policy debates; gradually the dual earner family has become the model, and the goal is to facilitate both roles, breadwinner and caregiver. This has brought with it a growing awareness that the position of women and men, in the home and the labour market, are linked; women's employment cannot just be considered in isolation. Apart from any question of men's and children's rights to spend time with each other, there has been growing recognition that reconciliation of work and family life must involve both parents in both domains, in particular the father taking on more responsibilities in the home.

First enacted in Sweden in 1974 and subsequently in the other Nordic countries, parental leave embodied the concept of the father's active role in parenting and a father's right (and even obligation) to take leave was increasingly established. The 'Swedish model' became a model to emulate and influenced policy aspirations if not directions in many countries. The dual earner family became the prototypical family, and the need to reconcile work and family life the overarching goal. The most recent phase of leave development has, therefore, focused much, perhaps most, attention on measures to permit, encourage or even compel men (see, for example, Chapter Thirteen on Portugal and Spain) to take leave, albeit with varying degrees of success often linked to the design of the policies.

But gender equity has not gone unchallenged. Throughout the history of leave policies has rumbled on a continual debate, which has had different traction on policies at different times and in different places: are women primarily responsible for the care of young children and do young children require full-time maternal care? Behind the contemporary rhetoric about fathers' participation in childcare, there remains a substantial constituency that argues that the mother's place is in the home and that policies should support this, even if only as an option. Gender equity versus maternalism has been one of the main conflicts in the politics of leave policies.

Path dependency

One other influence on policy making that should be noted is 'path dependency', the way that current policy decisions may be limited by the effects of past decisions, resulting in more of the same. Stressing the importance of path dependency, Pierson (2004) points out that once a country has started down a policy track, the cost of changing or reversing direction is very high. In identifying the factors shaping parental leave policies, the role of path dependency is apparent in many countries, hence the extent to which parental leave policies emerged first in countries with relatively generous maternity leave policies, the difficulty faced by Australia because of the absence of a history of social insurance, the stress on gender equity in the Nordic countries, and the consistency of long childrearing/childcare leaves in the countries experiencing the transition to market economies.

Yet there are instances of significant change occurring: in Germany, Iceland and Québec in the last decade, to give three examples discussed in the book. Slovenia in the 1990s is also a fascinating example of a country that nearly made a major policy shift – to a long period of leave – but in the end did not after several years of active political debate. One common theme in the three examples of major change that did occur was the importance of political consensus (or agreement across some major parties) that such change was needed, while change did not happen in Slovenia in part because of irreconcilable differences among key political actors. The trigger to that consensus may then vary. It may be a shared sense of crisis (demographic in the case of Germany) or concern (about the gender pay gap in Iceland); there may be strong forces for change (the courts in Iceland, civic society organisations in Québec); or it may arise from governance or regime change (the opportunities of a changing federal system for Québec, unification for Germany).

The components of the current leave policy debates

Today, a handful of countries still debate whether or not to have a statutory entitlement to maternity and/or parental leave (notably Australia and the United

States, although Chapter Two suggests that Australia may be about to resolve that debate). But most affluent (post)industrial countries have accepted the principle of parental leave policies. Contemporary debate, academic and political, is about policy design and the core components of leave. This includes: the duration of the (job-protected) leave; whether it is paid or unpaid; if paid, the level of the benefit; and whether fathers' use of leave should be actively encouraged or even obligatory. As yet, no consensus has emerged, so the results are diverse, as our contributions abundantly illustrate.

On duration, the issue is mainly between a shorter (about one year), high-paid leave or a longer (about 3 years) leave with lower levels of payment or unpaid periods. On payment, the issue is whether leave is paid or unpaid and, if paid, at what level. Despite the universality of a paid leave following childbirth (and usually adoption) and whether it is called a 'maternity' leave or not, and notwithstanding the strong encouragement of the European Commission (EC) and ILO, parental leaves are not paid in all countries. Where leave is paid, differences exist about whether it should be an earnings-related or a flat-rate benefit. One option to emerge in recent years is a policy that offers a trade-off between duration and benefit level, offering parents a number of options (see Chapters Three, Four, Twelve and Thirteen).

As far as fathers are concerned, the issue is whether some time should be mandated to them – an individual right replacing a family entitlement that parents choose how to use. With the individual entitlement, unless it is transferable, the principle of 'use it or lose it' comes into play, bringing some pressure or incentive on fathers to take leave. Norway and Sweden began the process by setting aside one or 2 months of well-paid leave for fathers, and it is important to note that such 'father's quotas' are widely used, but only if well paid. More recently, Iceland has introduced an advanced variant of this model, replacing separate parental leaves by a single 9 months' 'birth leave', divided equally into three parts: for fathers, for mothers and for the family to divide up as they choose.

Debates about leave policies have, in some cases, become embroiled in wider issues, in particular the issue of a mother's wage and whether there should be financial support for women caring for their own children at home. Examples are provided in Chapters Two and Twelve. This seems to confound two questions: what measures are needed to support parents' continued participation in the labour market, and should the costs of care by family members be recompensed to some extent?

Although there is widespread recognition of the relationship between leave and ECEC policies, this issue is largely unresolved; there are few examples of an explicit and coherent articulation between the two policies. Sweden, where an entitlement to ECEC follows the end of leave, and Finland, where there are concurrent entitlements to leave and ECEC services from a child's birth, are two exceptions. In most cases, however, leave and ECEC, located in different ministries and policy domains, show no such coordination.

The political factors

Context and values

Welfare regimes help define the boundaries of what is possible and the approach taken to leave policy. However, their influence should not be overstated to the point of determinism. Compare, for instance, the four Nordic countries featured in this book, and it becomes clear that their social democratic welfare regimes have produced leave policies that differ in significant ways and, more striking, policy-making processes that are quite distinctive.

Broad economic and social changes create new conditions that can call for new solutions (for example, the rapid rise in women's educational qualifications, the changing profile of employment, periods of high unemployment, demographic trends). Also significant contextually are prevalent ideas and attitudes about roles, relationships and practices. Is it generally accepted that mothers of young children should be employed? Are ECEC services seen as a last resort or necessary evil or as an integral part of a good childhood? Are men primarily viewed as breadwinners or as partners who should take an active part in domestic work? Differences here seem to have played an important part in the differences in leave policy between neighbouring Hungary and Slovenia.

These prevalent ideas and attitudes have helped shape two key value issues, influential in the politics of leave policies: first, the value placed on gender equity by the society and, therefore, the importance attached to designing leave policies that are effective in achieving high use by men; and second, the value attached to 'freedom of choice', between employment and childcare, for mothers (the rhetoric may refer to parents, but in practice the issue is about women and children).

As already argued, this should be seen as an issue distinct from leave policy, being about different purposes and aims. In practice, however, the two have often become connected, with 'childcare' or 'home care' allowances often being linked to an extended period of leave. Whether policies do in practice permit real choice between home and employment, and for men as well as women, is another matter; usually they do not. The question here is what effect these value wars have had on policy making.

Political actors and institutions

Political parties can adopt certain positions on leave policy or, more broadly, on policy concerning reconciliation of work and family life. Morgan and Zippel (2003) argue that centrist and conservative forces have been the primary advocates of care leaves (especially long leaves) and flat-rate cash benefits, while social democrats, trade unionists and feminists have been more likely to advocate ECEC services and briefer but earnings-related cash benefits. The significance of party political views is bound up with the history of parties in government (for example, the long-term role of the Social Democrats in Sweden and their strong support of ECEC services as well as the inclusion of fathers in leave policy) and also with whether national governments are usually drawn from a single party or require coalitions.

The social partners

Improving work–life balance is at the heart of the EU strategy for higher economic growth and jobs and the European Parliament and national governments have consistently stressed the need for stronger policies. But other interests also play an important role in shaping European policy. According to the EC press release referred to above (European Commission, 2008), in addition to the core components of the work–life policy package – adequate leave policies, sufficient supply of child care services and flexible working arrangements – "social partners at European, national and sectoral levels all have a role to play".

The term 'social partners' as defined by the ILO includes "all types of negotiation, consultation or simply exchange of information between, or among, representatives of governments, employers, and workers, on issues of common interest relating to economic and social policy". In the EU context, social partners representing employees and employers have been deputed responsibility for negotiating updated EU standards on parental leave, having set the existing standards in 1996; if social partners can reach agreement, the EU will incorporate this in new legislation. Just as the social partners have played an important role in shaping EU leave policies, so they have in several countries, as can be seen, for example, in the Chapters Six, Seven and Eleven.

Other actors

Other actors in the political process include churches and a variety of civil society organisations. The Catholic Church and Catholic organisations have often been active supporters of conservative leave policy, as in the Czech Republic, Hungary, Portugal and Spain. Civic organisations have played an important role in some countries, such as the family associations in France, and the childcare association in Slovenia, supporting the development of leave policies.

Governance

Federal states, or highly devolved unitary states, may provide some scope for local action to vary or supplement national policy; Spain and particularly Canada provide examples. Another potentially significant effect of governance may be the gender composition of legislators (and other policy makers). We quoted in Chapter One from research whose conclusions was "that having women in power is consistently associated with more generous child care and parental leave policies" (Lambert, 2008, p 317). This is illustrated by the high levels of female parliamentarians in the Nordic countries and their highly developed leave and ECEC policies.

International influences

Although no one organisation has had the authority to establish a uniform policy across national borders, international organisations have played an important role in shaping policies. Some work has been done through the projection of 'soft power', influencing national policy through cross-national comparisons, recommendations and setting international standards. In 1919, the ILO adopted its first convention on maternity protection, proposing a 12-week leave. The policy was significantly extended in 1952, to a 14-week leave at full wages. In 1985, the ILO stated that the main object of policy was "to protect the health of the future mother and child and to guarantee a continuing source of income and security of employment" (Kamerman, 2000, p 97). The OECD's cross-national reviews of ECEC policies and programmes (*Starting strong*; OECD, 2001, 2006) and on reconciling work and family life (*Babies and bosses*; OECD, 2003, 2004, 2005, 2006) both acknowledge the role that parental leave policies play, while Chapter Nine on Hungary and Slovenia shows how the OECD's economic reports on particular countries can influence policy debate.

The EU exerts both soft and hard power, through its competence to set legally binding standards, which it has used for both maternity and parental leaves, and is currently proposing to employ again to improve pan-European minimum levels of entitlement. Past EU directives have played an important role in shaping policies in some member states, especially among newer members (see the references to EU influence in Chapters Five and Nine).

Individual countries can also sometimes exert influence through example. An obvious example is Sweden, referred to in Chapters Five, Eight and Nine. But Chapter Three, on Canada, also points to the influence of Europe, in particular, France and Scandinavia, on the development of distinctive policies on leave and ECEC in Québec.

Looking ahead

Although the reconciliation of work and family life is high on the policy agenda in much of Europe, family policies (government actions affecting children and their families) incorporate far more than parental leave policies and need to be seen in a larger context. The policy components aimed at helping to reconcile work and family life include ECEC and family support services, family cash benefits and flexible working time as well as parental leave policies. Public expenditures on one component, maternity and parental leave benefits, have become increasingly significant; spending on them doubled between 1980 and 2001 in the OECD countries, while spending on family cash benefits generally declined slightly (albeit that spending on this item is much greater overall) (Gatenio–Gabel and Kamerman, 2006).

Leave policies need to be enhanced and designed to ensure that parental leave really is 'parental'. There needs to be full coverage for all new working parents (fathers as well as mothers), benefits need to be earnings-related to provide adequate economic support and a substantial portion of parental leave should comprise an individual entitlement. The 'Icelandic model' looks particularly interesting, with its division of a single postnatal leave period between mother, father and family use.

But looking forward, what else is likely to be on the future agenda for leave policies? How will the politics of leave policies develop? Five issues appear to be likely candidates, over and above the general enhancement of leave provisions.

First, gender lies at the heart of leave policies, now and in the future. How far can and should leave policies be a vehicle for promoting gender equality at work and in the home? And if they are to have this role, what does this mean for policy design? This involves, of course, changes in how men participate in the home, continuing the gradual but far from completed shift from assistant to equal partner in childcare and domestic work. But it also means changes in the workplace, towards new employment practices and expectations, in particular towards the time when the norm for employment is no longer based on the male breadwinner, working full time and continuously.

Second, the relationship between leave and ECEC policies will need to be explicitly articulated, to ensure that these areas of policy are complementary and coherent. This raises questions both about costs (short leaves will mean ECEC entitlements from an early age) but also about departmental responsibility. Should policy responsibility for both leave and ECEC policies be unified?

Third, far more attention will need to be given to how leave policies accommodate the increasing diversity in society, both in families and in work. Are leave policies sufficiently responsive to the great variety of family circumstances, and do they work for the growing numbers in the workforce engaged in 'atypical' employment, be that in terms of employment and contractual status, working hours or location of employment? What forms of flexibility in leave policies are relevant to and supportive of diversity in family life and employment? A starting point is to have better statistical information, accompanied by research studies, on eligibility for, use of and experiences in taking leave policies, including current forms of flexibility (for example, part-time leave options). Are certain groups disproportionately excluded from benefiting? Do some workers experience more disadvantage when using leave? For whom is it a progressive measure and for whom a pitfall?

Fourth, there is a need to consider how the interests of the child can be better represented in the formation of leave policy. The chapters in this book reveal the relative invisibility to date of the child in policy making, except as supporting actors in arguments about gender and parenthood and whether children do or do not need maternal care during their first 3 years. With the growing attention to children's rights and to ways in which even very young children can be listened to and their perspectives understood, the possibilities here seem promising, especially if a country or an international organisation sets an example. Parental leave is as much a children's issue as it is a family, employment and gender equality issue.

Finally, the future of leave policies may involve rethinking their whole concept. Distinctions between maternity, paternity and parental leave are already blurred, or have even disappeared, in some countries. But why stop there? Why not detach leave policies from their current focus on one particular point of the life course – parenting young children – and instead build them around a life-course approach? This could mean each citizen having an allocation of paid leave time to use over the course of his or her working life, either for a range of specified reasons or for any reason. If required, certain reasons for leave taking could be prioritised (so caring for children or older relatives could attract extra benefit payments) and the period of life-course leave might be supplemented according to the amount of caring undertaken by the citizen, a sort of care bonus.

Such a life-course approach, currently only found in Belgium as a national policy, would have several advantages for recipients, as well as perhaps easing some of the more intractable political issues. In those countries where there is some antipathy by non-parents towards benefits for parents, the former would now benefit. Parents could use some of their 'time credit' to take longer periods of child-related leave, if they so chose. It might, therefore, have the potential to properly integrate two policy areas: support for workers who have children, and recognition of the costs of informal care.

References

Derthick, M. (1975) *Policy making for social security*, Washington, DC: Brookings Institute.

European Commission (2006) 'First stage consultation of European social partners on reconciliation of professional, private and family life (SEC (2006) 1245)', available at http://ec.europa.eu/employment_social/news/2006/oct/consultation_reconciliation_en.pdf (accessed 21 October 2008).

European Commission (2007) 'Second stage of consultation of European social partners on reconciliation of professional, private and family life', available at http://ec.europa.eu/employment_social/social_dialogue/docs/reconciliation2_en.pdf (accessed 21 October 2008).

European Commission (2008) 'Work–life balance package (memo/08/603)', available at http://europa.eu/rapid/pressReleasesAction.do?reference=MEMO/08/603&format=HTML&aged=0&language=EN&guiLanguage=en (accessed 21 October 2008).

Gatenio-Gabel, S. and Kamerman, S.B. (2006) 'Investing in children: public commitment in 21 industrialized countries', *Social Service Review*, vol 80, no 3, pp 239-66.

Hayes, C.D. (ed) (1982) *Making policies for children*, Washington, DC: National Academy Press.

Neyer, G. (2006) 'Family policies and fertility in Europe', Paper presented at the Annual Meeting of the Population Association of America, Los Angeles, 30 March–1 April.

Kamerman, S.B. (2000) 'From maternity to parental leave policies; women's health, employment, and child and family well-being', *Journal of the American Medical Women's Association*, vol 55, no 2, pp 96–9.

Kamerman, S.B. and Kahn, A.J. (eds) (1991) *Child care, parental leaves, and the under 3s: Policy innovation in Europe*, Westport, CT: Auburn House.

Lambert, P. (2008) 'Comparative political economy of parental leave and child care: evidence from 20 OECD countries', *Social Politics*, vol 15, no 4, pp 315–44.

Morgan, K. and Zippel, K. (2003) 'Paid to care: the origins and effects of care leave policies in Western Europe', *Social Politics*, vol 10, no 10, pp 49–85.

Moss, P. and Deven, F. (eds) (1999) *Parental leave: Progress or pitfall? Research and policy issues in Europe*, The Hague/Brussels: NIDI/CBGS Publications.

OECD (Organisation for Economic Co-operation and Development) (2001) *Starting strong I*, Paris: OECD.

OECD (2002) *Babies and bosses: Reconciling work and family life, Vol 1: Australia, Denmark and the Netherlands*, Paris: OECD.

OECD (2003) *Babies and bosses: Reconciling work and family life, Vol 2: Austria, Ireland and Japan*, Paris: OECD.

OECD (2004) *Babies and bosses: Reconciling work and family life, Vol 3: New Zealand, Portugal and Switzerland*, Paris: OECD.

OECD (2005) *Babies and bosses: Reconciling work and family life, Vol 4: Canada, Finland, Sweden and the United Kingdom*, Paris: OECD.

OECD (2006) *Starting Strong II: Early childhood education and care*, Paris: OECD.

Pierson, P. (2004) *Politics in time: History, institutions and social analysis*, Princeton, NJ: Princeton University Press.

Pierson, P. (2005) 'The study of policy development', *Journal of Policy History*, vol 17, no 1, pp 34–51.

Plantenga, J. and Siegel, M. (eds) (2004) 'Child care in a changing world', Position paper prepared for Childcare in a Changing World Conference, Groningen, Netherlands, 28–31 October, available at www.childcareinachangingworld.nl (accessed 21 October 2008).

Ruhm, C. (1998) 'The economic consequences of parental leave: mandates; lessons from Europe', *Quarterly Journal of Economics*, vol 113, no 1, pp 285–318.

Shonkoff, J. and Phillips, D. (eds) (2000) *From neurons to neighborhoods: The science of early child development*, Washington, DC: National Academy Press.

Tanaka, S. (2005) 'Parental leaves and child health across OECD countries', *Economic Journal*, vol 115, no 501, F 7–28.

Tilly, C. (2005) 'Why and how history matters', in R.E Goodin and C. Tilly (eds) *Oxford handbook of contextual political analysis*, Oxford: Oxford University Press, pp 417–37.

Demographic, gender and early childhood policy indicators for case study countries (2005, 2006)

	Population (millions)	Fertility rate	Women's employment			Gender Development Index	Gender Empowerment Measure
			Mothers: % with child <3 years	Mothers: % with youngest child 3–5 years	All women: part-time as % all employment		
Australia	20.3	1.81	44	58	41	2nd	8th
Canada	32.3	1.53	59	68	26	4th	10th
Czech Rep	10.2	1.28	20	51	6	29th	34th
Estonia	1.3	1.4	No information			41st	31st
Finland	5.3	1.8	52	81	15	8th	3rd
France	60.9	1.94	54	64	23	7th	18th
Germany	81.8	1.34	36	55	39	20th	9th
Hungary	10.1	1.32	14	50	4	34th	50th
Iceland	0.3	2.05	84		26	1st	5th
Netherlands	16.3	1.73	69	68	60	6th	6th
Norway	4.6	1.84	No information		33	3rd	1st
Portugal	10.6	1.4	69	72	13	28th	22nd
Slovenia	2.0	1.2	No information			25th	41st
Spain	43.4	1.34	45	48	21	12th	41st
Sweden	9.0	1.77	72	81	19	5th	2nd

Sources: Population, fertility rate, women's employment (except Estonia and Slovenia) – OECD (2008) *Babies and bosses: A synthesis of findings for OECD countries*, Paris: OECD, Table 1.1; Gender Development Index, Gender Empower Measure (and population and fertility rate for Estonia and Slovenia) – United Nations Development Programme (2008) *The human development report 2007/2008*, New York, NY: United Nations Development Programme, Tables 25 and 27.

Index